THE
WATERFORD
WAY

THE
WATERFORD
WAR DEAD

A HISTORY OF THE CASUALTIES OF THE GREAT WAR

TOM BURNELL

First published 2010

The History Press Ireland
119 Lower Baggot Street
Dublin 2, Ireland
www.thehistorypress.ie.com

British Library Cataloguing in Publication Data.
A catalogue record for this book is available from the British Library.

ISBN 978 1 84588 996 8

Typesetting and origination by The History Press
Printed in Great Britain
Manufacturing managed by Jellyfish Print Solutions Ltd

Contents

Acknowledgements

Special thanks to Kevin Myers; Jimmy Taylor, Wexford Town; Ciarán Reilly, Edenderry; my daughter Kathlene Burnell, Holycross, Tipperary; Etta Coman and Sinéal O'Higgins of the Waterford City Library; Gordon Power, Waterford; Eddie Sullivan, Waterford; Emmet Kennedy, Kilnagrange Kilmacthomas; Ger Croughan, Dungarvan Central Library and Terry Denham of the Commonwealth War Graves Commission.

Sources

The Commonwealth War Graves Commission, Soldiers Died in the Great War, Soldiers of the Great War, The New Library and Archives Canada. The National Archives of Australia. Nominal Rolls of the New Zealand Expeditionary Force, De Ruvigny's Roll of Honour, The War Graves of the British Empire, Commonwealth War Graves Commission registers for the Irish Free State, Ireland's Memorial Records. *The Tipperary War Dead, The Wexford War Dead, The Wicklow War Dead, The Offaly War Dead*, University of St Andrews Roll of Honour, Souvenir of the Great Naval Battle, Call to Arms, Montreal's Roll of Honour, Croydon and the Great War, Artists Rifles Roll of Honour, Princes Patricia's Canadian Light Infantry, University of Edinburgh Roll of Honour, 1914-1919, Sligo 1914-1921, Irish at the Front, New Zealand Roll of Honour, Irish on the Somme, Tenth Irish Division in Gallipoli, The National Roll of the Great War, London, Blackrock College Roll of Honour, South Irish Horse Casualties, The First Five Hundred, Roscommon Soldiers who died in WW1, Roll of the sons and daughters of the Anglican Church, The Roll of Honour, *Five months on a German Raider, The Munster Express, The Waterford News, Journal of the Old Waterford Society, The People, Waterford and Thereabouts, The Southern Star, The Dungarvan Observer* and *Munster Industrial Advocate. Decies: Journal of the Waterford Archaeological & Historical Society, Waterford: Heroes, Poets and Villains.*

Foreword

As the ploughshares of Picardy and Flanders daily yield a fresh harvest of old bones of the nameless men who perished on those acres over ninety years ago, so too are researchers in Ireland retrieving our forgotten dead of the Great War. A monumental exercise in amnesia – entirely voluntary, and therefore all the more extraordinary – abolished the memory of the tens of thousands of young men – and a good few women – who lost their lives in 1914-1918. No western democracy has achieved such a melancholy feat of posthumous contempt – which can only serve to redouble our duty to those who – for whatever reason – lost their lives in that unspeakable calamity.

The deed of forgetting is now being systematically undone. County after Irish county have set about the same solemn duty of honouring our forgotten dead. Now it is Waterford's turn, from Abbot to Wixted alphabetically, and from 23 August 1914 until 1920 chronologically – though of course, the death toll has no finite bound until the last survivor has died. And even then, who can say what further calamities followed the families of those who had lost so much? What of the Collins brothers, six of whom served, with four of them falling? What tales did the next generation learn as they grew up? Or did the deadly silence of taboo supervene? And what poverty and trauma must perforce have followed such a calamity?

Colonel JMF Shine, of Tramore, Co. Waterford, and his wife Kathleen, came from different end of the social spectrum from the poor Collins brothers. They had three sons: John Denys, Hugh Patrick and James Owen. Captain John Shine, 26, Royal Irish Regiment, was one of the first soldiers killed in the war, on 25 August 1914. Eight months later, his brother, 2nd Lieutenant Hugh Patrick Shine, Royal Irish Fusiliers, was killed. And in August 1917, upon the evil, muddy slopes of Frezenberg Ridge, Captain James Owen, 26, Royal Dublin Fusiliers, laid down his young life. To be followed shortly thereafter, by their mother, Kathleen, who died of whatever it is that mothers die of when all their sons are dead. Colonel Shine went on to marry again, and had three more sons. Wiser souls might find a parable in such a tale: with three boys dead, and their mother also, I am beyond any such wisdom.

The most famous Waterford victim of the war is of course Private John Condon, aged 14, killed in action in May 1915. He was one of many Munster men with the Royal Irish Regiment who died in the great German gas attacks that ushered in a new and yet more terrible form of war that spring. And the great events of the war are now becoming imprinted on the collective consciousness of the Irish people after decades of an almost totalitarian amnesia: so the general outlines of the collective calamity are known, from the retreat from Mons, through to the gas or Gallipoli of 1915, the Somme of 1916, Third Ypres in 1917, and the great and final battles of 1918.

Yet some events can nonetheless sneak in catch you unawares. Until I read this moving and deeply illuminating tribute to the Waterford men and women who died in the Great War, I had never even heard of SS *Coningbeg*, sailing out of Glasgow. Yet thirty-five Waterford men went down on this vessel on 18 December 1917. The county can scarcely have known such a terrible day or ill-fated vessel in the entire twentieth century, yet this calamity nonetheless has passed from popular ken, hiding for ever the grieving that must have consumed so many Waterford homes that terrible Christmas.

The fate of those men lifts the curtain on so many other Waterford men who were killed outside the normally accepted parameters of the Great War, which form around the ranks of the British Army. In the pages that follow are the many other Merchant Marine and Royal Navy personnel, those of the Royal Flying Corps and the Royal Air Force, and finally, in the Commonwealth Forces: thus we find in this record that nine Waterfordmen died with the Australian army, and forty-three with the Canadians.

The first Waterford men to be killed at the front were Private John Connolly and Sergeant Denis Walsh, of the Royal Irish Regiment, who lost their lives in the very first fatal British engagement of the war, near Mons, on 23 August 1914. To add some proportion to those two very personal tragedies, the day before, the French army had lost 26,000 men killed in action in the 'Battle of the Frontiers'. Total French dead that week exceeded 60,000 men. And as many Turks were killed in a single doomed night-advance through the snow-clad Caucasus the following Christmas. The wolves of the slopes of Saramakesh grew fat that kindly winter. So above all else, it must always be remembered that Waterford's war was merely part of a truly terrible world war.

It is of course quite impossible to make any real sense of the losses that such a war entails. Each of us must therefore make do with what is within reach, and of which we can make sense. This is most easily done in our own local communities – wherever they be: from Alberta to Anatolia, Austria to Australia. But that said, it would be wrong and perverse, so long after the events, to fetishise these dead, or turn them into political tools for some modern agenda that they themselves would never have understood. They were merely victims of history, whose place therein was denied them to so long, in Ireland particularly. These pages that commemorate Waterford's war dead must therefore go by one simple, belated word: AMENDS.

Kevin Myers

Terminology

Killed in action: The soldier was killed during engagement with the enemy.

Died of wounds: The soldier was not killed outright and may have made it back to the Regiments Aid post or Casualty Clearing Station before he eventually died of his wounds.

Died at home: Death by drowning, suicide, accident or illness in the UK. Home in these cases means back in England and not necessarily where he lived. Many times I have come across this and it turned out to be that the soldier died in a UK hospital.

Died of wounds at home: The soldier was not killed outright and may have made it back to the Regiments Aid post or Casualty Clearing Station before he eventually died of his wounds back in the UK or Ireland.

Died: Can mean death by drowning, suicide, accident or illness.

A

ABBOTT, Charles Thomas: Rank: Company Quartermaster Sergeant. Regiment or Service: Royal Irish Regiment. Unit: 2nd Battalion. Age at death: 34. Date of death: 24 May 1915. Service No: 5808. Born in Secunderabad, East India. Enlisted in Birr while living in Carrick-on-Suir, Co. Tipperary. Killed in action.

Supplementary information: Son of the late H.G. Abbott, husband of Margaret Helen Abbott, of 9 The Terrace, Tramore, Co. Waterford. See F.R. Gorbey, his brother-in-law, also killed in action.

DE RUVIGNY'S ROLL OF HONOUR
Abbott, Charles Thomas, Company Quartermaster Sergeant, No 5080[*sic*], B Company, 2nd Battalion, Royal Irish Regiment. Son of Graves Abbott, Sergeant, 1st Battalion, Royal Scottish Fusiliers. Born in Secunderabad, India, 13th September, 1881. Enlisted 15th April-1896. Served in the South African War (Medal with clasps), in India and with the Expeditionary Force in France and Flanders. Killed in action 24 May-1915. He married at Karachi, 9th December 1908, Margaret Helen, daughter of John William Gorbey of Carrick-on-Suir and had a son and two daughters; Henry Graves, born Agra, 17th November 1910. Agnes May, born Agra, 2nd October-1909; and Ellen Rewa, born on the troopship 'RIWA' in the Bay of Biscay, 26th December-1911. Sergeant Abbott's brother-in-law, Corporal Frank R Gorbey, D.C.M., was killed in action 23 April-1915.

Grave or Memorial Reference: He has no known grave but is listed on Panel 33 on the Ypres (Menin Gate) Memorial in Belgium.

ABBOTT, John: Rank: Private. Regiment or Service: Gloucestershire Regiment. Unit: 8th Service Battalion. Date of death: 7 June 1917. Service No: 19603. Born in Waterford. Enlisted in St Paul's Churchyard, London while living in Waterford. Killed in action. Has no known grave but is commemorated on Panel 22 and 34 on the Ypres (Menin Gate) Memorial in Belgium.

ALLEN, Reginald Arthur Sinclair: Rank: Captain. Regiment or Service: Canadian Infantry (Saskatchewan Regiment). Unit: 5th Battalion. Age at death: 36. Date of death: 30 April 1915. Data from attestation papers:

In what Town, Township or Parish, and in what Country were you born? Blackheath, London, England.

What is the name of your next of kin? Gertrude Elizabeth Allen.

What is the address of your next of kin? 717 Nicola Street, Kamloops, British Columbia.

Charles Thomas Abbott. Taken from De Ruvigny's Roll of Honour.

What is the relationship of your next of kin? Wife.

What is the date of your birth? 27 May 1879.

What is your trade or calling? Prison Guard.

Are you married? Yes.

Are you willing to be vaccinated or re-vaccinated and inoculated? Yes.

Do you now belong to the Active Militia? Yes. If so, state particulars of former service. 3 years, Royal Irish Regiment, 3 years 2 months Royal Warwickshire Regiment including S.A.

Apparent age: 35 years 4 months.

Girth when fully expanded: 38 Ins

Range of expansion: 4 Ins

Complexion: light.

Eyes: blue.

Hair: brown.

Distinctive marks: gold filling upper jaw, several moles over shoulder blade, 3 vaccination left arm, scar left arm.

Date: 10 September 1914. Location. Valcartier.

Supplementary information: Son of Lt. Arthur James Allen, R.N., and Marion Barlow Allen, of Cheekpoint, Waterford. Husband of Gertrude Elizabeth Allen, of Church Cottage, Dunmore East, Co. Waterford. From the *Waterford News* 1915:

LOCAL AND DISTRICT GOSSIP.

WATERFORD OFFICER DIES OF WOUNDS.

The death has occurred at Boulogne of Captain Allen, son of Mrs Allen, Mighnaun, Cheekpoint. Deceased gentleman Died of wounds received at Ypres in the recent fighting.

Captain R.A.S. Allen, of the 5th Battalion, 2nd Canadian Brigade, was the only son of the late Lieutenant Arthur Allen, R.N., and grandson of the late Colonel R. Bligh Sinclair, Black Watch, Deputy Adjutant-General of the Militia Forces, Halifax, Nova Scotia. Educated at Cheltenham and Stubbington, he was gazetted to the 2nd Royal Warwickshire Regiment in 1900,

Reginald Arthur Sinclair Allen.

he served in the Boer War, having the Queen's medal with three clasps, and also accompanied his Regiment to Bermuda in charge of Boer prisoners. He afterwards went to Canada where he held a captaincy in the 31st British Columbia Horse.

Grave or Memorial Reference: II.B.27. Cemetery: Boulogne Eastern Cemetery in France. He is also listed on the Waterford and District Roll of Honour. Located in Christ Church Cathedral (Church of Ireland), Henrietta Street, Waterford.

ANDERSON, Francis Sainthill: Rank: Major. Regiment or Service: Royal Field Artillery. Unit: 'A' Battery. 15th Brigade. Age at death: 23. Date of death: 25 August 1918. Won the Military Cross and listed in the *London Gazette.*

Supplementary information: Son of Brig. Gen. Sir Francis Anderson and Lady Anderson, of Ballydavid, Rossduff, Waterford. Served in 'N' Battery. Royal Horse Artillery, 'The Eagle Troop' as subaltern and Capt. for nearly three years. From the *Journal of the Old Waterford Society*, No 49. Spring 1994:

ABBEY GRAVEYARD, KILCULLIHEEN.

ANDERSON: (inscription on wooden cross mounted on tablet in church) In proud memory of Major Francis Sainthill Anderson, MC, RHA, RFA, deeply loved younger son of Brig. General Sir Francis and Lady Anderson of Ballydavid House and grandson of Major O'Gorman. Major Anderson served in 'N' Battery RHA (the Eagle Troop) as subaltern and captain in France from April 1915 to Nov. 1917. As captain he greatly distinguished himself in temporary command of two separate RHA batteries near Lens. Promoted acting Major in Nov. 1917. He was appointed to the command of a field battery which he took to Italy, returning with it in April 1918 to France, where after 3 years 8 months gallant service he was killed in action August 25th 1918 at the age of 23. This cross marked his wayside grave. In memory of GRU Major F. S. Anderson (MC), 'A' Batty 15th Brigade RFA, killed in action 25-8-1918.

Grave or Memorial Reference: II.B.10. Cemetery: Queens Cemetery, Buoquoy in France.

ANDERSON, George Michael: Rank: Corporal. Regiment or Service: Royal Garrison Artillery. Unit: 112th Heavy Battery. Age at death: 27. Date of death: 19 March 1917. Service No: 29878. Born in Tallow, Co. Waterford. Enlisted in Clonmel while living in Leeds. Died.

Supplementary information: Son of the late John and Mary Anderson, of Tallow, Co. Waterford. Husband of Mary Anderson, of Evergreen Cottage, Lismore, Co. Waterford. From the *Waterford News*, March 1917:

KILLED IN ACTION.

News has been received at Lismore that Sergeant George Anderson, R.G.A., has been killed in action. Deceased, who was a native of the Tallow district, was married to Miss Ahearne, of Lismore, about 18 months ago.

Grave or Memorial Reference: II.L.45. Cemetery: Auchonvillers Military Cemetery in France.

ANDERSON, Hans: Rank: Private. Regiment or Service: Manchester Regiment. Unit: 20th Battalion. Previously he was with the Lancashire Fusiliers where his number was 4320. Date of death: 12 October 1916. Service No: 40273. Born in New Ross, Co. Wexford. Enlisted in Bury, Lancs while living in Waterford. Died of wounds. Age at death: 30. Grave or Memorial Reference: II.F.255. Cemetery: Bailleul Communal Cemetery Extension (Nord) in France.

ASPELL, Jeremiah: Rank: Private. Regiment or Service: Royal Irish Fusiliers. Unit: 2nd (Garrison) Battalion. Age at death: 49. Date of death: 13 March 1918. Service No: G/1478. Previously he was with the Royal Irish Regiment where his number was 5906. He won the Military Medal and is listed in the *London Gazette*. Born in Waterford. Enlisted in Waterford. Died in Salonika. Brother of James Aspell, of Smith's Lane, Ballybuchen, Waterford. From *Waterford News* 1914:

BACK FROM THE FRONT.
EXPERIENCES OF WATERFORDMEN.
Private Thomas Clemens, of the 2nd Royal Irish Regiment, arrived here in Waterford this week after nearly three months at the front. He left on August 6th with a batch of 150 to join his Regiment and landed at St Nazaire. They were joined on leaving the latter place by men of the Devons, Lincolns, Middlesex, and the Gordons.

They marched generally about twenty-five miles a day and had several minor touches with the enemy at Blaine and Vailly. At Blaine Quartermaster Sergeant Thomas Croke, Ballybricken man was wounded, and, Clemens thinks, was afterwards taken prisoner. Jeremiah Aspel, another Waterford man, was also wounded there and is now in a convalescent home outside Glasgow.

Grave or Memorial Reference: 1377. Cemetery: Salonika (Lembet Road) Military Cemetery in Greece.

ATTRIDGE, Daniel: Rank: Private. Regiment or Service: Royal Irish Regiment. Unit: 7th Battalion. Date of death: 7 March 1918. Service No: 4229. Born in St John's, Waterford. Enlisted in Waterford. Died of wounds.

Supplementary information: Brother of Mrs M. Allen, of Brown's Lane, Waterford. From the *Waterford News* 1915:

THREE HOURS UNDER SHELL FIRE.

The following letters from Drummer Daniel Attridge, C Company, 2nd Royal Irish Regiment, have been received by his relatives in Waterford, and describes his terrible experience under fire in one of the recent bloody engagements in which the British troops took part:

May 10th, 1915.
Somewhere in France.
Dear Father,
I received your parcels all right …I have a terrible tale to tell you. On Sunday the Germans shelled our trenches where I was. There were eleven men in the trenches with me. Ten got killed and my officer got wounded. I got through safe. They kept firing hell into our trench for three hours. All my comrades were buried in the trench. I had to pull out half of them by myself, and when I go them out they were dead. After that I had to get out of the trench and try to get away as safe as I could. I got out of the trench. They put two maxim guns on me, so I had to be in the open for six hours under shell-fire. I got away safe, thank God. I wish to thank the members of the Confraternity for their prayers, and also K---S--- for the Mass said for me. Just picture what it was to be in a trench and all in it dead but yourself, with nowhere to go, and expecting death every minute. But, thank God for hearing your prayers for me. It came night-time; I crept about

600 yards over to my other comrades, and when I got over there were heaps of dead and wounded there. In all those exciting hours I kept up my heart, and thought about you and I said; "Well, my fathers prayers were heard, and my little sister's. " I started to cry when I looked round and saw dead and wounded everywhere about me, and I heard the wounded crying for help. I had a lot of trophies and things in my kit-bag for the boss, but tell him that when the battle was over they were all buried in the trench. I am very sorry. Don't forget to buy the papers and you will see all the men we lost, and look for an officer, his name is Ramsay(?). He is the only one that got out safe with me.

The other letter describes the same experience, but given extra details:

May 11th.
Somewhere in France.
Dear K---
I would like to have answered your letter sooner, only I had not time to look around me on Sunday last. I will never forget it as long as I live. I was about to make tea, when the Germans started shelling us. There were eleven men in the trench with me. The first shell buried three men in the ground. After that they were firing for about an hour before another came in to our trench. The next one killed two men, and burned my face and hurt my back. The men who were left thought to get away and they crept out of the trench; but when they got out they were killed with maxims. I kept a cool head and remained in the trench with the dead and wounded. After a few minutes there was nobody left but one officer and myself. Another man who had been with me crept out for safety, and I never saw him until night-time when the last man that was wounded died. I crept out of the trench. My heart was beating like a clock. When I got out the Germans opened fire with a maxim, but I said a prayer, and I thought of the

Mass you got said for me. I got behind a dead calf for cover. I lay there under shell fire for six hours, when I came to myself and saw dead and wounded all about me, the wounded crying for help and for water. That will tell you the way I was. When night came I crept about 600 yards into another trench. When I got there it was cruel to see the heaps of dead in this trench. I had to leave here and go to another place for safety. When I found my comrades they had to give me water to bring me round. When I got better I had to go back for my officer who was wounded. I guided him down to a Red Cross station. When I got down it was morning. You may imagine the time I had, but, thank God, I got safely out of it all. It took me a full day to write this letter.

Grave or Memorial Reference: V.C.6. Cemetery: Tincourt New British Cemetery in France.

AYLWARD, Edward: Rank: Sapper. Regiment or Service: Corps of Royal Engineers. Unit: Railways (263rd Railway Company) Date of death: 13 April 1918. Age at death: 36. Service No: 256524 and R/256524. Formerly he was with the Royal Irish Rifles where his number was 1676. Born in Ballybricken, Co. Waterford. Enlisted in Waterford. Killed in action.

Supplementary information: Son of Thomas and Margaret Aylward, of 22 Southpark, Co. Kilkenny. Grave or Memorial Reference: On the West Side. Cemetery: La Motte-Brebiere Communal Cemetery in France.

AYLWARD, Hubert: Rank: Private. Regiment or Service: Royal Irish Regiment. Unit: 1st Battalion. Age at death: 18. Date of death: 6 December 1917. Service No: 6427. Born in Trinity Without, Waterford. Enlisted in Waterford. Died of wounds in Salonika.

Supplementary information: Son of John and Kate Aylward, of 6 Pump Lane, Barrack Street, Waterford. Grave or Memorial Reference: XIII.E.7. Cemetery: Gaza War Cemetery in Israel.

AYLWARD, Joseph: Rank: Private. Regiment or Service: Royal Irish Regiment. Unit: 1st Battalion. Age at death: 27. Date of death: 11 April 1915. Service No: 4697. Born in Newtown, Waterford. Enlisted in Waterford while living in Kilmacthomas, Co. Waterford. Died of wounds. Killed in action.

Supplementary information: Husband of Catherine Aylward, of Kilmoylan, Kilmacthomas. He has no known grave but is listed on Panel 33 on the Ypres (Menin Gate) Memorial in Belgium.

B

BACON, Thomas: Rank: Private. Regiment or Service: Royal Munster Fusiliers. Unit: 2nd Battalion. Age at death: 37. Date of death: 22 September 1916. Service No: 6167. Born in Carrigmore, Co. Tipperary. Enlisted in Cork while living in Tallow, Co. Waterford. Killed in action. Son of John and Euen Bacon, of West Street, Tallow. From the *Munster Express*:

> THE WAR.
>
> Corporal Patrick Sweeney, of the Royal Irish Regiment, a native of New Street, Lismore, was prayed for at Lismore R. C. Church on Sunday last. We also learn that Private Thomas Bacon has been killed in action and that Private Robert Scanlon of the Irish Guards, and Thomas Cripps, of the Leinster Regiment are both wounded.

He has no known grave but is listed on Pier and Face 16C of the Thiepval Memorial in France.

BARNETT, Patrick: Rank: Private. Regiment or Service: Royal Dublin Fusiliers. Unit: 8th Battalion. Date of death: 19 May 1916. Service No: 22977. Born in Clashmore, Co. Waterford. Enlisted in Merthyr. Died of wounds. Killed in action. He has no known grave but is listed on Panel 127 on the Loos Memorial in France.

BARRETT, Augustine: Rank: Stoker 1st Class. Regiment or Service: Royal Navy. Unit: HMS *Eaglet*. Age at death: 21. Date of death: 28 April 1920. Service No: K/43568.

Supplementary information: Son of Patrick and Mary Barrett, of 16 Presentation Row, Waterford. Grave or Memorial Reference: B.12.10. Cemetery: Haslar Royal Navy Cemetery, Gosport in Hamshire, UK.

BARRETT, Joseph: Rank: Private. Regiment or Service: Connaught Rangers. Unit: 2nd Battalion. Date of death: 19 October 1914. Service No: 4020. Born in Waterford. Enlisted in Galway while living in Waterford. Died of wounds. Grave or Memorial Reference: C.14. Cemetery, Soupir Communal Graveyard in France.

BARRON, John: Rank: Private. Regiment or Service: Royal Welsh Fusiliers. Unit: 8th Battalion. Age at death: 21. Date of death: 7 August 1915. Service No: 11756. Born in Kilmacthomas, Co. Waterford. Enlisted in Cardiff while living in Fishguard. Killed in action in Gallipoli.

Supplementary information: Brother of Maurice Barron, of Kilmacthomas, Co. Waterford. He has no known grave but is listed on Panel 77 to 80 on the Helles Memorial in Turkey.

BARRON, Timothy: Rank: Private. Regiment or Service: Black Watch (Royal Highlanders). Unit: 9th Battalion. Age at death: 22. Date of death: 28 September 1915. Service No: S/4871. Born in Kilcalf, Tallow, Co. Waterford. Enlisted in Tonypandy, Glamorganshire. Died of wounds.

Supplementary information: Son of Thomas Barron, of Kilcalf, Tallow. Grave or Memorial Reference: IV.G.5. Cemetery: Etaples Military Cemetery in France.

BARRON, Walter: Rank: Gunner. Regiment or Service: Royal Horse Artillery and Royal Field Artillery. Unit: 'D' Battery, 123rd Brigade. Date of death: 3 May 1917. Service No: 77365. Born in Waterford. Enlisted in Dungarvan. Killed in action. Brother of Gunner J. Barron R.G.A. and Corporal J. Barron serving on

HMS *Revenge*. Sons of John Baron, baker, Cappoquin. Grave or Memorial Reference: C.59. Cemetery: Cojeul British Cemetery, St Martin-Sur-Cojeul in France.

BARRY, Edward: Rank: Private. Regiment or Service: Irish Guards. Unit: Reserve Battalion and 49th Battalion. Date of death: 8 August 1918. Age at death: 20. Service No: 9218. Born in Cappoquin, Co. Waterford. Enlisted in Waterford. Died at Home.

Supplementary information: Son of John and Mary Barry, of 12 Martindale Road, Custom House, London. He has no known grave but is listed on Panel 154 to 159 and 163A on the Tyne Cot Memorial in Belgium.

BARRY, James: Rank: Rifleman. Regiment or Service: Royal Irish Rifles. Unit: 7th Battalion. Age at death: 21. Date of death: 16 August 1917. Service No: 7948. Born in Waterford. Enlisted in Waterford. Killed in action.

Supplementary information: Son of Richard and Mary Barry, of 36 Green Street, Waterford. He has no known grave but is listed on 138 to 140 and 162 to 162A and 163A on the Tyne Cot Memorial in Belgium.

BARRY, John: Rank: Private. Regiment or Service: Lancashire Fusiliers. Unit: 12th Battalion. Date of death: 23 December 1917. Service No: 11316. Born in Waterford. Enlisted in Salford in Lancashire while living in Waterford. Died of wounds in Salonika. Grave or Memorial Reference: 1324. Cemetery: Salonika (Lembet Road) Military Cemetery in Greece.

BARRY, Michael: Rank: Able Seaman. Regiment or Service: Mercantile Marine. Unit: SS *Coningbeg* (Glasgow). Age at death: 49. Date of death: 18 December 1917. Torpedoed by German Submarine U-62. There were no survivors.

Supplementary information: Son of the late Edward and Margaret Barry. Husband of Margaret Barry (*née* Dempsey), of 15 Parliament Street, Waterford. He has no known grave but is listed on the Tower Hill Memorial in the UK. He is also listed on the Formby-Coningbeg Memorial, Adelphi Quay in Waterford City.

BARRY, Michael: Rank: Fireman and Trimmer. Regiment or Service: Mercantile Marine. Unit: SS *Haulwen* (Cardiff). Age at death: 52. Date of death: 9 June 1917.

Supplementary information: Son of the late Patrick and Mary Barry. Husband of Mary Barry (*née* Kelly), of Parish Height, Carrickbeg, Co. Tipperary. Born at Tramore, Co. Waterford. The Steam Ship *Haulwen* was a 4,032grt, defensively armed British Merchant steamer. She was torpedoed without warning and sunk by German submarine U-43. 4,250 miles NW from the Fastnet, Ireland. *Haulwen* was en route from Montreal to Manchester. Four men died that day, two of which, **LANNIGAN, PATRICK FRANCIS,** and **BARRY, MICHAEL** were from Waterford. He has no known grave but is listed on the Tower Hill Memorial in the UK.

BARRY, Michael: Rank: Private. Regiment or Service: Royal Irish Fusiliers. Unit: 5th Battalion. Date of death: 16 September 1915. Service No: 17035. Previously he was with the Royal Irish Regiment where his number was 1681. Born in Clonmel. Enlisted in Clonmel while living in Kilmanahan Co. Waterford. Died of wounds in Gallipoli. Grave or Memorial Reference: III.C.7. Cemetery: Lala Baba Cemetery in Turkey.

BARRY, Patrick: Rank: Private. Regiment or Service: Connaught Rangers. Unit: 'D' Coy. 5th Battalion. Age at death: 29. Date of death: 11 November 1915. Service No: 5693. Born in Carrigbeg in Co. Waterford and enlisted in Carrick-on-Suir while living in Carrick-on-Suir. Died in Salonika.

Supplementary information: Son of Michael and Ellen Barry. Husband of Annie Barry, of Mass Road, Carrick Beg, Carrick-on-Suir, Co. Tipperary. Born at Carrick-on-Suir. Grave or Memorial Reference: C.39. Cemetery: Alexandria (Chatby) Military and War Memorial Cemetery in Egypt.

BARRY, Richard: Rank: Private. Regiment or Service: Royal Irish Regiment. Unit: 7th Battalion. Date of death: 21 March 1918. Service No: 1983. He won the Military Medal and is listed in the *London Gazette*. Born in St Patrick's, Waterford. Enlisted in Waterford. Killed in action. He has no known grave but is listed on Panels 30 and 31 on the Pozières Memorial in France.

BARRY, Thomas: Rank: Private. Regiment or Service: Royal Irish Regiment. Unit: 2nd Battalion. Date of death: 21 October 1914. Service No: 10731. Born in Lismore, Co. Waterford. Enlisted in Waterford while living in Knocknagopple, Co. Waterford. Killed in action. He has no known grave but is listed on Panels 11 and 12 on the Le Touret Memorial in France.

BARRY, W.: Rank: Mess Room Steward. Regiment or Service: Mercantile Marine. Unit: SS *Hollington* (London). Age at death: 16. Date of death: 2 June 1917. Sunk by a German submarine off the Faroe Islands.

Supplementary information: Son of Mrs M. Barry, of 3A Ben Jonson Street, Liverpool. Born in Waterford. He has no known grave but is listed on the Tower Hill Memorial in the UK.

BARRY, William: Rank: Private. Regiment or Service: Irish Guards. Unit: 2nd Battalion. Date of death: 1 November 1914. Service No: 2413. Born in Kilrossenty, Co. Waterford. Enlisted in Waterford. Killed in action. He has no known grave but is commemorated on Panel 11 on the Ypres (Menin Gate) Memorial in Belgium.

BASSETT, William Frederick: Rank: Lieutenant (T.P.) Regiment or Service: Black Watch (Royal Highlanders). He won the Military Medal and is listed in the *London Gazette*. Unit: 10th Battalion attached to the 2nd Battalion. Date of death: 27 October 1917. Age at Death. Killed in action. From the *Waterford News*, April 1915:

Mr William F. Bassett, son of Mr G.W. Bassett, wine merchant, Waterford, has received intimation from the War Office of his appointment as Second Lieutenant in the 10th (Service) Battalion, Black. [*sic*] He has been on service with the 6th (Territorial) Battalion in Scotland since mobilisation. His many friends in Waterford will be very pleased to hear of his success. Three of his brothers in Canada have also joined.

From the *Waterford News*, July 1916:

WATERFORD OFFICERS.
To our lists already published of Waterford officers the names of Lieutenant E. V. Meredith and Second Lieutenant Wm. F Bassett should be added.

The former is a son of Mr W. E. Meredith (Messrs Bassett and Meredith). He was gazetted Lieutenant in the Royal Warwickshire Regiment in October, 1914. After training at the Isle of Wight he was sent to Gallipoli, in 1915, in charge of a draft of the South Staffordshires, and there he joined the Royal Warwicks. He was twice lightly wounded, and in November, 1915, he was invalided as suffering from "trench feet" and sent to Malta and Palermo. He is at present attached to the 1st Garrison Battalion of the Royal Scots at Alexandria.

Second Lieutenant Bassett is a son of Mr Meredith's partner. He is with the Black Watch at Salonika.

Another Waterford officer is 2nd Lieutenant H. W. Strangman, son of Mr John Strangman, of Summerland, who has been serving in Flanders and France for the past twelve months in the 80th Brigade, Royal Field Artillery.

Grave or Memorial Reference: He has no known grave but is listed on the Archangel Memorial in the Russian Federation.

BATEMAN, Michael: Rank: Deck Hand. Regiment or Service: Royal Naval Reserve. Unit: HM Trawler *George Milburn*. Age at death: 30. Date of death: 12 July 1917. Service No: 10773DA.

Supplementary information: Son of William and Mary Bateman, of Helvick Head, Dungarvan, Co. Waterford. Grave or Memorial Reference: 24 on the Plymouth Naval Memorial, UK.

BATTERSON, Peter: Rank: Private. Regiment or Service: Royal Defence Corps. Unit: 402nd Protection Coy. Date of death: 6 January 1917. Service No: 34261. Born in Waterford. Enlisted in Finsbury while living in Trafford Park, Manchester. Died at home.

Supplementary information: Son of Adam Batterson, of Waterford, and the late Mary Ann Batterson. Served in the Soudan Campaign. Grave or Memorial Reference: Soldiers' Plot. 179 (Screen Wall). Cemetery: Moston (St Joseph's) Roman Catholic Cemetery, UK.

BEAUMONT-NESBITT, Wilfrid Henry: Rank: Captain, also listed as Lieutenant/Acting Captain. Regiment or Service: Grenadier Guards. Unit: No. 2 Coy. 2nd Battalion. Age at death: 23. Date of death: 27 November 1917. Awarded the Military Cross and listed in the *London Gazette*. Killed in action.

Supplementary information: Son of Edward and Helen Beaumont-Nesbitt, of Tubberdaly, Edenderry, King's Co. From De Ruvigny's Roll of Honour:

Beaumont-Nesbitt, Wilfred Henry, M. C., Capt., Grenadier Guards; 2nd son of Edward John Beaumont-Nesbitt, of Tubberdaly, Edenderry, King's County, by his wife, Helen, daughter of Frederick Freeman-Thomas. Born Eastbourne, Co. Sussex, 2 Sept, 1894. Educated at Ludgrove, Osbourne; Dartmouth Naval Colleges, and Trinity College, Cambridge. Gazetted Midshipman, and was invalided out of the Navy in 1912. Gazetted 2nd Lieutenant, in the Grenadier Guards in February, 1915. Promoted Lieutenant, 1916, and Capt, the same year. Served with the Expeditionary Force in France and Flanders from June, 1915, was wounded at Les Boeufs during the Somme Battle in Sept, 1916. On recovery, was appointed instructor to the Household Brigade Officers Cadet Battn. Returned to France in August, 1917, and was killed in action at Fontaine, near Bourlon Wood, 27 Nov, following. He was awarded the Military Cross for gallant and distinguished service in the field.

Grave or Memorial Reference: Panel 2. Memorial: Cambrai Memorial, Louveral in France.

BECHER, Edward Richard Fane: Rank: Lieutenant. Regiment or Service: Royal Munster Fusiliers. Unit: 8th Battalion. Age at death: 19. Date of death: 19 July 1916.

Supplementary information: Son of Edmund W. and Ella Becher, of Ardagh, Lismore, Co. Waterford. From the *Munster Express*:

Sympathy.
To Mr E W Becher, Lismore Castle, we tender our sympathy in the loss he has sustained by the death of his only son, Lieutenant E R F Becher, of the 8th R. M. Fusiliers, who Died of wounds received in France. Deceased was a popular and sporting young gentleman scarcely out of his teens. The Board of Guardians at their meeting passed a resolution of sympathy with Mr Becher, who is a member of that body.

From *The Irish on the Somme* (p. 159):

I can only mention a few typical cases of the officers of the Irish Brigade killed at Guillamont and Guinchy. Lieutenant E. R. F. Becher, of the Munster Fusiliers, was but nineteen, and the only child of

E.W. Becher, Lismore, Co. Waterford. He was decended in direct line from Colonel Thomas Becher, who was aide-de-camp to King William at the Battle of the Boyne, and was on that occasion presented by the King with his watch, which is still an heirloom in the family.

From the *Munster Express*:

GLOWING TRIBUTES.

Mr E.W. Beecher, Castlefarm House, Lismore, has received the following correspondence in connection with the death of his gallant son, Second Lieutenant, E.R.F. Beecher, of the 8th R.M.F., who was killed on the 19th July last while leading his men in a gallant charge against the enemy with the B.E.F. in France.

When it is understood that Mr Beecher heads the poll for the Lismore Urban District or Lismore Rural District Council one can grasp an idea of the popularity in which he is held at Lismore.

The following letters speak volumes for the young officer's gallantry and plucky conduct:

Headquarters, 16th Irish Division.

Dear Mr Beecher,

I must write to you to offer you my sincere sympathy in the loss of your very gallant son. I regret to tell you that he died in hospital and at Bethune at 4 o'clock this morning.

He had been severely wounded on the night of the 18th, and from reports I had received I hoped that he would have pulled through. His loss is a serious one to the Battalion and to the Division. He had already been brought to notice and in particular for 'gallant conduct and skilful leadership on the night of the 26th June, 'when he took part in a raid carried out by the Leinster Regiment.

I have again received a report from his Colonel on his behaviour on the night he was wounded and had he survived he would have been recommended for the Military Cross.

It must be a consolation to you to know that he has left behind him an honoured name, and that he did his duty nobly to the end.

Yours very truly;

W. B. Hickie (Major General).

Commanding 16th (Irish Division).

Headquarters, 46th Infantry Brigade.

Dear Mr Beecher,

I am very anxious to write to you my great grief at the loss of your boy. He was a splendid young officer, full of promise and had done splendid work while with this Brigade. Less than three weeks ago he took part in a big raid on the enemy's trenches. Although his Battalion was not actually engaged. He not only carried out his own duties but did a great deal more, volunteering to carry messages and to assist in moving the wounded, and the Commanding Officer, who had charge of the operations was very much impressed by his conduct and loud in his admiration and appreciation of what he had done; Colonel Monteagle Browne, his own Commanding Officer, has constantly pointed out to me how much he valued him. Whatever he did he did well, and I do not know whether to admire more his fearless courage or his devoton to duty.

On behalf of the Brigade and of myself personally, I wish to offer you my sincerest sympathy in your irreparable loss

Yours very truly.

George Periern. Brig. General.

Commanding 47th Inf. Brigade.

The Irish Brigade

Second Lieutenant, E. R. F. Beecher, 8th R/F. M.

I have read with much pleasure the reports of your Regimental Commander and Brigade Commander regarding your gallant conduct and devotion to duty in the field on 26th June, 1916, and have ordered your name to be entered in the record of the Irish Division.

W. B. Hickie, Major General.

Commanding 16th Irish Division.

Dear Mrs Beecher,

I hope you will forgive me, the Colonel commanding 8th R.M. Fusiliers for intruding upon your great sorrow over the death of your gallant son, Lieutenant. E. Beecher, but I am most anxious to convey to you in all sincerity the warm sympathy of all ranks in my Regiment in the irreparable loss you are called upon to bear.

Please try to be consoled to some extent by the knowledge that your son died the bravest of deaths from wounds received in the most gallant charge upon the enemy. His loss is a great blow from the fact that one of the cheeriest and best of good comrades has been taken from our midst.

I cannot speak too highly of your son's gallantry at all times, and his untiring energy, keenness and courage, quickly made me decide to promote him.

He has left an example to all subaltern officers which will continue to do good and never be forgotten by them, and his devotion to duty at all times lightened the responsibility of his seniors.

Again allow me to offer you, on behalf of the whole Regiment, our deepest sympathy and hope that God will sustain and strengthen you in your great trial.

Yours very truly.

E. Monteagle Browne

Grave or Memorial Reference: I.F.7. Cemetery: Mazingarbe Communal Cemetery Extension in France.

BELL, Rupert R.E.: Rank: Private. Regiment or Service: Royal Fusiliers. Unit: 23rd Battalion. Age at death: 25. Date of death: 8 February 1916. Service No: 1380 (CWGC), SPTS/1380 (SDGW). Born in Cathedral Waterford. Enlisted in Waterford while living at 85 Quay. Killed in action.

Supplementary information: Son of Isaac John and Maria Edith Bell, of 85 Quay, Waterford. From the *Waterford News* January 1915:

WATERFORD MEN VOLUNTEER.

A popular send-off was given on Monday evening to Mr Thomas Chambers, son of ex-Sergeant Chambers, South Parade, and Mr Rubert Bell, son of Mr J.J. Bel, the Quay, on the occasion of their departure for London to join the Sportsmen's Battalion Irish Fusiliers. Both young men are well and favourably known in Waterford. Mr Chambers was for a number of years in the office of Messrs H. Brandon and Co, Accountants, and it is satisfactory to learn that the firm are not only paying his salary for six months but they have agreed to retain his position for him. Mr Bell enjoys well-merited popularity among a wide circle of friends. The motor car of Mr William Hill, J. P., conveyed both young men to Waterford North Station, and there a large number of friends had gathered to give them a hearty send-off and wish them a safe and speedy return.

From the *Waterford News*, February 1916:

WATERFORD SOLDIER KILLED IN ACTION.

The death has occurred in action of Private Hubert [*sic*] E. Bell, son of Mr J.J. Bell, clothier, 81 The Quay, Waterford. The deceased was attached to the 23rd Battalion of the Fusiliers, Machine Gun Section, and was only twenty-five years of age. He volunteered shortly after the outbreak of war, and the news of his death will be learned of with regret and sympathy will go out to his parents in their loss.

Mr Bello learned of his son's death by a letter from Private Chambers who was alongside him, and by the following letter the chaplain; –

23rd Battalion, R. F.

B. E. F.

8th February, 1915.

My Dear Mr Ball,

The news of your son's death will, I know, come as a great shock to you. Although others will doubtless write to you of him

21

– others who knew him better and could speak with a more intimate knowledge of his sterling worth – yet I, too, would like to send you a word of heartfelt sympathy in this your hour of sorrow.

I laid your son to rest this afternoon in company with another lad of the 23rd Battalion. The Commanding Officer and others were present to pay their respects to those who had nobly made the greatest sacrifice for their King, their Country, and their God. The service was punctuated by the roar of guns – a fitting requiem for a gallant soldier. He was buried in a plot of ground set apart and carefully tended for our own soldiers, and lies there with many another who has laid down his life as we pray God not without avail for the advancement and betterment of the world. I know how hollow and unreal words of sympathy at a time like this often appear. I would have you feel, none the less, that my sympathy for you is great and my prayers real. May God give you strength – as indeed all those who have given their sons – to bear this trial. As to the actual military ability of your son, I leave that to others more competent to speak. From all I hear, he was respected by all, and endeared himself to his mates, who were very really touched by his death. A durable cross of wood, inscriped with his name, Regiment, etc.

From the *Waterford News*, February 1916:

HOW PRIVATE BELL DIED.

A Waterford soldier in a letter home describes how Private Hubert [*sic*] E Bell, son of Mr I. J. Bell, Quay, met his death at the front. He says "we have been in rather a warm portion of the line, and naturally have had more casualties than usual. I expect you have seen them in the papers from day to day. Poor Bell, who made up a quartet from Urbs Intacta, was killed early one morning whilst being pointed out the spot where O'Leary won the V. C. We regret him very much as he was a fine class of a chap, and we truly sympathise with his people at home."

Grave or Memorial Reference: II.K.7. Cemetery: Guards Cemetery, Windy Corner, Cuinchy in France. He is also listed on the Waterford and District Roll of Honour. Located in Christ Church Cathedral (Church of Ireland), Henrietta Street, Waterford.

BELLMAN, Arthur: Rank: Stoker, 1st Class. Regiment or Service: Royal Irish Regiment. Unit: HMS *Monmouth*. Date of death: 1 November 1914. Service No: K/190206. 'A nicely-mannered and popular inhabitant of Lismore.' Grave or Memorial Reference: 3. He has no known grave but is listed on the Plynouth Naval Memorial. UK.

BIGGANE, Michael Daniel: Rank: Private. Regiment or Service: Canadian Army Service Corps. Date of death: 10 October 1918. Service No: 2738. Data from enlistment documents:

In what Town, Township or Parish, and in what Country were you born? Stradbally, Waterford, Ireland.

What is the name of your next of kin? Patrick Biggane (father),

What is the address of your next of kin? Bonmahon, Ireland.

What is the date of your birth? 8 October 1893.

What is your trade or calling? Chauffeur. Are you married? No.

Are you willing to be attested to serve in the Canadian Over-Seas Expeditionary Force? Yes.

Apparent age: 21 years, 5 months.

Height: 5 Ft 10½ Ins.

Girth when fully expanded: 36½ Ins.

Range of expansion: 2½ Ins.

Complexion: dark

Eyes: grey

Hair: black.

Drowned on the HMS *Leinster*.

Grave or Memorial Reference: Near North-East corner. Cemetery: Ballylaneen (St Anne) Catholic Churchyard, Co. Waterford.

BIGGS, Colin: Rank: Private. Regiment or Service: Canadian Army. Unit: Canadian Infantry (Manitoba Regiment). Date of death: 13 June 1916. Age at death: 19. Service No: 420827. Killed in action.

Supplementary information: Son of Capt. Thomas J. Biggs, of The Imperial War Graves Commission, Camp Anglaise, Armentieres, Nord, France. From 'Our Heroes'. 1916:

Mr Colin Biggs, 16th Canadian Scottish Regiment, who was killed in action about June 13th, was the third son of Lieutenant Thomas J Biggs, R.E., and Mrs Biggs, Dungarvan, and grandson of the Rev. John Bain, M.A., late Rector of Dungarvan, and the Rev Thomas Biggs.LL.D., late of Templemartin, County Cork. He went to Canada in 1912, but on the outbreak of the war joined the Canadian Scottish and had spent over ten months in the trenches when he fell in action in his 20th year.

He has no known grave but is listed on Panel 24.26.28.30 on the Ypres (Menin Gate) Memorial in Belgium.

BISHOP, Walter: Rank: Private. Regiment or Service: Household Cavalry and Cavalry of the line including the Yeomanry and Imperial Camel Corps. Unit: 2nd Dragoon Guards (Queens Bays). Date of death: 13 May 1915. Service No: 3577. Born in Enniscorthy, Co. Wexford. Enlisted in Kilkenny. Killed in action. Age at death: 33.

Supplementary information: Son of Thomas Bishop of Shee Institute, Manor Street, Waterford. The Life Guards are a unit of the Household Cavalry. From the *Enniscorthy Guardian* in 1915:

WEXFORDMAN AND DUBINMAN IN THE LIFE GUARDS.

The following interview took place between a well known Wexfordman and a Dublinman who joined the Life Guards. Business took me out early one morning in the City of Dublin last week and just as

I was on the steps of my club the steward's son came, and shook my hand. He was only a lad when I knew him first and he donned khaki in the month of August 1914 just as the war broke out. His father was a soldier, and his mother says she would be a soldier too if it were possible and the three boys are still well off although they have been fighting since the war started.

He looked browned, hale and hearty, and was in tip top spirits. He told me he had not been home for ten months and during all that time he lived between the trenches and death. Out of his Battalion of 600 Life Guards, the biggest and the best, only 37 survived, and out of his own particular squadron of 200, 7 were alive to tell the tale of how their comrades nobly fell. Jack said he had some narrow escapes. He has had four horses killed under him.

One horse was struck with a shell, the poor animal was killed instantly and Jack's clothes and tunic were torn asunder, but he himself escaped without a scratch. Then again he was in the trenches one evening and the whole trench appears to have been blown up by an undermine. Apparently, he was left unconscious, and when he regained consciousness he found that the trench was gone and also that his comrades had gone to Heaven, for their bodies were mangled and in pieces and all around him were their legs, heads, arms and fragments of their bodies. He rested himself for an hour until he became quite conscious, and then set out in the dusk of the evening and went back to another Regiment, for his own had been no more. He thinks his mothers prayers helped him a lot, but I suggested to him that it was his sweetheart's, he said no, that he could not afford to have a sweetheart till the war was over.

He had only a week's holidays which will be up by the time this paper will appear and he should have gone back again with vigour and determination renewed. He assured me that the Irish soldiers were the talk of the whole front, indeed, the Germans were glad to be made prisoners by them, and by their

British comrades, but for some reason best known to the Germans, they don't care to fall into the hands of the French.

We shook each others hand and I expressed a hope that he would get a V.C, which he has so well earned but he told me that it was not his game that that was too high for him and all he wanted was to go and fight and when the war is over to come back again and tell his soldier father and good mother how he well and nobly did his bit. As we bade each other farewell, he said, "Rest assured the Germans are bled to death, for I myself have taken prisoners, boys of 15 years of age and old men of more than 50 summers. They were all glad to lift their hands in surrender and then to shake ours for mercy. In my opinion the war cannot last any longer than three months".

Grave or Memorial Reference: He has no known grave but is listed on Panel 3 on the Ypres (Menin Gate) Memorial in Belgium.

BLUETT, Joseph: Rank: Lance Sergeant. Regiment or Service: Royal Munster Fusiliers. Unit: 1st Battalion. Date of death: 9 July 1915. Age at death: 30. Service No: 8637. Born in Cappoquin, Co. Waterford. Enlisted in Youghal, Co. Cork, while living in Youghal. Died of wounds in Gallipoli.
Supplementary information: Son of Mary Bluett, of 151 Clinton Street, Portsmouth, New Hampshire, USA., and the late James Bluett. He has no known grave but is listed on Panel 185 to 100 on the Helles Memorial in Turkey.

BOBBIN, William Groom: Rank: B.Q.M.S. Regiment or Service: Royal Horse Artillery and Royal Field Artillery. Unit: 42nd Battery, 2nd Brigade. Date of death: 16 June 1916. Age at death: 34. Service No: 38701. Born in Kings Lynn, Norfolk. Enlisted in Chesterfield, Derby. Died.
Supplementary information: Husband of Rosa Bobbin, of 65A Fairlight Road, Tooting, London. I am not sure of the Waterford con-

nection but he is listed on the Waterford and District Roll of Honour. Located in Christ Church Cathedral (Church of Ireland), Henrietta Street, Waterford. Grave or Memorial Reference: II.C.2. Cemetery: Poperinghe New Military Cemetery in Belgium.

BOLAND, Daniel: Rank: Private. Regiment or Service: Royal Irish Regiment. Unit: 2nd Battalion. Date of death: 3 September 1916. Service No: 6550 and 2-6650. Born in Carrickbeg, Co. Waterford. Enlisted in Clonmel while living in Carrick-on-Suir, Co. Tipperary. Killed in action. Grave or Memorial Reference: XIV.J.7. Cemetery: Delville Wood Cemetery, Longueval in France.

BOLAND, Maurice: Rank: Lance Sergeant. Regiment or Service: Royal Munster Fusiliers. Unit: 2nd Battalion. Age at death: 32. Date of death: 25 September 1916. Service No: 747 Born in Dungarvan, Co. Waterford. Enlisted in Merthyr, Glamorganshire while living in Merthyr. Died of wounds. He won the Military Medal and is listed in the *London Gazette*.
Supplementary information: Son of Patrick Boland and Ann Lynch Boland, of Inchindrisla, Dungarvan, Co. Waterford. Grave or Memorial Reference: III.C.14. Cemetery: Dernancourt Communal Cemetery Extension in France.

BOR, Thomas Humphrey: Rank: Lieutenant. Regiment or Service: Royal Naval Reserve. Unit: H.M. Submarine E.5. Date of Death: 11 March 1916.
Supplementary information: Son of Edward N.C. Bor and Mabel Bor, of Rilcoran House, Callan, Co. Kilkenny. From 'Our Heroes':

Lieutenant T.H. Bor, R.N.R., was drowned at sea whilst on active service, about March 11th, 1916. he was the eldest son of Mr and Mrs Bor, Bank of Ireland, Maryborough, and was educated at Kilkenny College. He entered the Mercantile Marine when 14 years of age and secured his captain's certificate at 22. On the outbreak of the war he offered his services and obtained a Commission in the Royal Naval Reserve.

From De Ruvigny's Roll of Honour:

Eldest son of Edward Norman Cavendish Bor, of the Bank of Ireland, Maryborough, Queen's County, by his wife, Mabel, daughter of Isaac Thornton of Waterford, solicitor/ Born Tramore, County Waterford, 12th Feb, 1892. Educated in Kilkenny College, entered the Mercantile marine age the age of 14, and received his captain's certificate at the age of 22. Offered his services after the outbreak of war and was gazetted Lieutenant, Royal Naval reserve in September, 1914. He was employed in the Submarine Service from that time, his depot ship being H. M. S. Maidstone, and was lost in action 5th or 6th of March, 1916. His Captain wrote on 25 March, 1916; "We only know that the boat should have returned before dark on the 11th, and has never arrived. The two possibilities are that she either struck a mine, or was rammed by one of the German ships that we know passed over her patrol station on the night of the 5th or 6th. Your son had been here almost since the outbreak of war, and had done excellent service, and he was always keen."

From the *Leinster Express*:

DEATH OF LIEUTNENAT BOR.

The large circle of friends and acquaintances of Mr E.N.C. Bor, agent of the bank of Ireland, Maryborough, were grieved to learn that his eldest son, Lieutenant Thomas H. Bor, had lost his life in the service of his country while on naval duty. Lieutenant Bor was educated in Kilkenny College, from whence he passed into the mercantile marine service. The fact that he was granted a captain's certificate at

22 years of age is sufficient evidence of Lieutenant Bor's ability, and of his special aptitude for the profession he adopted. While in the mercantile service he travelled practically over the whole world, having visited China, Japan, South Africa, New Zealand, etc.

At the outbreak of the war Lieutenant Bor volunteered his services, and subsequently he received a Commission in the Royal Naval Reserve. He was only a few weeks Second Lieutenant, promotion following quickly on his connection with the Royal Navy, and the rank of Lieutenant was conferred upon him. Lieutenant Bor was actively engaged in the naval warfare, chiefly in connection with the most dangerous section of it—the submarine—and while thus engaged it is not revealing any secret to realise that his craft was instrumental in sending some enemy ships to the bottom. That he was an expert gunner is also evidenced by the fact that he fired an air-craft gun which injured a Zeppelin. Lieutenant Bor was a young man whose life was upright and blameless. He was beloved by his parents and all who knew him, it is regrettable that his brilliant, bu all to brief career---one which promised such a bright and useful future—should be prematurely destroyed. But his case is unfortunately only one of thousands that are grieved for to-day.

The utmost sympathy is felt for Lieutenant Bor's family in their great sorrow. A second son of Mr Bor's is on active service in the army.

The following telegram has been received by Mr E. N. C. Bor, Maryborough;

'The King and Queen deeply regret the loss you and the Navy has sustained by the death of your son in the service of his country. Their Majesties truly sympathise with you in your sorrow.

"Keeper of the Privy Purse. "

From the *Waterford News*, 1916:

LIEUTENANT T. H. BOR.

Lieutenant T.H. Borr, R.N.R. , whose death on active service has been notified, was the son of Mr E.N.C. Bor, Bank of Ireland, Maryborough. He received his early education at Kilkenny College, and at the age of 14 entered the Merchantile Marine, receiving his captain's certificate at 22. At the outbreak of hostilities he offered his services to his country, was accepted, and got a commission in the Royal Navy Reserve. The deceased officer gave promise of a brilliant career. Mr. Bor was for many years stationed in Waterford, and his many friends will, we are sure, with him in his bereavement.

Carlow Sentinel, April 1916:

LIEUTENANT T. H. BOR.

The death on active service at sea is announced of Lieutenant T.H. Bor, R. N.R. Lieutenant Bor, who was 24 years of age, was the eldest son of Mr E.N.C. Bor, Agent of the Bank of Ireland, Maryborough, and formerly of Kilkenny. His brother, Lieutenant N.L. Bor, is at present in France serving with the Connaught Rangers.

(His brother, Lieutenant N.L. Bor was wounded in September of the same year with the Connaught Rangers. He is a son of Mr. E.N.C. Bor, Maryborough, a cousin of the late General J.N. Bor, of Lieutenant-Colonel Hobbs. Submarine E. 5 was lost, cause unknown, in March 1916 with all hands, the wreck has never been located, Author.)

Grave or Memorial Reference:22. Cemetery: Plymouth Naval Memorial, UK.

BOWERS, Charles: Rank: Sapper. Regiment or Service: Royal Engineers. Unit: Base Signal Depot. Age at death: 25. Date of death: 4 May 1917. Service No: 152470.

Enlisted in Dungarvan, Co. Waterford while living in Portlaw. Died in Egypt.

Supplementary information: Son of John Henry and Elizabeth Jane Bowers, of Annes Court, Co. Waterford. From the *Waterford News* 1916:

WATERFORD G.P.O. MEN WITH THE COLOURS.

Three more young men on the clerical staff of the Waterford G.P.O. have now joined the signal company of the Royal Engineers as expert telegraphists. They are Messrs H. St. John Joseph Barden, and J. P. Clarke. Mr Bowers, of the clerical staff of office, has also joined the same unit. Waterford G.P.o. can boast of as good a record in the matter of giving men to the army as any other post office in Ireland. Up to the present over fifty postal employees in the Waterford postal district have joined the colours, no less than 13 of these being clerks, many of whom are already serving with the Engineers in France and other theatres of war. Lance-Corporal Duggan. Royal Engineers, who joined from the clerical staff of the GPO., and has been in France for a considerable time is home on short leave this week.

Grave or Memorial Reference: C.7. Cemetery: Savona Town Cemetery in Italy.

BOWMAN, Walter: Rank: Private. Regiment or Service: Hampshire Regiment. Unit: 1st Battalion. Date of death: 22 May 1915. Service No: 9480. Born in Piltown, Carrick-on-Suir, Co. Tipperary. Enlisted in Clonmel while living in Waterford. Killed in action. Age at death: 35. He has no known grave but is listed on Panel 35 on the Ypres (Menin Gate) Memorial in Belgium.

BRAWDERS, Richard: Rank: Private. Regiment or Service: Canadian Machine Gun Corps. Unit: 2nd Battalion. Age at death: 26. Date of death: 15 November 1917 Service No:

428182 Awards: Military Medal. Data from attestation papers:

> In what Town, Township or Parish, and in what Country were you born? Luffany, Kilkenny.
>
> What is the name of your next of kin? (brother) Malcolm, Brawders.
>
> What is the address of your next of kin? 22 Phillips Street, Salem, Mass.
>
> What is the date of your birth? 3 July 1893.
>
> What is your trade or calling? Labourer.
>
> Are you married? No.
>
> Do you now belong to the Active Militia? Yes, 11th I. F.
>
> Do you understand the nature and terms of your engagement? Yes.
>
> Apparent age: 22 years, 9 months.
>
> Height: 5 Ft, 6 ¾ Ins.
>
> Girth when fully expanded: 40Ins.
>
> Complexion: medium.
>
> Eyes: grey.
>
> Hair: light.
>
> Distinctive marks: four vaccination marks on left arm.
>
> Date: 20 March 1915.

Son of John and Mary Brawders. Native of Mooncoin, Waterford, Ireland. Grave or Memorial Reference: XII.B.16. Cemetery: Dozinghem Military Cemetery in Belgium.

BREEN, James: Rank: Private. Regiment or Service: Royal Irish Regiment. Unit: 2nd Battalion. Date of death: 1 July 1916. Service No: 4705. Born in St John's Waterford. Enlisted in Waterford. Killed in action. Grave or Memorial Reference: K.20. Cemetery: Carnoy Military Cemetery in France.

BREEN, Matthew: Rank: Lance Corporal. Regiment or Service: Guards Machine Gun Regiment. Unit: 4th Battalion. Date of death: 11 October 1918. Service No: 1844. Previously he was with the South Irish Horse where his number was 9529. Born in Templetown, Co. Wexford. Enlisted in Ayr, Ayrshire while living

in Fethard, Co. Tipperary. Died of wounds. Age at death: 23.

Supplementary information: Son of Mrs Margaret Breen, of Herrylock, Fethard, Waterford. Grave or Memorial Reference: I.D.5. Cemetery: Masnieres British Cemetery, Marcoing in France.

BREEN, Martin: Rank: Mate. Regiment or Service: Unknown. Unit: River Steamer *Duncannon*. Date of death: 24 December 1914.

Supplementary information: About 8pm on Christmas Eve, during a heavy fog he fell whilst attempting to put out the Gangway at Passage he fell overboard and drowned. His body was recovered two hours later. He leaves a wife and a large family. There is no burial information available.

BREEN, Walter: Rank: Mate. The only information I have on this sailor is contained in the below. From the *Waterford News*, 1915:

SEAMAN DROWNED IN WATERFORD HARBOUR.

Widows Claim for Compensation.

At Waterford Quarter Sessions before Judge Brerton Barry.

Catherine Breen, *Duncannon*, widow of the late Walter Breen, sued the owners of the S.S. *Duncannon* for compensation in respect of the loss of her husband who, as a mate on the vessel, was drowned. Mr P.A. Buggy, solicitor, appeared for the applicant, and Mr O'Connor, solicitor (acting for Mr McCoy, solicitor, Waterford), for the respondents. Mr Buggy said the drowning occurred on the voyage from Waterford to Passage East. The deceased, who left a widow and six children, was in receipt of 25s a week. Mr O'Connor submitted that his Honour had no jurisdiction on as the ship was registered in Waterford and in Waterford the man was drowned. Mr Buggy produced the ship's log to show that the man was drowned at sea and the case was within his Honour's jurisdiction. The applicant also resided in the County Wexford. They were also claiming £204. Mr O'Connor said he would agree to an order for £165 or 22s weekly. Mr Buggy aid he would take £195. His Honour made an order for this amount, allocating one-third for the widow to be paid quarterly and retaining the balance for the children. On the application of Mr Buggy, £3 15s witnesses expenses were allowed. Mr Buggy stated that he had to pay Mr French, M.P., Coroner, £1 for copies of the depositions taken at the inquest.

BREGAN, Paul: Rank: Private. Regiment or Service: Royal Munster Fusiliers. Unit: 1st Battalion. Date of death: 21 August 1915. Age at death: Service No: 9370. Born in St John's, Cappoquinn, Co. Waterford. Enlisted in Tralee, Co. Kerry while living in Dublin. Killed in action in Gallipoli. He has no known grave but is listed on Panel 185 to 190 on the Helles Memorial in Turkey.

BRENNAN, Kieran Joseph: Rank: Private. Regiment or Service: City of London Regiment (Royal Fusiliers). Unit: 1st Battalion. Date of death: 31 July 1917. Service No: 50140. Formerly he was with the Royal Fusiliers where his number was STK/2627. Born in Waterford. Enlisted in Camberwell while living in Southwark. Killed in action. Grave or Memorial Reference: Panel 6 and 8. Memorial: Ypres (Menin Gate) Memorial in Belgium.

BRETT, Patrick: Rank: Private. Regiment or Service: Royal Irish Regiment. Unit: 2nd Battalion. Date of death: 25 January 1916. Service No: 4877. Born in Tramore, Co. Waterford. Enlisted in Clonmel. Died at Home. From the *Munster Express* and the *Waterford News*:

WATERFORD SOLDIER'S SAD DEATH.

The sad circumstances attending the death of Private Patrick Brett, of the 2nd Royal Irish Regiment, who died in the hospital at Newport (South Wales), as a result of injuries received in the Newport tunnel were investigated on Friday. It was stated that the deceased was travelling to his home at Williamstone, Waterford. A ticket collector who travelled with the train from Paddington said that six or seven soldiers returning from the front were on the train and some were more or less intoxicated. When he punched their tickets between reading and Bath some of them were noisy and the others were trying to persuade them to sit down. They were noisy at Bristol but not quarrelsome. He thought they fell asleep after leaving Bristol. The train passed through Newport and the tunnel about 8 o'clock, but witness knew of nothing amiss until they reached Fishguard when he saw he had a wire asking if a solder was missing. He did not know for soldiers were getting in and leaving at all the stations. At Fishguard it was found impossible to rouse the soldiers and they were got out by their friends. Dr. Champrey, of the Newport Hospital, said the he thought deceased fell from one train and was run over by another. On deceased's identification disc, which was fastened to his right hand, was the word 'died' but no date.

The coroner remarked that the word was scratched on with a pin or something of that sort and appeared to have been done some months ago.

Replying, Mr A. J. Williams, of the National Union of Railwaymen said that the deceased smelt as if he had intoxicants. A shunter stated that when the express left Newport one of the doors was open, but a signalman in a box near the tunnel said that when the express passed his box no door was open. The driver of a train on the top line said he felt his engine pass over something in the tunnel at nine minutes past eight, but found no marks on the engine at the next station. The jury returned a verdict that death was due to injuries received by the deceased being run over but whether as a result of an accident or not there was not sufficient evidence to show.

From the *Waterford News*, January 1916:

WATERFORD SOLDIER'S SAD END.
Killed on his way home from the front.
Patrick Brett, Royal Irish Rifles, aged 30, died in hospital at Newport, Mon, on Tuesday as a result of an accident on the railway. He was found in the Newport tunnel about 10 o'clock with a fractured skull and one leg practically severed, and had apparently fallen out of the train while on his way to Williamstown, Waterford. He was on leave from France.

The deceased formerly lived at Moonamintra. He was a farm labourer and worked in the Williamstown district, a brother of his being at present employed at Mr Barron's, Williamstown. He was in the army reserve, and joined the colours at the outbreak of war.

From the *Waterford News*, March 1916:

LETTER FROM THE TRENCHES.
D Company, 2nd Battalion, Royal Irish Regiment. B. E. F.
28th February, 1916.
Dear Editor,
Will you kindly make space in your paper of which we Waterford men are constant readers, and which we are glad to be able to see our local paper put around the trenches every week. I write just to leave the relatives of Private Brett, late of our company, know that we have heard of his death by accident while proceeding on leave for his native city to enjoy a well-earned rest with his parents and afterwards to return back again to continue his task with his comrades and bring a murderous and treacherous enemy to his knees. However, we hope and trust that he was prepared to join the ranks of his fellow comrades in the land above and enjoy everlasting rest in peace and happiness. We send our deepest sympathy to the relatives of Private Brett in their loss of a good fighting soldier.

Sent on behalf of all the Waterford boys and other comrades who knew him.
Corporal M Butler.

Grave or Memorial Reference: 24.RC.144.
Cemetery: Newport (St Woolos) Cemetery, UK.

BRIEN, David: Rank: Private. Regiment or Service: Royal Irish Regiment. Unit: 2nd Battalion. Date of death: 19 October 1914. Service No: 6615. Born Knockbeg, Co. Waterford. Enlisted in Waterford. Killed in action.

BRIEN, Michael: Rank: Private. Regiment or Service: Royal Irish Regiment. Unit: 2nd Battalion. Date of death: 24 August 1918. Service No: 8178. Born in Kereen, Co. Waterford. Enlisted in Dungarvan while living in Kereen. Killed in action. Grave reference; Special Memorial 1. Cemetery; St Symphorien Military Cemetery in Belgium

BRIEN, William Thomas: Rank: Private. Regiment or Service: Royal Irish Regiment. Unit: 'A' Coy. 5th Battalion. Age at death: 23. Date of death: 16 August 1915. Service No: 3428. Born in Randalstwon, Co. Meath. Enlisted in Longford while living in Portlaw. Killed in action in Gallipoli.

Supplementary information: Son of William Thomas and Sarah Sophia Brien, of Ardkeen, Waterford. He has no known grave but is listed on Panel 55 on the Helles Memorial in Turkey.

BROWN, Hubert William: Rank: Lieutenant. Regiment or Service: Royal Irish Regiment. Unit: attached to the 2nd Nigeria Regiment, W.A.F.F. Date of Death: 19 September 1914. Died of wounds. De Ruvigny's Roll of Honour:

...son of the late John Mosse Brown. Born in Greenville, Waterford, 11 January 1890. Educated at Aravon, Bray; St Faughan's College, County Cork, and at Cheltenham

College. Gazetted 2nd Lieutenant Royal Irish Regiment, 6 November 1909, and promoted Lieutenant, 9 March 1910. Served with the Indian Expeditionary Force, and died in September 1914 from wounds received in action while fighting in the Cameroons.

Grave or Memorial Reference: He has no known grave but is listed on the Lokoja Memorial in Nigeria.

BROWN, John: Rank: Private. Regiment or Service: 2nd Dragoons (Royal Scots Greys). Age at death: 35. Date of death: 2 November 1914. Service No: 5230. Born in Glencairn, Thornhill, Dumfriesshire. Enlisted in Dumfries while living in Glencairn. Died.

Supplementary information: Son of the late William and Sarah Brown, of Moss-Side, Dunscore, Dumfriesshire. Born at Woodhead, Glencairn, Co. Waterford. Grave or Memorial Reference: Wervicq Road. German Cemetery Memorial. 31. Cemetery: Zantvoorde British Cemetery in Belgium.

BROWN, John: Rank: Lance Corporal. Regiment or Service: Royal Irish Rifles. Unit: 23rd Entrenching Battalion, late 14th Battalion. Age at death: 33. Date of death: 23 March 1918. Service No: 5259. Born in Carbally, Co. Waterford. Enlisted in Cardiff, Glamorgan while living in Dunmore East, Co. Waterford. Killed in action.

Supplementary information: Son of Mrs Anne Brown, of Ballymacaw, Dunmore East, Co. Waterford. Grave or Memorial Reference: 74 to 76 on the Pozières Memorial in France.

BROWN, John: Rank: Private. Regiment or Service: Irish Guards. Unit: 1st Battalion. Date of death: 17 September 1916. Service No: 9566. Born in Carrick Beg, Co. Waterford. Enlisted in Killeater, Co. Waterford. Killed in action. He has no known grave but is listed on Pier and Face 7D on the Thiepval Memorial in France.

Patrick Brown. Image above courtesy of Millie Murphy, Hillview, Waterford. Information on the back says, 'Pat Brown, Couse, Waterford, 17 years. Killed 2nd Battle of Loos, 01-05-1916.'

BROWN, Patrick: Rank: Private. Regiment or Service: Royal Irish Regiment. Unit: 6th Battalion. Date of death: 1 May 1916. Service No: 11232. Born in St John's, Waterford. Enlisted in Waterford. Killed in action. Grave or Memorial Reference: I.J.19. Cemetery: Dud Corner Cemetery, Loos in France.

BROWN, Patrick: Rank: Cattleman. Regiment or Service: Mercantile Marine. Unit: SS *Coningbeg* (Glasgow). Torpedoed by German Submarine U-62. There were no survivors. U-62 surrendered in November 1918. Age at death: 57. Date of death: 18 December 1917.

Supplementary information: Son of the late Patrick and Ellen Brown. Born in Waterford. Grave or Memorial Reference: He has no known grave but is listed on the Tower Hill Memorial in the UK. He is also listed on the Formby-Coningbeg Memorial, Adelphi Quay in Waterford City.

BROWN, Richard: Rank: Private. Regiment or Service: Royal Dublin Fusiliers. Unit: 1st Battalion. Date of death: 30 June 1915. Service No: 18496. Born in Waterford. Enlisted in Portlaw, Co. Waterford. Killed in action in Gallipoli. Grave or Memorial Reference: Panel 190 to 195. Memorial: Helles Memorial in Turkey.

BROWNER, John: Rank: Private. Regiment or Service: Royal Irish Fusiliers. Unit: 8th Battalion. Date of death: 9 May 1917. Service No: 43014. Formerly he was with the Royal Irish Regiment where his number was 6043. Born in Waterford. Enlisted in Waterford. Killed in action. From the *Waterford News*, May 1917:

PRIVATE BROWNER KILLED IN ACTION.
Mrs Browner, New Street, Waterford, received notification on Tuesday from the War Office that her husband, Private John Browner, Royal Irish Regiment, had been recently killed in action. The deceased, who was through many important engagements, was home for six weeks last summer suffering from dysentery.

Grave or Memorial Reference: II.A.5. Cemetery: Elzenwalle Brasserie Cemetery in Belgium.

BUCKLEY, John: Rank: Lance Corporal. Regiment or Service: Royal Irish Fusiliers. Unit: 7th/8th Battalion. Age at death: 24. Date of death: 7 June 1917. Service No: 43018. Previously he was with the Royal Irish Regiment where his number was 7648. Born in Waterford. Enlisted in Waterford. Killed in action.
Supplementary information: Son of James and Mary Anne Buckley, of 34 Doyle Street, Waterford. Grave or Memorial Reference: XV.K.20. Cemetery: Voormezeele Enclosure No. 3 in Belgium.

BUGGY, Joseph: Rank: Private. Regiment or Service: Canadian Infantry (Eastern Ontario Regiment) Age at death: 34. Date of death: 3 May 1918 Service No: 3057423. Joseph's attestation papers are not available.
Supplementary information: Son of Michael Buggy, of Waterford. Grave or Memorial Reference: Plan 4. Grave 7. Cemetery: Kingston (St Marys) Cemetery, Ontario, Canada.

BURKE, Edward: Rank: Able Seaman Regiment or Service: Mercantile Marine Unit: SS *Formby* (Glasgow). Date of death: 16 December 1917.
Supplementary information: Son of the late William and Mary Burke. Husband of the late Mary Burke. Born at Portally, Dunmore East. He has no known grave but is listed on the Tower Memorial, UK. He is also listed on the Formby-Coningbeg Memorial, Adelphi Quay in Waterford City.

BURKE, John: Rank: Private. Regiment or Service: Royal Dublin Fusiliers. Unit: 1st Battalion. Date of death: 7 July 1915. Service No: 17588. Born in Waterford. Enlisted in Merthyr while living in Penrhiweeiber, Glam. Killed in action in Gallipoli. Grave or Memorial Reference: VII.F.7. Cemetery: Twelve Tree Copse Cemetery in Turkey.

BURKE, Michael: Rank: Private. Regiment or Service: Royal Irish Regiment. Unit: 2nd Battalion. Date of death: 7 June 1917. Service No: 8763. Born in Trinity Without, Waterford. Enlisted in Waterford. Died of wounds. Grave or Memorial Reference: I. A. 4. Cemetery: Locre Hospice Cemetery in Belgium.

BURKE, Richard Joseph: Rank: Lieutenant. Regiment or Service: Canadian Forestry Corps Age at death: 56. Date of death: 8 September 1918. Data from attestation papers:

What is your present address? 104 University Avenue, Toronto, Canada, changed to 425 Quebec Avenue, Toronto, Canada.

In what Town, Township or Parish, and in what Country were you born? Waterford, Ireland.

What is the name of your next of kin? Annie Burke.

What is the address of your next of kin? Hudson Road, Aldion, Brisbane. Queensland, Australia, changed to Vallambrasa Street, St John's Road, Hyde, Isle of Wight.

What is the relationship of your next of kin? Wife.

What is the date of your birth? 2 September (also listed as 8 September) 1868. What is your trade or calling? Soldier.

Are you married? Married.

Do you now belong to the Active Militia? Yes. If so, state particulars of former service. 1st King's Liverpool Regiment, 22½ years, Sergeant Major.

Have you ever served in any Military Force? Yes A.A.S.C., 2 years Sergeant Major, 1st King's Liverpool Regiment, 22 ½ years, Sergeant Major.

Are you willing to be attested to serve in the Canadian Over-Seas Expeditionary Force? Yes.

Apparent age: 47 years, 8 months.

Height: 5 Ft, 8Ins.

Girth when fully expanded: 39½ Ins.

Range of expansion: 3Ins.

Complexion:med.

Eyes: blue.

Hair: dark.

Date: 5 May 1916.

Supplementary information: Son of the late Richard J. and Mary Burke. Husband of Anny Burke. Served in the South African War with 8th Battalion. The King's Liverpool Regiment. Died when the Steamship *Missanabie* was torpedoed in the English Channel. Grave or Memorial Reference: Panel 2 on The Halifax Memorial, Nova Scotia, Canada.

BURKE, William: Rank: Private. Regiment or Service: Royal Irish Regiment. Unit: 1st Battalion. Date of death: 26 April 1915. Age at death: 26. Service No: 9689. Born in St

Patrick's, Waterford. Enlisted in Waterford. Killed in action.

Supplementary information: Son of Anastatia Burke, of 9 Stephen Street., Waterford. Has no known grave but is commemorated on Panel 33. Memorial: Ypres (Menin Gate) Memorial in Belgium.

BURNS, John: Rank: Able Seaman. Regiment or Service: Mercantile Marine. Unit: SS *Formby* (Glasgow) The ship was lost with all hands and never located during a fierce storm. Age at death: 30. Date of death: 16 December 1917.

Supplementary information: Son of Martin and Alice Burns. Husband of Anne Burns (*née* Phelan), of Cheek Point, Co. Waterford. Born at Cheek Point. He has no known grave but is listed on the Tower Hill Memorial in the UK. He is also listed on the Formby-Coningbeg Memorial, Adelphi Quay in Waterford City.

BURNS, William: Rank: Lance Sergeant. Regiment or Service: Royal Irish Rifles. Unit: 2nd Battalion. Age at death: 22. Date of death: 26 October 1914. Service No: 9945. Born in Cork. Enlisted in Dublin while living in Waterford. Killed in action.

Supplementary information: Son of William and Marian Burns, of 105 Barrack Street, Waterford. Grave or Memorial Reference: 42 and 43 on the Le Touret Memorial in France.

BURNS, William: Rank: Corporal. Regiment or Service: Royal Irish Rifles. Unit: 2nd Battalion. Date of death: 26 October 1914. Age at death: 22. Service No: 9945. Born in Cork. Enlisted in Dublin while living in Waterford. Killed in action.

Supplementary information: Son of William and Marian Burns, of 105, Barrack Street, Waterford. He has no known grave but is listed on Panels 42 to 43 on the Le Touret Memorial. He is also listed on the Waterford and District Roll of Honour. Located in Christ Church Cathedral (Church of Ireland), Henrietta Street, Waterford.

BUTLER, Joseph: Rank: Private. Regiment or Service: Royal Inniskilling Fusiliers. Unit: 1st Battalion. Date of death: 1 July 1916. Service No: 17041. Born in Portlaw, Co. Waterford. Enlisted in Manchester while living in Droylesden. Killed in action. He has no known grave but is listed on Pier and Face 4D and 5B on the Thiepval Memorial in France.

BUTLER, Matthew: Rank: Private/Lance Corporal. Regiment or Service: Royal Irish Regiment. Unit: 2nd Battalion. Date of death: 27 August 1916. Service No: 4772. Born in Trinity Without, Waterford. Enlisted in Waterford. Killed in action. From the *Waterford News* and the *Munster Express* 1915:

A CARRICK MAN'S EXPERIENCES.

Private J. Fahy, of the Royal Irish Regiment, writing from Dublin Castle Hospital to his father in Carrick-on-Suir, gives the following vivid account of his experiences at the battle of St Eloi, in which he was wounded.

"I got wounded about 3 o'clock on Monday at the attack on St Eloi. We had a rough time of it there. We had to retire at First. Then we counter attacked and got back four of the trenches. The Germans had six of them belonging to us. The number killed was terrible. The Germans shelled us going up. I will never forget it. The stretcher-bearers could not get in to take away the wounded. Some of them had to be left there, to bleed to death. When I got hit I threw off my rifle, equipment and all and scrambled over dead and wounded on my hands and one knee for about four hundred yards, dragging my leg after me. A chap from Waterford, named Matty Butler carried me on his back to the dressing station. He afterwards got six wounds in the hands and legs bringing back more wounded. The cries and moans of the wounded were terrible. I cried a bit myself too."

From the *Waterford News*, 9 April 1915:

WOUNDED WATERFORDMAN'S GALLANTRY.

A Waterfordman, Lance Corporal Matt Butler (Royal Irish Regiment), writing from a hospital at Harrogate to a chum, says; "Yes, I took you back and dressed your wounds to keep you from bleeding to death, and continued to dress until I had seven of my comrades done …. If our gallant Major Lillie had been spared there would be something about it, as he asked me would I continue to dress. I said yes. He said that he would remember me. However, I got my reward, as can be seen. I got wounded in both arms, both thighs, and right leg. I didn't get hit in the stomach or head, so you can see the Almighty God saved me for saving the lives of my comrades; that was my reward. "

(See letter sent to parents of **BRETT, Patrick.**) He has no known grave but is listed on Pier and Face 3 A on the Thiepval Memorial in France.

BUTLER, Maurice: Rank: Carpenter. Regiment or Service: Mercantile Marine. Unit: SS *Formby* (Glasgow). Age at death: 28. Date of death: 16 December 1917. The ship was lost with all hands and never located during a fierce storm.

Supplementary information: Son of Maurice and Ellen Butler. Husband of Ellen Butler (*née* Keating), of 15 St Alphonsus Road, Waterford. Born in Waterford. He has no known grave but is listed on the Tower Hill Memorial in the UK. He is also listed on the Formby-Coningbeg Memorial, Adelphi Quay in Waterford City.

BUTLER, Nicholas: Rank: Private. Regiment or Service: Royal Irish Regiment. Unit: 'C' Coy. 1st Battalion. Age at death: 39. Date of death: 4 February 1916. Service No: 7049. Born in Ballybricken, Co. Waterford. Enlisted in Waterford. Killed in action. Died in Salonika.

Supplementary information: Husband of Bridget Butler, of 3 Walshe's Lane, Waterford. Served in the South African Campaign. Grave or Memorial Reference: 77. Cemetery: Salonika (Lembet Road) Military Cemetery in Greece.

BUTLER, Pierce: Rank: Rifleman. Regiment or Service: Royal Irish Rifles. Unit: 1ˢᵗ Battalion. Age at death: 25. Date of death: 29 June 1916. Service No: 9535. Born in Waterford. Enlisted in Waterford. Died of wounds.

Supplementary information: Son of Michael and Mary Butler, of 47 Slieve-Keale, Waterford.

LOCAL WAR NEWS.

HOW A WATERFORD SOLDIER DIED.

Mrs Butler of 14 Slievekeale, Waterford, has received a letter from Sister N.E. Vernon Harcourt who is I charge of No 36 Casualty Clearing Station, B.E.F., France, notifying here of the death of her son, Rifleman P. Butler, 9536. The letter runs, "I am grieved to have to tell you of the death of your son. He was admitted early this morning (29ᵗʰ June) to this hospital. He had been badly wounded in the left leg just below the knee. The artery was severed and he was suffering from shock and loss of blood. They had given him morphia at the field ambulance to save him pain, and he was consequently in a very weak, drowsy condition and did not speak. He did not appear to be suffering. The doctors did all they could for him, but it was of no avail; he never rallied and passed away very peacefully at 2pm. I sent for the priest as soon as I saw your son this morning an he came at once and did what he could for him, and will bury him to-morrow in the military cemetery hard by this camp where so many of his fellow-soldiers already lie at peace. I pray God comfort you in your bereavement. I am sending you a lock of his hair which I think you will like to have."

Grave or Memorial Reference: I F.7. Cemetery: Heilly Station Cemetery, Mericourt-L'Abbe in France.

BUTLER, William: Rank: Private. Regiment or Service: Irish Guards. Unit: 1ˢᵗ Battalion. Date of death: 1 November 1914. Service No: 558. Born in Aglish, Co. Waterford. Enlisted in Dowlais, Glamorganshire while living in Bedminster, Glos. Killed in action. He has no known grave but is listed on Panel 11 on the Ypres (Menin Gate) Memorial in Belgium.

BUTLER William: Rank: Private. Regiment or Service: Australian Infantry, A.I.F. Unit: 26th Battalion. Date of death: 8 August 1918. Service No: 283. Enlisted in Ennogera on 16 April 1915, Taken on strength, 26ᵗʰ Battalion, 24 May 1915. Killed in action on the Somme. Over his career he was awarded various punishments of Field punishment No 2, forfeiture of pay and detention for being absent without official leave, drunkenness at Etaples, absent from detention roll call, breaking camp while under field punishment No 2, A.W.O.L. and incurring a taxi fare, being out of bounds in Etaples, damaging Government property, contracting VD, absent from billets at Tattoo, breaking camp, and being absent from guard mounting. Hospitalised with trench foot, VD, epididymitis, enlarged testicle, Tuberculosis, non venereal Palillomata. From his records.

In or near what Parish or Town were you born? Waterford, Ireland.

Are you a natural born British subject or a Naturalised British subject? Natural Born British Subject.

What is your age? 23 years, 4 months.

What is your trade or calling? Cordial Maker.

Are you, or have you been an Apprentice? No. If so where, to whom, and for what period?

Are you married? Single.

Who is your next of kin? (Father) James Butler, Beau Street, Waterford. [Later changed to his brother Patrick Butler, Roanmore Terrace, Waterford and then changed to wife, (on the 6 December 1916) Mrs A Butler, 29 North Quay, Manley, Sydney. She proved to be untraceable. His medals were finally issued to his brother.]

Have you ever been convicted by the Civil Power? No.

Distinctive marks, tattoo on right arm 'Harp with 'Erin go Bragh' and a tattoo on the left arm of a rose.

Age, 23 years, 4 months.

Height 5 feet, 10½ inches.

Weight, 11st, lbs.

Chest measurement: 32–34½ inches.

Complexion: fair.

Eyes: brown.

Hair: red.

Religious denomination: R.C.

Grave or Memorial Reference: I.E.21. Cemetery: Adelaide Cemetery, Villers-Bretonneux in France.

BYRNE, John Alphonsus: Rank: Private. Regiment or Service: Australian Infantry, A.I.F. Unit: 53rd Battalion. Date of death: 19 July 1916. Service No: 1664. Admitted to hospital at various times for Dysentry, Diarrhoea and being wounded in action.

In or near what Parish or Town were you born? St John's, Waterford.

Are you a natural born British subject or a Naturalised British subject? Natural Born.

What is your age? 24 years, 3 months.

What is your trade or calling? Groom.

Are you, or have you been an Apprentice? If so where, to whom, and for what period? No.

Are you married? No.

Who is your next of kin? Frank Byrne (father), 44 Patrick Street, Waterford.

Age: 24 years, 3 months.

Height 5 feet, 5 1/8 inches.

Weight: 143 lbs.

Chest measurement: 31–34 ½ inches.

Complexion: fair.

Eyes: grey.

Hair: fair.

Religious denomination: R.C.

Listed as 'wounded and missing'. Later this was changed to 'Killed in action' by a Court of Enquiry 'in the field' on 2 September 1917. The memorial plaque and scroll were sent to his father. Pension of 20 shillings per fortnight issued to his father, Mr Francis Byrne, 44 Patrick Street, Waterford from 4 October 1917. The pension was reversed in October 1918 when his father died He has no known grave but is listed on the V.C. Corner Australian Cemetery Memorial in Fromelles in France.

BYRNE, Patrick Arthur: Rank: Lance Corporal. Regiment or Service: Royal Army Medical Corps. Unit: 98th (County Palatine) Field Amb. Age at death: 24. Date of death: 22 April 1917. Service No: 339148. Born in Wallasey, Cheshire. Enlisted in Liverpool, Lancashire while living in County Wallasey. Died of wounds.

Supplementary information: Son of Edward and Isabella Byrne, of Kilmacow, Waterford. Grave or Memorial Reference: I.A. 22. Cemetery: Bucquoy Road Cemetery, Ficheux in France.

C

CAHILL, James: Rank: Private. Regiment or Service: Royal Irish Regiment. Unit: 2nd Battalion. Date of death: 19 October 1914. Service No: 5723. Born in St Patrick's, Co. Waterford. Enlisted in Waterford. Killed in action. He has no known grave but is listed on Panels 11 and 12 on the Le Touret Memorial in France.

CAHILL, Patrick: Rank: Private. Regiment or Service: Household Cavalry and Cavalry of the line including the Yeomanry and Imperial Camel Corps. Unit: 19th (Queens Alexandra's Own Royal) Hussars. Age at death: 38. Date of death: 24 May 1915. Service No: 5187. Born in Waterford. Enlisted in Cardiff while living in Waterford. Killed in action.

Supplementary information: Son of Margaret Cahill, of Carrick-on-Suir. Mobilized 4 August 1914. Fourteen years' service. Served in the South African Campaign. Grave or Memorial Reference: Panel 5. Memorial: Ypres (Menin Gate) Memorial in Belgium.

CAHILL, William: Rank: Able Seaman. Regiment or Service: Mercantile Marine. Unit: SS *Coningbe* (Glasgow). Torpedoed by German Submarine U-62. There were no survivors. U-62 surrendered in November 1918. Age at death: 57. Date of death: 18 December 1917.

Supplementary information: Son of the late William and Margaret Cahill. Husband of Ellen Cahill (*née* Crowley), of Market Street, Tramore, Co. Waterford. Born in Waterford. He has no known grave but is listed on the Tower Hill Memorial in the UK. He is also listed on the Formby-Coningbeg Memorial, Adelphi Quay in Waterford City.

CALLAGHAN, Michael John: Rank: Sergeant. Regiment or Service: Machine Gun Corps (Infantry). Unit: 36th Coy. He was previously with the Royal Sussex Regiment where his number was 459. Age at death: 23. Date of death: 16 February 1916. Service No: 20301. Born in Grange in Tipperary and enlisted in Horesham in the UK while living in Clonmel, Co. Waterford. Killed in action.

Supplementary information: Son of Patrick and Mary Anne Callaghan, of Knocklofty, Demesne, Clonmel, Co. Tipperary. Grave or Memorial Reference: B.26. Cemetery: Quarry Cemetery, Vermelles in France.

CALLAGHAN, William: Rank: Private. Regiment or Service: Irish Guards. Unit: 2nd Battalion. Date of death: 12 April 1918. Service No: 11167. Born in Newtown, Co. Waterford. Enlisted in Waterford. Killed in action. Grave or Memorial Reference: I.BB.34. Cemetery: Aval Wood Military Cemetery, Vieux-Berquin in France.

CANTY, Thomas: Rank: Private. Regiment or Service: Royal Irish Regiment. Unit: 1st Battalion. Date of death: 28 December 1917. Service No: 7325. Born in St John's, Waterford. Enlisted in Waterford while living in Grantstown, Waterford. Killed in action in Palestine. Grave or Memorial Reference: A.26. Cemetery: Jerusalem War Cemetery, Israel.

CARBERRY, James: Rank: Private/Lance Corporal. Regiment or Service: Royal Irish Regiment. Unit: 2nd Battalion. Date of death: 21 August 1918. Service No: 7609. Born in St Patrick's, Waterford. Enlisted in Waterford. Killed in action. He won the Military Medal and is listed in the *London Gazette*.

Supplementary information: Son of Thomas Carberry, of 42 Newports Lane, Waterford. Grave or Memorial Reference: 5 on the Vis-En-Artois Memorial in France.

CARBERRY, Michael: Rank: Private. Regiment or Service: Royal Irish Regiment. Unit: 2nd Battalion. Date of death: 19 October 1914. Service No: 6690. Born in St Patrick's, Co. Waterford. Enlisted in Waterford. Killed in action. He has no known grave but is listed on Panels 11 and 12 on the Le Touret Memorial in France.

CARBERY, William: Rank: Sapper. Regiment or Service: Royal Engineers. Unit: 97th Field Coy. Age at death: 36. Date of death: 2 October 1917. Service No: 63504. Enlisted in London. Killed in action.

Supplementary information: Son of Marianne Dee (formerly Carbery), of 37 Brown St, Portlaw, Co. Waterford, and the late William Carbery. Grave or Memorial Reference: XLI.B.24. Cemetery: Tyne Cot Cemetery in Belgium.

CAREW, Edward: Rank: Sapper. Regiment or Service: Corps of Royal Engineers. Unit: 5th Reserve Battalion, Royal Engineers. Battalion. Age at death: 28. Date of death: 10 October 1918. Service No: 46134. Born in Waterford. Enlisted in Dublin. Died at Sea. The SS *Leinster* sank on this day. He may have been a passenger as he 'died at sea'.

Grave or Memorial Reference: RC. 611. Cemetery: Grangegorman Military Cemetery in Dublin.

CAREW, Robert Thomas: Rank: Colonel. Regiment or Service: Leinster Regiment. Age at death: 56. Date of death: 11 February 1917.

Supplementary information: Husband of Mary Carew, of Ballydavid, Rossduff, Co. Waterford. From the *Waterford News*, October 1916:

> Colonel R.T. Carew, D. L., of Ballinamona Park, has been lying dangerously ill in an hospital in Alexandria for some time past. We are glad to state that he has sufficiently recovered to leave the hospital, and is not on his way home in an hospital

ship. Colonel Carew was serving with the British Expeditionary Force at Salonika.

He is listed on the Carew Memorial. Located in Christ Church Cathedral (Church of Ireland), Henrietta Street, Waterford. The memorial reads:

> In ever loving memory of Colonel Robert Thomas Carew, D. L. Of Ballinamona Park, Waterford.
> Sometime commanding the Waterford Artillery Militia
> Who died in his 57th year on the 11th February 1917. From disease contracted on active service abroad as a Draft Conducting Officer, in response to the call of His King and Country.
> From his wife Mary Carew.

Grave or Memorial Reference: 530. Cemetery: Waterford Protestant Cemetery, Co. Waterford.

CAREY, Patrick: Rank: Driver. Regiment or Service: Royal Army Service Corps. Unit: 20th Reserve Park. Age at death: 18. Date of death: 11 August 1918. Service No: T4/086558. Born in Four Mills, Co. Waterford. Enlisted in Clonmew while living in. Kilmanahan, Co. Waterford. Died at Home.

Supplementary information: Son of Thomas and Mary Carey. Grave or Memorial Reference: Commonwealth War Dead. Cemetery: Netheravon (All Saints) Churchyard in Wiltshire.

CARLTON, Thomas: Rank: Ordinary Seaman. Regiment or Service: Royal Navy. Unit: HMS *Defence*. Age at death: 26. Date of death: 31 May 1916. Service No: J/30577. HMS *Defence* was an armoured cruiser and was sent to the bottom by the Naval guns of a German battleship during the battle of Jutland. HMS *Defence*'s magazine exploded when it was hit by a German shell. The magazine explosion triggered off other explosions which almost blew the ship apart and she went down with the entire crew of 903 men. There were no survivors. Five Waterford men died with this ship on that day.

Supplementary information: Son of Thomas and Bridget Carlton, of Fallacoolmore, Dungarvan, Co. Waterford. Grave or Memorial Reference: 12 on the Plymouth Naval Memorial, UK.

CARPENDALE, George: Rank: Fireman. Regiment or Service: Mercantile Marine. Unit: SS *Formby* (Glasgow). Age at death: 35. Date of death: 16 December 1917. The ship was lost with all hands and never located during a fierce storm.

Supplementary information: Son of Elizabeth Carpendale and the late George Carpendale. Husband of Mary Carpendale (*née* Stephens), of 40 Ferrybank, Waterford, Co. Kilkenny. Born at Leicester. He has no known grave but is listed on the Tower Hill Memorial in the UK. He is also listed on the Formby-Coningbeg Memorial, Adelphi Quay in Waterford City.

CARRIGAN, Stephen: Rank: Private. Regiment or Service: Royal Irish Regiment. Unit: 'C' Company, 6th Battalion. Date of death: 2 August 917. Age at death: 21. Service No: 6394. Born in Irish town, Clonmel. Enlisted in Nenagh while living in Waterford. Killed in action in the third battle of Ypres.

Supplementary information: Son of Martin and Ellen Carrigan, of Waterford. Husband of Mary Carrigan (*née* Corr), of 4 Pump Lane, Waterford. Grave or Memorial Reference: I.A.3A. Cemetery: Aeroplane Cemetery in Belgium.

CARROLL, James: Rank: Private. Regiment or Service: Royal Munster Fusiliers. Unit: 6th Battalion. Age at death: 22. Date of death: 9 August 1915. Service No: 2901. Enlisted in the Curragh Camp while living in Kilmacow, Co. Kilkenny. Killed in action in Gallipoli.

Supplementary information: Son of William and Ellen Carroll, of Lower Kilmacow, Waterford, Co. Kilkenny. He has no known grave but is listed on Panel 185 to 190 on the Helles Memorial in Turkey.

CARTER, Alfred: Rank: Private. Regiment or Service: Household Cavalry and Cavalry of the line including the Yeomanry and Imperial Camel Corps. Unit: Corps of Lancers. 5th (Royal Irish). Date of death: 24 May 1915. Service No: 5341 (Soldiers died in the Great War) and L/15341 (The Commonwealth War Graves Commission). Born in Gracedien, Waterford. Enlisted in Dublin while living in Waterford. Killed in action. Grave or Memorial Reference: III.D.7. Cemetery: Ypres Town Cemetery in Belgium.

CASEY, James: Rank: Seaman. Regiment or Service: Unknown. Unit: Schooner *Morning Star*. The only information I have on this sailor is contained in the below. article. He is not in any of the War Dead databases. From the *Waterford News*, September 1915:

WRECK OF THE *MORNING STAR*.
INTERVIEW WITH SURVIVOR.
DUNGARVAN, SATURDAY NIGHT.

This afternoon I journeyed to Dungarvan or Boatstrand as the locality is more commonly called, to view the scene of the wreck of the Morning Star, a sailing vessel of a registered tonnage of 94, which traded between Cardiff and Cork harbour, and which was driven on to a reef of rocks in the storm of Thursday night off Dunabrattin Head, becoming a total wreck some two hours afterwards. The *Morning Star* carried five hands, including the Captain, and of these only one survivor remains to tell the tale of that terrible night. His name is Denis Flynn. He is a native of Abbeyside, Dungarvan, and held the post of mate on board the vessel. Captain Augustine Christopher who was lost was a native of Abbeyside also. He was a young man having only attained the age of 34 years. Active and athletic he possessed a thorough knowledge of all matters pertaining to navigation, and on more than one occasion his abilities in this direction were put to the test. He was part owner of the *Morning Star* himself, a Mr Fitzpatrick of Lapp's Quay, Cork, having a share in the velles also. The other victims of the disaster were James Casey, Dungarvan, seaman, Michael Sullivan, Courymacsherry, seaman and John Falvey, of 3 Paul's Avenue Cork, cook.

On my arrival at the scene of the catastrophe at about 4p.m. today there was little to be seen of the schooner. The coast for some distance around the little harbour or Boatstrand was strewn with wreckage. Parts of the deck, the jib-book, and mald mast, and the topsail yard and portions of the crew's clothing were lying along the quay, and looking out to sea between the jetty and the pier and at about 100 yards from the shore some floating spars were all that was visible of the *Morning Star*. The rocks to the south of Dunabrattin Head with their beautiful formations and the cliffs towering above them with the sea lapping their base presented a scene of peace and tranquillity. It would be hard to make oneself believe that here was enacted only some hours previously such a scene of pathos and disaster. Three men were engaged on the quay in turning a capstan and raising one of the terrible night – foggy wet, dark and stormy. The wind was from the south and there was a heavy sea running. They could discern a dark object at about 200 yards from the shore off Dunabrattin Head. Some minutes afterwards they heard men's voices shouting for help coming from that direction. Then they knew that some ship had been wrecked on the reef of rocks that runs in that vicinity. During a slight lull in the storm one sail was visible on the doomed vessel, and from what they could judge they thought it was a mainsail. Those on the pier kept shouting back to the sailors but to do anything in the nature of rescue work was impossible. Sometimes they could not see the hull of the ship at all when she was probably washed by a swell of the sea. They could hear the masts breaking and the ship cracking away and stayed watching her until no more could

be heard or seen. Then they ran for the rocks with lanterns and picked up one man who was completely exhausted. The Bonmahon Coastguards then arrived with the life saving apparatus but alas too late. The vessel wan then gone to pieces. The Coastguards of Tramore were also on the scene.

I then proceeded to the house of Mr John O'Gorman which stands on the summit of the cliff and directly over the quay. Mr O'Gorman who is a coal merchant and who supplies the district with that commodity received me with all possible hospitality. It was in his house that Denis Flynn, was lying in bed recovering from the shock of his thrilling experiences. Through the courtesy of Miss O'Gorman I was enabled to interview him. His mother who had travelled to Boatstrand with all possible speed on learning of the occurrence was in the room with him tending him with a motherly care and anxiety. He was very weak, as was natural to expect, considering all he had gone through, but was able to give the following account of his adventures.

We left Cardiff on Tuesday evening at 4.30 bound for Ballinacurra with a cargo of coal. All went well until Thursday night. We were off Mine Head when the storm came down on us. The skipper tried to make pool for shelter, but we could not pick up … clear of the boom she shipped another sea that swept the decks 'fore and aft. As soon as the skipper saw the red light on the pier at Boatstrand he took it for Dunmore. "Hard up," I said; "Hard up." The skipper said to me. "Lower the peak of the mainsail." We did so and she wasn't well off before the wind when she struck. All hands then took to the rigging, and we were two hours there shouting and roaring for assistance. We could hear the men on the pier shouting back to us. We all said the Rosary there in the rigging, and when we found the masts going from under us the skipper took my hand and said "we may as well have a go for it, Diny." We jumped together, the skipper and I into the water, and the last I knew of him was that he gave a terrible road and I could not account for what happened to him. I saw no more of him after that. I was the only one of the crew who had a lifebelt on at the time. After jumping into the sea I felt myself carried along towards land by a wave and felt myself held on the beach by two men. They asked me "Are you dead or alive?" and I said "I am all right, but the rest of my mates I think are all gone. After that I remembered no more until I found myself here in bed" Asked is Casey was a passenger on the ship Flynn said "No he was not. He signed on as a member of the crew in Cardiff."

After hearing this story from Denis Flynn I visited a shed some 50 yards away fro Mr O'Gormans house where the body of John Falvey picked up this morning was waking. The undertaker was there waiting to convey the corpse to the railway station to have it brought home to Cork. Several persons from the neighbourhood of Dunabrattin and some police constables from Annestown were about the place. On enquiring amongst them I learned that Casey's body was then on its way to Dungardan for internment there. The funeral had left after an inquest which was held by Coroner Power of Tramore earlier in the day.

To obtain news of what transpired at the inquest I travelled to Annestown to interview the sergeant there. Arrived at the police barracks Sergeant McDonagh treated me with every courtesy and he and Constable Harrington gave me the following particulars of the inquest:

The inquest was held at Boatstrand at 2.10p.m. on the bodies of James Casey and John Falvey by Coroner Power of Tramore. Sergeant McDonagh watched the proceedings on behalf of the police authorities. Patrick Morrissey, Dunabrattin was foreman of the jury. Michael Flynn, Knockaun East, deposed that at about 10p.m. on Thursday night ne observed a black object outside

Dunabrattin quay which he believed to be a large vessel in distress. He immediately went to the R.I.C. Barracks as Annestown and reported the matter. The vessel was about 200 yards off the quay and the night was very dark and stormy. Michael Morrissey deposed that he with Constable Harrington and a few fishermen from the neighbourhood found the body of Denis Flynn, the survivor being washed ashore. They were attracted by cries for assistance coming from him. They found him washed ashore and lying prostrate between the rocks. He was alive and had a lifebelt on at the time. They conveyed him to the house of Mr John O'Gorman, coal merchant, Dunabrattin, where he received every kind treatment and attention, and where he still remained in bed.

Continuing witness said that he found the body of James Casey on Friday morning at about 10 o'clock lying on the beach. He was dead. He had no lifebelt on. On Saturday morning at about the same hour witness with others found the body of John Falvey. It was lying in a large pool of water between the rocks at Dunabrattin. Life was extinct. He had a pair of boots, a pants, and a khaki jacket on him at the time but had no lifebelt.

A verdict was found as follows; death from drowning caused by the foundering of the *Morning Star* owned by Messrs Christopher and Fitzpatrick.

The Coroner said that the people of Boatstrand deserved every credit for their kindness on the occasion, and for rendering all the aid they possibly could. Mr John O'Gorman and family in particular deserved special mention for their thoughtful and timely hospitality. Mt John Morrissey also deserved to be mentioned for his promptitude and for the trouble he went to in going twice to Bonmahon – once for the doctor and another for the life-saving apparatus which unfortunately arrived too late on the scene to be of any assistance. The survivor Denis Flynn is receiving every care and attention that could be given him from Mr O'Gorman. He is being attended regularly by Dr Foley of Bonmahon, and it is to be hoped that in a short time he will be quite well again despite the terrible privations that he has suffered. A constant search is being kept for the two bodies, that of Captain Christopher and Michael O'Sullivan amongst the rocks and cliffs but up to the time of writing neither of these has been found. The sad occurrence has cast a gloom over the little townland of Boatstrand and the surrounding localities, and the scenes on Thursday night will remain for a long time to come in the minds of those persons who witnessed them.

Denis Flynn never recovered from his injuries and died in bed in November 1915.

CASEY, Michael Francis: Rank: Captain. Regiment or Service: Royal Munster Fusiliers. Unit: 9th Battalion. Age at death: 35. Date of death: 18 July 1916. Killed in action.

Supplementary information: Son of James and Mary Ann Casey, of Park, Stradbally, Co. Waterford. From the *Waterford News*, July 1916:

MR CASEY KILLED.

The deepest sympathy is felt with Mrs Casey, mother of Mr Casey, who has been killed at the front. He was an employee of the County Council, and volunteered his position being kept for him. He was a splendid type of young Irish man. A vote of condolence was passed by the County Council for Lieutenant [*sic*] Casey in the *Munster Express*, August 26, 1916.

Grave or Memorial Reference: I.F.8. Cemetery: Mazingarbe Communal Cemetery Extension in France.

CASEY, MICHAEL J.: Rank: First Mate/Acting Captain. Regiment or Service: Unknown. From the *Waterford News*, December 1917:

WATERFORD CAPTAIN'S SAD END.

Much regret will be felt in Waterford at the tragic death, which occurred recently at a French port, of Mr Michael J. Casey, son of Mr John Casey, Summerland, Waterford. Deceased was First Mate on a merchant vessel, and was Acting-Captain at the time he met his end. As a result of a severe accident he received his two legs were amputated. He was in the prime of life, and had spent most of his years at sea. The deceased was a very popular and capable officer, was brother-in-law of Mr Godwin, manager Messrs O'Grady's, Kilkenny.

A full report of the accident is reported in the *Munster Express*, December 1917. This man is not in any of the War Dead Databases. The only reference I can find to him is the above.

CASEY, Nicholas: Rank: Gunner. Regiment or Service: Royal Garrison Artillery. Unit: 1st Mountail Battery. Date of death: 1 September 1914. Service No: 14535. Born in Wexford. Enlisted in London while living in Tramore, Co. Waterford. Died in India. Grave or Memorial Reference: 4.A.25. Cemetery: Rawalpindi War Cemetery in Pakistan.

CASEY, Patrick: Rank: Able Seaman. Regiment or Service: Mercantile Marine. Unit: SS *Dotterel* (Cork). Age at death: 73. Steamship *Dotterel* struck a mine and sank, killing five of her crew. Date of death: 29 November 1915.

Supplementary information: Son of the late John and Bridget Casey. Husband of Elizabeth Casey (*née* Flood), of 58 Dublin Street, Liverpool. Born at Stradbally, Co. Waterford. He has no known grave but is listed on the Tower Hill Memorial in the UK.

CASEY, Patrick: Rank: Private. Regiment or Service: South Wales Borderers. Unit: 5th Battalion. Age at death: 28. Date of death: 5 July 1916. Service No: 17661. Born in

Kill, Co. Waterford. Enlisted in Gorseinon, Glamorganshire while living in Kill. Killed in action.

Supplementary information: Son of Edmond and Ellen Casey, of Kilbarrymeaden Hill, Co. Waterford. He has no known grave but is listed on Pier and Face 4A of the Thiepval Memorial in France.

CASEY, Patrick: Rank: Yeoman of Signals. Regiment or Service: Royal Navy. Unit: HMS *Glowworm.* Age at death: 33. Date of death: 25 August 1919. Service No: 227466. HMS *Glowworm* went to the assistance of a barge that was burning on a bank of the Dvina River. As the *Glowworm* came along side the barge, unknown to the *Glowworm* it was laden with explosives. It exploded killing *Glowworm*'s Captain (Commander Sebald Green, who was also commanding the flotilla) and seventeen of the officers and men of the *Glowworm*'s crew.

Supplementary information: Son of John Casey, of Summerland Square, Waterford. Husband of Doris Lilian Grace Casey, of St George, Bristol (buried Semenovka (Bereznik) Cem. Extension). Grave or Memorial Reference: Sp. Mem. B20. Cemetery: Archangel Allied Cemetery in the Russian Federation.

CASHIN, Edward: Rank: Private. Regiment or Service: Royal Irish Regiment. Unit: 1st Battalion. Date of death: 10 March 1918. Service No: 10106. Born in Kilmacow, Co. Kilkenny (Soldiers died in the Great War). Enlisted in Waterford while living in Kilmacow, Co. Kilkenny. Killed in action in Palestine. Grave or Memorial Reference: A.68. Cemetery: Jerusalem War Cemetery, Israel.

CASTLES, William: Rank: Sergeant. Regiment or Service: Duke of Cornwalls Light Infantry. Unit: 1st Battalion. Age at death: 33. Date of death: 15 September 1914. Service No: 5983. Born in Ardmore, Waterford. Enlisted in Lurgan, Co. Armagh. Killed in action.

Supplementary information: Son of the late Benjamin and Rose Castles. Grave or Memorial Reference: He has no known grave but is listed on the La Ferté-sous-Jouarre Memorial in France.

CAVANAGH, Edward: Rank: Gunner. Royal Horse Artillery and Royal Field Artillery. Unit: 6th Ammunition Column. Date of death: 27 September 1916. Service No: 52432. Born in Waterford, Ireland. Enlisted in Warrington. Died in Mesopotamia. Grave or Memorial Reference: XXI. A.6. Cemetery: Baghdad (North Gate) War Cemetery Iraq.

CHAMBERS, Robert Francis: Rank: Sergeant and Acting Sergeant. Regiment or Service: Leinster Regiment. Unit: 7th Battalion. Age at death: 21. Date of death: 7 June 1917. Service No: 3302. Born in Waterford. Enlisted in Waterford while living in Waterford. Killed in action.

Supplementary information: Son of John and Matilda Chambers, of The Square, Portlaw, Co. Waterford. Native of Kilmacthomas, Co. Waterford. From the *Munster Express*, July 1917:

KILLED IN ACTION.
Sergeant R. Chambers, Leinster's, son of Sergeant Chambers, R.I.C., Kilmacthomas, has been killed in action. He was in several big engagements and for his gallantry was awarded the D.C.M., and was also mentioned in despatches. Prior to joining the colours he was employed in Messrs Hearne and Co. Quay.

Grave or Memorial Reference: II.AA.12. Cemetery: La Laiterie Military Cemetery in Belgium.

CHEASTY, Michael: Rank: Fireman. Regiment or Service: Mercantile Marine. Unit: SS *Highbury* (London). Age at death: 34. Date of death: 31 May 1917.

Supplementary information: Son of Jeffrey Cheasty, of 17 The Glen, Waterford, and the late Bridget Cheasty. He has no known grave but is listed on the Tower Hill Memorial in the UK.

CHEEVERS, Matthew: Rank: Private. Regiment or Service: The King's (Liverpool Regiment). Unit: 12th Battalion. Age at death: 23. Date of death: 27 March 1917. Service No: 14211. Born in Carrigbyrne, Co. Wexford. Enlisted in Llanelly, Wales while living in Cambelelo, Co. Waterford. Died of wounds.

Supplementary information: Son of James and Catherine Cheevers (*née* Hanlon) of Horeswood, Campile, Co. Wexford. From *The People*, 1916:

HORESWOOD SOLDIERS WOUNDED;
The following soldiers from Sutton's Parish were recently wounded in the fighting lines: Private James Whitty, Ballinamona, on the hand; Private M Cheevers, Horeswood, on the arm, and Private James Shea, Great Island, on the hand.

Grave or Memorial Reference: II.B.40. Cemetery: Hermies Hill British Cemetery in France.

CHEEVERS, Patrick: Rank: Sergeant. Regiment or Service: Kings Liverpool Regiment. Unit: 13th Battalion. Age at death: 26. Date of death: 3 May 1917. Service No: 14122. Born in Carrigbyrne, Co. Wexford. Enlisted in Llanelly, North Wales while living in Waterford. Killed in action.

Supplementary information: Son of James and Catherine Cheevers of Horeswood, Campile, Waterford. He has no known grave but is listed in Bay 3 on the Arras Memorial in France.

CHESTNUTT, John: Rank: 3rd Engineer. Regiment or Service: Mercantile Marine. Unit: SS *Coningbeg* (Glasgow). Torpedoed by German Submarine U-62. There were no survivors. U-62 surrendered in November 1918. Age at death: 41. Date of death: 18 December 1917.

Supplementary information: Son of Rachel Chestnutt and the late John Chestnutt. Husband of Janet Mary Chestnutt (*née* Bain), of 28 John Street, Waterford. Born in Waterford. He has no known grave but is listed on the Tower Hill Memorial in the UK. He is also listed on the Formby-Coningbeg Memorial, Adelphi Quay in Waterford City.

CHITTICK, Thomas: Rank: Rifleman. Regiment or Service: Royal Irish Rifles. Unit: 2nd Battalion. Date of death: 26 August 1914. Service No: 9995. Born in Ardmore, Waterford. Enlisted in Cork. Killed in action. Born at Ardmore, Co. Waterford in about 1894.

Supplementary information: Son of William and Margaret Chittick, 5 Parliament Street, Cork. Enlisted at Cork into the Corps of Lancers of the Line. Flour factory labourer. His siblings were William J. (HMS *Defiance*), Vincent, Gerard, and a sister Mary Frances Dixon. Trained at Belfast until he moved to 2nd RIR at Tidworth. A report by Capt. Master and Lt. Hutcheson described him as 'sober, honest, trustworthy and clean, is very keen to learn'. KIA at Caudry. He has no known grave but is listed on the La Ferté-sous-Jouarre Memorial in France.

CHRISTOPHER, Augustine: Rank: Captain. Regiment or Service: Unknown. Unit: Schooner *Morning Star*. The only information I have on this ships Captain is contained in the attached to **CASEY, James:** Rank: Seaman. He is not in any of the War Dead databases.

CLANCY, William: Rank: Private. Regiment or Service: Royal Irish Regiment. Unit: 2nd Battalion. Date of death: 25 May 1915. Service No: 5584. Born in Carrigmore, Co. Tipperary. Enlisted in Piltown Co. Kilkenny while living in Carrigbeg, Co. Waterford. Died of wounds. Grave or Memorial Reference: I.F.70. Cemetery: Bailleul Communal Cemetery Extension (Nord) in France.

CLARKE, Richard: Rank: Private. Regiment or Service: Irish Guards. Unit: 1st Battalion. Date of death: 4 September 1914. Service No: 2297. Born in Waterford. Enlisted in Waterford. Killed in action.

Supplementary information: Cousin of Mrs Mary Power, of 2 Conduit Lane, Quay, Waterford. Grave or Memorial Reference: 30. Cemetery: Guards Grave, Villers Cotterets Forest in France.

CLARKE, William: Rank: Sergeant. Regiment or Service: Connaught Rangers. Unit: 3rd Battalion. Date of death: 25 May 1915. Service No: 5449. Born in Waterford. Enlisted in Waterford while living in Waterford. Died at Home. Grave or Memorial Reference: IV.II.23. Cemetery: Ballygunner (St Mary) Catholic Churchyard in Co. Waterford.

CLAWSON, James: Rank: Able Seaman. Regiment or Service: Mercantile Marine. Unit: SS *Formby* (Glasgow). Age at death: 56. Date of death: 16 December 1917. The ship was lost with all hands and never located during a fierce storm.

Supplementary information: Son of William and Annie Clawson. Husband of Bridget Clawson (*née* Sullivan), of Cheek Point, Co. Waterford. Born in Waterford. He has no known grave but is listed on the Tower Hill Memorial in the UK. He is also listed on the Formby-Coningbeg Memorial, Adelphi Quay in Waterford City.

CLEARY, Daniel: Rank: Fireman. Regiment or Service: Mercantile Marine. Unit: SS *Coningbeg* (Glasgow). Torpedoed by German Submarine U-62. There were no survivors. U-62 surrendered in November 1918. Age at death: 45. Date of death: 18 December 1917.

Supplementary information: Son of the late Timothy and Johanna Cleary. Husband of Ellen Cleary (*née* Plasteon), of 13 Henrietta Street, Waterford. Born in Co. Clare. He has no known grave but is listed on the Tower Hill

Memorial in the UK. He is also listed on the Formby-Coningbeg Memorial, Adelphi Quay in Waterford City.

CLEARY, Thomas: Rank: Sapper. Regiment or Service: Corps of Royal Engineers. Unit: 59th Field Company, Royal Engineers. Date of death: 13 November 1918. Service No: 13320. Born in Waterford. Enlisted in Waterford. Died of wounds.

Supplementary information: Husband of Ethel Cleary, of 104 Upper Milton Road. Gillingham, Kent. Grave or Memorial Reference: X.A.12A. Cemetery: Mount Huon Military Cemetery, Le-Treport in France.

CLEMENTS, William: Rank: Driver. Regiment or Service: Royal Field Artillery. Unit: 'D' Battery. 315th Brigade. Age at death: 24. Date of death: 19 December 1918. Service No: 119438.

Supplementary information: Son of Thomas and Mary Clements, of 61 Hall Place, Edgware Road, Paddington, London. Native of Waterford. Grave or Memorial Reference: I.F.18. Cemetery: Solesmes British Cemetery in France.

COADY/CODY, John: Rank: 2 Lt. Regiment or Service: Connaught Rangers. Unit: Attached to the 2nd Battalion Royal Irish Regiment. Age at death: 37. Date of death: 21 August 1918.

Supplementary information: Croix de Geurre (Belgium). Son of James and Margaret Coady. Husband of Florence Mary Dounes (formerly Coady), of Duncannon, Waterford. Killed in action. From a Wexford newspaper:

LIEUTENANT CODY KILLED.

Regret was felt in Duncannon when the sad news arrived to Mrs Cody that her husband, Lieutenant Cody, had been killed in action. The deceased Officer was promoted only a few months ago from the ranks for conspic-uous bravery on the field. Besides his service on the Western Front he had also seen serv-ice formerly in South Africa where he also won distinction for bravery. While gallantly leading his platoon on 22nd of August last on the Lys sector he fell. Lieutenant Cody belonged to a Kilkenny family, but had recently married a Duncannon Lady.

From *The Free Press*, 1918.

The promotion of Mr John Coady to commissioned rank has been a source of gratification to his many friends in Duncannon. A Kilkenny man by birth, he married a Duncannon lady and made it his future home. When war broke out he was Regimentals Sergeant Major to the R. I. R, and has since been awarded the parchment, certificates, and Belgian Croix de Guere for bravery in the field. He has been awarded a commission in the Connaught Rangers as a further testimony to his gallantry.

He has no known grave but is listed on the Vis-En-Artois Memorial in France.

COADY, Michael: Rank: Private. Regiment or Service: Welsh Regiment. Unit: 1st Battalion. Age at death: 24. Date of death: 2 October 1915. Service No: 36159. Previously he was with the 4th Battalion, South Wales Borderers where his number was 12438. Born in Ballybricken. Enlisted in Brecon, Breconshire while living in Waterford Waterford. Killed in action.

Supplementary information: Son of Stephen and Hannah Coady, of 29 Newports Lane, Waterford. Grave or Memorial Reference: 77 and 78 on the Loos Memorial in France.

COADY/ CODY, Patrick Moses: Rank: Private. Regiment or Service: Royal Irish Regiment. Unit: 2nd Battalion. Age at death: 32. Date of death: 6 May 1915. Service No: 6692. Born in Portlaw, Co. Waterford. Enlisted in Waterford while living in Portlaw. Killed in action.

Supplementary information: Son of William and Bridget Sullivan Cody. Awarded Tibet Medal and clasp. Served twelve years in 7th

Mountain Battery. Royal Garrison Artillery. Born in Waterford. Grave or Memorial Reference: Special Memorial. 7. Cemetery: New Irish Farm Cemetery in Belgium.

COFFEE, Francis Warren: Rank: Second Lieutenant. Regiment or Service: Royal Irish Rifles. Unit: 5th Battalion attached to the 14th Battalion. Date of death: 16 August 1917. Age at death: 28. Killed in action.

Supplementary information: Son of Francis Richard and Evelyn Coffee, of 8 Fairfield Park, Rathgar, Dublin. Born 20 November 1888 at Whitechurch, Kilkenny. Entered Trinity College in 1906. From *Irish Life* October 1917:

… was killed in an advanced position whilst gallantly leading his men forward during an attack on the enemy's lines on August 16th, 1917, was the eldest and only surviving son of Mr F.R. Coffee, Inspector, Board of Works, of 8 Fairfield Park, Rathgar. He was educated at Bishop Foy's School, Waterford; Fermoy College, and Trinity College. He was gazetted to the Royal Irish Rifles in October 1915, proceeded to France in June 1916 and went through the Somme campaign of that year. He again arrived in France in January last and was on active service there until his death.'

Listed on the Bishop Foy School Memorial located in Christ Church Cathedral (Church of Ireland), Henrietta Street, Waterford. He has no known grave but is listed on Panel 138 to 140 and 162 to 162A and 163A on the Tyne Cot Memorial in Belgium.

COFFEY, Thomas: Rank: Able Seaman. Regiment or Service: Mercantile Marine. Unit: SS *Formby* (Glasgow). Age at death: 28. Date of death: 16 December 1917. The ship was lost with all hands and never located during a fierce storm.

Supplementary information: Son of Thomas and Catherine Coffey. Husband of Mary Coffey (*née* McGuire), of 85 Poleberry, Waterford. Born in Waterford. He has no known grave but is listed on the Tower Hill Memorial in the UK. He is also listed on the Formby-Coningbeg Memorial, Adelphi Quay in Waterford City.

COGHLAN, Gerald N.: Rank: Private. Regiment or Service: Household Cavalry and Cavalry of the line including the Yeomanry and Imperial Camel Corps. Unit: Special Cavalry Reserve, 1st King Edwards Horse. Date of death: 19 August 1917. Service No: 981. Born in Waterford. Enlisted in Liverpool while living in Waterford. Killed in action.

Supplementary information: Son of Matthew Patrick and Mary Ellen Coghlan, of New Rath Lodge, Waterford. From *Waterford News*, May 1917:

THE NEWS IN THE TRENCHES.
STRANGE FIND IN A CAPTURED
DUG-OUT.

We received the following interesting letter this morning.

7th June, 1917.
Dear Mr Downey,
During the course of duty a few days ago in the recently evacuated German area, I happened to enter one of the dug-outs, and on looking round I noticed on the top of an ammunition box, and English newspaper (as I thought) which had evidently been doing duty for a tablecloth. Curiosity prompted me to further investigate the paper. Need I say that I was mildly surprised to find that it was an old copy of "*The Waterford News*." The only conclusion which I could come to was that it had been forgotten by some of our boys when they rented this part of the country from Fritz for the summer months. Assuming that it would be a matter of interest to you to know that your widely-read paper even penetrates the German trenches. I take this opportunity of sending this brief account of the incident.
Sincerely yours.
Gerald N Coghlan,
1st King Edwards Horse,
K.O.D.R., B.E.F., France.

Grave or Memorial Reference: I.H.1. Cemetery: Gwalia Cemetery in Belgium.

COGHLAN, Joseph James: Rank: Petty Officer Stoker. Regiment or Service: Royal Navy. Unit: HMS *Indefatigable*. Age at death: 34. Date of death: 31 May 1916. Service No: 303132. During the Battle of Jutland the German Battlecruiser *Van Der Tann* fired 11-inch shells at the *Indefatigable*. The first two entered 'X' magazine area and blew out the bottom of the ship and she began sinking by the stern. More 11-inch shells from the *Van Der Tann* destroyed 'A' turret and also blew up the forward magazine and she then sank. There were only two survivors of her crew of 1,017 men. The *Van Der Tann* was scuttled in Scapa flow in June 1919. Three Waterford men died on the ship that day.

Supplementary information: Son of James and Catherine Coghlan, of Co. Waterford. Husband of Minnie Coghlan, of 84 Butler Street, Belfast. Grave or Memorial Reference: 14 on the Plymouth Naval Memorial, UK.

COLBERT/CULBERT, James: Rank: Sergeant. Regiment or Service: Royal Irish Regiment. Unit: 2nd Battalion. Date of death: 31 May 1915. Service No: 6299. Born in Ballinamela, Co. Waterford. Enlisted in Dungarvan, Co. Waterford while living in Cappoquin Co. Waterford. Died of wounds. Grave or Memorial Reference: A. 2. Cemetery: Gent City Cemetery in Belgium.

COLBERT, John: Rank: Gunner. Regiment or Service: (Cork) Royal Garrison Artillery. Unit: 119th Battery. Date of death: 17 September 1916. Service No: 3566. Born in Lismore, Co. Waterford. Enlisted in Lismore. Died. Grave or Memorial Reference: Officers, B.18.27. Cemetery: St Sever Cemetery, Rouen in France.

COLBERT/CULBERT, Patrick: Rank: Private. Regiment or Service: Loyal North Lancashire Regiment. Unit: 10th Battalion.

Date of death: 10 April 1917. Service No: 2638. Born in Killea, Waterford. Enlisted in Preston while living in Waterford. Killed in action. Grave or Memorial Reference: I.D.7. Cemetery: Windmill British Cemetery, Monchy-Le-Preux in France.

COLBERT, Thomas: Rank: Private. Regiment or Service: Royal Irish Regiment. Unit: 2nd Battalion. Date of death: 25 September 1914. Service No: 10007. Born in Aglish, Co. Waterford. Enlisted in Clonmel, County Tipperary while living Dungarvan, Co. Waterford. Died of wounds. Grave or Memorial Reference: 1.12. Cemetery: Le Gonards Cemetery, Versailles in France.

COLEMAN, Michael: Rank: Private. Regiment or Service: Royal Irish Regiment. Unit: 2nd Battalion. Date of death: 20 November 1917. Service No: 9605. Born in Dungarvan, Co. Waterford. Enlisted in Dungarvan. Killed in action. He has no known grave but is listed in Bay 5 on the Arras Memorial in France

COLLINS, James: Rank: Private. Regiment or Service: Royal Irish Regiment. Unit: 2nd Battalion. Date of death: 26 August 1918. Service No: 8366. Born in Trinity Without, Waterford. Enlisted in Waterford while living in Charleville, County Cork. Killed in action. Grave or Memorial Reference: II.B.14. Cemetery: St Symphorien Military Cemetery in Belgium.

COLLINS, John: Rank: Private. Regiment or Service: Royal Munster Fusiliers. Unit: 1st Battalion. Date of death: 9 September 1916. Service No: 14033. Formerly he was with the Connaught Rangers where his number was 10218. Born in Trinity Without, Waterford. Enlisted in Waterford while living in Waterford. Killed in action. He has no known grave but is listed on Panel and Face 16C on the Thiepval Memorial in France.

COLLINS Joseph: Rank: Private. Regiment or Service: Royal Irish Regiment. Unit: 1st Battalion. Date of death: 26 April 1915. Service No: 9893. Born in Trinity Without, Waterford. Enlisted in Waterford. Killed in action. He has no known grave but is listed on Panel 33 on the Ypres (Menin Gate) Memorial in Belgium.

COLLINS, Patrick: Rank: 2nd Corporal. Regiment or Service: Royal Engineers. Unit: 173rd Tunnelling Coy. Age at death: 30. Date of death: 29 March 1918. Service No: 79980. Previously he was with the Connaught Rangers (173rd Tunnelling Company, Royal Engineers) where his number was 9616. Born in Waterford. Enlisted in Waterford.

Supplementary information: Son of Mrs Agnes Collins, of 1 Philip Street, Waterford. One of six brothers who served, four of whom fell. Grave or Memorial Reference: 10 to 13 on the Pozières Memorial in France.

COLLINS, Stephen: Rank: Private. Regiment or Service: Royal Irish Regiment. Unit: 2nd Battalion. Age at death: 16. Date of death: 19 October 1914. Service No: 6347. Born in Trinity Without, Waterford. Enlisted in Waterford. Killed in action.

Supplementary information: Son of Mrs Agnes Collins, of 1 Philip Street, Waterford. One of six brothers who served, four of whom fell. Grave or Memorial Reference: 11 and 12 on the Le Touret Memorial in France.

COLLINS, Thomas: Rank: Private. Regiment or Service: Leinster Regiment. Unit: 7th Battalion. Date of death: 9 September 1916. Service No: 10378. Born in Waterford. Enlisted in Dungarvan, Co. Waterford. Residence Cappoquin. Killed in action. He has no known grave but is listed on Pier and Face 16C on the Thiepval Memorial in France.

COLTHORPE, George: Rank: Sergeant. Regiment or Service: Royal Irish Regiment.

Unit: 1st Battalion. Date of death: 16 March 1915. Service No: 6236. Born in Corbally, Co. Waterford. Enlisted in Waterford. Killed in action. He has no known grave but is listed on Panel 33 on the Ypres (Menin Gate) Memorial in Belgium.

COMERFORD (Alias, true family name is **MORAN**), **James:** Rank: Private. Regiment or Service: Royal Irish Regiment. Unit: 2nd Battalion. Age at death: 34. Date of death: 19 October 1914. Service No: 6486. Born in Dungarvan, Co. Waterford. Enlisted in Kilkenny. Killed in action.

Supplementary information: (Served as Comerford) Son of the late Mr and Mrs Moran, of King's Street, Kilkenny. Husband of Mrs Moran of New Building Lane, Kilkenny. He has no known grave but is listed on Panels 11 to 12 on the Le Touret Memorial in France.

COMERFORD, Laurence: Rank: Able Seaman. Regiment or Service: Mercantile Marine. Unit: SS *Coningbeg* (Glasgow). Torpedoed by German Submarine U-62. There were no survivors. Age at death: 39. Date of death: 18 December 1917.

Supplementary information: Born in Fethard-on-Sea in 1878. Son of Patrick and Catherine Comerford. Husband of Anastasia Comerford (*née* Hawkins) of 5 Presentation Row, Waterford. Laurence's brother Patrick is also mentioned on the Tower Memorial. Able Seaman Patrick Comerford drowned on the SS Clune Park in 1941, aged 52. Patrick's death in the Second World War brought an end to the male line of the Comerfords of Dungulph. The Submarine U-62 that sunk the *Coningbeg* surrendered in November 1918. It was broken up on Bo'ness in 1920 for scrap. SS Clune Park was one of the nineteen ships in the unescorted convoy SLS64 when it was attacked by the German Crusier *Admiral Hipper* on the 12 February 1941. The *Admiral Hipper* was scuttled in dock in Germany in May 1945. Memorial: Laurence is listed on the Tower Hill Memorial UK. He is also listed on the Formby-Coningbeg Memorial, Adelphi Quay in Waterford City.

CONDON, John: Rank: Private. Regiment or Service: Royal Irish Regiment. Unit: 2nd Battalion. Age at death: 14. Date of death: 24 May 1915. Service No: 6322. Born in Trinity Without, Waterford. Enlisted in Waterford. Killed in action.

Supplementary information: Son of John and Mary Condon, of Waterford. Youngest known battle casualty of the war. From the *Munster Express:*

A special court was held in the Court House on Saturday morning before Judge Gerald Griffin, R.M., at which a man named Thomas Ryan, residing at Harrington's Lane, was brought up in custody on a charge of fraud in connection with the effects of a soldier killed in action. The allegation was that the defendant got hold of a Office form and drew a sum coming to the father of John Condon, the deceased. The charge was as follows: "That he did between the 2nd July 1915 and the 12th December-1915, forge and utter two documents, viz, Army Form No 39 and a War Office money order for £4-9s-9d, in the name and prejudice of one John Condon, and did obtain the said sum by fraud and false pretences."

Mr Maxwell, D. I. Prosecuted. John Condon was the first witness examined. He corroborated the deposition made by him on which defendant was arrested. None of the eight letters produced were written by him. He wrote to the War Office about his dead son's effects, but did not ask them to address the reply to him in the care of Thomas Ryan. He never signed Army Form, No 39, which purported to bear his signature.

When asked had he any question to put to the witness, defendant said he was guilty, and added that he was prepared to pay the money back in instalments.

His mother, who was in court, he was guilty because he had not enough money for drink.

Rev. M. F. Walsh, C.C., Convent Hill stated-I remember a man calling to the Presbytery last July with an Army form. I did not know him. He said his son was killed in the war and he wanted to get his effects. He showed me a form (produced) and asked me to fill it up. He said his name was John Condon. I filled the form for him and I believe he signed it in my presence. It is my usual practice to get people tendering me such forms to write their names when the form is already signed. When I returned off holidays I found that the form had been sent back to be completed. I searched for Condon but could not find him. After some months I again got a letter from the War Office about the same matter. This referred me to John Condon, of 7 Harrington's Lane, I went there and found the man that gave the name of John Condon. He is defendant now present. I completed the form and gave it to him. Some weeks ago I met him in Barrack Street. I spoke to him and he said "I got that money".

Sergeant Scollard gave evidence of arrest. When cautioned the accused said "You made a mistake. There are more Ryans in Harrington's Lane than me. " Sergeant Thomas Murphy, Recruiting Sergeant, stated that in July last defendant enlisted in the 7th Leinster's. He identified the man's signature. Defendant denied that he joined the Leinster's at that time. He had been discharged from the Royal Irish . Accused and remanded till Monday.

On Monday morning Mr Gerald Griffin, R. M., sitting in the City Court, resumed the magisterial investigation into this case. Mrs Ryan, Postmistress at the Barrack Street Office, stated:I see War Office money order No, 68601 for £4-9s-9d (produced). It was initialled y me and paid in my office in December last, but the date of the month I cannot make out. It purports to be made out to John Condon, but I do not recollect who drew the money. I don't recollect seeing the prisoner in the office. This form of money order is only used by the War Office.

This was all the evidence offered, and the accused, who made no statement, was returned for trial to the Quarter Sessions.

Grave or Memorial Reference: LVI.F.8. Cemetery: Poelcapelle British Cemetery in Belgium.

CONDON, Michael: Rank: Private. Regiment or Service: Royal Dublin Fusiliers. Unit: 2nd Battalion. Age at death: 19. Date of death: 8 July 1915. Service No: 19510. Born in Waterford. Enlisted in Waterford. Died of wounds.

Supplementary information: Son of Patrick and Margaret Condon, of 5 Water Street, Waterford. From the *Waterford News*, July 1915:

YOUNG WATERFORD SOLDIER'S DEATH AT THE FRONT.

Intimation was received from the War Office yesterday of the death from wounds received in action of Private Michael Condon, 2nd Royal Dublin Fusiliers, a native of this city. The fallen soldier, who had barely reached his nineteenth year, was a son of Mr Patrick Condon. Water Street and prior to joining the army four months ago was a foreman in the employment of Mr Graves, timber merchant, Williams Street. He had been three weeks in the trenches in Flanders and participated in the heavy fighting which marked the beginning of this month. He was wounded on the 7th inst., and died in hospital "somewhere in France" on the following day. His mother had received a letter a short time ago from a comrade in the same Battalion telling her that her son had been slightly wounded. Subsequently she received another message from the same individual saying that Private Condon was more seriously wounded than he liked to tell her, and then came the official news of his death. To the bereaved parents, brothers, sister and friends the sympathy of all will be extended in the cruel blow they have sustained.

Grave or Memorial Reference: B.14. Cemetery: Hospital Farm Cemetery in Belgium.

CONDON, Stephen: Rank: Private. Regiment or Service: East Lancashire Regiment. Unit: 13th Battalion. Age at death: 23. Date of death: 22 August 1918. Service No: 33119. Formerly he was with the Royal Welsh Fusiliers where his number was 5180. Born in Ballybricken, Waterford. Enlisted in Cardiff. Killed in action.

Supplementary information: Son of Mary and Stephen Condon. Has no known grave but is commemorated on Panel 5 and 6 on the Ploegsteert Memorial in Belgium.

CONDON, Thomas: Rank: Fireman. Regiment or Service: Mercantile Marine. Unit: SS *Formby* (Glasgow). Age at death: 50. Date of death: 16 December 1917. The ship was lost with all hands and never located during a fierce storm.

Supplementary information: Son of John and Mary Ann Condon. Husband of Johanna Condon (*née* Diggins), of 27 Roanmore Road, Waterford. He has no known grave but is listed on the Tower Hill Memorial in the UK. He is also listed on the Formby-Coningbeg Memorial, Adelphi Quay in Waterford City.

CONDON, Thomas Joseph: Rank: Leading Deck Hand. Regiment or Service: Royal Naval Reserve. Unit: HMS *Victory*. Age at death: 29. Date of death: 12 July 1919. Service No: 234SD.

Supplementary information: Son of William Joseph and Elizabeth Condon, of 12 The Mall, Waterford. Grave or Memorial Reference: III.B.7. Cemetery: Mazargues War Cemetery, in France.

CONNELL, Richard: Alias, see **FITZGERALD, Richard:**

CONNELL, Thomas: Rank: Private/Lance Corporal. Regiment or Service: Royal Irish Regiment. Unit: 1st Battalion. Date of death: 24 April 1915. Service No: 9487. Born in St John's, Waterford. Enlisted in Clonmel, Co. Tipperary while living in Waterford. Killed in action. He has no known grave but is listed on Panel 33 on the Ypres (Menin Gate) Memorial in Belgium.

CONNERS, John: Rank: Corporal. Regiment or Service: Royal Irish Rifles. Unit: 1st Battalion. Date of death: 1 July 1916. Service No: 7295. Born in Waterford. Enlisted in Lancaster while living in Waterford. Killed in action. He has no known grave but is listed on Pier and Face 15A and 15B on the Thiepval Memorial in France.

CONNOLLY, John: Rank: Private/Lance Corporal. Regiment or Service: Royal Irish Regiment. Unit: 1st Battalion. Date of death: 12 March 1915. Service No: 4886. Born in Dungarvan, Co. Waterford. Enlisted in Cahir, Co. Tipperary. Killed in action. He has no known grave but is listed on Panel 33 on the Ypres (Menin Gate) Memorial in Belgium.

CONNOLLY, John: Rank: Private. Regiment or Service: Royal Irish Regiment. Unit: 'B' Coy. 2nd Battalion. Age at death: 24. Date of death: 23 August 1914. Service No: 7622. Born in Ferrybank, Co. Waterford. Enlisted in Waterford. Killed in action.

Supplementary information: Son of John and Margaret Rome Connolly, of Ferrybank. Grave or Memorial Reference: II.F.22. Cemetery: Caudry British Cemetery in France.

CONNOLLY, Patrick: Rank: Private. Regiment or Service: Royal Irish Regiment. Unit: 2nd Battalion. Date of death: 14 July 1916. Service No: 10633. Born in Tramore, Co. Waterford. Enlisted in Clonmel. Killed in action. He has no known grave but is commemorated on Pier and Face 3 A and 10 A. Memorial: Thiepval Memorial in France.

CONNOLLY, William: Rank: Private. Regiment or Service: Royal Irish Regiment. Unit: 2ⁿᵈ Battalion. Date of death: 19 October 1914. Service No: 7755. Born in Trinity Without, Waterford. Enlisted in Waterford. Killed in action. He has no known grave but is listed on Panels 11 and 12 on the Le Touret Memorial in France.

CONNORS, John: Rank: Able Seaman. Regiment or Service: Mercantile Marine. Unit: SS *Coquet* (London). Steamship *Coquet* was 200 miles east from Malta when she was captured and sunk by bombs from German submarine U34. Age at death: 35. Date of death: 4 January 1916.

Supplementary information: Son of Mary Anne and John Connors. Husband of the late Mary Connors. Born at Passage East, Co. Waterford. He has no known grave but is listed on the Tower Hill Memorial in the UK.

CONNORS, Michael: Rank: Private. Regiment or Service: Royal Irish Regiment. Unit: 2ⁿᵈ Battalion. Age at death: 20. Date of death: 19 October 1914. Service No: 6341. Born in Trinity Without, Waterford. Enlisted in Waterford. Killed in action.

Supplementary information: Son of Mrs Hannah Connors, of 3 May Lane, Waterford. Grave or Memorial Reference: 11 and 12 on the Le Touret Memorial in France.

CONNORS, Thomas: Rank: Private. Regiment or Service: Canadian Railway Troops Age at death: 43. Date of death: 21 April 1920 Service No: 1102334. Data from attestation papers:

What is your present address? American House, York Street, Toronto, Canada.

In what Town, Township or Parish, and in what Country were you born? Waterford, Ireland.

What is the name of your next of kin? Bridget Grubb.

What is the address of your next of kin? Tramore, Waterford, Ireland.

What is the relationship of your next of kin? cousin.

What is the date of your birth? 24 May 1876.

What is your trade or calling? Labourer. Are you married? single.

Apparent age: 40 years, 10 months.

Height: 5 Ft, 7½Ins.

Girth when fully expanded: 36Ins.

Range of expansion: 2Ins.

Complexion: medium.

Eyes: brown.

Hair: brown.

Distinctive marks: lost little finger on left hand.

Son of Thomas and Bridget Connors, of Somerhill, Tramore, Co. Waterford. Grave or Memorial Reference: Sec. 17. Lot 295. Gr. 9. Cemetery: Toronto (Mount Hope) Cemetery in Canada.

CONROY, Denis Augustine: Rank: Private. Regiment or Service: South Staffordshire Regiment. Unit: 'A' Coy, 4ᵗʰ Special Reserve Battalion. Age at death: 35. Date of death: 9 October 1918. Service No: 41600. Previously he was with the Royal Flying Corps where his number was 33616. Born in Waterford. Enlisted in Whitehall, Middlesex while living in Stoke Newington, Middlesex. Died.

Supplementary information: Son of Patrick and Kate Conroy, of 85 Newrath, Co. Waterford. Husband of Kathleen Faith Conroy, of 85 Winston Road, Green Lanes, Stoke Newington, London. Grave or Memorial Reference: VII.C.2. Cemetery: Grand-Seraucourt British Cemetery in France.

CONWAY, James: Rank: Private. Regiment or Service: Royal Army Service Corps. Unit: 1ˢᵗ Reserve Motorised Transport Depot. Date of death: 1 September 1916 (Soldiers died in the Great War and Irelands Memorial Records) 1 September 1916 (Commonwealth War

Graves Commission). Service No: M2/130587. Born in Waterford. Enlisted in Dublin while living in Waterford. Died at Home. Grave or Memorial Reference: Near the South West Boundary. Cemetery: Ferrybank Catholic Churchyard, Kilkenny.

CONWAY, James: Rank: Sergeant. Regiment or Service: Royal Irish Regiment. Unit: 1st Battalion. Date of death: 6 October 1916. Service No: 10001. Born in Trinity Without, Waterford. Enlisted in Waterford. Died of wounds at home. From the *Munster Express*:

> HOME FROM THE FRONT.
> Private James Conway Tullahought, was home from Salonika on ten day's furlough and returned on Thursday last. Private Martin Shea, Tullahought, is expected home soon. He has been thrice wounded, last time at the Somme from shrapnel.

Grave or Memorial Reference: Screen Wall. 72. 16114. Cemetery: Reading Cemetery, Berkshire, UK.

CONWAY, John: Rank: Company Sergeant Major Regiment or Service: Princess Patricia's Light Infantry. Unit: Eastern Ontario Regiment. Age at death: 30. Date of death: 2 June 1916. Service No: 249. Killed in action during fighting in Sanctuary Wood. Promoted Cpl. in August but reverted to Private 20 October 1914 after being severely reprimanded for creating a disturbance in the billets. Arrived in England with the 1st Canadian Contingent October 1914. Crossed to France with the Regiment on 20 December 1914. Promoted to Cpl. 16 March 1915 and to Lance/ Sergeant 7 April 1915 General action, 2nd Battle Ypres, Battle of Frezenberg. Promoted to Sgt 14 May 1915. Hospitalised with illness 9 August but returned to Unit 14 August 1915. Hospitalised with bronchitis 21 February 1916. Returned to Unit 28 February and was promoted CSM 26 Apr 1916. Data from enlistment documents:

In what Town, Township or Parish, and in what Country were you born? Waterford, Ireland.

What is the name of your next of kin? Patrick Conway.

What is the address of your next of kin? 50 North Sinai Avenue.

What is the date of your birth? 12 January 1886.

What is your trade or calling? Hotel Porter.

Are you married? Yes.

Apparent age: 27 years, 6 months.

Height: 5 Ft, 11 Ins.

Girth when fully expanded: 41 Ins.

Range of expansion: 2½ Ins.

Complexion: fresh.

Eyes: grey.

Hair: brown.

He has no known grave but is listed on Panel 10 on the Ypres (Menin Gate) Memorial in Belgium.

COOKE, Michael: Rank: Private. Regiment or Service: Royal Irish Regiment. Unit: 2nd Battalion. Date of death: 15 March 1915. Service No: 16300. Born in Trinity Without, Waterford. Enlisted in Waterford. Killed in action. There are no burial details available for this man at this time.

CORBOY, Thomas Francis: Rank: Private. Regiment or Service: Australian Infantry, A.I.F. Unit: 51st Battalion. Date of death: 3 August 1916. Service No: 2618A. Enlisted on 17 August 1915 in Blackboy Hill, Western Australia. Reported missing in action 9 September 1916. His records then add a note that he was hospitalised with mumps in the North Western Hospital in London on 6 November 1916. Later a Court of Enquiry on the 23 April 1917 found that he was in fact killed in action. His death plaque and scroll were sent to his brother in 1922. His medals were also issued. Data from enlistment documents:

In or near what Parish or Town were you born? Waterford, Ireland.

What is your age? 33 years 2 months.

What is your trade or calling? Labourer.

Are you married? No.

Who is your next of kin? Mr James Corboy [brother], Ferry Park [also listed as Ferry Bank], Waterford.

Have you stated the whole, if any, of your previous service? Yes.

Age: 33 years, 2 months.

Height: 5 feet, 5 inches.

Weight: 133 lbs.

Chest measurement: 33-35 inches.

Complexion: fair.

Eyes: blue.

Hair: fair.

Religious denomination: RC.

Killed at Moquet farm, Pozières. He has no known grave but is listed on the Villers-Bretonneux Memorial in France.

CORCORAN, Matthew: Rank: Private. Regiment or Service: Royal Irish Regiment. Unit: 2nd Battalion. Date of death: 24 May 1915. Service No: 4684. Born in Kilmacthomas, Co. Waterford. Enlisted in Waterford while living in Kilmacthomas. Killed in action. He has no known grave but is listed on Panel 33 on the Ypres (Menin Gate) Memorial in Belgium.

CORCORAN, Patrick: Rank: Private. Regiment or Service: Household Cavalry and Cavalry of the line including the Yeomanry and Imperial Camel Corps. Unit: 6th Dragoons (Inniskillings.) Date of death: 11 February 1915. Service No: 5400. Born in Lismore, Co. Waterford. Enlisted in Dublin while living in Naas, Co. Kildare. Killed in action. Grave or Memorial Reference: II. C.6. Cemetery: Ypres Town Cemetery Extension in Belgium.

CORCORAN, R.A.: Rank: Worker. Regiment or Service: Queen Mary's Army Auxiliary Corps. Unit: Receiving Depot (Dublin). Date of death: 20 December 1918. Service No: 51688.

Supplementary information: Daughter of Mrs J. Conway, of 12 Five Alley Lane, Waterford. Grave or Memorial Reference: RC.637. Cemetery, Grangegorman Military Cemetery in Dublin.

CORERI, Francis: Rank: Private. Regiment or Service: Royal Munster Fusiliers. Unit: 4th Battalion. Service No: 7334. Born in Waterford. Enlisted in Cork while living in Cork. Died at home. Date of death: 27 December 1916. Service No: 4/7334. From *Waterford News*, December 1917:

SHOCKING RAILWAY ACCIDENT.
SOLDIER KILLED AT LIMERICK JUNCTION.
A fatal accident occurred at Limerick Junction on Wednesday evening. As the limited mail train to Dublin was moving out from the platform at 5. 30p.m. Private Francis Coreri, 4th Battalion, Munster Fusiliers, married, aged about 30, was seen running from the military free buffet portable table with a cup of tea in his hand, apparently for somebody in the train. He slipped between the footboard and the platform, and his left leg and arm were caught in a carriage wheel, and the man's body was seen to revolve along the platform edge for about 25 yards, within which distance the train was stopped. Railway officials disentangled the body from the wheel, and placed it flat between the rails, and when the train moved off the man was found to be dead. The left arm and leg were broken. He was not travelling by the train. Papers on his body showed his wife to be residing at 29 Francis Street Cork, and Lieutenant Shirgroe, Tipperary, who happened to be on the platform, identified the man as having been stationed at Berehaven six weeks ago.

SOLDIERS SAD DEATH–INQUEST.
A inquest was held at Limerick Junction yesterday afternoon by Mr E. Cummins,

J. P., Coroner, Brookhill, Fethard on the body of Francis Corieri, Cork City, a private in the Royal Munster Fusiliers, who was killed the previous evening, and whose death is reported on page 2 of this issue.

Mrs Mary Wilson, Tipperary, stated that as the mail train from Cork to Dublin was leaving the Limerick Junction platform at 5. 30 p. m. she saw a soldier running along the platform with a cup of tea in his hand. The cup fell from his hand as he was apparently trying to board the train. The next thing she saw was the soldier's head appearing over the kerbstone of the platform. When she looked again the body had disappeared. When she saw him running along the platform before the accident he appeared to be quite sober.

Mr Thomas Brewer, stationmaster at Limerick Junction, stated that after the mail train began to get in motion he heard the sound of what he thought was breaking glass, and then a woman's scream. He saw a soldier caught between the footboard and the platform, and revolving with the motion of the wheels. From the time he saw the body it was dragged about 15 yards, but it was dragged altogether about 25 yards. The guard immediately stopped the train, and the body was found between the inside rail and the platform, lengthwise, and face upward, the head turned towards the engine and the left arm across the rail. The man was quite dead. Witness had the body removed on a stretcher. Before the train started witness was satisfied that all carriage doors were locked.

James Kelly, Dublin, guard on the train, stated that he saw the soldier running along the platform, apparently trying to enter a carriage. Immediately he saw the man fall he pulled up the train. The Foreman (Mr James White, D.C.) said it was a dangerous practice for people to rush from the refreshment rooms with cups of tea in their hands, trying to board a moving train. The Stationmaster said that the company's servants did their best

Francis Coreri.

to stop this practice, but it was virtually impossible to do so, The Coroner said that, considering the great number of people who passed through Limerick Junction daily it was remarkable that accidents were so few. Doctor Blackburn, Tipperary, stated that death was due to shock from the injuries received. The jury found accordingly, attaching no blame to anybody.

Grave location: E.H.98. Cemetery: St Michaels New Cemetery, Tipperary Town.

CORMACK, Michael: Rank; Private. Number 9902, 3rd Battalion, Royal Irish Regiment. Born in Holycross. Also listed as McCormack. Enlisted in Clonmel while living in Holycross (other records say Waterford). Died on Thursday, 20 January 1916, aged 19. Son of William and Brigid McCormack of Holycross. Buried in Holycross Abbey and moved during renovations to the left of the path in the graveyard. Official records say he died at home but oral tradition indicate his remains were brought home for burial.

COSTIGAN, Michael: Rank: Private. Regiment or Service: Royal Irish Regiment. Unit: 2nd Batalion. Date of death: 15 October 1914. Service No: 3824. Born in St John's, Kilkenny. Enlisted in Tipperary while living in Waterford. Killed in action. He has no known grave but is commemorated on Panel 11 and 12 on the Le Touret Memorial in France.

COSTIGAN, Patrick: Rank: Private. Regiment or Service: Connaught Rangers. Unit: 5th Battalion. Date of death: 8 June 1918. Service No: 5205 and 4/5205. Born in Thomastown, Co. Kilkenny. Enlisted in Waterford while living in Carrick, Co. Tipperary. Died in Egypt. I include this man as he is mentioned in *Waterford: Heroes, Poets and Villains*, 'Pete Sarsfield … escaped from a Prison Camp with the help of Tom Torpey who attacked the guards. Paddy Costigan was killed in this escape attempt.' I cannot see any Waterford connection other than he enlisted there. Grave or Memorial Reference: C.76. Cemetery: Alexandria (Hadra) War Memorial Cemetery in Egypt.

COSTIGAN, Richard: Rank: Private/Lance Corporal. Regiment or Service: Royal Irish Regiment. Unit: 2nd Battalion. Age at death: 35. Date of death: 2 March 1916. Service No: 4822. Born in St Nicholas, Carrick-on-Suir, Co. Waterford. Enlisted in Carrick-on-Suir. Died.

Supplementary information: Husband of Ellen Costigan, of Pill Road, Carrick-on-Suir. Grave or Memorial Reference: Plot 2, Row L, Grave 1B. Cemetery: Le Treport Military Cemetery in France.

COTTER, Harry: Rank: Private. Regiment or Service: Irish Guards. Unit: 2nd Battalion. Age at death: 20. Date of death: 11 October 1915. Service No: 7268. Born in Waterford. Enlisted in Waterford. Died of wounds.

Supplementary information: Son of John and Kate Cotter, of 8 St Alphonsus Road, Waterford. From *Waterford News*, October 1915:

WATERFORD SOLDIER
KILLED AT THE FRONT.

Official intimation had bees received in the city of the death of Private Harry Cotter, Irish Guards, who was killed in the recent heavy fighting in Northern France. The fallen soldier, who was a tailor in the employment of Messrs Robertson, Ledlie and Ferguson's and resided at Alphonsus Road, enlisted at the time of the recruiting rally in the city early this year.

From the *Waterford News*, November 1915.

WATERFORD GUARDSMAN DIES OF WOUNDS. TOUCHING DETAILS FROM A COMRADE.

We regret to have to announce the death at the front of Private Henry [sic] Cotter, of the Irish Guards, who died on October 11th from the effects of a gunshot wound. Much sympathy is felt for deceased's father and mother and other relatives, who were informed of their sad bereavement in the following kindly letters:-

12th October, 1915.
Dear Mrs Cotter,

You will be surprised to hear from me, a stranger. Yesterday the 11th October, at five minutes past nine in the morning, your son, Harry Cotter, of the 2nd Irish Guards, slipped away at ease, having Died of wounds. He died on my barque, and I thought you would like to know just what kind of an end he had. I also assure you that he will have a good funeral. On my return I will visit his grave. We travel on the canals from the firing line to the different bases. Your son died when we were half way, so you may be sure he will be buried with full honours.

Believe me,
Yours faithfully.
J Blair, Sergeant.

20th October, 1915.
Dear Mrs Cotter,

So pleased to hear from you, but, owing to being very busy since I wrote you last,

I have been unable to visit your son's grave. I write by return to assure you that your son died very happy. He had a gun-shot wound in the thigh, and had he lived he would have been short a leg. He was a good patient, very quiet, and conscious to the end. He spoke freely until he fell asleep, and with a smile passed quietly away. No clergy were in attendance, as we are a mobile unit, always on the go, but you can take my word he is happy where he is. So the reason why I write to you is to assure you that he is happy, having had every attendance available before leaving this earth. But God has taken him once. I am unable to forward you anything regarding your son's personal belongings, as when we transfer the body to the mortuary we transfer the kits and valuables, etc. So I am unable owing to duty to oblige that way. But on visiting his grave I will forward you something from it, even if it be a blade of grass, so as to oblige you. You have my prayers and sympathy.
Yours sincerely.
Sergeant J. Blair.

Grave or Memorial Reference: I.C.8. Cemetery: Aire Communal Cemetery in France.

COUCH, Stanley Arthur: Rank Bombardier. Regiment or Service: Royal Field Artillery. Unit: 53rd Battery. Age at death: 23. Date of death: 9 August 1915. Service No: 57175. Born in Marleybone and enlisted in Newport, Monmouthshire. Died of wounds.

Supplementary information: Son of Richard and Sarah Couch, of Danhurst Street, Fulham Palace Road, London. Husband of Margaret Couch, of Bank Place, Waterford. Grave or Memorial Reference: I.C.3A. Cemetery: Lijssenthoek Military Cemetery in Belgium. He is also listed on the Waterford and District Roll of Honour. Located in Christ Church Cathedral (Church of Ireland), Henrietta Street, Waterford.

COUGHLAN, John: Rank: Private. Regiment or Service: Royal Irish Regiment. Unit: 2nd

Battalion. Date of death: 19 October 1914. Service No: 4803. Born in St John's Clonmel, Co. Tipperary. Enlisted in Tipperary while living in Kilmacuma, Co. Waterford. Killed in action. He has no known grave but is listed on Panels 11 and 12 on the Le Touret Memorial in France.

COUGHLAN, Michael: Rank: Private. Regiment or Service: Royal Munster Fusiliers. Unit: 1st Battalion. Date of death: 9 September 1916. Service No: 7110. Born in St John's, Waterford. Enlisted in Cork while living in Cork. Killed in action. Grave or Memorial Reference: III.D.10. Cemetery: Guillemont Road Military Cemetery, Guillemont, France.

CROKE, David: Rank: Private. Regiment or Service: Royal Irish Regiment. Unit: 1st Battalion. Date of death: 21 November 1916. Service No: 7496. Born in Ballybricken, Co. Waterford. Enlisted in Waterford. Killed in action in Salonika. Grave or Memorial Reference: VI.H.8. Cemetery: Struma Military Cemetery in Greece.

CROKE, J.: Rank: Private. Regiment or Service: Worcestershire Regiment. Unit: 4th Battalion. Date of death: 29 June 1921. Service No: 5242257.

Supplementary information: Son of Mrs Anne Croke, of 4 Walshers Place Ballybricken, Co. Waterford. Alternative Commemoration: buried in Raithpatrick Old Graveyard, Co. Kilkenny. Grave or Memorial Reference: 6 (Screen Wall) on the Grangegorman Memorial in Blackhorse Avenue in Dublin.

CROKE, Martin: Rank: Aircraftman 1st Class. Regiment or Service: Royal Air Force. Age at death: 34. Date of death: 5 August 1919. Service No: 288203.

Supplementary information: Son of Thomas and Ellen Croke, of Waterford. Husband of Kathleen Kearns (formerly Croke, of 121 High Street, Brentford, Middlesex). Grave or

Memorial Reference: Family Plot, just inside entrance. Cemetery: Killea (Holy Cross) Catholic Church in Waterford.

CROKE, Michael: Rank: Lance Corporal. Regiment or Service: Connaught Rangers. Unit: 1st Battalion. Date of death: 27 April 1916. Service No: 9203. Born in Waterford. Enlisted in Waterford while living in Waterford. Died in Mesopotamia. This man is in Ireland's Memorial Records twice with the same information. Grave or Memorial Reference: XX.B.2. Cemetery: Amara War Cemetery in Iraq.

CROKE, Thomas: Rank: Rifleman. Regiment or Service: Royal Irish Rifles. Unit: 2nd Battalion. Date of death: 9 July 1916. Service No: 5233. Born in Waterford. Enlisted in Waterford. From the *Waterford News*, 1915:

LETTERS FROM IMPRISONED
WATERFORDMEN IN GERMANY.
Councillor John Hearne has received the following letter:

Limburg, Lahn, Germany.
11th February, 1915.
Dear Mr H,
Just as Tom and myself were chatting to-day the subject turned to yourself. So vividly did he bring back old memories that I decided to write at once, enquiring how Mrs Hearne and yourself are doing; also Mary, her husband and family. I suppose Father Time had been very good to each one of you and bountifully given you the sweets of this world–aye, in lavish profusion. In any case, 'tis my sincere hope that He has, and I assure you that he has not been one bit better than I would wish.

Have you heard how narrowly we escaped destruction in the war? Perhaps you have not. Well, we were both wounded, and, strangely enough, in the right shoulder. The bullet in Tom's case went right through, but in my case it remained inside. Tom is now (T.G.) com- pletely recovered, but an operation will be necessary to set me right again. The prayers of those at home, no doubt, are largely responsible for our providential escape. Time hangs on us rather heavily here, doing next to nothing from one end of the day to the other. We daily expect a parcel or letter from home, but, through no fault of our friends, we seldom get any. Should we be amongst the fortunate few, our elation you can't imagine. On the other hand, when no news reaches us we have a tough job to conceal our feelings of disappointment. When you are again pass- ing P. M. Doyle's I trust you'll remember that a "Player" often brings solace in abun- dance, but only to those who know how to appreciate them, and I assure you the exiles named below can do that to per- fection. –With every kind of esteem and regard, I am, yours very sincerely.
Daniel J. Croke.

From the *Waterford News*, 1915:

MORE LETTERS FROM LIMBURG.
The following letters have been received by Mr Alexander Croke, T. C., Stephen Street, from his uncles, who are prisoners of war in Limburg, Germany:

Dear Sandy,
Tom and I are prisoners of war here, and are keeping fit, thought we miss our usual smoke. Does it ever strike you, when pass- ing P. M. Doyle's, that you have two uncles out here. I am sure not, but you can't think of everything in your busy life. How is uncle Johnnie? Give him my kindest regards, also father and mother,
Dan Croke

Dear Sandy,
We are both looking forward to a good time after this. Have you heard we were both very nearly knocked out? Well near enough. Anyway we are still in the pink. We saw Joe's son, Tommy on the 26th August just for a minute. Have you heard

of him since? We should like to hear from you occasionally, and would enjoy some of your fags (Player's preferred) over a evening chat. You would be surprised how a cigarette and a few lines lift the exile's spirits. Write when you can, and send us what news you can – excluding war news. Kindest regards to all old friends, including Mr MacD, at Ferrybank, and all old friends on the Quay.

Tom Croke.

Dear Mr Hearne–Dan has not left me much space; still I have much pleasure in using what is left to hope that this may find you, Mrs, and Mary enjoying good health and happiness. To Mr MacD, and all your employed give my kind regards. This is a lonely life, but we are looking forward to brighter days in our old home. Good-bye. God Keep you all. --Your very sincerely.

Tom Croke.

From *Waterford News*, 1915.

FROM A PRISONER OF WAR.

Mr John Hearne, T. C. has received from his nephew, Colour-Sergeant Croke, the following postcard dated April 9th. The writer of the postcard is a prisoner at Limburg at Lahn:

Dear Mr H.,

Your letter of 21st March to hand, also two fine boxes of cigarettes from Goodbody's" Dublin. For both – at present at least – I can only ask you to accept the warmest thanks of Tom and myself. Had also a line from M, and another excellent parcel which I acknowledged immediately conveying my astonishment and thanks. Tom is keeping very well (and myself) thank God, and sends you all good wishes. More news next week.

Yours sincerely.

Dan Croke.

Died of wounds. Grave or Memorial Reference: III.B.5. Cemetery: Pozières British Cemetery, Ovillers-La Boisselle in France.

CROKE, William: Rank: Gunner. Regiment or Service: Royal Garrison Artillery. Unit: 19th Trench Mortar Battery. Age at death: 22. Date of death: 4 November 1916. Service No: 3432. Born in St Patrick's, Waterford. Enlisted in Waterford while living in Cork. Killed in action. Previously he was with the Cork Royal Garrison Artillery.

Supplementary information: Son of William and Bridget O'Brien, of 6 Kerny Hall Avenue, St Mary's Road, Cork. Born in Waterford. Grave or Memorial Reference: II.B.12. Cemetery: Sailly-Au-Bois Military Cemetery in France.

CRONE, Percy Alexander: Rank: Lieutenant. Regiment or Service: Royal Munster Fusiliers. Unit: 4th Battalion and 7th Battalion. Age at death: 22. Date of death: 8 September 1916. Killed in action.

Supplementary information: Son of the Revd Alexander Crone, B.A., and Emily Laura Crone, of Clifton, Strand, Youghal, Co. Cork. I am not sure of the Waterford connection but he is listed on the Bishop Foy School Memorial located in Christ Church Cathedral (Church of Ireland), Henrietta Street, Waterford. He has no known grave but is listed on the Doiran Memorial in Greece.

CRONIN, James: Rank: Bombardier. Regiment or Service: Royal Horse Artillery and Royal Field Artillery. Unit: 70th Battery, 34th Army Brigade. Date of death: 4 October 1917. Service No: 58297. Born in Tallow, Co. Waterford. Enlisted in Newport. Killed in action. Grave or Memorial Reference: IX.F.15 Cemetery: Vlamertinghe New Military Cemetery, Ieper in Belgium.

CRONIN, P.: Rank: Private. Regiment or Service: Royal Irish Regiment. Unit: 2nd Battalion. Age at death: 35. Date of death: 3 November 1920. Service No: 7109546.

Supplementary information: Son of Mrs Ellen Cronin, of 6 Rockshire Road, Ferrybank, Waterford. Grave or Memorial Reference: 8.A.21. Cemetery: Delhi War Cemetery in India.

CRONIN, Timothy: Rank: Private. Regiment or Service: Cheshire Regiment. Unit: 1/6th Battalion. Date of death: 31 July 1917. Age at death: 19. Service No: 24484. Born in Waterford. Enlisted in Wallasey, Cheshire. Killed in action.

Supplementary information: Son of John and Minnie Cronin, of 72 Guildford Street, Egremont, Cheshire. He has no known grave but is listed on Panel 19-22 on the Ypres (Menin Gate) Memorial in Belgium.

CROTTY, Lawrence: Rank: Gunner. Regiment or Service: Royal Field Artillery. Unit: 87th Battery. Age at death: 24. Date of death: 4 July 1915. Service No: 62614. Born in Waterford. Enlisted in Waterford. Killed in action.

Supplementary information: Son of Michael Crotty and Hannah Crotty, of Ballynamintra, Kilmacomb, Co. Waterford. Grave or Memorial Reference: A.14. Cemetery: Potijze Chateau Wood Cemetery in Belgium.

CROTTY, Michael: Rank: Private. Regiment or Service: Royal Defence Corps. Unit: 268th Coy. Date of death: 8 August 1918. Service No: 36513. Born in Portland, Waterford. Enlisted in Finsbury while living in Merthyr Vale. Died at Home.

Supplementary information: Husband of Mary A. Crotty, of 4 William Street, Portlaw, Co. Waterford. Grave or Memorial Reference: EB. 48. Cemetery: Cardiff (Cathays) Cemetery UK.

CROWE, Francis Gerald: Rank: Sergeant. Regiment or Service: Royal Munster Fusiliers. Unit: 2nd Battalion. Age at death: 35. Date of death: 18 October 1918. Service No: 6940. Born in Cappaquin, Co. Waterford. Enlisted in Bandon, Co. Cork while living in Cappaquin. Killed in action.

Supplementary information: Son of John and Bridget Crowe (*née* Stack), of Cappoquin. In 2000 his 1914-15 star (medal) was among a lot of three medals auctioned in by Dix Noonan Webb in London from the Chris Murphy Collection for £50. There is an extremely interesting long letter in the *Munster Express*, July 1915, written by Sergeant Crowe. Grave or Memorial Reference: III.A.6. Cemetery: Highland Cemetery, Le Cateau in France.

CROWLEY, James: Rank: Private. Regiment or Service: Royal Irish Fusiliers. Unit: 7th Battalion. Age at death: 20. Date of death: 3 August 1916. Service No: 17029. Previously he was with the Royal Irish Regiment where his number was 1698. Born in Waterford. Enlisted in Waterford. Died of wounds.

Supplementary information: Son of Thomas and Catherine Crowley, of Ballycashin, Butlerstown, Co. Waterford. Grave or Memorial Reference: H.3. Cemetery: Bois-Carre Military Cemetery, Haisnes in France.

CUDDIHY, Patrick: Rank: Petty Officer Stoker. Regiment or Service: Royal Naval Reserve. Unit: HMS *Tiger*. Age at death: 35. Date of death: 28 April 1918. Service No: 2242T.

Supplementary information: Son of Mrs Kate Cuddihy, of 1 Castle St, Waterford. Grave or Memorial Reference: General L.3.27. Cemetery: Ford Park Cemetery (Formerly Plymouth Old Cemetery) (Pennycomequick) UK.

CUDDIHY, Patrick: Rank: Private. Regiment or Service: Royal Munster Fusiliers. Unit: 8th Battalion. Date of death: 9 September 1916. Service No: 4388. Born in Ballybricken, Co. Waterford. Enlisted in Waterford while living in Waterford. Killed in action. He has no known grave but is listed on Pier and Face 16C on the Thiepval Memorial in France.

CUFFE, Patrick: Rank: Private. Regiment or Service: Machine Gun Corps. Unit: Infantry, 7th Company. Date of death: 24 March 1918. Service No: 18139. Formerly he was with the Royal Irish Rifles where his number was 13915. Born in Tallow, Co. Waterford. Enlisted in Cardiff while living in Waterford. Killed in action. Grave or Memorial Reference: XII.F.7.

Cemetery: Grevilliers British Cemetery in Pas-De-Calais, France.

CULLEN, Gerald Sommerville Yeats: Rank: Second Lieutenant. Regiment or Service: Royal Irish Fusiliers. Unit: 1ˢᵗ Battalion. Age at death: 19. Date of death: 10 April 1917. Killed in action.

Supplementary information: Son of Jane Anita Cullen, of 3 Langford Place, Cork, and the late Revd James Edward Cullen, M.A., Trinity College, Dublin. Born at Ballyheigue, Co. Kerry. I am not sure of the Waterford connection but he is listed on the Bishop Foy School Memorial located in Christ Church Cathedral (Church of Ireland), Henrietta Street, Waterford. He is also listed in 'Roll of the sons and daughters of the Anglican Church clergy throughout the world and of the naval and military chaplains of the same who gave their lives in the Great War, 1914-1918'. Grave or Memorial Reference: III.D.6. Cemetery: Brown's Copse Cemetery, Roeux in France.

CULLEN, Joseph: Rank: Private. Regiment or Service: Royal Munster Fusiliers. Unit: 2ⁿᵈ Battalion. Date of death: 14 July 1915. Service No: 6409. Born in Ballybricken, Co. Waterford. Enlisted in Borrisokane, County Tipperary while living in Waterford. Died at Home. Grave or Memorial Reference: J.R.C.1428. Cemetery: Tynemouth (Preston) Cemetery, Northumberland, UK.

CULLEN, Michael: Rank: Private. Regiment or Service: Irish Guards. Unit: 1ˢᵗ Battalion. Date of death: 18 May 1915. Service No: 2193. Born in Dunmore, Co. Waterford. Enlisted in Waterford. Killed in action. Grave or Memorial Reference: He has no known grave but is listed on Panel 4 on the Le Touret Memorial in France.

CULLEN, Patrick: Rank: Fireman. Regiment or Service: Mercantile Marine. Unit: SS *Coningbeg* (Glasgow). Torpedoed by German

Submarine U-62. There were no survivors. U-62 surrendered in November 1918. Age at death: 31. Date of death: 18 December 1917.

Supplementary information: Son of Alice Cullen, and the late Walter Cullen. Husband of Anne Cullen (*née* O'Keeffe), of 7 Chapel Lane, Ballybricken, Waterford. Born in Waterford. He has no known grave but is listed on the Tower Hill Memorial in the UK. He is also listed on the Formby-Coningbeg Memorial, Adelphi Quay in Waterford City.

CULLEN, Walter: Rank: Cattleman. Regiment or Service: Mercantile Marine. Unit: SS *Coningbeg* (Glasgow). Torpedoed by German Submarine U-62. There were no survivors. U-62 surrendered in November 1918. Age at death: 42. Date of death: 18 December 1917.

Supplementary information: Son of the late Walter and Alice Cullen. Husband of Margaret Cullen (*née* Morrissey), of 1 Newport's Lane, Waterford. He has no known grave but is listed on the Tower Hill Memorial in the UK. He is also listed on the Formby-Coningbeg Memorial, Adelphi Quay in Waterford City.

CULLETON, James: Rank: Private. Regiment or Service: Royal Dublin Fusiliers. Unit: 8ᵗʰ Battalion attached to the 1ˢᵗ Battalion. Age at death: 332. Date of death: 1 July 1916. Service No: 12291. Born in Ferrybank, Co. Waterford. Enlisted in Dublin. Killed in action.

Supplementary information: Son of the late Patrick Culleton. Husband of Mary Culleton, of 18 Belvedere Avenue, North Circular Road, Dublin. Grave or Memorial Reference: XIX.F.11. Cemetery: Serre Road Cemetery No 2 in France.

CULLETON, Martin: Rank: Private. Regiment or Service: Irish Guards. Unit: 1ˢᵗ Battalion. Age at death: 36. Date of death: 6 November 1914. Service No: 1458. Born in Ballybricken, Co. Waterford. Enlisted in Waterford. Enlisted in Whitehall, Middlesex while living in Waterford. Killed in action.

Supplementary information: Son of Bridget Culleton, of 14 The Glen, Waterford. He has no known grave but is listed on Panel 11 on the Ypres (Menin Gate) Memorial in Belgium.

CUMMINS, John: Rank: Private. Regiment or Service: Royal Irish Regiment. Unit: 2nd Battalion. Date of death: 5 July 1916. Service No: 11033. Born in St Patrick's, Waterford. Enlisted in Waterford. Killed in action. He has no known grave but is listed on Pier and Face 23A on the Thiepval Memorial in France.

CUMMINS, Michael: Rank: Private. Regiment or Service: Irish Guards. Unit: 1st Battalion. Age at death: 29. Date of death: 11 October 1915. Service No: 6321. Born in Kill, Co. Waterford. Enlisted in Waterford. Killed in action.

Supplementary information: Son of Thomas and Kate Casey, of Kilsteague, Annestown, Waterford. Grave or Memorial Reference: XV.A.14. Cemetery: Loos British Cemetery in France.

CURRAN, Bartholomew Joseph: Rank: Sapper Regiment or Service: Australian Tunnelling Corps Unit: 3rd Coy. Age at death, 38. Date of death: 22 February 1917 Service No: 5003. Enlisted 20 January 1916 at Black Boy Hill, Western Australia while living at Kalgoorli. What is your name? Bartholomew Joseph Curran.

In or near what Parish or Town were you born? Dungarvan, Ireland.

What is your age? 37.

What is your trade or calling? Bootmaker.

Are you, or have you been an Apprentice? Yes to above, five years. If so where, to whom, and for what period?

Are you married? No.

Who is your next of kin? (mother) Ellen Curran, Clare, South Australia.

Have you stated the whole, if any, of your previous service? Yes.

Age: 37 years, months.

Height: 5 feet, 8 inches.

Weight, 140 lbs.

Chest measurement: 32-35 inches.

Complexion: medium. Eyes: blue.

Hair: brown.

Religious denomination: R. C.

Admitted to the 50th Field Ambulance, 17 February 1917 with Pneumonia, transferred next day to hospital. Died in the 33rd Casualty Clearing Station on 22 February 1917 from Disease (Pneumonia). Buried by Revd L. Green, attached to the 8th Battalion, Somerset Light Infantry. His mother was granted a pension of £2 per fortnight from 1 May 1917.

He came to Australia when he was six months old.

Supplementary information: Son of John and Ellen Curran, of Clare, South Australia. Grave or Memorial Reference: I.G.16. Cemetery: Hersin Communal Cemetery Extension, Pas de Calais in France.

CURRAN, M.: Rank: Air Mechanic 2nd Class. Regiment or Service: Royal Air Force. Unit: Aero Service Unit. Age at death: 22. Date of death: 2 March 1919. Service No: 291713.

Supplementary information: Son of Richard and Jane Curran, of Teperstown, Dunmore East, Co. Waterford. Grave or Memorial Reference: II.A.42. Cemetery: Huy (La Sarte) Communal Cemetery in Belgium.

CURRAN, Michael: Rank: Private. Regiment or Service: Irish Guards. Unit: 2nd Battalion. Age at death: 24. Date of death: 15 September 1916. Service No: 6619. Born in Waterford. Enlisted in Dublin, while living in Seraham, Co. Waterford. Died of wounds.

Supplementary information: Son of James and Bridget Curran, of Scrahan, Dungarvan, Co. Waterford. He was wounded in the left arm in July 1916. Grave or Memorial Reference: II.D.63. Cemetery: La Neuville British Cemetery, Corbie in France.

D

DALEY, James: Rank: Seaman. Regiment or Service: Royal Naval Reserve. Unit: HMS *Indefatigable*. During the Battle of Jutland the German Battlecruiser *Van Der Tann* fired 11-inch shells at the *Indefatigable*. The first two entered 'X' magazine area and blew out the bottom of the ship and she began sinking by the stern. More 11-inch shells from the *Van Der Tann* destroyed 'A' turret and also blew up the forward magazine and she then sank. There were only two survivors of her crew of 1,017 men. The *Van Der Tann* was scuttled in Scapa Flow in June 1919. Three Waterford men died on the ship that day. Age at death: 31. Date of death: 31 May 1916. Service No: 3610C.

Supplementary information: Son of Margaret Daley, of Passage East, Co. Waterford. Grave or Memorial Reference: 18 on the Plymouth Naval Memorial, UK.

DALTON, Edward: Rank: Private. Regiment or Service: Royal Irish Regiment. Unit: 2nd Battalion. Date of death: 3 May 1915. Service No: 4321. Born in St Nicholas, Carrick-on-Suir, Co. Tipperary. Enlisted in Carrick-on-Suir while living in Carrickbeg, Co. Waterford. Died of wounds. Son of Mr and Mrs Dalton, Carrigbeg. His father also served at the front. Grave or Memorial Reference: V.C.14. Cemetery: Klein-Vierstraat British Cemetery in Belgium.

DALTON, John: Rank: Private. Regiment or Service: Royal Irish Fusiliers. Unit: 2nd Battalion. Age at death: 17. Date of death: 13 May 1915. Service No: 17742. Born in Waterford. Enlisted in Glasgow while living in Govan, Glasgow. Killed in action.

Supplementary information: Son of Edward and Mary Dalton, of 110 Queen Street, Govan, Glasgow. He has no known grave but is listed on Panel 42 on the Ypres (Menin Gate) Memorial in Belgium.

DALTON, Patrick: Rank: Private. Regiment or Service: Royal Army Ordnance Corps. Unit: 118th Coy. Age at death: 40. Date of death: 7 April 1919. Service No: S/3635.

Supplementary information: Son of William and Bridget Dalton, of Waterford. Served in the South African War. Grave or Memorial Reference: RC.662. Cemetery, Grangegorman Military Cemetery in Dublin.

DALTON, Thomas: Rank: Private. Regiment or Service: Royal Irish Regiment. Unit: 2nd Garrison Battalion. Age at death: 50. Date of death: 31 March 1916. Service No: 6589. Formerly he was with the Royal Field Artillery. Born in St Mary's, Dungarvan. Enlisted in Dungarvan. Died at home.

Supplementary information: Son of Mr and Mrs John Dalton, of Patrick Street, Dungarvan. Grave or Memorial Reference: In the north-west part. Cemetery: Kilgobnet Catholic Churchyard, Waterford.

DALY, John: Rank: Private. Regiment or Service: Bedfordshire Regiment. Unit: 1st Garrison Battalion. Age at death: 36. Date of death: 13 November 1919. Service No: 32461.

Supplementary information: Son of Mrs Bridget Daly, of 18 Lower Newtown, Waterford. Grave or Memorial Reference: In north-east part. Cemetery: Faithlegg Catholic Churchyard in Waterford.

DALY, Michael: Rank: Private. Regiment or Service: Irish Guards. Unit: 1st Battalion. Age at death: 30. Date of death: 1 November 1914. Service No: 1926. Born in Kilrossenty, Co. Waterford. Enlisted in Bristol while living in Kilrossenty, Co. Waterford. Killed in action.

Supplementary information: Son of Patrick and Bridget Daly. He has no known grave but is listed on Panel 33 on the Ypres (Menin Gate) Memorial in Belgium.

grave but is listed on the La Ferté-sous-Jouarre Memorial in France.

DALY, Patrick: Rank: Gunner. Regiment or Service: Royal Garrison Artillery. Unit: 4th Mountain Battery. Age at death: 32. Date of death: 11 January 1915. Service No: 26577. Born in Kilmacthomas, Co. Waterford. Enlisted in Portlaw, Co. Waterford while living in Kilmacthomas. Died in India.

Supplementary information: Son of Patrick and Bridget Daly, of Cutteen, Kilrossanty, Kilmacthomas. Buried in Quetta Govt. Cemetery 1660. Grave or Memorial Reference: Face 1. Cemetery: Delhi Memorial (India Gate) in India.

DALY, Patrick: Rank: Private. Regiment or Service: Royal Irish Regiment. Unit: 6th Battalion. Date of death: 3 June 1916. Service No: 11113. Born in Cappoquin, Co. Waterford. Enlisted in Dungarvan, Co. Waterford while living in Cappoquin. Killed in action. From the *Munster Express*, 'Killed. A Cappoquin man in the person of Pte Daly, of the Royal Irish Regiment, son of Mr Patrick Daly, of Bank Street, has been killed in action.' Grave or Memorial Reference: II.K.2. Cemetery: Dud Corner Cemetery, Loos in France.

DAMER, Timothy: Rank: Private. Regiment or Service: Royal Munster Fusiliers. Unit: 2nd Battalion. Date of death: 24 March 1918. Service No: 6956. Born in St Patrick's, Waterford. Enlisted in Dublin while living in Dublin. Died of wounds. Grave or Memorial Reference: II.D.7. Cemetery: Honnechy British Cemetery in France.

DANIELS, James: Rank: Private. Regiment or Service: Royal Irish Regiment. Unit: 2nd Battalion. Date of death: 26 August 1914. Service No: 8285. Born in Portlaw, Co. Waterford. Enlisted in Waterford while living in Portlaw. Killed in action. He has no known

DARLING, Claude Henry Whish: Rank: Second Lieutenant. Regiment or Service: Royal Irish Rifles. Unit: 3rd Battalion. Attached to the 2nd Battalion. Age at death: 20. Date of death: 12 December 1915.

Supplementary information: Son of the Revd Oliver Warner and Edith (*née* Dunn) Darling. Native of Duncannon, Co. Wexford. From an in a Wexford newspaper:

Scarcely had the sorrow felt by Mrs Darling, Chelsea Lodge, Duncannon, for the loss of her eldest stepson began to wane when the sad news reached her that the second had fallen. The gallant Lieutenant was serving with the Royal Irish Rifles in France, where he was killed on the 12th inst. He was second son of Rev Oliver W Darling, Rector of All Saints, Duncannon, and was most popular in the district.

From De Ruvigny's Roll of Honour:

attached to the 2nd (86th Foot), Battalion, The Royal Irish Rifles. Second son of the late Rev, William Oliver Darling, Rector of Killesk, Duncannon, Co Waterford, by his wife, Edith, 2nd daughter of George Newman, Dunn, of Kinsale, Co Cork, M. D.; and brother to Lieutenant William Oliver Fortescue Darling (q. v.) Born in Winkle, Co Chester, 13 Apri, 1895. Educated at Braidlea, Stoke Bishop, Bristol; Monkton Coombe School, near Bath, where he was a member of the O.T.C, and on the Worcester, training ship for the Mercantile Marine; but while in training there his eyesight was found not to be sufficiently good, and he was obliged, to his great disappointment, to give up that life. Subsequently he was destined for the Colonies, but found the preparation distasteful, and joined the 8th Hussars as a trooper, being sent to the 4th Hussars at the Curragh Camp. On the outbreak of war he applied for a commission, and was gazetted 2nd Lieutenant, 3rd Royal Irish Rifles 10 March 1915. Went to France at the end of Sept, and was killed in action on 12 December, following. Buried in the Far Military Cemetery, Touquet des Mages, near Bols Grenier, south of Armentieres.

His Commanding Officer wrote of his, when in training in Dublin: "Your boy has done exceedingly well, and I lose a good and promising officer" He was killed by a sniper's bullet whilst in the trenches with his men-shot through the head while he was looking after the men's welfare. " A brother officer also wrote: "Your son was a general favourite, and his loss is most keenly felt by both officers and men. His death was a great blow to me. It is one consolation, however, that he gave his life in fighting for his country against the enemies of civilization, and we must remember 'Dulce et decorum est pro patria mori.'"

Grave or Memorial Reference: I.G.10. Cemetery: Tancrez Farm Cemetery in Belgium.

DARCY, Daniel: Also down as **DARCY, O.:** Rank: Private. Regiment or Service: Household Cavalry and Cavalry of the Line. Unit: 6th Dragoons (Inniskillings). Age at death: 39. Date of death: 15 February 1918. Service No: 21029. Born in Tramore, Waterford. Enlisted in Waterford while living in Kiltegan, Co. Wicklow. Died.

Supplementary information: Son of James Darcy. Husband of Kate Darcy, of Feddang Kiltegan, Co. Wicklow. Grave or Memorial Reference: VI.J.29. Cemetery: Tincourt New British Cemetery in France.

DAVIN, Thomas Joseph: Rank: Private. Regiment or Service: Irish Guards. Unit: 2nd Battalion. Age at death: 26. Date of death: 31 July 1917. Service No: 10568. Born in Carrickbeg, Co. Waterford and enlisted in Clonmel. Killed in action.

Supplementary information: Son of Thomas Davin (Solicitor) and Mrs Davin, of Carrick Beg, Carrick-on-Suir, Co. Tipperary. Has no known grave but is commemorated on Panel 11. Memorial: Ypres (Menin Gate) Memorial in Belgium.

DAWNAY/DAWNEY, (The Hon.) Hugh: Rank: Major. Regiment or Service: 2nd Life Guards. Age at death: 39. Date of death: 6 November 1914 Awards: D.S.O. He is not listed in Officers died in the Great War.

Supplementary information: Second son of the 8th Viscount Downe, Husband of Lady Susan Dawnay, of Whitfield Court, Waterford. From De Ruvigny's Roll of Honour:

DAWNAY, THE HON. HUGH, D.S.O. Major, 2nd Life Guards. Second son of Sir Hugh Richard Dawnay, the Viscount Downe, K.C.V O., C.B., by his 1st wife, Lady Cecilia Maria Charlotte, V.A. (Lady of the Bedchamber to Queen Victoria), only daughter of Charles William, 3rd Earl of Sefton. Born 19 Sept. 1875. Gazetted 2nd Lieutenant. Rifle Brigade 2 October 1895. Promoted Lieutenant. 1 January. 1898, Capt. 18 March 1901, and Major in the Life Guards 18 January. 1911. Served (1) in the Nile Expedition 1898 (mentioned in Despatches; Fourth Class of the Medjidie; Egyptian Medal with clasp, and Medal). (2) in the South African War 1899-1900 (mentioned in Despatches (London Gazettes, 8 February. and 10 Sept. 1901). Queen's Medal with clasp, and D.S.O.. (3) in East Africa (Somaliland) 1908-10, mentioned in Despatches (London Gazette, 17 June 1910, and Medal with clasp.) (4) Went with the Expeditionary Force to France and Flanders, and was killed in action 6 Nov. 1914. Major Dawnay was mentioned in Despatches (London Gazette, 19 October. 1914] by F.M. Sir John (now Lord) French, for gallant and distinguished service in the field. He married 28 April. 1902, Lady Susan de la Poor Beresford of 109, Gloucester Place, W. Daughter of John

Henry, 5th Marquess of Waterford, and had four sons: David, b. 10 July, 1903 ; Peter, b. 14 August. 1904; Ronald, b. 2 February. 1908. and Michael. b. 24 October. 1912.

The Bond of Sacrifice Volume 1:

Major the Honorable. Hugh Dawnay, D.S.O., p.s.c., 2nd Life Guards, who was killed in action on the 6 November 1914, was the second son of Viscount Downe. He was born on the 19 September 1875, and received his commission in the Rifle Brigade in October, 1895, becoming Lieutenant in January, 1898; from February, 1899, to November, 1900, he was Adjutant of his battalion. He became a Captain in the Rifle Brigade in March, 1901, and in February of that year was appointed A.D.C. to the Commander-in-Chief, retaining the position till February, 1904, and from April, 1904, to January, 1905, was A.D.C. to the G.O.C., North West District. He took part in the Nile Expedition, being present at the Battle of Khartoum, and being mentioned in Despatches, "London Gazette" 30 September 1898; received the medal, 4th class of the Order of Medjidieh, and the Egyptian medal with clasp. He next served in the South African War, 1899-1900, while Adjutant of his Battalion, being present at operations in Natal, including actions at Lombard's Kop; the defence of Ladysmith, including sortie of the 10th December, 1899, and action of the 6 January 1900. He was twice mentioned in Despatches ("London Gazette" 8 February and 10 September 1901); was awarded the D.S.O.., and received the Queen's medal with clasp. He also served in East Africa, Somaliland Expedition, 1908-10 for which he was mentioned in Despatches (" London Gazette, " 17 June, 1910), and received the medal with clasp. In the Great War, Major Dawnay was serving as General Staff Officer, 2nd grade, and was mentioned in Sir John French's Despatch of the 8 October 1914. Major Dawnay married, in 1902, Lady Susan Beresford, daughter of the fifth Marquess of Waterford, and left four sons.

From Distinguished Service Order 1886-1915:

DAWNAY, THE HONOURABLE HUGH, Lieutenant., was born on the 19 Sept. 1875, second son of Viscount Downe and Lady Cecilia Maria Charlotte Molyneux, V. A. (who died in 1910), daughter of the Earl of Sefton. He received his commission in the Rifle Brigade in October. 1895, and became Lieutenant in January. 1898, and took part in the Nile Expedition, being present at the Battle of Khartum, and being mentioned in Despatches (London Gazette, 30 Sept. 1898). He received the Medal; the 4th Class of the Order of the Medjidie, and the Egyptian Medal with clasp. From February. 1899, to Nov. 1930, he was Adjutant of his battalion, and in that capacity served in the South African War in 1899 and 1900, being present at operations in Natal, including actions at Lombard's Kop; the Defence of Ladysmith, including sortie of the 10 December 1899, and action of the 6 January 1900. He was twice mentioned in Despatches (London Gazette, 8 February. and 10 Sept. 1901.) Received the Queen's Medal with clasp, and was created a Companion of the Distinguished Service Order (London Gazette, 27 Sept. 1901.) "The Honourable Hugh Dawnay, Lieutenant., The Rifle Brigade. In recognition of services during the operations in South Africa." The Insignia were presented by the King 29 October 1901. He became Captain in the Rifle Brigade in March, 1901, and in February of the same year was appointed A.D.C. to the Commander-in-Chief. Major Dawnay was transferred to the 2nd Life Guards, and served in the European War. He was killed in action on the 6 November 1914. In 1902 he married Lady Susan Beresford, daughter of the 5th Marquess of Waterford, and they had four sons.

Grave or Memorial Reference: XVII.A.14. Cemetery: Harlebeke New British Cemetery in Belgium.

DAY, John: Rank: Rifleman. Regiment or Service: Royal Irish Rifles. Unit: 1st Battalion. Date of death: 30 November 1917. Service No: 5228. Born in Waterford. Enlisted in Waterford. Died of wounds.

Supplementary information: Won the D.C.M. *London Gazette* 26 January 1918: 'For conspicuous gallantry and devotion to duty. During an enemy attack all the Lewis guns in the front line had been rendered useless. He ran back to the support line and returned with a Lewis gun under very heavy machine gun fire. He then opened fire and held up the enemy advance.' Grave or Memorial Reference: Coll, Grave II.C. Cemetery: White House Cemetery, St Jean-Les-Ypres in Belgium.

DAY, John Edward: Rank: Captain. Regiment or Service: Royal Irish Regiment. Unit: 'A' Coy. 6th Battalion. Age at death: 22. Date of death: 6 April 1917. Died of wounds.

Supplementary information: Son of the Very Revd Maurice W. Day and Katherine L.F. Day, of Culloden, Bray, Co. Wicklow. Born at Newport, Co. Tipperary. From *Waterford News*, September 1915:

Mr Geoffrey William Day, second son of the Very Rev the Dean of Waterford, has just received a commission in the Army. He was in Canada at the outbreak of the war, and in October last he enlisted in the 20th Canadians. He had been gazetted a Commission in the 3rd (Special reserve) Battalion Cheshire Regiment. Another son of Dean Day's. Lieutenant Day, is in the Royal Irish Regiment.

De Ruvigny's Roll of Honour:

Son of the Very Revd Maurice William Day, Dean of Waterford, by his wife, Kathlene Louisa Frances, daughter of the late Charles Garfit, J.P. Born in St John's Rectory, Newport, Co Tipperary, 1 December 1894. Educated at Hamilton House, Rath, Marlborough College and Trinity College, Dublin. Gazetted 2nd Lt, Royal Irish Regiment, 15 August 1914. Promoted Lieutenant, 30 Nov following, and Capt, 6 April 1916, served with the Expeditionary Force in France from 18 December 1915, was severely wounded, 8 April 1916. Returned to France in Sept, and died 6 April 1917, from wounds received in action while in command of a raid near Wytschaete. Buried in Bailleul. Brigadier-General Pereira, commanding the 47th Infantry Division wrote: "He was such a splendid young officer in every way. I have always had the highest opinion of a trust him, and I feel that his place cannot be filled. He was absolutely fearless, and led his men into action with splendid coolness. Besides being a gallant, capable and most conscientious officer, he was beloved by his men. Thanks in great measure to him, the operation was completely successful", and Major Hutcheson; "Everyone of us loved your son most dearly, and we all feel your loss, and will do so for a long time. He will never be forgotten in the Regiment. Your son was senior officer in the attack, and was leading the Regiment on the night of the 5th. The attack was a very great success. The Regiment has received the congratulations from the Army and the Corps Commanders.

Day Memorial, Christ Church Cathedral (COI), Henrietta Street, Waterford:

SIC ITUR AD ASTRA
In loving memory of the Very Revd, Maurice William Day; M.A. Dean of this Cathedral; and Rector of Holy Trinity Parish 1913-1916.

Who died at Courtmacsherry, County Cork, August 29 1916. Aged 58 years. Also of his sons, Maurice Charles Day; B.A. Senior Scholar, Trinity College, Cambridge; Bell University Scholar, 1911; Wrangler 1913; Lieutenant 13th Rajputs. Killed in action at Tanga, German East Africa, November 3, 1914 aged 23 years. And John Edward Day, Captain 6th Service

Battalion, The Royal Irish Regiment. Died of wounds received in action near Wytschaete on Good Friday, April 6 1917, aged 22 years.

This tablet is placed here by Katherine L.F. Day; wife and mother.

From the *Waterford News*, March 1916:

ANOTHER APPEAL FROM THE TRENCHES.
A.S.C.
On Active Service.
March 9th, 1916.
My dear Mr Editor,
Just a line hoping that you shall spare me space in your old and well-esteemed paper of the old City of Waterford. We are all going on well.

We are five of the R.I. Regiment, one of the R. I. Rifles, one of the Connaught Rangers, and one of the North Irish Horse; and we just thought that we would write one line to you and ask if you would put an appeal in your paper to get some kind friend to send us out an old gramophone or accordion box, as we have some trying times here, and one little bit of music would pass away the time for us. A football would also help to do likewise. I will close for now, as we have not much to say; so we hope that some kind friend will answer our appeal. Hoping that your paper shall meet with success, and hoping also to hear from you in the near future,

We remain, yours faithfully. 7374, Private Clayton, Connaught Regiment [sic], 4884 Private Murphy, 2nd R.I. Regiment, 6163 Private Patrick Walsh, 1st R.I. Regiment, 8973 Private Jack Moore, 2nd R.I. Rifles, 73985 Private J Kelly, NI. Horse.

P.S. We all hope to get news from you papers soon. Please address your letter to: The Treasurer of the Company, 6163 Private P Walsh, 1st Battalion, R.I. Regiment attached to 32 Company, M.T., Repair Depot, A.S.C., B.E.F., France.

From the *Waterford News*, March 1916:

LOCAL WAR NEWS.
A WATERFORD FOOTBALL.
Lieutenant John E Day, 6th Battalion, Royal Irish Regiment, wishes to thank the kind Waterford friends who have sent his a splendid football for the Battalion. He writes; "The men are delighted with it. I only had it about five minutes before they were kicking it about." "From Waterford" is inscribed on the football. The funds were kindly collected by Mrs Mitchell, Michael Street, who has also made a weekly penny collection by which 3,300 cigarettes have been sent to the Battalion since the beginning of the year. The last request has been for mouth organs to start a band, and a dozen ("Made in Japan") were forwarded this week. On behalf of the Battalion, Lieutenant Day wishes to send most cordial thanks to Mrs Mitchell and all the kind friends.

From the *Waterford News*, February 1917:

SECOND LIEUTENANT G. W. DAY.
As already stated briefly in the "Evening News" Second Lieutenant Geoffrey W. Day, son of the late Very Rev. M. W. Day, Dean of Waterford, and Mrs Day, has been wounded in action at the front. Second Lieutenant Day is attached to the Cheshire Regiment, and has been at the front for a considerable time. His wounds which were received on the night of the 27th January, are reported to be somewhat severe, and are located in the shoulder.

From the *Waterford News*, April 1917:

CAPTAIN J. E. DAY MORTALLY WOUNDED.
Captain John Edwrad Day, Royal Irish Regiment, has Died of wounds received in action. Captain Day, who was the son of the lat Dean Day, of Waterford, was 22 years of age, and was educated at Maryborough College and Trinity College, Dublin. He was gazetted second Lieutenant on April 6, 1916. On April 8,

1916, he was severely wounded. His eldest brother was killed in action in East Africa in November, 1914. The Major-General of Captain Day's Division, in a letter to Mrs Day, offers his most sincere sympathy in the loss of her very gallant and excellent son. The officers of the Regiment and his Brigadier, the letter continues, will have told you of the manner of his death, and how by his skilful leadership he brought back his men when, in their ardour and enthusiasm they had passed their objective. Captain Day's Brigadier-General says of his "The more I saw of him the more I admired him. He was absolutely fearless, and led his men into action with a splendid coolness."

Grave or Memorial Reference: III.B.60. Cemetery: Bailleul Communal Cemetery Extension (Nord) in France.

DAY, Michael: Rank: Gunner. Regiment or Service: Royal Horse Artillery and Royal Field Artillery. Unit: 6th Ammunition Supply Park. Date of death: 20 August 1917. Service No: 32908. Born in Waterford. Enlisted in Waterford. Died. Grave or Memorial Reference: IV.A.44. Cemetery: St Venant Communal Cemetery in France.

DAY, Maurice Charles. Rank: Second Lieutenant. Regiment or Service: Shekhawati Regiment. Unit: 13th Rajputs. Date of death: 3 November 1914. The image above is taken from De Ruvigny's Roll of Honour.

Supplementary information: Son of the Dean of Waterford. This information is taken from 'Roll of the sons and daughters of the Anglican Church clergy throughout the world and of the naval and military chaplains of the same who gave their lives in the Great War, 1914-1918'. He is also listed on the Waterford and District Roll of Honour and on the Day Memorial. These are located in Christ Church Cathedral (Church of Ireland), Henrietta Street, Waterford. The memorial reads:

SACRED TO THE MEMORY OF
2ND LIEUTENANT MAURICE CHARLES DAY
13th Rajputs,
Killed in action at Tanga, German East Africa
On 3rd Novr, 1914, aged 23 years.

From the *Freeman's Journal*:

DEAN OF WATERFORD'S SON KILLED.
WATERFORD, MONDAY.
A telegram was received here on yesterday from the War Office intimating that Second Lieutenant Maurice Charles Day, of the Indian Army, eldest son of the Protestant Dean of Waterford, had been killed in East Africa. Dean Day has two other sons, one in the Canadian Army and the other, the youngest, Second Lieutenant J Day, of the Royal Irish Regiment, stationed at Fermoy. The deceased was 23 years of age.

From De Ruvigny's Roll of Honour:

Day, Maurice Charles, Lieutenant, 13th Rajputs, Indian Army. Eldest son of the Very Rev, Maurice William Day, Dean of Waterford, by his wife, Katherine Louisa Frances. Daughter of Charles Garfit and grandson of the late Right Rev. Maurice Day, Bishop of Cashel. Born the Palace, Waterford, 26 February 1891. Educated Aravon, Bray (1902-5), Marlborough College (1905-10), Foundation Scholarship, Senior Scholarship, (Leaving

Maurice Charles Day.

Exhibition), and Trinity College, Cambridge (1910-13), Exhibition T. C. 1910; Senior Scholarship, T. C. 1913. Bells University Scholarship, 1912. Wrangler, B. A. 1913 and was gazetted 2nd Lieutenant to the unattached list for the Indian Army, 5 September, 1913, to rank as from 5 September, 1911, being awarded six months seniority for his University candidate. He was attached to the Royal West Kent Regiment for his first year and was stationed at Multan and Dalhousie. He was promoted Lieutenant 28 September, 1914 (to rank from 5 December, 1913), and the same day joined his Indian Regiment, the 13th Rajputs. They started on active service the day after he joined and left Bombay with the Expeditionary for East Africa on 16 October. He fell in action at Tanga, German East Africa, 3 November, 1914, the morning they landed. Lieutenant-Col Stewart wrote; "The Commandant, Lieutenant Col H.W. Codrington, and the Adjutant Capt E. Clothire, and Major B Corbett were all hit at the same time and place. Your son was buried by the Germans subsequently. Mr Day joined us before we came on service, and when we landed was acting as Brigade Transport Officer. During the short time he was with us, we realised what a keen and promising officer he was. There can be no doubt that he would have made a name for himself, and that soon"; and Lieutenant-Col H.W. Codrington; "First I must tell you that your son, although he only joined the Regiment on the day before we started from Agra had become a great favourite, and that his loss is very keenly felt by all. It was a great blow to me personally, as I had taken a great fancy to him. Professionally he was a most exceptionally able, keen and promising young officer. His brother officers would very much like is we may put up a small memorial brass to the memory of your son in your church. We shall be so glad if you will allow us to do this." Capt. Cole also wrote; "Your son was in my double company and I was with him when he was killed. Colonel Codrington, the Adjutant, your son, and myself had just got on to a small hillock to have a look around when a machine gun opened up on us at close range and the first three named went down instantaneously. Your son was killed outright. I cannot tell you how very deeply we mourn his loss, for although he had been with us such a short time we knew him for a brave, capable and resourceful boy." Previous to joining the Army he worked in the Trinity Mission at Camberwell, and the Vicar of St George's there (the Rev. H.G.D. Latham) wrote; "Your son when at Trinity was one of those who would not be content simply to get the best out of life for ourselves. He came here to do hard mission work among our people and to share with those who had not had his privileges whatever of Cambridge spirit can be shared by a simple and sincere friendliness, and so he has helped to sweeten life for many and to make the strained relations between class and class easier, and he has helped on the good Cambridge tradition of coming to South London. There are many here who will feel his loss as a personal blow, while they will be proud to have had his friendship."

Grave or Memorial Reference: Tanga Memorial Cemetery in Tanzania.

DAYE, John: Rank: Private. Regiment or Service: Royal Inniskilling Fusiliers. Unit: 7th Battalion. Age at death: 18. Date of death: 27 April 1916. Service No: 27703. Previously he was with the Royal Irish Regiment where his number was 11393. Born in Kilmacthomas, Waterford. Enlisted in Dungarvan while living in Waterford. Killed in action.

Supplementary information: Son of William Daye, of Cooltubbrid, Kilmacthomas. Grave or Memorial Reference: 60 on the Loos Memorial in France.

DAY/DAYE, Richard: Rank: Private. Regiment or Service: Royal Irish Regiment. Unit: 2nd Battalion. Date of death: 9 May 1915. Age at death: 50. Service No: 6443. Born in

Mooncoin, Co. Kilkenny Soldiers died in the Great War), Mooncoin, Co. Waterford (Ireland' Memorial Records). Enlisted in Waterford while living in Mooncoin. Killed in action. He has no known grave but is listed on Panel 33 on the Ypres (Menin Gate) Memorial in Belgium.

DEAN, Patrick: Rank: Fireman and Trimmer. Regiment or Service: Mercantile Marine. Unit: SS *Thracia* (Liverpool). Age at death: 37. Date of death: 27 March 1917. The Steamship *Thracia* was on a voyage from Bilbao to Ardrossan stuffed with a cargo of iron ore when she was torpedoed by German Submarine UC69 in the Bay of Biscay 12 miles north of Belle Isle. Thirty-six of her crew died, the only survivor of the sinking being 15 year old Cadet Douglas V Duff. The submarine was a Type UCII coastal minelayer which later sank after it collided with German submarine (U96) in 1917.

Supplementary information: Son of the late Henry and Mary Ann Dean. Husband of Josephine Dean (*née* Grayson), of 59 Waterloo Road, Liverpool. Born in Waterford. He has no known grave but is listed on the Tower Hill Memorial in the UK.

DELAHUNTY, John: Rank: Private. Regiment or Service: Irish Guards. Unit: 2nd Battalion. Date of death: 15 September 1916. Service No: 8073. Born in Waterford. Enlisted in Glasgow, Lanarkshire while living in Waterford. Killed in action. From *Waterford News*, January 1917, 'In the Casualty Lists. In this week's casualty lists appears the name of Private J Delahunty (8073) Irish Guards, Waterford, previously reported missing, now killed.' He has no known grave but is listed on Pier and Face 7D on the Thiepval Memorial in France.

DELANEY, James: Rank: Sapper. Regiment or Service: Corps of Royal Engineers. Unit: Inland Water Transport, Royal Engineers. Date

of death: 20 May 1917. Service No: 205530. Born in Waterford. Enlisted in Cardiff while living in Islington, Middlesex. Died. Grave or Memorial Reference: II.C.6. Cemetery: Suzanne Military Cemetery, No. 3 in France.

DENN, John Joseph: Rank: Private. Regiment or Service: Royal Irish Regiment. Unit: 2nd Battalion. Age at death: 25. Date of death: 26 May 1915. Service No: 10164. Born in Ballybricken, Waterford. Enlisted in Cork while living in Waterford. Died of wounds.

Supplementary information: Son of Nicholas and Mary Denn, (*née* Ruth), of 1 Costelloe's Lane, Waterford. Grave or Memorial Reference: VIII.A.48. Cemetery: Boulogne Eastern Cemetery in France.

DENNEHY, James: Rank: Private. Regiment or Service: Irish Guards. Unit: 1st Battalion. Date of death: 3 September 1917. Service No: 9537. Born in Dungarvan, Co. Waterford. Enlisted in Dungarvan. Killed in action. Grave or Memorial Reference: I.H.37. Cemetery: Bleuet Farm Cemetery in Belgium.

DESMOND, Thomas: Rank: Signal Boy. Regiment or Service: Royal Naval Reserve. Unit: HM Trawler *Amroth Castle*. Age at death: 17. Date of death: 29 August 1918. Service No: 2079SB.

Supplementary information: Son of Alexander and Catherine Desmond, of 22 Philip St, Waterford. Grave or Memorial Reference: 29 on the Plymouth Naval Memorial, UK.

DEVEREUX, William Patrick: Rank: Sapper. Regiment or Service: Royal Engineers. Unit: 14th Signals. Age at death: 23. Date of death: 20 August 1915. Service No: 58571. Born in Kilmacon, County Kilkenny. Enlisted in Waterford while living in Ferrybank, County Kilkenny. Died of wounds.

Supplementary information: Son of Patrick and Margaret Devereux, of Mount Sion, Ferrybank, Waterford. Grave or Memorial Reference: III.C.21A. Cemetery: Lijssenthoek Military Cemetery in Belgium.

DEVINE, William Francis: Rank: Private. Regiment or Service: Household Cavalry and Cavalry of the line including the Yeomanry and Imperial Camel Corps. Unit: 16th Lancers (The Queen's). Date of death: 24 February 1915. Service No: 283. Born in Tallow, Co. Waterford. Enlisted in London. Died of wounds. Grave or Memorial Reference: III.A.36. Cemetery: Hazebrouck Communal Cemetery, Nord, in France.

DEWAR, Tyrie: Rank: Second Lieutenant. Regiment or Service: Royal Irish Rifles. From the *Waterford News*, February 1917:

THE ROLL OF HONOUR.

We learn with deep regret that Second Lieutenant Tyrie Dewar, of the Royal Irish Rifles, has been killed in action. This gallant young officer was the eldest son of Mrs Deward, of Mount Street, Dublin, who is a daughter of the late Mr P MacKenna, of Parade Quay, Waterford.

The Commanding Officer of the Regiment has sent a sympathetic letter to the gallant young officer's father, Mr James Dewar (of the Registrar-General's Office), in the course of which he says; "Like all his brother officers, I had already taken a great liking for your son. I know that Colonel Savage and Major Waring had the highest opinion of him as a most gallant and always cheerful soldier. Only to-day his company commander was saying how extraordinarily popular he was with his men. They would do anything for him".

This man is not in any of the War Dead Databases including the Royal Irish Rifles in the Great War. The only reference I can find to him is the above.

DILLON, William: Rank: Private. Regiment or Service: Royal Irish Regiment. Unit: 2nd Battalion. Date of death: 19 October 1914. Service No: 6622. Born in Trinity Without, Waterford. Enlisted in Waterford while living in Dungarvan, Co. Waterford. Killed in action. He has no known grave but is listed on Panels 11 and 12 on the Le Touret Memorial in France.

DINNEEN, Daniel: Rank: Lance Corporal. Regiment or Service: Hampshire Regiment. Unit: 2/5th Battalion. Date of death: 10 April 1918. Age at death: 40. Service No: 241953. Born in Modligo [*sic*], Co. Waterford. Enlisted in Winchester while living in Portsmouth. Killed in action in Egypt.

Supplementary information: Son of Daniel and Margaret Dinneen. He has no known grave but is listed on panels 28 and 29 on the Jerusalem Memorial in Israel.

DOBBS, William Cary/Carey: Rank: Captain. Regiment or Service: Middlesex Regiment. Unit: 'D' Coy. 2nd Battalion. Age at death: 46. Date of death: 31 July 1917. Killed in action.

Supplementary information: Son of Robert Conway Dobbs, J.P., and Edith Juliana Dobbs, of Camphire, Cappoquin, Co. Waterford. Twice previously wounded. Educated at Winchester College and Trinity College Cambridge. From the *Waterford News*, August 1917:

Captain William C. Dobbs, of the Middlesex Regiment, was killed in action on July 31st. He was 46 years of age and the eldest son of the late Mr R. Conway Dobbs and of Mrs Dobbs, of Camphire, Cappoquin, Co. Waterford.

He has no known grave but is listed on Panel 49 and 51 on the Ypres (Menin Gate) Memorial in Belgium.

DOBBIN, William Leonard Price: Rank: Lieutenant Regiment or Service: Royal Irish

Rifles. Unit: 2nd Battalion also listed as 3rd Battalion. Age at death: 20. Date of death: 21 March 1918. Awarded the Military Cross.

Supplementary information: Son of Maj. William Wood and Emily Josephine Cuzens Dobbin, M.B.E., of Osborne, Dunmurry, Co. Antrim. I am not sure of the Waterford connection but he is listed on the Dobbin Memorial located in Christ Church Cathedral (Church of Ireland), Henrietta Street, Waterford. The Memorial reads:

TO THE GREATER GLORY OF GOD.
In loving memory of Lieutenant William Leonard Price Dobbin, M. C.
Killed in action at Contes Court, 21st March 1918 in his 21st year.
Only son of Major William Wood Dobbin, M. B. E.

From the *Waterford News*, April 1917:

ANOTHER MILITARY CROSS.
Waterford continues to earn considerable distinction in the battlefield. On Tuesday we noted the distinction conferred on 2nd Lieutenant Dobbyn.

He has no known grave but is listed on Panels 74 and 76 on the Pozières Memorial in France.

DOBBYN, Michael: Rank: Private. Regiment or Service: Royal Irish Regiment. Unit: 6th Battalion. Age at death: 28. Date of death: 6 June 1916. Service No: 1885. Born in Kilmacow, Co. Kilkenny. Enlisted in Dungarvan, Co. Waterford. Killed in action.

Supplementary information: Son of Michael and Mary Dobbyn, of Kilmacow, Co. Kilkenny. Husband of E. Dobbyn, of 39 Queen Street, Portlaw, Co. Waterford. Grave or Memorial Reference: 44 on the Loos Memorial in France.

DOBBYN, Robert Newport: Rank: Second Lieutenant. Regiment or Service: Royal Flying Corps and General List, New Armies. Date of death: 23 November 1916.

Born in Waterford. Killed in a flying accident. From the *Waterford News*, December 1916.

LATE LIEUTENANT, R. N. DOBBYN.
The funeral took place on Monday, with full military honours, of the late Lieutenant, R. N. Dobbyn, R. F. C., only son of the late Mr Robert Dobbyn, Ballinakill House. The remains arrived at Waterford on Sunday from Croydon, where deceased was accidentally killed, and were conveyed to Ballinakill Church.

On Monday the funeral took place from the church to the ancient burial ground attached to the family residence, Ballinakill House. The attendance at the funeral was thoroughly representative, and showed how widespread is the regret at the demise of this popular young gentleman.

The chief mourners were Mrs Dobbyn (mother), Miss Dobbyn, Miss Irish Dobbyn and Mrs Wm, Mackesy (sisters), Messrs, Newport (2) (uncles), Mr, W.A. Dobbyn, Clerk of the Crown and Peace (first cousin), Lieutenant, AS.L. Dobbyn, M.C.; Mr, M.H. Dobbyn, Mr Francis Jones, and Mr Herbert Goff (cousins). The band of the 5th Lancers played the Dead March along the route, and the Last Post was sounded over the grave and three volleys fired, the firing party consisting of men of the Royal Irish Regiment from Clonmel. The Rev. Canon Greenstreet and the Rev. Mr, Young officiated at the graveside. A number of floral tributes were laid on the grave.

From the *Waterford News*, November 1916.

MR ROBERT N. DOBBYN KILLED.
One of the saddest tragedies we have had to chronicle since the outbreak of the war is the death of Mr Robert Newport Dobbyn, Second Lieutenant in the Royal Flying Corps, only son of the late Mr Robert Dobbyn, Ballinakill House. He was killed as the result of an accident at Croydon. Thus, at the age of twenty-three, has passed away one of the few male repre-

sentatives of two most important Waterford families connected with this city for centuries, and linking present-day Waterford with historic events and personages of the past. For instance, the Dobbyn family and the family of Luke Wadding were related, whilst the romantically situated mansion at Banninakill is said to have been the last refuge of King James II, in his flight overseas after that defeat at the Battle of the Boyne. The Newport family, to which deceased was related on his mothers side, has been identified with the public life of Waterford since the middle of the 17th century when Captain Newport came to Waterford from Carrick-on-Suir, then Ormonde's town. The late Lieutenant R. N. Dobbyn may therefore be described as the repository of some of Waterford's oldest and most treasured traditions, which makes his death doubly tragic. A young man of such promise, he had been educated at Clister College, and, with numbers of his old school friends, joined the Public School Corps in the early stages of the war. For a considerable time he served in Flanders, where he took part in many an memorable engagement. Subsequently returning to England, he obtained a commission in the Royal Flying Corps. It was while undergoing a course of training in this famous corps that he met his death, but no details have yet been received of the accident in which he lost his life. The news of his death has been received with the deepest regret, not only by those who knew him but also by all who are responsive to the claims of long decent and connection with Waterford's storied past.

The funeral will take place next Monday from Ballinakill Church to the ancient family graveyard, which is adjacent to Ballinakill House, surrounded by an enclosing wall.

From the *Waterford News*, November 1916:

HOW LIEUTENANT DOBBYN WAS KILLED. When a verdict of accidental death was returned at Hounslow on Lieutenant R. N. Dobbyn, Royal Flying Corps, son of the late Mr Dobbyn, solicitor, Waterdford, Captain Fuller said he believed that Lieutenant Dobbyn, who was returning from Brooklands, lost speed whilst turning down, causing a nose dive. Colonel White, R.A. M.C, said death was due to concussion and burns.

From the *Waterford News*, November 1916.

Lieutenant Dobbyn's father was Robert Dobbyn, for many years the leading solicitor in Waterford. He was the son of Michael Dobbyn, Barrister-at-Law, commonly called Councellor Dobbyn, who lived at Woodlands. Before his retirement from business in 1882, Mr Robert Dobbyn leased the old Dobbyn family mansion from its owner, Mr Hubert Power, of Faithlegg. He died in 1911, and was buried in the old churchyard at Ballinakill, where his son was laid to rest last Monday.

Grave or Memorial Reference: On the south-east boundary. Cemetery: Ballinakill House Private Burial Ground, Waterford.

DOBBYN, Thomas: Rank: Cattleman. Regiment or Service: Mercantile Marine. Unit: SS *Coningbeg* (Glasgow). Torpedoed by German Submarine U-62. There were no survivors. U-62 surrendered in November 1918. Age at death: 51. Date of death: 18 December 1917.

Supplementary information: Son of the late Patrick and Mary Dobbyn. Born at Newtown, Kilmacthomas, Co. Waterford. He has no known grave but is listed on the Tower Hill Memorial in the UK. He is also listed on the Formby-Coningbeg Memorial, Adelphi Quay in Waterford City.

DOBBYN, William Augustus Nelson: Rank: Second Lieutenant. Regiment or Service: Lancashire Fusiliers. Unit: 15th Battalion. Age at death: 20. Date of death: 4 February 1917.

Supplementary information: Son of Mr W.A. Dobbyn, of Riverdale, Newtown, Waterford. From the *Waterford News*, September 1916:

LIEUTENANT DOBBIN.

2nd Lieutenant W. L. P. Dobbin was examined yesterday at the ----------session of the Sheehy-Skeffington -------is a son of Major Dobbin CK--- formerly Governor of Waterford ----- [missing words are obscured by an ink blot.]

Lieutenant Dobbin was commander of the guard on the occasion of the Portobello shooting, His evidence was given yesterday after he had been brought back from the fighting line in France for the purpose, and he stated that Captain Colthurst ordered the prisoners out of the guardroom and said; "I am going to shoot them, Dobbin; I think it the right thing to do." He admitted that a grave irregularity had been committed both in regard to the holding of Mr Skeffington as a hostage and respecting the shooting of the three men; but he was not in a position to say to his superior officer that what he was doing was right or wrong.

He is also listed on the Bishop Foy School Memorial in the Church of Ireland Cathedral, Henrietta Street, Waterford City and also on the Dobbyn Memorial in the same location. The Memorial reads:

Dulce et decorum est patria mori. In loving memory of William Augustus Nelson Dobbyn, 2nd Lieutenant. Lancashire Fusiliers, eldest son of William A. and Eleanor A. Dobbyn of Waterford. Accidentally killed in the performance of his duty at Montrelet, France on 4th January, 1917 in his twenty first year.

Call him not dead who fell at duty's feet And passed thro' light where earth and heaven meet

Call him not dead, thy fallen soldier-son But say "the warfare waged, the victory won.

From De Ruvigny's Roll of Honour:

Dobbyn, William Augustus Nelson, 2nd Lieutenant, 22nd (Service) Battalion. The Lancashire Fusiliers, eldest son of William Alexander Dobbyn, of Riverdale. Waterford. Clerk of the Crown and Peace for the County and City of Waterford. by his wife, Eleanor Adelaide, only daughter of Alexander Nelson, of Waterford. J.P., D.L., born 9 June. 1896. Educated. High School, Waterford; Monkton Cumbe, near Bath, and Trinity College, Dublin, where he was studying for the Bar when war broke out. Obtained a commission in 16th Battalion, The King's (Liverpool Regiment.) 20 October 1915. Transferred to the Lancashire Fusiliers in June 1916; served with the Expeditionary Force in France and Flanders from 14 July following, and was accidentally killed at Beauval 4 January 1917. by the bursting of a Mills' grenade in the hand of one of his men while instructing a bombing class. Buried in Bonneville Communal Cemetery, near Amiens. Lieutenant-Col. H.G. Harrison wrote: "Your son came to my notice as one of the smartest and best of officers both in work and play," and his Company Commiander, Caitt. E. B. Lord: "He was in my company (2) for a month or so before he went on to Headquarters, and his bright and sunny nature endeared him to all. He was irrepressibly merry even in the most dreary moments and acted like a tonic to us all. "Capt and Adjutant Frank A. Boyton also wrote: "I had known your son during the whole of his time with the battalion, and looked upon him as a most painstaking and promising officer. Had he lived he would. I feel sure, have justified my belief in him If it is any consolation for you to know, your son always showed great courage and coolness when in the trenches before the enemy, "and the Chaplain, tile Rev. R. French: "He was instructing a class in bombing this morning when there was a premature explosion, and a piece of the bomb pierced his heart, killing him Instantaneously. I can hardly realize yet that it is true: he was always so cheery and bright and full of life, and left everyone the happier for having met him."

Grave or Memorial Reference: Near south-west corner. Cemetery: Bonneville Communal Cemetery in France. He is also listed on the Bishop Foy School Memorial in the Church of Ireland Cathedral, Henrietta Street, Waterford City.

DOBSON, Robert: Rank: Gunner. Regiment or Service: Royal Field Artillery. Unit: 13th Battery. Secondary Regiment: Labour Corps Secondary. Unit: transferred to (633150) 995th Coy. Age at death: 46. Date of death: 28 July 1919. Service No: 37276.

Supplementary information: Son of John Dobson, of Wigan, Co. Waterford. Hhusband of Mary Dobson, of Steeple Ashton. Grave or Memorial Reference: South of west end of Church. Cemetery: Steeple Ashton (St Mary) Churchyard, Wiltshire, UK.

DOHERTY, Patrick: Rank: Corporal. Regiment or Service: Royal Irish Regiment. Unit: 1st Battalion. Date of death: 27 April 1915. Service No: 6446. Born in St John's Waterford. Enlisted in Waterford. Died of wounds. Grave or Memorial Reference: III.A.63. Cemetery: Hazebrouck Communal Cemetery, Nord, in France.

DOHNEY/DOHENY, Martin: Rank: Guardsman. Regiment or Service: Scots Guards. Unit: 3rd Battalion. Date of death: 31 October 1915. Service No: 5471. Born in Waterford. Enlisted in Edinburgh while living in Waterford. Died of wounds at home. From the *Waterford News*, November 1915:

TRAGIC OCCURRENCE.

Waterfordman Dies on way to the Front.

The death took place under tragic cir-

cumstances on Saturday night of Private Martin Doheny, Scots Guards, a native of this city.

The deceased, who was aged about 30 years, and was a splendid type of Irish manhood, was born in Barrack Street, but latterly lived with his wife at Tanyard Arch.

Being on the reserve, he was called up at the outbreak of the war and participated for close on a year in the fighting in Belgium and France. He received a bullet wound in the chest several months ago. After coming home on *sick* leave he again went away to all intents and purposes fully recovered. It appears, however, that the bullet was never extracted, and his relatives attribute death to this. A few weeks ago he again returned to Waterford on furlough, and left on Saturday night en route for the front.

On Sunday his bereaved widow received news of his death, and from the telegrams it seems that at Cardiff he was suddenly taken ill and removed to one of the infirmaries there where he died.

THE INQUEST.

On Tuesday last the Cardiff Coroner held an inquest on Martin Doheny, aged 31, a private in the 3rd Battalion (Reserve) Scots Guards, who died while returning from Ireland to duty on Sunday. According to the evidence deceased had been in the Army twelve years, and had been home to Waterford after being wounded in France. He left home on Saturday night to journey to London. Some time after nine o'clock on Sunday morning an inspector at the Great Western railway Station ar Cardiff received a message from Bridgend (another Welsh town) to get an ambulance ready as a soldier had been taken ill on the boat-train. Deceased was taken in the ambulance to a military hospital in Cardiff but death had occurred on the way. The medical testimony was that death was due to haem-orrhage from shrapnel wounds accelerated by vomiting. The jury returned a verdict accordingly. The Coroner on behalf of himself and the jury expressed sympathy with the relatives who had journeyed from Ireland to be present at the inquiry.

THE FUNERAL.

The remains of the late Private Doheny arrived in this city at 9. 30 o'clock on Wednesday morning from Cardiff. They were met by a large number of deceased's comrades and by the members of the Erin's Hope Fire and Drum Band. Some of the military were also in attendance.

Grave or Memorial Reference: E.B. 54. Cemetery: Ballynaneshagh (St Otteran's) Catholic Cemetery in Waterford.

DONNELLY, Maurice: Rank: Private. Regiment or Service: Royal Inniskilling Fusiliers. Unit: 2nd Battalion. Date of death: 27 June 1916. Service No: 8747. Born in Crook, Co. Waterford. Enlisted in Cardiff while living in Waterford. Killed in action. From the *Waterford News*, July 1916:

BRAVE COUNTY WATERFORD
SOLDIER'S DEATH.

Mrs Donnelly, late of Ballycanvan, Passage east, has received news of the death of her son, Private M Donnelly, 2nd Royal Inniskilling Fusiliers, who was killed at the front on the 27th ult. The Rev. John Coghlan, Chaplain to the Forces, in informing mrs Donnelly of her son's death writes: 'It took place during a bombardment of our front line trenches. Your poor son was hurrying up to attend to a wounded comrade when he was hit and killed. To-day I buried him in the little military cemetery at Authuile. I have a nice cross erected over his grave, and when I get the opportunity I shall offer up Holy Mass for the repose of his soul. Though it is indeed sad news for you will, I am sure, be much consoled when I tell you your son received Holy Communion three or four times during the week before he died. He was a good soldier and very popular with all, but above all he was a grand Catholic. Whenever opportunity offered

he was always to be seen attending to his religious duties, and now I feel certain he is in heaven.'

Grave or Memorial Reference: F. 7. Cemetery: Authuile Military Cemetery in France.

DONOGHUE, John: Rank: Private. Regiment or Service: South Lancashire Regiment. Unit: 1/5th Battalion. Date of death: 11 September 1916. Service No: 4470. Born in Stradbally, Waterford. Enlisted in St Helens, Lancashire while living in Dungarvan, Co. Waterford. Died of wounds. Grave or Memorial Reference: IV.C. 57. Cemetery: Heilly Station Cemetery, Mericourt-l'Abbe in France.

DONOVAN, Michael: Rank: Private. Regiment or Service: Canadian Infantry (Central Ontario Regiment). Unit: 102nd Battalion. Age at death: 25. Date of death: 2 November 1918 Service No: 3105437. Data from attestation papers:

What is your present address? 808 Cass(Rush?) Street, Chicago, Ill, USA.

In what Town, Township or Parish, and in what Country were you born? Watergord, Ireland.

What is the name of your next of kin? Margaret Donovan.

What is the address of your next of kin? 818 Rush Street, Chicago, Ill, USA.

What is the relationship of your next of kin? Sister.

What is the date of your birth? 15 August 1895.

What is your trade or calling? Cook.

Are you married? No.

Apparent age: 22 years, 2 months.

Height: 5 Ft, 3 Ins.

Girth when fully expanded: 3Ins

Range of expansion: 4Ins

Complexion: medium.

Eyes: brown.

Hair: dark brown.

Date: 22 October 1917.

Headstone of Michael Donavan.

DORGAN, John: Rank: Private. Regiment or Service: Royal Munster Fusiliers. Unit: 1st Battalion. Date of death: 9 September 1916. Service No: 4767. Born in Mallow, County Cork. Enlisted in Mallow while living in Mallow. Killed in action.

Supplementary information: Brother of Miss Helena Dorgan, of Ballygalane, Lismore, Co. Waterford. He has no known grave but is listed on Pier and Face 16 C of the Thiepval Memorial in France.

DOUCH, Albert Edward: Rank: Private. Regiment or Service: Royal Dublin Fusiliers. Unit: 7th Battalion. Date of death: 27 September 1915. Age at death: 40. Service No: 12459. Born in Waterford. Enlisted in Liverpool. Killed in action in Gallipoli.

Supplementary information: Son of Martin Douch. Husband of Catherine Douch, of 3 Court, 4 House, Clay Street., Great Howard Street, Liverpool. Has no known grave but is commemorated on Panel 190 to 196. Memorial: Helles Memorial in Turkey.

Supplementary information: Son of Michael and Bridget Donovan, of Knockaun Pike, Tallow, Co. Waterford, Ireland. Grave or Memorial Reference: B.2.6. Cemetery: Aulnoy Communal Cemetery, Nord in France.

DOODY, Patrick: Rank: Private. Regiment or Service: Royal Irish Fusiliers. Unit: 7th Battalion. Date of death: 6 September 1916. Service No: 16477. Formerly he was with the Royal Irish Regiment where his number was 360. Born in Slieverue, Co. Waterford. Enlisted in Waterford while living in Perrybank, Co. Waterford. Died of wounds. Grave or Memorial Reference: II. C. 25. Cemetery: La Neuville British Cemetery, Corbie in France.

DOWER, James: Rank: Sapper. Regiment or Service: Royal Engineers Secondary Regiment: Labour Corps Secondary. Unit: transferred to (348305) 653rd Home Service Employment Coy. Age at death: 48. Date of death: 6 July 1918. Service No: 163344. Born in Killen, County Kilkenny. Enlisted in Waterford while living in Ballinamore, Co. Kilkenny. Died at home.

Supplementary information: Husband of A. Dower, of Ballinamona, Ferrybank, Waterford. Born at Kilea. Grave or Memorial Reference: In north-west part. Cemetery: Kilbride Graveyard in County Kilkenny.

DOWER, Patrick: Rank: Private. Regiment or Service: Royal Munster Fusiliers. Unit: 2nd Battalion. Age at death: 44. Date of death: 15 July 1916. Service No: 4412. Born in Ballybricken, Co. Waterford. Enlisted in Waterford while living in Waterford. Died of wounds.

Supplementary information: Husband of Bridget Connors (formerly Dower), of 13 Brown's Lane, Waterford. Grave or Memorial Reference: D.8. Cemetery: Meulte Military Cemetery in France.

DOWER, William: Rank: Fireman. Regiment or Service: Mercantile Marine. Unit: SS *Coningbeg* (Glasgow). Torpedoed by German Submarine U-62. There were no survivors. U-62 surrendered in November 1918. Age at death: 41. Date of death: 18 December 1917.

Supplementary information: Husband of Honora Dower (*née* Malone), of 23 Newport Lane, Waterford. Born at Port Law, Co. Waterford. He has no known grave but is listed on the Tower Hill Memorial in the UK. He is also listed on the Formby-Coningbeg Memorial, Adelphi Quay in Waterford City.

DOWLING, Michael: Rank: Sergeant. Regiment or Service: South African Infantry. Unit: 2nd Regiment. Date of death: 14 October 1918 Service No: 11738.

Supplementary information: Son of Thomas and Mary Dowling, of 2 Lower Yellow Road, Waterford. Born at Dromkare, Waterville. Grave or Memorial Reference: XIX.A.4. Cemetery: Harlebeke New British Cemetery in Belgium.

DOWNEY, William Edmund: Rank: Captain. Regiment or Service: Royal Army Ordnance Corps/Army Ordnance Department. Date of death: 19 July 1917. Drowned. The only Waterford reference I can find to this man is in the below. From the *Waterford News*, July 1915.

LETTER FROM AN OFFICER.

To the Editor of the "*Waterford News*"

Dear Sir,

As a constant reader of your paper, and as a soldier just returned from the front, perhaps a few impressions might be of interest to your readers. I might add, too, that the writing of this letter has helped towards relieving the tedium of hospital life.

I must say that the first thing that struck me most on this my first campaign was the splendid arrangement with regard to transport. I was second in command of a full-strength service company, comparatively speaking quite a small body of men. We were proceeding "overseas" for active service and the arrangements for transport and comfort were perfect for transport in every detail. The second thing that appealed to me greatly and which gave me no inconsiderable pride and satisfaction was the fact that during the four days and four nights we were travelling that we did not save a single "casualty" in the company. This is remarkable when one considers that the company was made up entirely of new service men, the average length of service being seven months and a "casualty" in this case, meaning the "pulling up" of any man for a breach of discipline, etc. The thing that strikes me most forcibly about the campaign is the hopeless failure of Germany as a great military nation. I don't say this without due consideration and thought. I have turned over in my mind at considerable length many things that I'd have seen, heard and read, and it is the quiet consideration of these things that has brought me to this conclusion. To enumerate some of these points; (1) Germany has been preparing seriously for this present war for at least 20 years. (2) At the outbreak of the war and up to quite recently Germany had more men in the fighting line than the combined forces of the Allies. (3) Germany has always been able to fire at least six shells from any big gun while we fire one. (4) Germany dictated the form of warfare that was to be the order of the day both for infantry and artillery. The Allies in the beginning had to adopt and learn these methods. (4) Germany has had all along more guns of all sizes and bigger guns than the Allies possess. They can always put up at least 6 machine guns to one of ours. (6) When war broke out every single manufacturing shop or works in Germany started at once to manufacture some munitions or war wonderful people, Yes it appears they are wonderful people because they were so much better prepared at the outbreak of the war than the Allies after 20 years earnest preparation. Their Frightfulness is wonderful, and they have put wonderful ingenuity into their methods of destroying human life. But I also venture to say that when the history of this war is written, on their present showing, Germany's military part in this war will be written down as the Greatest Military Debacle since the world began. The British Empire's achievement of raising and training a voluntary army about 2 1/5 million of men in a little over six months is the finest military and greatest patriotic achievement in the history of war. I must not take up too much of your valuable space, but I like to say something about the magnificent and courageous work done by our Girls in Khaki who drive some of our Red Cross Ambulance wagons. These ambulance wagons are manned by two of these young khaki clad girls (some of them, I am sure, are not more that 20 years of age), and when necessary they go right up to the trenches and bring wounded to those hospitals. I have seen one of these wagons on a shell swept road hit, and the girls get down as calmly as possible, repair the damage, and move on. It was one of the finest things I've seen. I am not ashamed to say that I have wept tears of shame to see these plucky and indomitable young girls doing what, we men, have always considered men's work, and to know so many of my young able bodied male acquaintances are shirking at home.

The burses and doctors in hospitals are deserving of praise that is impossible to express in words. They are constantly at work on the most horrible side of this ghastly war and must be always cool and collected and see or feel none of the excitement or variety that one sees in the firing line. Our hospitals at the front are perfect in every arrangement, and one cannot help thinking everywhere one turns what an enormously wealthy nation we are.

There is a humorous side to almost everything, and such a war as the present one, horrible as it is, has its humorous side issues. So Perhaps before "I pull down the blind" as Little Litch (I beg his pardon, Little Titch) would say a humorous incident will not be out of place.

One night, not so many weeks ago, a fatigue party was making its way through a narrow cutting to prepare some trenches at the further end. The cutting was the only way through. It was therefore necessary to send forward parties under cover of night,. Machine guns and snipers were very active on this particular occasion and it was a matter of necessity for every man to "bob down" and seek cover when the enemy's starlight rockets burst overhead one of our men was rather slow in getting down, and some enthusiastic pal behind shouted at the hardy cove "Hi, you blankety blank. Get darn, do ye want to get us orl bust"

The hardy cove immediately rises in his wrath and shouts in bloodcurdling and broad "Brummeger" dialect. "Who calls me blankety blank? Naw man calls me blankety blank. "There and then a very violent "scrap" took place between the two boyohs and continued amidst the bursting shells, sometime after the main party had advanced and numerous starlights had gone aloft.

Apart from its humorous side this also illustrates the extraordinary incongruities of war. Imagine two comrades punching each other for all they are worth in this manner and death shrieking all around them.

Since I returned from the front, invalided, I had an unexpected visit from one of the most popular novelists of the day. He happened to mention that he had a son in the trenches who, a few weeks ago, wrote home to say that his life had been saved by his respirator. It so happened that it was I who had on this particular occasion supplied the respirators, and almost immediately after our men had been furnished with them the Huns rolled down gas on them.

Apologising for having trespassed on your valuable space for so long.

I am Yours faithfully

W.E.D.

He has no known grave but is listed on the Doiran Memorial in Greece.

DOWNEY, James: Rank: Private. Regiment or Service: Royal Irish Regiment. Unit: 7th Battalion (South Irish Horse). Age at death: 32. Date of death: 21 March 1918. Service No: 7357. Born in Grange, Co. Waterford. Enlisted in Clonmel, Co. Tipperary while living in Piltown, Co. Waterford. Killed in action.

Supplementary information: Son of Mrs Seaward, of Piltown, Kinsalebeg, Youghal, Co. Cork. He has no known grave but is listed on Panels 30 and 31 on the Pozières Memorial in France.

DOWNEY, James: Rank: Gunner. See **JAMES, John:**

DOYLE, Daniel: Rank: Stoker. Regiment or Service: Royal Naval Reserve. Unit: HMS *Indefatigable*. During the Battle of Jutland the German Battlecruiser Van Der Tann fired eleven-inch shells at the *Indefatigable*. The first two entered 'X' magazine area and blew out the bottom of the ship and she began sinking by the stern. More 11 inch shells from the *Van Der Tann* destroyed 'A' turret and also blew up the forward magazine and she then sank. There were only two survivors of her crew of 1017 men. The *Van Der Tann* was scuttled in Scapa flow in June 1919. 3 Waterford men died on the ship that day. Age at death: 47. Date of death: 31 May 1916. Service No: 690V.

Supplementary information: Son of Daniel and Mary Doyle, of Waterford. Hhusband of Mary Doyle, of 11 Newport Street, Grangetown, Cardiff. Grave or Memorial Reference: 19 on the Plymouth Naval Memorial, UK.

DOYLE, John: Rank: Rifleman. Regiment or Service: Royal Irish Regiment. Unit: 1st Battalion. Date of death: 16 August 1917. Service No: 10322. Born in Waterford. Enlisted in Waterford. Killed in action. He has no known grave but is listed on Panel 138 to 140 and 162 and 162A and 163A on the Tyne Cot Memorial in Belgium.

DOYLE, M.: Rank: Trimmer. Regiment or Service: Royal Naval Reserve. Unit: HMS *Eaglet III* Age at death: 23. Date of death: 11 March 1920. Service No: 81855.

Supplementary information: Son of Thomas Doyle, of 8 Gaffney's Lane, Waterford. Grave or Memorial Reference: R. Ba. 35. Cemetery: Ballynaneashagh (St Otteran's) Catholic Cemetery in Co. Waterford.

DOYLE, Patrick: Rank: Able Seaman. Regiment or Service: Mercantile Marine. Unit: SS *Formby* (Glasgow). The ship was lost with all hands and never located during a fierce storm. Age at death: 55. Date of death: 16 December 1917.

Supplementary information: Son of the late James and Mary Doyle, Husband of Catherine Doyle (*née* Whitby) of 37 Doyce Street, Waterford City, Waterford. Born at Kilmore, Co. Wexford. Memorial: Tower Hill Memorial UK. He is also listed on the Formby-Coningbeg Memorial, Adelphi Quay in Waterford City.

DOYLE, Patrick: Rank: Pantryman. Regiment or Service: Mercantile Marine. Unit: SS *Umgeni* (London). The ship was lost to German Submarine U-22 during very bad weather in Robin Hood Bay, Yorkshire. It was also supposed to have been lost at sea during bad weather while part of a convoy. Age at death: 39. Date of death: 9 December 1917.

Supplementary information: Son of Michael and Bridget Doyle. Husband of Kate Doyle (*née* MacDonald) of Great Island, Campile, Co. Wexford. Born at Tramore, Co. Waterford. Memorial: Tower Hill Memorial UK.

DOYLE, Patrick: Rank: Sergeant. Regiment or Service: Royal Garrison Artillery. Age at death: 49. Date of death: 17 February 1918. Service No: 4025. This man is not listed in the Commonwealth War Graves Commission or Ireland's Memorial Records.

Supplementary information: Son of Mrs Mary Doyle, of Ballybricken, Waterford. Grave or Memorial Reference: 2U. 387. Cemetery: Sunderland (Southwick) Cemetery, UK.

DOYLE, Thomas: Rank: Unknown. Regiment or Service: Irish Volunteers. Date of Death: September 1914. Died of typhoid fever. The only information found is contained in an article from the *Munster Express*, September 1914.

CARRICK VOLUNTEERS FUNERAL.
Mr Thomas Doyle, Well Road, Carrick-on-Suir, a very popular and active member of the Carrich-on-Suir Battalion of the Irish Volunteers, succumbed on Sunday last to an attack of typhoid fever. He was given a military funeral by his colleagues, who assembled in full strength and walked four deep behind the hearse, accompanied by the local brass band playing the Dead March. At the graveside a firing party from the Volunteers fired a volley when the grave had been closed in. This is the third member of the local volunteer corps who has died from typhoid during the past few weeks.

DRAKE, Denis: Rank: Sergeant. Regiment or Service: Royal Garrison Artillery. Unit: 90th Heavy Battery. Date of death: 10 June 1917. Age at death: 33. Service No: 17431. Born in Ballynoe, Waterford. Enlisted in Waterford. while living in Ballyone [*sic*]. Killed in action.

Supplementary information: Son of Edward and Catherine Drake, of Ballynoe, Co. Cork. Grave or Memorial Reference: II.J.20. Cemetery: St Quentin Cabaret Military Cemetery in Belgium.

DRISCOLL, Augustine: Rank: Private. Regiment or Service: Royal Irish Regiment. Unit: 2nd Battalion. Age at death: 20. Date of death: 2 May 1915. Service No: 10345. Born in Dungarvan, Co. Waterford. Enlisted in Clonmel, Co. Tipperary while living in Dungarvan. Killed in action.

Supplementary information: Son of Alice Driscoll, of 2 Davis Street, Dungarvan, Co. Waterford. He has no known grave but is listed on Panel 33 on the Ypres (Menin Gate) Memorial in Belgium.

DRISCOLL, Denis: Rank: Private. Regiment or Service: Royal Irish Fusiliers. Unit: 3rd Reserve Garrison Battalion. Age at death: 22. Date of death: 10 October 1918. Service No: G/22680 and 22680. Born in Waterford. Enlisted in Dundee while living in Waterford. Died at Home.

Supplementary information: Son of Mrs J. Driscoll, of 5 Michael Street, Waterford. Memorial: Hollybrook Memorial, in Southampton, UK.

DROHAN, Michael: Rank: Private. Regiment or Service: Royal Irish Regiment. Unit: 1st Battalion. Date of death: 15 March 1915. Service No: 4082. Born in Carrickbeg, Co. Waterford. Enlisted in Clonmel while living in Carrick-on-Suir, Co. Tipperary. Killed in action. Age at death: 19.

Supplementary information: Son of David and Bridget Drohan. He has no known grave but is listed on Panel 33 on the Ypres (Menin Gate) Memorial in Belgium.

DUCEY, Martin: Rank: Private. Regiment or Service: Irish Guards. Unit: 1st Battalion. Date of death: 18 May 1915. Service No: 5834. Born in Modeligo, Co. Waterford. Enlisted in Maesteg, Glam, while living in Cappagh, Co. Waterford. Killed in action. He has no known grave but is listed on Panel 4 on the Le Touret Memorial in France.

DUGGAN, Maurice: Rank: Private. Regiment or Service: Royal Irish Regiment. Unit: 6th Battalion. Age at death: 19. Date of death: 7 June 1917. Service No: 11252. Born in Kill Co. Waterford. Enlisted in Waterford while living in Bonmahon, Co. Waterford. Died of wounds.

Supplementary information: Son of Thomas and Johanna Duggan, of Kildwan, Bonmahon, Kilmacthomas, Co. Waterford. Grave or Memorial Reference: III.C.237. Cemetery: Bailleul Communal Cemetery Extension (Nord) in France.

DUGGAN, William: Rank: Private. Regiment or Service: Royal Irish Fusiliers. Unit: 5th Battalion. Date of death: 15 September 1916. Service No: 16497. Formerly he was with the Royal Irish Regiment where his number was 1704. Born in Waterford. Enlisted in Waterford. Killed in action. Grave or Memorial Reference: II.F.9. Cemetery: Struma Military Cemetery in Greece.

DUMPHEY, Michael: Rank: Private. Regiment or Service: Machine Gun Corps. Unit: Infantry. Date of death: 19 August 1918. Service No: 128656. Formerly he was with the Royal Army Service Corps where his number was T4/062287. Born in St Annes, Waterford. Enlisted in New Ross while living in Waterford. Died in India. He has no known grave but is listed on Face II of the Kirkee 1914-18 Memorial in India.

DUNN James John: Rank: Corporal. Regiment or Service: Australian Infantry, A.I.F. Unit: 18th Battalion. Date of death: 5 May 1917. Service No: 5578. Hospitalised in France only twice with a sprained ankle (notes say, 'soldier not to blame'), fatigue and when he was wounded in action. Enlisted in Liverpool, New South Wales on 24 November 1915. Will states 'In the event of my death I leave all I possess to my father, Mr Hugh Dunne, c/o 15 Rockhouse Street, Rocky Lane, Anfield, Liverpool, England.' Died of wounds received in action at No 3 Casualty Clearing Station, France. Killed in action. Buried by Revd K.J. Cullen.

In or near what Parish or Town were you born? Waterford, Ireland.

What is your age? 28 Years.

What is your trade or calling? Chef.

Are you, or have you been an Apprentice? No. If so where, to whom, and for what period? No.

Are you married? No.

Who is your next of kin? (Father) Hugh Dunne, C/O Little Sisters of the Poor, Parkfield Avenue, Birkenhead, England Have you ever been convicted by the Civil Power? No.

Age: 28 years, 6 months.

Height: 5 feet, 5 inches.

Weight: 9st 11lbs.

Chest measurement: 37 inches.

Complexion: Fair.

Eyes: Hazel.

Hair: Auburn.

Religious denomination: RC.

On 12 February 1917 he writes home:

Dear Dad.

Your welcome letter to hand. Pleased to hear you are well. I also received a letter from Emily. I am glad that you enjoyed your Xmas dinner and trust that you will have many more. My Xmas dinner consisted of a biscuit and a bit of tinned beef, but it was better than nothing and as I was very hungry I enjoyed it very much and could have eaten more. I have wrote to Emily and have told her to let you have the two shillings a week as promised and I will see that you receive it regularly. I am sorry that you wrote to headquarters as things cannot be altered now but in case of anything happening to me you will get all that belongs to me and as soon as the war is over I hope to be in the position to do something better for you. At present you are better off where you are as I know that you are comfortable and it takes a lot of worry off my mind and everything will come right later on. Our Battalion has been up to the firing line and have had a pretty rough time of it with more to come. We hoe to get out of the line very shortly and will have a good rest and will write you a longer letter later on. The weather he is very cold with a hard frost and one can hardly hold the pencil to write with. I received a parcel from Emily with some cake and pudding and was very glad to get it. I almost forgot to tell you that I am a private now but have been recommended for promotion and expect to get it very shortly, all of our (N. C. Os) reverted to the ranks on joining the Battalion to make room for senior men, but expect it again our rank very soon [sic]. Well Dad I must conclude now as I have no more to say but will write again shortly and will have something to tell you next time. Trusting that this will find you well.

I remain your loving son.

Jim.

Au Revoir

Write soon.

A pension of 20 shillings per fortnight was awarded to his sister Emily, 15 Rockhouse Street, Liverpool commencing 22 November 1917 and was reversed 20 November 1919 and a pension of 40 shillings per fortnight was awarded to his father Hugh Dunn, C/o The Little Sisters of the Poor, Parkfield Avenue, Birkinhead, Cheshire from the 12 November 1917 and was reversed on 21 November 1918. Grave or Memorial Reference: III.B.10. Cemetery: Grevilliers British Cemetery in Pas-De-Calais, France.

DUNNE, Edward Patrick: Rank: Private. Regiment or Service: Royal Irish Fusiliers. Unit: 1st Battalion. Date of death: 6 July 1915. Age at death: 34. Service No: 8950. Born in Tinahely, Co. Wicklow. Enlisted in Waterford while living in Ballytruckle, Co. Waterford. Killed in action.

Supplementary information: Son of Mr and Mrs Patrick Dunne, of Waterford. Grave or Memorial Reference: III.D.10. Cemetery: Artillery Wood Cemetery in Belgium.

DUNNE, James: Rank: Private. Regiment or Service: Royal Irish Regiment. Unit: 2nd Battalion. Age at death: 19. Date of death: 15 October 1914. Service No: 10901. Born in Dungarvan, Co. Waterford. Enlisted in Waterford while living in Dungarvan. Killed in action.

Supplementary information: Son of John and Mary Dunne, of Mitchell Street, Dungarvan, Co. Waterford. From the *Waterford News*, 1914:

FROM THE FRONT.

News arrived some time ago from the War Office to the parents of James Dunne who live at Upper Mitchell Street, that their son, who belonged to the Royal Irish Regiment, had been killed at the front. The mother of William Riordan, Shandon Street, has received a post card from a camp in Germany that her son is a prisoner of war there and in good health. He also belongs to the Royal Irish Regiment.

Grave or Memorial Reference: 11 and 12 on the Le Touret Memorial in France.

DUNNE, James: Rank: Private. Regiment or Service: Royal Munster Fusiliers. Unit: 2nd Battalion. Date of death: 25 April 1915. Service No: 8379. Born in St Johns, Waterford. Enlisted in Waterford while living in Waterford. Killed in action in Gallipoli.

Supplementary information: Son of the late Thomas and Ellen Dunne. Grave or Memorial Reference: He has no known grave but is listed on Panel 185 to 190 on the Helles Memorial in Turkey.

DUNNE, Martin: Rank: Gunner. Regiment or Service: Royal Garrison Artillery. Unit: 23rd Heavy Battery. Age at death: 34. Date of death: 24 August 1916. Service No: 6940. Born in Dungarvan, Co. Waterford. Enlisted in Seaforth while living in Piltown, County Kilkenny. Killed in Acton.

Supplementary information: Son of Thomas and Bridget Dunne, of Grange, Mooncoin, Waterford. Native of Dungarvan, Co. Waterford. Grave or Memorial Reference: II.A.12. Cemetery: Contalmaison Chateau Cemetery in France.

DUNNE, William: Rank: Private. Regiment or Service: Leinster Regiment. Unit: 2nd Battalion. Date of death: 2 May 1915. Service No: 9973. Born in Lismore, Co. Waterford. Enlisted in Drogheda, County Louth. Died of wounds. Grave or Memorial Reference: I.A.2. Cemetery: Erquinghem-Lys Churchyard Extension in France.

DWYER, David James: Rank: Carpenter's Mate, Second Class (A), Regiment or Service: United States Navy. Enlisted in Buffalo, New York 15 December 1917. Died in the Naval hospital, League Island, Pa., 4 April 1918 of Broncho Pneumonia. Next of kin: Father, Thomas Dwyer, Belly Facey, Glenmore, Waterford, Ireland. The information above is taken from Soldiers of the Great War (the USA's version of Soldiers Died in the Great War). Burial details on this man are not available to me.

DWYER John: Rank: Private. Regiment or Service: Australian Infantry, A.I.F. Unit: 26th Battalion. Date of death: 29 July 1916. Service No: 300. Enlisted in Townsville, Queensland on12 April 1915. Hospitalised in Greece and Egypt with a facial injury, pneumonia, and rheumatism. Charges brought against him included drunkenness, drunk on active service and absence.

In or near what Parish or Town were you born? City of Waterford, Ireland.

Are you a natural born British subject or a Naturalised British subject? Yes.

What is your age? 43 and one month.

Who is your next of kin? (brother)

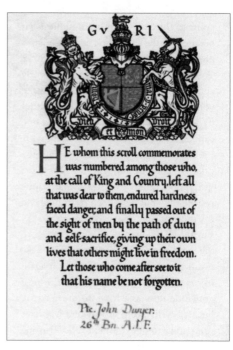

John Dwyer's memorial scroll that would normally be issued with the death plaque.

Maurice Dwyer, j'Quaqui, Argentine, South America. Later changed to Iquique, Chili, South America. (After John's death his next of kin could not be traced.)

What is your trade or calling? Labourer.

Are you, or have you been an Apprentice? No. If so where, to whom, and for what period?

Are you married? No.

Height: 5 feet, 5 ½ inches.

Weight: 9st 10 lbs.

Chest measurement: 35-36 ½ inches.

Complexion: dark.

Eyes: grey. Hair: brown.

Religious denomination: RC.

After a Court of Enquiry dated 29 June 1917 his papers record, 'Previously reported missing now reported killed in action. Statement from Private P.W.A. Murphy regarding the death of Private Dwyer':

MISSING 29TH JULY 1916.

'I knew Dwyer well–He was my mate and we were in the same platoon. We were attacking the German trenches. After capturing the first trench we went on to the second. I was wounded close to the second trench and started to come back. I saw Dwyer lying wounded in a shell hole, hit either in the hip or knee. I never saw him again after that. The ground was being shelled by the guns on both sides. We lost the ground and it was taken a week later.

Letter from the Official Secretary. Commonwealth of Australia, Australia House, Strand, W.C.2. :

300 Pte J Dwyer, 26th Battalion, A.I.F. 29 July-1916.

I am directed to inform you that as the result of investigation which has been made, it is believed that the burial place of the above-mentioned soldier has been identified. In the course of the work of removing the bodies of soldiers who were buried in isolated or scattered graves to cemeteries where the graves could be cared for and maintained, the body of an unknown soldier was found in the vicinity of Pozières, and the remains were carefully and reverently reburied in Serre Road Cemetery No 2, Beaumont Hamel, Plot 1, Row A. Grave 2. When the removal was carried out a knife marked "J.D." and Australian titles were found. As the result of an examination of the casualty list of soldier who bore the initials "J.D." it has been concluded that the only one who could possibly refer is Private J Dwyer, as the Battalion with which he was serving was at that time operating in the area in which the body was found. The Commission will therefore in due course erect a permanent memorial over the grave bearing his name and full Regimental particulars.

I am to ask you to be good enough to forward this information to his next-of-kin and ascertain at the same time whether they desire the words 'Believed to be' omitted from the headstone.
(Sgd) P. Lowe.
for Principal Assistant Secretary.
Imperial War Graves Commission.
82 Baker Street.
London, W. C. 1.

As his next of kin could not be traced, his medals, death plaque and scroll could not be issued. Grave or Memorial Reference: XXI.A.2. Cemetery: Serre Road Cemetery No. 2 in France.

DWYER, Martin: Rank: Stoker 1st Class. Regiment or Service: Royal Navy. Unit: H. M. S/M "E47". Age at death: 22. Date of death: 20 August 1917. Service No: K/22432. Was lost in the North Sea.

Supplementary information: Son of Martin and Johanna Nolan (formerly Dwyer), of Ballymacaw, Dunmore East, Co. Waterford. Grave or Memorial Reference: 23. Memorial: Chatham Naval Memorial in England.

DWYER, Michael: Rank: Private. Regiment or Service: Royal Irish Regiment. Unit: 1st Battalion. Age at death: 35. Date of death: 17 October 1916. Died in Salonika. Serial Number: 7286. Enlisted in Clonmel while living in Kilmacoma, Co. Waterford.

Supplementary information: Son of John and Bridget Dwyer of Kilmacomma, Clonmel. Grave or Memorial Reference: 595. Cemetery: Salonika (Lambet Road) Military Cemetery in Greece.

E

EARL/EARLE, Daniel Robert: Rank: Lance Corporal. Regiment or Service: Irish Guards. Unit: 1st Battalion. Age at death: 21. Date of death: 15 September 1916. Service No: 4228. Born in Waterford. Enlisted in Dundalk.

Supplementary information: Son of Richard and Elizabeth Earl, of Brohatna, Mount Pleasant, Dundalk, Co. Louth. He has no known grave but is listed on Pier and Face 7D on the Thiepval Memorial in France.

EGAN, Claude Edwin: Rank: Private Regiment or Service: Australian Infantry, A.I.F. Unit: 19th Battalion. Age at death: 22. Date of death: 4 May 1917. Enlisted 28 February 1916 in the Royal AS Showgrounds, New South Wales. Service No: 5333.

Supplementary information: Son of John and Rosanna Egan, of 56, Mount Joy Square, Dublin, Ireland. Born at Dungarvan, Co. Waterford, Ireland. Reported wounded and missing in action on 3 May 1917. After a Court of Enquiry held on 11 December 1917 this was changed to Killed in action. His personal effects consisted of ten photographs and nothing else. These were sent to 56 Mountjoy Square, Dublin after his death.

In or near what Parish or Town were you born? Dungarvan, Waterford, Ireland.

Are you a natural born British subject or a Naturalised British subject? Natural Born.

What is your age? 21 years 1 month.

What is your trade or calling? Sacristan (in a Church in Dublin).

Are you, or have you been an Apprentice? No. If so where, to whom, and for what period?

Are you married? No.

Who is your next of kin? (father) John Egan, 56 Mountjoy Square, Dublin, Ireland.

Height: 5 feet, 11 ¾ inches.
Chest measurement: 31-35 inches.
Complexion, fair.
Eyes: hazel.
Hair: dark brown.
Religious denomination: R.C.

From *The Cruel Clouds of War*:

The seventy former pupils and teachers of Belvedere College who lost their lives in military conflicts of the 20th century:

Claude Edwin Egan, 19th Battalion, 2nd Division, Australian Force. Died 4 May 1917. Claude Egan born on 23 January 1895 in Dungarvan, Co Waterford. The family later moved to Galway (where Cluade was educated by the Jesuits at St Ignatius' College) and then to Dublin. He was one of several brothers who attended Belvedere. They were the sons of John and Rosanna Egan of St James' Villas, Upper Drumcondra, Dublin and later of 56 Mountjoy Square - a few hundred yards from the school. He was in Australia when the war broke out, and it was there that he joined the army. He was posted in France near Amiens. On Friday 4 May, 1917, Claude Egan received an injury to his leg and an arm. He was then attended to and sent off in a motor ambulance with two other wounded soldiers. While travelling up a hill on the way to the hospital, the ambulance was struck by a shell. Nothing more was seen of any of its occupants. Claude Egan was 22 at the time of his death. He is commemorated on the Villiers-Bretonneux Memorial at the Somme in France. His name is inscribed there, along with 10, 700 Australian soldiers who died in these parts during the First World War.

He has no known grave but is listed on the Villers-Bretonneux Memorial in France.

ELLIOTT, Christopher: Rank: Fireman. Regiment or Service: Mercantile Marine. Unit: SS *Hollington* (London). Sunk by a German submarine off the Faroe Islands. Age at death: 36. Date of death: 2 June 1917.

Supplementary information: Son of the late Thomas and Mary Elliott. Born in Waterford. He has no known grave but is listed on the Tower Hill Memorial in the UK.

ELLIOTT, Gerald Ewen/Even: Rank: Captain. Regiment or Service: Gloucestershire Regiment. Unit: 'B' Company, 1st/6th Battalion also listed as the 6th Battalion. Age at death: 26. Date of death: 21 July 1916. Killed in action.

Supplementary information: Son of J.C. and M.E.M. Elliott. From the *Munster Express*:

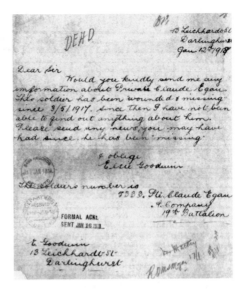

Claude Edwin Egan.

WATERFORD OFFICER
KILLED IN ACTION.
Captain Gerald Ewen Elliott, Gloucester Regiment, was killed in action July 21st leading his company. He was aged 26, seventh son of the late J. C. Elliott, J. P., Rathcurby, County Kilkenny, and Mrs Elliott, Hollywood Gardens, Waterford. The following facts relating to the death of Captain Gerlad Ewen Elliott have been received by the Elliott family in a letter from the doctor of his battalion; "He died like a gallant gentleman at the head of his company. He wore his best clothes and started his charge with bright buttons and clean gloves. From the accounts of his brother officers and men he was right ahead when he was first shot through the thigh and stomach. His servant tried to get him back, but he would sit up to cheer his men on, and he received another shot through the head. His battalion has lost a very fine officer and I have lost a very dear friend. I wish I could have been present at his funeral, but I was far too busy looking after his wounded men." Previous to the war he served eight years in the territorials and volunteered for foreign service at the outbreak of the war.

He has no known grave but is listed on Pier and Face 5A and 5B of the Thiepval Memorial in France.

ENGLISH, James: Rank: Private. Regiment or Service: Royal Munster Fusiliers. Unit: 9th Battalion. Age at death: 38. Date of death: 27 March 1916. Service No: 4414. Born in Waterford. Enlisted in Waterford while living in Waterford. Killed in action.

Supplementary information: Son of James and Catherine English (*née* O'Keefe). Husband of Catherine English (*née* Whelan), of 5 Thomas Avenue, Waterford. Grave or Memorial Reference: 127 on the Loos Memorial in France.

EUSTACE, Edward: Rank: Private. Regiment or Service: Royal Irish Regiment. Unit: 2nd Battalion. Age at death: 21. Date of death: 4 July 1916. Service No: 7514. Born in Waterford. Enlisted in Waterford. Killed in action.

Supplementary information: Son of Mr M. and Mrs E. Eustace. He has no known grave but is listed on Pier and Face 3A on the Thiepval Memorial in France.

Gerald Ewen/Even Elliott.

EUSTACE, John: Rank: Private. Regiment or Service: Royal Irish Regiment. Unit: 2nd Battalion. Date of death: 5 September 1916. Age at death: 23. Service No: 7536 (Soldiers died in the Great War), 7556 (Ireland's Memorial Records and The Commonwealth War Graves Commission). Born in Waterford. Enlisted in Waterford. Killed in action.

Supplementary information: Son of Mr M. and Mrs E. Eustace. He has no known grave but is listed on Pier and Face 3A on the Thiepval Memorial in France.

EUSTACE, Martin: Rank: Cattleman. Regiment or Service: Mercantile Marine. Unit: SS *Formby* (Glasgow). Age at death: 57. Date of death: 16 December 1917. The ship was lost with all hands and never located during a fierce storm.

Supplementary information: Son of the late Patrick and Catherine Eustace. Husband of the late Ellen Eustace. Born in Waterford. He has no known grave but is listed on the Tower Hill Memorial in the UK. He is also listed on the Formby-Coningbeg Memorial, Adelphi Quay in Waterford City.

EVANS, James Francis: Rank: Wireless Operator. Regiment or Service: Mercantile Marine. Unit: SS *Belgian Prince* (Newcastle). Sunk by German submarine U-55, 39 lives were lost. Age at death: 23. Date of death: 31 July 1917.

Supplementary information: Son of Patrick and Bridget Evans, of St Mary's Street, Dungarvan, Co. Waterford. He has no known grave but is listed on the Tower Hill Memorial in the UK.

F

FAHEY, Denis: Rank: Corporal and Acting Corporal. Regiment or Service: Royal Irish Regiment. Unit: 'B' Coy. 6th Battalion. Age at death: 21. Date of death: 12 August 1917. Service No: 5394. Born in Waterford. Enlisted in Tipperary while living in Waterford. Killed in action.

Supplementary information: Son of Ellen Fahey, of 1 Castle Terrace, Waterford. He has no known grave but is listed on Panel 33 on the Ypres (Menin Gate) Memorial in Belgium.

FAHY, William John: Rank: Sergeant. Regiment or Service: Royal Irish Regiment. Unit: 2nd Battalion. Date of death: 3 September 1916. Service No: 10157. He won the Military Medal and is listed in the *London Gazette*. Formerly he was with the Royal Scots where his number was 1854. Born in Waterford. Enlisted in Linlithgow while living in Londonderry. Killed in action. He has no known grave but is listed on Pier and Face 3A on the Thiepval Memorial in France.

FANNING, Frederick: Rank: 3rd Engineer. Regiment or Service: Mercantile Marine. Unit: SS *Rhineland* (Liverpool). Mined and sank SE of Southwold. Age at death: 27. Date of death: 11 November 1915.

Supplementary information: Son of John William and Helen Fanning, of South Mall, Lismore, Co. Waterford. Born at Lismore. There is an article in the *Waterford Star*, November 1915 regarding his death etc. He has no known grave but is listed on the Tower Hill Memorial in the UK.

FANNING, Michael: Rank: Private. Regiment or Service: Royal Irish Regiment. Unit: 6th Battalion. Date of death: 3 September 1916. Service No: 5393. Born in Ballybricken, Co. Waterford. Enlisted in Clonmel, County Tipperary while living in Waterford. Killed in action. He has no known grave but is listed on Pier and Face 3A on the Thiepval Memorial in France.

FARRELL, Edward: Rank: Driver. Regiment or Service: Army Service Corps and Royal Army Service Corps. Unit: 924th H.T. Coy. 54th Div. Train. Age at death: 26. Date of death: 11 August 1917. Service No: T4/083315. Enlisted in Waterford while living in Tramore, Co. Waterford. Died in Egypt.

Supplementary information: Son of James and Louisa Farrell. Born at Tramore, Co. Waterford. Grave or Memorial Reference: M. 143. Cemetery, Cairo War Memorial Cemetery in Egypt.

FARRELL, Michael: Rank: Private. Regiment or Service: Royal Irish Regiment. Unit: 2nd Battalion. Date of death: 14 July 1916. Service No: 4189. Born in Waterford. Enlisted in Cork. Died of wounds.

Supplementary information: Grave or Memorial Reference: IV.G.2. Cemetery: Abbeville Communal Cemetery in France.

FAUSSET/FAUSSETT, Vivian H.: Rank: Private. Regiment or Service: Royal Dublin Fusiliers. Unit: 'D' Company, 7th Battalion. Date of death: 19 August 1915. Age at death: 32. Service No: 14181. Born in Waterford. Enlisted in Dublin while living in Waterford. Died of wounds in Gallipoli.

Supplementary information: Youngest son of the Revd Charles Fausset, B.A., and Ellen F.O. Lane. B.A. (Trinity College, Dublin). Grave or Memorial Reference: II.G.110. Cemetery: East Mudros Military Cemetery in Greece.

FENTON, James: Rank: Gunner. Regiment or Service: Royal Garrison Artillery. Unit: 112th Heavy Battery. Date of death: 4 November 1917. Service No: 41953. Born in Lismore, Co. Waterford. Enlisted in Bargoed while living in Kilmore, Tallow, Co. Waterford. Killed in action. Grave or Memorial Reference: III. F17. Cemetery: Canada Cemetery, Tilloy-Les-Cambrai in France.

FERNIE, Noel/Robert Noel:. Rank: Private/ Lance Corporal. Regiment or Service: Royal Irish Regiment. Unit: 'C' Coy. 2nd Battalion. Age at death: 17. Date of death: 19 October 1914. Service No: 10518. Born in Kilmacow, Co. Kilkenny. Enlisted in Waterford while living in Tramore. Killed in action. Awards: D.C.M.

Supplementary information: Son of John Fernie, of Rosemount, Tramore, Co. Waterford. From 'Our Heroes':

Lance-Corporal Noel Fernie, 2nd Battalion, Royal Irish Regiment, who has been mentioned in Sir John French's Despatches and promoted Lance-Corporal, is a son of Mr Fernie, Rosemount, Tramore, Waterford and of Mrs Fernie, Waterford. Noel Fernie is only 18 years of age.

From *Waterford News*, 1914:

WATERFORD MAN MENTIONED IN DESPATCHES.

On Monday last there was published a long list of names of officers, non-commissioned officers, and men brought forward for special mention for services in the field from the beginning of the campaign to October 8th. The list included the name of Private N. Fernie, of the 2nd Royal Irish Regiment, son of Mrs Fernie, fruiterer, High Street.

From *Waterford News*, 1914:

MEDALS FOR WATERFORD SOLDIERS.

Amongst the names of the soldiers to whom the medal for distinguished conduct in the field has been awarded we notice the name of Private N Fernie (now Lance Corporal), of the 2nd Battalion Royal Irish Regiment. Mr Fernie is son of Mrs Fernie, High Street, and was recently mentioned in despatches. He receives the medal for having at Vailly repeatedly shown great coolness and gallantry when conveying messages under heavy fire. We understand that Private J. Doherty, Royal Irish Regiment, another of the soldiers to whom the medal has been awarded, is also a Waterford man.

Grave or Memorial Reference: 11 and 12 on the Le Touret Memorial in France. He is also listed on the Waterford and District Roll of Honour. Located in Christ Church Cathedral (Church of Ireland), Henrietta Street, Waterford.

FIELD, John: Rank: Private. Regiment or Service: Royal Irish Fusiliers. Unit: 6th Battalion. Age at death: 34. Date of death: 16 August 1915. Service No: 16793. Born in Waterford. Enlisted in Waterford. Previously he was with the Connaught Rangers where his number was 1210. Killed in action in Gallipoli.

Supplementary information: Son of Michael and Catherine Field. Husband of Margaret Field, of 7 Tanyard Arch, Waterford. He has no known grave but is listed on Panel 178 to 180 on the Helles Memorial in Turkey.

FINN, Michael: Rank: Sergeant. Regiment or Service: Royal Garrison Artillery. Unit: 83rd Siege Battery. Age at death: 27. Date of death: 19 February 1918. Service No: 40718. Born in Rathgormack, Co. Waterford. Enlisted in Merthyr Tydfil while living in Waterford. Killed in action.

Supplementary information: Son of Thomas and Mary Finn, of Ballynock, Carrick-on-Suir, Co. Tipperary. Grave or Memorial Reference: XIII.E.20. Cemetery. Poelcapelle British Cemetery in Belgium.

FISHBOURNE, Derrick Haughton Gardiner: Rank: Second Lieutenant.

Regiment or Service: Royal Garrison Artillery. Unit: 99th Siege Bty. Age at death: 20. Date of Death: 6 May 1917. Killed in Action. Supplementary information: Son of John Gardiner Fishbourne and Sarah Elizabeth Fishbourne, of Burrin House, Carlow.

Carlow Sentinel, May 1917:

Roll of Honour.

2nd Lieutenant D. H. G. Fishbourne.

We regret to learn that another gallant young officer closely connected with Carlow has been added to the long Roll of Honour. Second Lieutenant Derrick Haughton Gardiner Fishbourne, Royal Garrison Artillery, was killed in action on the 6th inst, in his 21st year. He was the only son of Mr and Mrs J. G. Fishbourne, bank of Ireland, Tralee, and nephew of Mr John William Haughton, J. P, Burrin House, Carlow. Lieutenant Fishbourne was educated at Russell School, Lancashire, from which he entered Trinity College, Dublin, with the view of qualifying for the Medical Profession. On the outbreak of the war he joined the T. C. D. Officer's Training Corps, obtained his commission, and went with his Regiment to France over a year ago, and fell gallantly fighting for King and Country, but to the great grief of a large circle of relatives and friends, with whom we join in heartfelt sympathy with his bereaved parents.

De Ruvigny's Roll of Honour:

...only son of John Gardiner Fishbourne, of Tralee, Agent, Bank of Ireland, by his wife, Sarah Elizabeth, daughter of Frederick Haughton. Born Bellville, Newtown, Waterford. Educated at Castle Park, Dalkey, County Dublin, and Rossall, co. Lancaster. Was a resident student at Trinity College, Dublin. Obtained a commission, 29-December-1915. Served with the Expeditionary Force in France and Flanders, and was killed in action near Monchy 04-May-1917, while acting as sectional commander. Buried in Faubourg

d'Amiens Cemetery, Arras. The General Commanding wrote; "He has shown a spirit of devotion to duty which is the true soldierly spirit which is going to win the war. His calmness and cheerfulness in the battery under fire showed courage of the highest order, which reacted on the men. He did credit to his country and his name, " and his Major; " I can only assure you he is most deeply and sincerely mourned by us all, officers, N. C. O.'s and men, both for his cheerful spirit and keenness in everything connected with the battery. " A brother officer also wrote; " I feel I have lost one of the best friends I have ever had; he was always so cheerful and brave, and was, in fact, the life and soul of the battery. He never lost his cheerfulness under the most adverse circumstances. He has bucked me up many times by his cheery example. All the men liked him, he never lost his temper, he was always the same; . He did not understand the meaning of the word 'fear'."

Grave or Memorial Reference: IV.G.11. Cemetery: Faubourg D'Amiens Cemetery, Arras in France.

FISHER, Hubert Patrick: Rank: Second Lieutenant. Regiment or Service: King's Shropshire Light Infantry. Unit: 9th Battalion attached to the 1/4th Battalion. Date of death: 9 July 1916. Born in Waterford. Killed in action. From the *Waterford News*. July 1916:

MEMOIR OF WATERFORD OFFICER KILLED IN ACTION.

The first intimation was received by post to Mrs Fisher, and was from the Officer Commanding the Gloucester Regiment. It seems that when Lieutenant Fisher arrived in France with his own Regiment some three weeks ago he was drafted into the Gloucesters owing to the shortage of officers, and it was whilst serving with the latter Regiment he was killed. The Commanding Officer speaks very highly of Lieutenant Fisher's capabilities as an officer, and describes how he met his death while leading a platoon into a front line trench. His body was recovered and laid to rest in a little cemetery in the vicinity. The late Lieutenant was second son of the Editor of the "Galway Express" and Mrs Marry [sic] D. Fisher, Taylor's House. Lieutenant Fisher was born just years ago at Butlerstown Castle, Waterford, and was educated at the School, Waterford, and Chesterfield College, Birr. He was a skilful telegraphist and signalling officer, and, before obtaining his commission, spent a lengthened period at the Marconi Wireless Offices, Strand, London, and had a first-class certificate for wireless. When his commission arrived he was on board a large liner bound for Brazil, and was in charge of the Marconi instruments. He had great difficulty in getting out of his engagement, but at the last moment succeeded in finding a substitute. His signalling ability was recognised by General Friend, who, at the parade in Trinity College, strongly advised him to volunteer as Signalling Officer when he was sent to the front. He was of a most loveable nature, generous to a fault, and greatly attached to animals. He was a brilliant horseman, and when only ten hours of age used to follow the famous Curraghmore Hunt. May God comfort his sorrowing mother, father, sisters, and brothers. He died like a brave and gallant soldier, and died the death he often wished for.

There is another short article about him in the *King's County Chronicle* in July 1916. Grave or Memorial Reference: I.I.64. Cemetery: Sucrerie Military Cemetery, Colinclamps in France. He is also listed on the Bishop Foy School Memorial in the Church of Ireland Cathedral, Henrietta Street, Waterford City.

FISHER, (The Revd) **Oswald Garrow:** Rank: Chaplain, 4th Class. Regiment or Service: Army Chaplains Department. Date of death: 4 November 1920. Born in Waterford. Died in Persia.

Supplementary information: He is listed several times in 'Calender, The Dublin Year 1920-1921/' Grave or Memorial Reference: VIII.A.9. Cemetery: Baghdad (North Gate) War Cemetery - Iraq.

FITZGERALD, Edward: Rank: Private. Regiment or Service: Royal Irish Regiment. Unit: 2nd Battalion. Age at death: 26. Date of death: 16 August 1917. Service No: 9481. Born in Kilmacthomas, Co. Waterford. Enlisted in Portlaw, Co. Waterford while living in Kilmacthomas. Killed in action.

Supplementary information: Son of John and Kate Fitzgerald, of Ballinanogue, Kilmacthomas. Grave or Memorial Reference: 51 to 52 on the Tyne Cot Memorial in Belgium.

FITZGERALD, James: Rank: Private. Regiment or Service: Royal Munster Fusiliers. Unit: 2nd Battalion. Age at death: 20. Date of death: 9 May 1915. Service No: 10012. Born in Stradbally, Co. Waterford. Enlisted in Waterford while living in Kilmacthomas, Co. Waterford. Killed in action.

Supplementary information: Son of John and Kate Fitzgerald, of Ballyogoarty, Kilmacthomas. Grave or Memorial Reference: 43 and 44 on the Le Touret Memorial in France.

FITZGERALD, Jeremiah: Rank: Private. Regiment or Service: Royal Irish Regiment. Unit: 2nd Battalion. Age at death: 19. Date of death: 30 December 1917. Service No: 11879. Previously he was with the Royal Field Artillery where his number was 120056. Born in St Mary's Clonmel. Enlisted in Waterford. Died at sea.

Supplementary information: Son of William and Ellen Fitzgerald, of 23 Emmet Place, Waterford. He has no known grave but is listed on the Chatby Memorial in Egypt.

FITZGERALD, John: Rank: Private. Regiment or Service: Royal Irish Regiment. Unit: 5th Battalion. Date of death: 19 August 1915. Service No: 89. Born in Trinity Without, Waterford. Enlisted in Waterford. Resided at Newport Lane. Killed in action in Gallipoli. Killed at Suvla. He has no known grave but is listed on Panel 55 on the Helles Memorial in Turkey.

FITZGERALD, M.: Rank: Private. Regiment or Service: Royal Fusiliers. Unit: 47th Battalion. Age at death: 42. Date of death: 29 May 1920. Service No: 140437.
Supplementary information: Husband of B. Fitzgerald, of 3 May Lane, Waterford. Grave or Memorial Reference: O. Ba. 109. Cemetery: Ballynaneashagh (St Otteran's) Catholic Cemetery in Co. Waterford.

FITZGERALD, Michael: Rank: Private. Regiment or Service: Irish Guards. Unit: 1st Battalion. Date of death: 20 October 1915. Service No: 7556. Born in Clashmore, Co. Waterford. Enlisted in Cork, County Cork. Died of wounds.
Supplementary information: Son of Mrs Kate Fitzgerald, of Clashmore, Youghal, Co. Waterford. Grave or Memorial Reference: IV.D.13. Cemetery: Lillers Communal Cemetery in France.

FITZGERALD, Patrick: Rank: Private. Regiment or Service: Devonshire Regiment. Unit: 1st Battalion attached to the Machine Gun Section, General Headquarters, 3rd Echelon. Age at death: 41. Date of death: 21 May 1917. Service No: 22144. Born in Waterford. Enlisted in Llandrindod Wells, Wales while living in Hanwell, Wales. Died of wounds.
Supplementary information: Son of Thomas and Mary Ellen Fitzgerald, of Tavistock, Devon. Grave or Memorial Reference: A. 13B. Cemetery: Bois Guillaume Communal Cemetery in France.

FITZGERALD, Richard: Rank: Private. Regiment or Service: Grenadier Guards. Unit: 4th Battalion. Age at death: 25. Date of death: 25 October 1915. Service No: 12337. Born in Faha, Waterford. Enlisted in Chester. Killed in action.
Supplementary information: (Served as Connell) Son of the late Thomas Fitzgerald and of Mrs Alice Cummins (formerly Connell), of Tan Yard Arch, Michael Street, Waterford. Grave or Memorial Reference: 5 to 7 on the Loos Memorial in France.

FITZGERALD, Walter: Rank: Seaman. Regiment or Service: Royal Naval Reserve. Unit: HMS *Laurentic*. Age at death: 36. Date of death: 25 January 1917. Service No: 2465C.
Supplementary information: Son of Catherine Fitzgerald, of Ballymacaw, Dunmore East, Co. Waterford, and the late John Fitzgerald. Grave or Memorial Reference: 23 on the Plymouth Naval Memorial, UK.

FITZPATRICK, Andrew: Rank: Private. Regiment or Service: Royal Irish Regiment. Unit: 6th Battalion. Date of death: 12 August 1917. Born in Waterford. Enlisted in London while living in Kennington in Surrey. 10029. Killed in action. Grave or Memorial Reference: Panel 33. Memorial: Ypres (Menin Gate) Memorial in Belgium.

FITZPATRICK, James: Rank: Private. Regiment or Service: Royal Irish Regiment. Unit: 6th Battalion. Date of death: 10 September 1916. Service No: 1963. Born in Fethard. Enlisted in Waterford while living in Fethard. Killed in action. From the *Waterford News*, October 1916:

ANOTHER FERRYBANK SOLDIER KILLED.
A loving friend writes: It is with deep regret we announce the death of another Ferrybank soldier, Private 1963 James Fitzpatrick, A Company, 6th Battalion, Royal Irish Regiment, who Died of wounds received in action on 10th

September. He was the second eldest son of Mrs Catherine Fitzpatrick, Dobbyn's Square, Ferrybank, to whom the King and Queen sent a message of sympathy in her sorrow. Deceased had been two years serving with the British Expeditionary Force in France, and was formerly employed by Mr S. Morris, Newrath. He was a native of Fethard, County Tipperary, and was 27 years of age. May he and those who fell on the battlefield rest in peace.

Grave or Memorial Reference: II.B.51. Cemetery: Bronfay Farm Military Cemetery, Bray-Sur-Somme in France.

FITZPATRICK, Matthew: Rank: Private. Regiment or Service: Royal Irish Regiment. Unit: 'B' Coy. 2nd Battalion. Age at death: 49. Date of death: 21 March 1918. Service No: 10123. Born in Slieverue Co. Kilkenny. Enlisted in Waterford. Killed in action.

Supplementary information: Son of Patrick and Margaret Fitzpatrick, of Ferrybank, Waterford. Grave or Memorial Reference: I.B.30. Cemetery: Templeux-Le-Guerard British Cemetery in France.

FITZPATRICK, Martin: Rank: Carpenter. Regiment or Service: Mercantile Marine. Unit: SS *Princess Royal* (Glasgow). Age at death: 30. Date of death: 26 May 1918.

Supplementary information: Son of Thomas and Ellen Fitzpatrick. Husband of Annie Fitzpatrick (*née* Houlihan), of Bellevue House, Waterford. Born in Waterford. He has no known grave but is listed on the Tower Hill Memorial in the UK.

FITZPATRICK, Patrick: Rank: Gunner. Regiment or Service: Royal Garrison Artillery. Unit: 77th Siege Battery. Age at death: 25. Date of death: 25 December 1916. Service No: 3280. Born in Kill, Co. Waterford. Enlisted in Curraghmore while living in Kill. Died.

Supplementary information: Son of Michael Fitzpatrick, of Ballyvohalane, Kill, Co. Waterford. Grave or Memorial Reference: V.C.18. Cemetery: Couin British Cemetery in France.

FITZPATRICK, Richard: Rank: Private/Lance Corporal. Regiment or Service: Royal Irish Regiment. Unit: 1st Battalion. Date of death: 23 February 1915. Service No: 9630. Born in Passage East, Co. Waterford. Enlisted in Clonmel, Co. Tipperary while living in Cappoquin, Co. Waterford. Killed in action. Richard is buried beside Tipperaryman Private Thomas Morris from Ballingarry, who died three days after him. Grave or Memorial Reference: I.C.3. Cemetery: Elzenwalle Brasserie Cemetery in Belgium.

FIVES, Patrick: Rank: Private. Regiment or Service, South Wales Borderers. Unit: 4th Battalion. Date of death: 9 April 1916. Service No: 13459. Born in Waterford. Enlisted in Newport, Monmouthshire. Killed in action in Mesopotamia. Grave or Memorial Reference: Panel 16 and 62. Memorial: Basra Memorial in Iraq.

FLAHERTY, Michael: Rank: Private. Regiment or Service: South Lancashire Regiment. Unit: 1/5th Battalion. Date of death: 13 July 1918. Service No: 26456. Born in Waterford. Enlisted in Widnes in Lancashire while living in Waterford. Killed in action.

Supplementary information: Brother of Mrs S. Grant, of 223 Glebe Road., Letchworth, Herts. Grave or Memorial Reference: III.C.9. Cemetery: Houchin British Cemetery in France.

FLANAGAN, James: Rank: Pioneer. Regiment or Service: Royal Engineers. Unit: 12th Labour Battalion. Age at death: 46. Date of death: 5 October 1916. Service No: 163362. Born in Ballybricken, Co. Waterford. Enlisted in Waterford. Died in Salonika.

Supplementary information: Son of John and Mary Flanagan, of Carrick-on-Suir, Co. Tipperary. Husband of Margaret Flanagan, of 3 Pump Lane, Waterford. Grave or Memorial Reference: 522. Cemetery: Salonika (Lembet Road) Military Cemetery in Greece.

FLANNERY, Thomas John: Rank: Private. Regiment or Service: Royal Dublin Fusiliers. Unit: 10th Battalion. Date of death: 13 November 1916. Age at death: 19. Service No: 26829. Born in Ferrybank, Co. Waterford. Enlisted in Limerick. Killed in action.
Supplementary information: Son of John and Marianne Flannery, of Sunville Park, Thomondgate, Limerick. He has no known grave but is listed on Pier and Face 16C on the Thiepval Memorial in France.

FLAVIN, Michael: Rank: Sapper. Regiment or Service: Royal Engineers. Unit: 16th (Coast Battalion.) Coy. Age at death: 37. Date of death: 12 April 1915. Service No: 741. This man is not listed in Soldiers died in the Great War or Irelands Memorial Records.
Supplementary information: Son of Michael and Catherine Flavin, of Mayor's Walk, Waterford. Served in the South African Campaign. Grave or Memorial Reference: 416. 40214. Cemetery: Hull Western Cemetery, UK.

FLAVIN, Thomas: Rank: Private. Regiment or Service: Australian Infantry, A.I.F. Unit: 11th Battalion. Date of death: 15 April 1917. Killed in action. Service No: 2269. Enlisted in Perth, Western Australia on 9 March 1915. Was admitted to hospital three times in Alexandria with a lacerated shoulder, a cut forehand and neuralga.

In or near what Parish or Town were you born? Waterford, Ireland.
Are you a natural born British subject or a Naturalised British subject? Yes.
What is your age? 32 (1882).
What is your trade or calling? Sleeper Cutter.

Are you, or have you been an Apprentice? No. If so where, to whom, and for what period?
Are you married? No.
Who is your next of kin? [Mother] Mrs Julia Flavin, Portlaw, Co. Waterford. [Mother died and Next of Kin was changed to (Brother) James Flavin, 12 William Street, Portlaw Co. Waterford.]
Age, 32 years.
Height 5 feet, 4 inches.
Weight: 150 lbs.
Chest measurement: 36-38 inches.
Complexion, med dark.
Eyes: blue.
Hair: dark brown.
Religious denomination: RC.

At a Field General Court Martial Private Flavin was charged with being absent without leave while on active service (12th-15th May 1916) at Sailly for three days. He pleaded guilty and was sentenced to two year's imprisonment but this was later commuted to 90 days field punishment number 1. This included being tied spread-eagled to a wagon wheel for long periods. He has no known grave but is listed on the Villers-Bretonneux Memorial in France.

FLEMING, John: Rank: Seaman. Regiment or Service: Royal Naval Reserve. Unit: HMS *Laurentic*. Age at death: 25. Date of death: 25 January 1917. Service No: 2320/A (Dev).
Supplementary information: Son of John Fleming, of Lower Dunmore East, Co. Waterford. Grave or Memorial Reference: Upper Fahan (St Mura's) Church of Ireland Cemetery, County Donegal.

FLEURY, William Henry: Rank: Second Mate. Regiment or Service: Mercantile Marine. Unit: SS *Lismore* (Cork). Age at death: 55. Date of death: 12 April 1917.
Supplementary information: Son of the late Caesar and Marianne Fleury. Born at Tramore, Waterford. He has no known grave

but is listed on the Tower Hill Memorial in the UK.

FLYNN, Charles Christopher: Rank: Private. Regiment or Service: Household Cavalry and Cavalry of the line including the Yeomanry and Imperial Camel Corps. Unit: 8th (King's Royal Irish) Hussars. Date of death: 30 November 1917. Service No: 1475 and H/14765. Born in Waterford. Enlisted I.E.14. Cemetery: Gouzeaucourt New British Cemetery in France.

FLYNN, Declan: Rank: Petty Officer. Regiment or Service: Royal Navy. Unit: HMS *Salmon*. Age at death: 37. Date of death: 18 September 1919. Service No: 198423 Awards: D S M.

Supplementary information: Son of Thomas and Alice Flynn, of Bohodoon, Dungarvan, Co. Waterford. Grave or Memorial Reference: R.N. Plot. 141. Cemetery: Shotley (St Mary) Churchyard, Suffolk, UK.

FLYNN, Denis: Rank: Unknown. The only reference I have to this man is contained in an article from the *Munster Express*, November 1915:

SEQUEL TO A COUNTY
WATERFORD WRECK.

The only survivor from the wreck of the 'Morning Star', Denis Flynn, a young man from Abbeyside, has just died. It may be remembered that about six weeks ago the vessel was wrecked at Boatstrand, and Denis Flynn, the only survivor out of five of a crew, gave some particulars of the loss of the vessel. Since that time he has not recovered from his injuries. He was taken home to Dungarvan, but was obliged to remain in bed all the time, and never completely rallying he succumbed to the effects of the injuries he received on that fatal night. He died at home, and much regret is felt at the awfully unfortunate occurrence.

FLYNN, Edmund: Rank: Private. Regiment or Service: Royal Irish Regiment. Unit: Depot. Born in Coolnamuck, Co. Waterford. Enlisted in Carrick-on-Suir, Co. Tipperary while living in Coolnamuck. Date of death: 6 November 1918. Service No: 7381. Cemetery, Clonmel, St Patrick's Cemetery. Grave location: 4.E.119

FLYNN, James: Rank: Private. Regiment or Service: Leinster Regiment. Unit: 2nd Battalion. Date of death: 8 September 1915. Service No: 2581. Born in Nenagh. Enlisted in Birr. Died of wounds. Age at death: 44.

Supplementary information: Son of the late Michael and Margaret Flynn, of 3 Waterside, Waterford. Husband of Johanne Flynn, of 2 The Manor, Waterford. Grave or Memorial Reference: III.B.36. Cemetery: Lijssenthoek Military Cemetery in Belgium.

FLYNN, James: Rank: Able Seaman. Regiment or Service: Mercantile Marine. Unit: SS *Australdale* (Brisbane). Age at death: 28. Date of death: 19 October 1917. While sailing in convoy she was torpedoed and sunk by German Submarine U-22.

Supplementary information: Son of the late Patrick and Ellen Flynn. Born at Dunmore East, Co. Waterford. He has no known grave but is listed on the Tower Hill Memorial in the UK.

FLYNN, James: Rank: Private. Regiment or Service: Royal Irish Regiment. Unit: 2nd Battalion. Age at death: 50. Date of death: 19 October 1914. Service No: 6524. Born in Ballybricken, Co. Waterford. Enlisted in Waterford. Died.

Supplementary information: Son of Richard and Bridget Flynn, of 38 Smith's Lane, Waterford. Husband of Catherine Flynn, of 38 Smith's Lane, Waterford. Grave or Memorial Reference: 11 and 12 on the Le Touret Memorial in France.

FLYNN, James: Rank: Seaman. Regiment or Service: Royal Naval Reserve. Unit: HMS *Goliath*. Age at death: 39. Date of death: 13 May 1915. Service No: 2052D. HMS *Goliath* was sunk by three torpedoes from German destroyer *Muvanet-I-Milet*, she blew up and capsized immediately taking 570 of her 750 crew including the Captain to a watery grave. Ten Waterford men died on the *Goliath* that day.

Supplementary information: Son of William and Ellen Flynn, of Carballymore, Dunmore East. Huband of Martha Flynn, of Carballymore, Dunmore East, Co. Waterford. Grave or Memorial Reference: 8 on the Plymouth Naval Memorial, UK.

FLYNN, John: Rank: Private. Regiment or Service: Royal Irish Regiment. Unit: 1st Battalion. Date of death: 24 April 1915. Service No: 9208. Born in Tramore, Co. Waterford. Enlisted in Waterford while living in Knockhouse, Co. Waterford. Killed in action. He has no known grave but is listed on Panel 44 on the Ypres (Menin Gate) Memorial in Belgium.

FLYNN, Joseph: Rank: Rifleman. Regiment or Service: Royal Irish Rifles. Unit: 2nd Battalion. Age at death: 19. Date of death: 9 July 1916. Service No: 8981. Born in Ballybricken, Co. Waterford. Enlisted in Waterford. Killed in action.

Supplementary information: Son of Mrs Mary Aspell, of 1 Smith's Lane, Waterford. He has no known grave but is listed on Pier and Face 15 A and 15 B of the Thiepval Memorial in France.

FLYNN, Martin: Rank: Private. Regiment or Service: Royal Irish Regiment. Unit: 1st Battalion. Age at death: 23. Date of death: 11 January 1916. Service No: 7438. Born in Carrigbeg Co. Waterford and enlisted in Carrick-on-Suir. Died in Salonkia.

Supplementary information: Son of Mr and Mrs Martin Flynn, of Carrick-on-Suir, Co. Tipperary. Grave or Memorial Reference: 47. Cemetery: Salonika (Lembet Road) Military Cemetery in Greece.

FLYNN, Michael: Rank: Seaman. Regiment or Service: Royal Naval Reserve. Unit: HMS *Goliath*. Age at death: 35. Date of death: 13 May 1915. Service No: 3580C. HMS *Goliath* was sunk by three torpedoes from German destroyer *Muvanet-I-Milet*, she blew up and capsized immediately taking 570 of her 750 crew including the Captain to a watery grave. Ten Waterford men died on the *Goliath* that day.

Supplementary information: Son of William and Ellen Flynn, of Carbally. Husband of Margaret Ellen Flynn, of Carbally Beg, Dunmore East, Co. Waterford. Grave or Memorial Reference: 8 on the Plymouth Naval Memorial, UK.

FLYNN, Patrick: Rank: Private. Regiment or Service: Royal Irish Regiment. Unit: 2nd Battalion. Age at death: 23. Date of death: 19 October 1914. Service No: 6130. Born in Abbeyside, Co. Waterford. Enlisted in Dungarvan, Co. Waterford. Killed in action.

Supplementary information: Son of Patrick and Mary Flynn, of King's Street, Abbeyside, Dungarvan, Co. Waterford. Grave or Memorial Reference: 11 and 12 on the Le Touret Memorial in France.

FLYNN, Patrick: Rank: Stoker 1st Class. Regiment or Service: Royal Navy. Unit: H. M. S/M "E22". Age at death: 25. Date of death: 25 April 1916. Service No: K/21302. Killed in action with a German Submarine.

Supplementary information: Son of Patrick and Margaret Flynn, of Ballinahassary, Dungarvan, Co. Waterford. Grave or Memorial Reference: 15 on the Plymouth Naval Memorial, UK.

FLYNN, Patrick: Rank: Private. Regiment or Service: Irish Guards. Unit: 1st Battalion.

Date of death: 4 September 1917. Service No: 11233. Born in Aglish, Co. Waterford. Enlisted in Dungarvan, Co. Waterford. Died of wounds. Grave or Memorial Reference: IV.F.11. Cemetery: Dozinghem Military Cemetery in Belgium.

FLYNN, Patrick: Rank: Private. Regiment or Service: Otago Regiment, N.Z.E.F. Unit: 2nd Battalion. Age at death: 35. Date of death: 23 December 1917. Service No: 47524. Occupation on Enlistment, Teamster. Next of kin; John Flynn (brother), Glendaligan, Kilrossanty, Co. Waterford. Killed in action in Ypres.

Supplementary information: Son of Mrs Alice Flynn, of Glendaligan, Kilrossanty, Kilmacthomas, Co. Waterford. The following letter was sent to his relatives in Waterford:

On Active Service.
New Zealand Expeditionary Force.
Presbyterian Church of N. Z.
Chaplains Department.
Belgium 28-12-17.
Dear Mr Flynn.
I am sorry to say that it is necessary for me to write to you to tell you of the death of your brother, 47524 Pte P. Flynn of 2nd Otago Regiment, N. Z. E. F. He and two others were killed by shellfire while in their bivvy in the support line trench on the 23rd inst and their bodies have been buried near where they died.

As I have not been long with this Battalion I am sorry that I have not got to know him by name although I probably knew him quite well by appearance.

In this great cause he has done what he could and now he rests beyond all power of shellfire in peace. Will you please accept the sympathy of his Battalion, in the hour of your grief.
Yours Sincerely.
D Cherron,
Chaplain.

Grave or Memorial Reference: XLV.H.14. Cemetery: Tyne Cot Cemetery in Belgium.

FLYNN, William: Rank: Private. Regiment or Service: Royal Irish Regiment. Unit: 5th Battalion. Age at death: 30. Date of death: 24 January 1918. Service No: 7874. Born in Four Mile Water, Co. Waterford. Enlisted in Clonmel, Co. Tipperary while living in Ballinamult, Co. Waterford. Died at Sea.

Supplementary information: Son of William and Ellen Flynn, of Ballinagulkee, Ballinamult, Co. Waterford. He has no known grave but is listed on the Chatby Memorial in Egypt.

FLYNN, William: Rank: Sergeant. Regiment or Service: Royal Irish Regiment. Unit: 2nd Battalion. Date of death: 21 October 1915. Service No: 10079. Born in St John's, Waterford. Enlisted in Clonmel, Co. Tipperary while living in Waterford. Killed in action. He has no known grave but is listed on Pier and Face 3A on the Thiepval Memorial in France.

FLYNN, William Francis: Rank: Private. Regiment or Service: Argyll and Sutherland Highlanders. Unit: 12th Battalion. Age at death: 25. Date of death: 19 September 1918. Service No: S/20101. Born in Stradbally, Queen's Co. Enlisted in Dungareen [sic], Co. Waterford while living in Kilmackthomas, Co. Waterford. Killed in action in Salonika.

Supplementary information: Son of Michael and Kate Flynn, of Durrow, Kilmacthomas, Co. Waterford. Grave or Memorial Reference: III.D.12. Cemetery: Doiran Military Cemetery in Greece.

FLYNN, William Francis: Rank: Private. Regiment or Service: Royal Irish Regiment. Unit: 5th Battalion. Age at death: 20. Date of death: 24 January 1918. Service No: 7874. Born in Four Mile Water, Co. Waterford. Enlisted in Clonmel, Co. Tipperary while living in Ballinamult, Co. Waterford. Died at Sea.

Supplementary information: Son of William and Ellen Flynn, of Ballinagulkee, Ballinamult, Co. Waterford. He has no known grave but is listed on the Chatby Memorial in Egypt.

FOLEY, David: Rank: Private. Regiment or Service: The King's (Liverpool Regiment). Unit: 1st/8th Battalion. Age at death: 21. Date of death: 10 June 1917. Service No: 307021. Born in Aglish, Co. Waterford. Enlisted in Liverpool while living Boston, Lincs. Killed in action.

Supplementary information: Son of Mrs Catherine Foley, of Mount Stewart, Aglish, Cappoquin, Co. Waterford. From the *Waterford News*, September 1916, 'D. Foley, Cappoquin - King's Liverpool Regiment - missing.' Grave or Memorial Reference: II.E.8. Cemetery: Cologne Southern Cemetery in Germany.

FOLEY, Thomas Francis: Rank: Sick Berth Attendant 1st Class. Regiment or Service: Royal Navy. Unit: HMS *Aboukir*. Sunk along with two others by German submarine, U-9. Age at death: 21. Date of death: 22 September 1914. Service No: M/5213.

Supplementary information: Son of Patrick and Catherine Foley, of Dungarvan, Co. Waterford. Joined the service two years previous to his death. Grave or Memorial Reference: 6. Memorial: Chatham Naval Memorial in England.

FOLEY, Thomas Francis: Rank: Listed as Acting Farrier Sergeant and Farrier Sergeant. Regiment or Service: Royal Army Service Corps. Unit: Date of death: 12 August 1917. Service No: RTS/7604. Born in Carrick-on-Suir, Co. Waterford. Enlisted in Woolwich while living in Woolwich. Died at home.

Supplementary information: Grave or Memorial Reference: Screen Wall. BB. 5. Cemetery: Leeds Roman Catholic Cemetery, UK.

FORBES, John: Rank: Lance Corporal. Regiment or Service: Sherwood Foresters (Nottinghamshire and Derbyshire Regiment). Unit: 9th Battalion. Age at death: 23. Date of death: 26 September 1916. Service No: 13106. Born in Castle Pollard, Co. Westmeath. Enlisted in Derby while living in Ballymacarberry Co. Cork. Killed in action.

Supplementary information: Son of Mr and Mrs Archibald Forbes, of Newcastle, Clonmel, Co. Tipperary. From the the *Waterford News*, November 1916, 'Casualty lists this week. Lce-Corporal G. Forbes, Sherwoods, Waterford, 13106'. He has no known grave but is listed on Pier and Face 10 C, 10 D and 11A of the Thiepval Memorial in France.

FORDE, Frank: Rank: Private. Regiment or Service: Royal Dublin Fusiliers. Unit: 'D' Coy. 10th Battalion. Age at death: 16. Date of death: 10 September 1916. Service No: 26437. Born in Dungarvan, Co. Waterford. Enlisted in Waterford while living in Wexford. Killed in action.

Supplementary information: Son of John and Margaret Forde of Patrick Square, Wexford. From the *Enniscorthy Guardian*:

WEXFORD SOLDIER KILLED

The sad news of the death of Private Francis Forde, eldest son of Mr John Forde,

Frank Forde (Photograph courtesy of Mrs Margaret Walsh Themistocleous. Middlesex. Frank Forde's niece).

St Patrick's Square, has been officially received by his parents on Sunday morning. Private Forde, who was barely 17 years old, joined the Pals battalion of the Royal Dublin Fusiliers in the end of March last, and he was only about a month on active service. Prior to his joining the army he was one of the clerical staff in the office of the Millroad Ironworks, and he was a great favourite with all his companions. The deepest sympathy is felt for his sorrowing parents. Second Lieutenant, A.W. Henchy, in conveying the sad news to Private Fordes mother says; –"I regret to have to inform you of the death of your son, Private Francis Forde, while in the execution of his duty on the morning of the 10th inst. He died on his way to the dressing station shortly after being wounded. I may mention that in the early morning of the day he entered the trenches he attended his religious duties and received Holy Communion. I attended the funeral service at which was present a number of his friends. He was buried in the cemetery behind the firing line and a wooden cross neatly inscribed marks his grave. You will be informed of his burial ground at some later time. As his platoon Commander, I assure you that I am indeed very sorry to lose such a fine courageous fellow and a gallant soldier of whom his family should be proud."

From another in a Wexford newspaper:

Private Francis Forde, son of Mr John Forde, ex-Sgt, R. I. C, of St Patrick's Square, Wexford was killed in action and notification to this effect was received by his parents on Saturday last. Private Forde, who was a member of the Wexford Boro Battalion, National Volunteers, enlisted at the age of 15, but on account of his extreme youth was subsequently discharged. At the end of last March, when he had passed his sixteenth birthday, he again volunteered for active service joining the 10th (Commercial batt) Royal Dublin Fusiliers. During his period

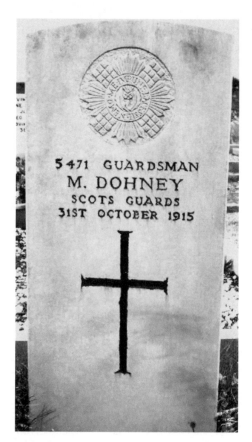

Henry Rawson Forde. From the London Gazette 17 April 1917.

of training at Dublin, Private Forde, with his Pals Batt, participated in the work of quelling the Sinn Fein Insurrection. Grave or Memorial Reference: J. 9. Cemetery: Tranchee De Mecknes Cemetery, Aix-Noulette in France.

FORDE, Henry Rawson: Rank: Captain. Regiment or Service: King's Own Yorkshire Light Infantry. Unit: 'D' Coy. 2nd Battalion. Age at death: 22. Date of death: 2 December 1917. He won the Military Cross and is listed in the *London Gazette*.

Supplementary information: Only son of Sir Henry Forde and Lady Forde, of The Manor of St John, Waterford. Educated at Clifton College and Sandhurst. From the *Waterford News*, July 1916.

LIEUTENANT FORDE.

2nd Lieutenant H.R. Forde, K.O.T.L.I. (son of Mr H.J. Forde, J.P., Manor of St John), has been wounded at the front. Lieutenant Forde is a popular young gentleman, and his return to health is earnestly wished for by his friends.

De Ruvigny's Roll of Honour:

Forde, Henry Rawson, M. C. Captain, 2nd Battalion (105th Foot) The King's Own (Yorkshire Light Infantry). Only son of Henry J. Forde of the Manor of St John, Waterford, J. P, by his wife, Annie Catherine, daughters of Richard Rawson. Born in Tramore, Co. Waterford on 24 June 1895. Educated at Clifton College and the Royal Military College, Sandhurst. Gazetted 2nd Lieutenant, The King's Own (Yorkshire Light Infantry) on 12 January 1915. Promoted Captain on 3rd December 1916. Served with the Expeditionary Force in France and Flanders from the following October. Killed in action near Passchendale on 2 December 1917 and buried where he fell. A brother officer wrote; "It was an awful blow to us all…for he was looked upon by everyone as a true friend. He is a great loss to the Battalion." And another; "A brave and gallant officer has been taken by God, but he did his work, and he was a man among men when danger lurked about." An officer of another Regiment wrote; "All his company officers had been killed, and he was rallying his men when a German sniper hit him in the head, and, poor lad, he was killed at once." He was awarded the Military Cross (London Gazette, 17 April 1917), the official record stating; "He led his men in the attack with great gallantry, and captured an enemy line of strong posts, together with 40 prisoners. He had previously done fine work."

From the *Waterford News*, April 1917:

ANOTHER MILITARY CROSS.

Waterford continues to earn considerable distinction in the battlefield. On Tuesday we noted the distinction conferred on 2nd Lieutenant Dobbyn. To-day we learn that Captain H Rawson Forde, son of Mr H.J. Forde, J.P., of the Manor of St John, Waterford, has been awarded the Military Cross for gallantry in the field. This young officer was gazetted from Sandhurst in January, 1915, to the 3rd Battalion King's Own Yorkshire Light Infantry. In the following October he was sent to France, and was appointed to the second Battalion to which he has been attached since. Captain Forde has taken part in many of the great battles on the Western Front during the past year.

From the *Waterford News*, April 1917:

NOTES OF THE WEEK.
HOW WATERFORD OFFICERS WON DECORATIONS.

In a recent issue we mentioned the fact that Captain H Rawson Forde, 2nd King's Own Yorkshire Light Infantry, son of Mr H.J. Forde, J.P., Manor of St John, Waterford, had gained the Military Cross. The official notice in the "Gazette" states, "He led his men in the attack with great gallantry, and captured an enemy line of strong posts, together with 45 prisoners. He had previously done fine work."

From the *Munster Express*, April 1917:

WATERFORD OFFICER AWARDED THE MILITARY CROSS.

Captain H. Rawson Ford, son of Mr H.J. Forde, J.P., Manor of St John, Waterford, has been awarded the Military Cross for gallantry in the field. The young officer was gazetted from Sandhurst in January 1915, to the 3rd battalion King's Own Yorkshire Light Infantry. In the following October, Captain Ford was sent to France and was appointed to the second Battalion to which he has been attached since.

CAPTAIN H.R. FORDE, M.C., KILLED.

The sad news was received in Waterford on Saturday evening by his father, Mr H.J. Forde, J.P., H.C., that his only son, Captain Henry Rawson Forde, was killed in action on 2nd inst., in France, when rallying his men. Captain Forde, who was attached to the King's Own Yorkshire Light Infantry, joined the army on the outbreak of the war, being first attached to the remount depot at Waterford, and afterwards going for the completion of training to the Military College, Sandhurst. He had seen a good deal of fighting in France and last summer was awarded the Military Cross for gallantry and devotion to duty. He was only about 23 years of age, and as an officer his qualities are highly spoken of. By his death, a brilliant and brave career has been cut short, and the deepest sympathy is felt in Waterford for his bereaved parents and friends.

Grave or Memorial Reference: IX E. 23. Cemetery: Tyne Cot Cemetery in Belgium. He is also listed on the Waterford and District Roll of Honour and also on the Forde Memorial. These are located in Christ Church Cathedral (Church of Ireland), Henrietta Street, Waterford.

FORSEY, Frederick: Rank: Private. Regiment or Service: Royal Irish Regiment. Unit: 'B' Company, 2nd Battalion. Date of death: 19 October 1914. Age at death: 27. Service No: 5612. Born in St John's, Waterford. Enlisted in Waterford. Killed in action.
Supplementary information: Husband of Bridget Forsey, of 6, Newports Lane, Waterford. He has no known grave but is listed on Panel 11 and 12 on the Le Touret Memorial in France.

FOUNDS, James Maurance: Rank: Able Seaman. Regiment or Service: Royal Navy.

Unit: HMS *Indefatigable*. Date of death: 31 May 1916. Age at death: 25. Service No: J7618. Born in Dunmore.
Supplementary information: Son of J. Founds (Coastguardsman), of Co. Galway. Grave or Memorial Reference: 12. He has no known grave but is listed on the Plymouth Naval Memorial. Devon, UK.

FOWLER, Michael: Rank: Private. Regiment or Service: Royal Irish Regiment. Unit: 2nd Battalion. Date of death: 8 May 1915. Service No: 10788. Born in Killea, Co. Waterford. Enlisted in Waterford while living in Rossduff, Co. Waterford. Killed in action. He has no known grave but is listed on Panel 33 on the Ypres (Menin Gate) Memorial in Belgium.

FRAHER, Patrick: Rank: Private. Regiment or Service: Royal Dublin Fusiliers. Unit: 7th Battalion. Service No: 21949. Formerly he was with the Royal Inniskilling Fusiliers where his number was 16811. Born in Waterford. Enlisted in Belfast while living in Waterford. Died of wounds. Killed in action in Gallipoli. He has no known grave but is listed on Panel 190 to196 on the Helles Memorial in Turkey.

FRANKLIN, Patrick: Rank: Private. Regiment or Service: King's (Liverpool Regiment.) Unit: 4th Battalion. Date of death: 28 October 1916. Service No: 34741. Born in Waterford. Enlisted in Liverpool while living in Liverpool. Killed in action. Has no known grave but is commemorated on Pier and Face 1D 8B and 8C. Memorial: Thiepval Memorial in France.

FRENCH, Patrick: Rank: Private. Regiment or Service: Royal Irish Regiment. Unit: 'E' Coy. 2nd Battalion. Age at death: 22. Date of death: 10 January 1917. Service No: 5533. Born in Tallow, Co. Waterford. Enlisted in Lismore while living in Tallow. Killed in action.

Supplementary information: Son of William and Hannah French, of Chapel Street, Tallow, Co. Waterford. Grave or Memorial Reference: X. 51. Cemetery: Kemmel Chateau Military Cemetery in Belgium.

FURLONG, Edward: Rank: Corporal. Regiment or Service: Royal Horse Artillery and Royal Field Artillery. Unit: 38th Brigade. Ammunition Column. Age at death: 41. Date of death: 30 July 1915. Service No: 15932. Born in Taghmon, Co. Wexford. Enlisted in Wexford.
Supplementary information: Son of John and Annastatia Furlong of Foghmon, Co. Wexford. Husband of Elizabeth Furlong of 48 Slievekeale, Waterford. Served in China (1900) and in the South African Campaign. Grave or Memorial Reference: I.G.3. Cemetery: Poperinghe New Military Cemetery in Belgium.

FURLONG, Thomas: Rank: Private. Regiment or Service: Royal Irish Regiment. Unit: 2nd Battalion. Age at death: 45. Date of death: 19 October 1914. Service No: 6775. Born in St Patrick's, Waterford. Enlisted in Cahir, Co. Tipperary while living in Waterford. Killed in action.
Supplementary information: Husband of Catherine Furlong, of 2 Blake's Lane, Waterford. Grave or Memorial Reference: 11 and 12 on the Le Touret Memorial in France.

G

GAFFNEY, Adam: Rank: Private. Regiment or Service: Royal Irish Regiment. Unit: 7ᵗʰ Battalion. Date of death: 21 March 1918. Service No: 25311. Formerly he was with the South Irish Horse where his number was 2388. Born in St John's, Waterford. Enlisted in Waterford. Killed in action. He has no known grave but is listed on Panels 30 and 31 on the Pozières Memorial in France.

GALLOWAY, Harold Bessemer: Rank: Major. Regiment or Service: Seaforth Highlanders. Unit: 7ᵗʰ Battalion. Age at death: 47. Date of death: 25 September 1915. Killed in action.

Supplementary information: Son of Charles J. Galloway, of Thorneyholme, Knutsford, Cheshire. Husband of Sybil Galloway, of Blervie, Forres, Morayshire. Served in the Hazara Expedition (1891), Chitral Campaign (1895), and in the South African Campaign. Awarded the Royal Humane Society's Medal for saving life from drowning. Article from 'Our Heroes':

7ᵗʰ Seaforth Highlanders, of Annestown, Waterford, was killed in action in Flanders on Septemebr 25ᵗʰ last. He was a keen follower of the Waterford Hunt, and his death is a loss to the Irish Hunting Field. Major Galloway was the only surviving son of Mr Charles Galloway, Thorneyholme, Knutsford. He joined the 2ⁿᵈ Battalion Seaforth Highlanders in 1888, and served in the Hazara Expedition in 1891 (medal and clasps), the relief of Chitral, 1895 (medal and clasps), and in the South African War, 1901–2, attached to Lovat's Scouts, for his services in which he received the medal and three clasps. At the outbreak of the war Major Galloway was in the reserve of Officers, but joined the 7ᵗʰ Seaforth Highlanders and was promoted Major.

From the *Waterford News*, April 1917:

MEMORIAL TABLET TO CO. WATERFORD OFFICER.

Mrs Galloway has erected a memorial in Annestown Protestant Church to the memory of her husband, the late Major Galloway, who was killed in the battle of Loos. The tablet consists of grey Aberdeen granite on a polished black ground, and is placed on the north wall of the church, between the two memorial windows. The inscription is as follows; --" In ever-loving memory of Harold Bessemer Galloway, major 7ᵗʰ Seaforth Highlanders, of Blervie Rafford, Morayshire, who fell in action at the battle of Loos on September 25ᵗʰ, 1915, aged 47 years. He joined the 2ⁿᵈ Seaforth Highlanders in 1888, and served in the Hazare Expedition, 1891 (medal and clasp), in the Chitral Expedition, 1895 (medal and clasp) and with Lovat's Scouts in South

Harold Bessemer Galloway. From 'Our Heroes'.

Africa (Queen's medal and three clasps). He joined the reserve of officers in 1902, and at the outbreak of the war in 1914 he rejoined the Seaforth Highlanders and was promoted Major in the 7th Battalion. Erected by his loving wife, Sybil Galloway, of Annestown.

Grave or Memorial Reference: 112 to 115 on the Loos Memorial in France.

GALVIN, Bartholomew: Rank: Lance Coproral. Regiment or Service: Royal Irish Rifles. Unit: 7th Battalion. Date of death: 26 September 1916. Service No: 3395. Born in Limerick. Enlisted in Waterford while living in Limerick. Killed in action. From the *Waterford News*, October 1916:

WATERFORDMEN
IN THE CASUALTY LISTS.
Mr Galvin of 17 Doyle Street, has received official information that his son, Private B. Galvin, R.I. Rifles, was killed in action in France on the 26th September. Deceased was only 20 years of age and before joining the army in March, 1915, he was employed by Messrs J. Wallis and Sons. He had been at the front since 18th December 1916 [*sic*].

Grave or Memorial Reference: Cemetery near Rossignol Estaminet, Kemmel, Mem. 5. Cemetery: Wytschaete Military Cemetery in Belgium.

GALVIN, Richard: Rank: Private. Regiment or Service: Leinster Regiment. Unit: 2nd Battalion. Date of death: 13 August 1915. Service No: 8265. Born in Portlaw, Co. Waterford. Enlisted in Portlaw. Died of wounds. Grave or Memorial Reference: I.G.7. Cemetery: Poperinghe New Military Cemetery in Belgium.

GAMBLE, William: Rank: Lance Corporal. Regiment or Service: Royal Irish Fusiliers. Unit: 7th Battalion. Age at death: 28. Date of death: 30 April 1916. Service No: 16507. Born in Ballyduff, Co. Waterford. Enlisted in Portlaw, Co. Waterford. Died of wounds.

Supplementary information: Son of William and Jane Gamble, of Cullinagh, Kilmeaden, Co. Waterford. From the *Waterford News*, May 1916:

ROLL OF HONOUR.
We have learned with great regret of the death of Lance Corporal William Gamble, which occurred as a result of wounds received in action and gas poisoning. Deceased was son of Mr William Gamble, P.L.G., Cunninagh, and was only about 27 years of age. He joined the Royal Irish Fusiliers about eighteen months ago, and he had been promoted to the rank of Lance Corporal. In the district where he resided he had many friends, who learned of his demise with the greatest regret, and to his parents and other relatives sincere sympathy is extended in their bereavement. The official notification of his son's death, sent to Mr gamble by the officer in charge of records, Dublin, reads as follows: "It is my painful duty to inform you that a report has this day been received from the War Office notifying the death of No 166507, Lance Corporal William, Gamble, Royal Irish Fusiliers, which occurred at No 1 Casualty Clearing Station, France, on the 30th day of April, 1916. I am to express to you the sympathy and regret of the Army Council. The cause of death was wounds and gas poisoning received in action." The Waterford Board of Guardians passed a resolution of condolence with Mr William Gamble on the death of his son; and Mr Gamble also received a message of sympathy from the King and Queen.

Grave or Memorial Reference: I.J.6. Cemetery: Chocques Military Cemetery in France.

GARREY, Stephen: Rank: Private. Regiment or Service: Royal Dublin Fusiliers. Unit: 1st Battalion. Date of death: 22 December 1915. Service No: 21863. Born in Waterford. Enlisted in Dunfermline. Killed in action in Gallipoli. Grave or Memorial Reference: II.E.5. Cemetery: Twelve Tree Copse Cemetery in Turkey.

GATWARD, Robert Horace: Rank: Lance Corporal. Regiment or Service: Duke of Cornwall's Light Infantry. Unit: 1st Battalion. Age at death: 23. Date of death: 23 July 1916. Service No: 11464. Born in Waterford. Enlisted in St Pancras, London while living in Hornsey, London. Killed in action.

Supplementary information: Son of the late Robert Gatward (S.M. 10th Hussars) and Hannah Gatward. Grave or Memorial Reference: Pier and Face 6B. Memorial: Thiepval Memorial in France.

GATWARD, William James Martin: Rank: Lance Corporal. Regiment or Service: Household Cavalry and Cavalry of the line including the Yeomanry and Imperial Camel Corps. Unit: City of London Yeomanry (Rough Riders). Date of death: 14 November 1917. Service No: 40731. Born in Waterford. Enlisted in Putney while living in Welwyn, Herts. Died of wounds in Palestine. Grave or Memorial Reference: X. 41. Cemetery: Jerusalem War Cemetery, Israel.

GAULE, Martin: (listed as **GAULE, W.R.** in the The Commonwealth War Graves Commission) Rank: Private. Regiment or Service: Royal Irish Regiment. Unit: 2nd Battalion. Date of death: 31 May 1915. Service No: 10006. Born in Trinity Without, Waterford. Enlisted in Waterford. Died of wounds. Grave or Memorial Reference: II.E.4. Cemetery: Roeselare Communal Cemetery in Belgium.

GAULE, Martin: Rank: Lance Corporal. Regiment or Service: Royal Irish Regiment. Unit: 2nd Battalion. Age at death: 24. Date of death: 24 May 1915. Service No: 10045. Born in Ballybricken, Co. Waterford. Enlisted in Clonmel. Killed in action.

Supplementary information: Husband of Bridget Gaule, of 103 Castle Terrace, Waterford. He has no known grave but is listed on Panel 33 on the Ypres (Menin Gate) Memorial in Belgium.

GAULE, William: Rank: Sergeant. Regiment or Service: Royal Irish Regiment. Unit: 2nd Battalion. Age at death: 29. Date of death: 3 September 1916. Service No: 8726. Born in Trinity Without, Co. Waterford. Enlisted in Clonmel, Co. Tipperary while living in Waterford. Killed in action.

Supplementary information: Son of Martin and Alice Gaule, of 6 John's Lane, Waterford. He has no known grave but is listed on Pier and Face 3A of the Thiepval Memorial in France.

GAULE, William: Rank: Private. Regiment or Service: Royal Irish Regiment. Unit: 2nd Battalion. Age at death: 38. Date of death: 28 May 1918. Service No: 6074. Born in Dungarvan, Co. Waterford. Enlisted in Liverpool while living in Dungarvan, Co. Waterford. Died.

Supplementary information: Husband of Alice Gaule, of Kilbarry, Co. Waterford. Grave or Memorial Reference: IV.B.29. Cemetery: Caudry British Cemetery Nord in France.

GAVIN, Martin: Rank: Private. Regiment or Service: Royal Irish Regiment. Unit: 6th Battalion. Date of death: 12 September 1916. Service No: 7545. Born in St Patrick's, Waterford. Enlisted in Waterford. Died of wounds. Grave or Memorial Reference: B.21.6. Cemetery: St Sever Cemetery, Rouen in France.

GEARY, Patrick: Rank: Private. Regiment or Service: Irish Guards. Unit: 1st Battalion. Age at death: 23. Date of death: 22 October 1915. Service No: 3760. Born in Waterford. Enlisted in Waterford. Killed in action.

Supplementary information: Son of Michael and Bridget Geary, of 28 Patrick Street, Waterford. From the *Waterford News*, May 1915:

WATERFORD SOLDIER'S PART
IN A BIG BATTLE.

"The day ended in a victory for us", so writes Private Patrick Geary to his mother, Mrs Geary, Patrick Street, in a letter describing the horrors he went through during one of the recent battles in Flanders. "Pat" Geary, not yet twenty-four ages of age, was called up at the very beginning of the war and went to the front with the first Expeditionary Force in August. He belongs to No (?) Company of the First Battalion of the Irish Guards. He has been in numerous engagements, but was only wounded once, at Ypres on November 1st. His letter is as follows.

23rd May, 1915.
Mr Dear Mother,
Just a few lines to let you know I am all right, thank God. We are just after having a big battle, and we are having a few days rest. Young Harris of Poleberry was killed. We had a very rough time of it, and a lot of casualties. I expect you will have read about it by the time you get this. Well, mother, I thought my own time had come at last, as it seemed an impossibility to escape. Thank God, I got through without a scratch. It was so awful, mother, that for three hours I did not know whether I was dead or alive. It was simply Hell let loose all of a sudden. They did all they could to cut up us with their artillery, but we went on and gained ground in spite of them. The saddest sight of all was to see our poor chaps, with broken legs and arms, creeping in and out of the way. Even then, the cowardly beggars did all in their power to kill them. They shot down our stretcher bearers who were carrying the wounded to the rear. The day ended in a victory for us, and I think our losses could not be compared with the German losses. Once again the Irish Guards have proved themselves one of the best Regiments England ever had.
Love to all at home.
PADDY.

From the *Waterford News*, January 1916:

DEATH OF LIEUTENANT GEARY.

It is with the deepest regret that we heard to-day of the death of Lieutenant Ronald Fitzmaurice Geary, who was killed on the 15th inst. Lieutenant Geary obtained a commission in the First Surrey Rifles at the outbreak of the war, and was a most promising and most gallant young officer. On the 15th inst, he set out to discover the whereabouts of a party of German snipers, and, having obtained the desired information, he was returning from his perilous expedition when he was shot in the head and died instantly. An officer who sent home information of his death said that it might be some consolation to know that twenty Germans were killed as the result of the information obtained by the ill-fated officer.

Lieutenant Geary was a second cousin of the editor of this paper, and a nephew of Mr Richard H Geary, or Cork, who was born in this city and who has many friends here.

Grave or Memorial Reference: I.K.1. Cemetery: Vermelles British Cemetery in France.

GEOGHEGAN, John: Rank: Gunner. Regiment or Service: Royal Garrison Artillery. Unit: 270th Siege Battery. Age at death: 25. Date of death: 30 June 1917. Service No: 53643. Born in Waterford. Enlisted in Maryborough while living in Borris-in-Ossary, Queen's County. Killed in action.

Supplementary information: Son of Bernard Geoghegan, of Borris-in-Ossory, Queen's Co. Grave or Memorial Reference: Plot 3. Row F. Grave 27. Cemetery: Ferme-Olivier Cemetery in Belgium.

GEOGHEGAN, William: Rank: Gunner. Regiment or Service: Royal Field Artillery. Unit: 48th Battery. Secondary Regiment: Labour Corps Secondary. Unit: transferred to (Pte. 411041) 787th Area Employment Coy.

Age at death: 43. Date of death: 17 February 1919. Service No: 88469. He won the Military Medal and is listed in the *London Gazette*.

Supplementary information: Son of Peter and Ellen Geoghegan. Grave or Memorial Reference: In North-East part. Cemetery: Butlerstown (St Anne) Catholic Churchyard, Co. Waterford.

GIBSON, Patrick: Rank: Private. Regiment or Service: Argyll and Sutherland Highlanders. Unit: 12th Battalion. Date of death: 19 September 1918. Service No: S/20133. Born in Waterford. Enlisted in St Pancras, London. Killed in action in Salonika. Grave or Memorial Reference: III.B.4. Cemetery: Doiran Military Cemetery in Greece.

GLAVIN, Patrick: Rank: Stoker 2nd Class. Regiment or Service: Royal Navy. Unit: HMS *Vivid*. Age at death: 17. Date of death: 3 August 1915. Service No: K/26347.

Supplementary information: Son of Mr and Mrs Glavin, of Green Street, Cappoquin, Co. Waterford. Grave or Memorial Reference: General L.10.0. Cemetery: Ford Park Cemetery (Formerly Plymouth Old Cemetery) (Pennycomequick) UK.

GLEESON, Joseph: Rank: Corporal. Regiment or Service: Royal Munster Fusiliers. Unit: 3rd Battalion. Date of death: 18 February 1919. Service No: 1/6525.

Supplementary information: Husband E.E. Gleeson, of District Asylum, Waterford. He was previously wounded at the Dardanelles in June 1915 and spent time in a hospital in Coventry. From the *Waterford News*, 1915:

OFF TO THE FRONT.

Corporal Joseph P Gleeson (1st Royal Munster Fusiliers) Lismore, a correspondent to this paper fifteen years ago, paid us a visit on his way home to Lismore from Rangoon, Punjab, previous to his going to the front.

Grave or Memorial Reference: E. North 19. 7. Cemetery: Cork (St Finbar's) Cemetery in Cork.

GLEESON, Kieran/Kiernan: Rank: Sapper. Regiment or Service: Royal Engineers. Unit: 9th Field Coy. Age at death: 22. Date of death: 21 December 1916. Service No: 23026. Born in Slieverue, Co. Kilkenny. Enlisted in Waterford. Died of wounds.

Supplementary information: Son of James and Annie Gleeson, of Ballyvalla, Ferrybank, Waterford. Grave or Memorial Reference: III.D.23. Cemetery: Peronne Road Cemetery, Maricourt in France.

GLODY, Thomas: Rank: Private. Regiment or Service: The King's (Liverpool Regiment). Unit: 13th Battalion. Age at death: 28. Date of death: 15 May 1917. Service No: 35195. Enlisted in Bootle while living in Bootle. Died of wounds.

Supplementary information: Son of Thomas Glody, of Dunmore East, Co. Waterford. Grave or Memorial Reference: XVIII.N.15. Cemetery: Etaples Military Cemetery in France.

GLYNN, John: Rank: Corporal. Regiment or Service: Leinster Regiment. Unit: 2nd Battalion. Age at death: 24. Date of death: 22 August 1916. Service No: 397. Born in Athboy, Co. Meath. Enlisted in Carlow. Died of wounds.

Supplementary information: Son of Robert and Mary J. Glynn, of Lismore, Co. Waterford. From the *Munster Express*:

KILLED.

Mr Robert Glynn, Castlefarm, Lismore Castle, has received notification that his son, Corporal John Glynn, of the 2nd Leinster Regiment, has died from the wounds received in action in France. Corporal Glynn, prior to the outbreak of war was a grocer's assistant employed at Cappoquin and Carlow and volunteered in response to Lord Kitchener's appeal. He was a nice-mannered and popular young

Lismore man, and his younger brother is also at the front serving with the Leinster's. Much sympathy is expressed with Mr and Mrs Glynn in their bereavement.

Grave or Memorial Reference: II.A.45. Cemetery: La Neuville British Cemetery, Corbie in France.

GOGGIN/GOGGINS, Michael: Rank: Private. Regiment or Service: Royal Irish Regiment. Unit: 'C' Coy. 2nd Battalion. Age at death: 42. Date of death: 24 May 1915. Service No: 4272. Born in Ballybricken, Co. Waterford. Enlisted in Wexford. Killed in action.

Supplementary information: Son of Patrick Goggins of Mary's Lane, Wexford and the late Catherine Goggins. Husband of Elizabeth Goggins of Wetherheld's Court, Bride Street. Wexford. A snippet from the *People,* 'A Wexford soldier, Private M. Goggin, Watery Lane, who served with the Royal Irish Regiment, is reported missing since 26th of May last.' Grave or Memorial Reference: Panel 33. Memorial: Ypres (Menin Gate) Memorial in Belgium.

GORBEY, Francis Rueben: Rank: Private. (Lance Corporal). Regiment or Service: Royal Irish Regiment. Unit: 1st Battalion. Date of death: 23 April 1915. Service No: 8930. Born in Villierstown, Co. Waterford. Enlisted in Aldershot, Hants while living in Carrick-on-Suir, Co. Tipperary. Killed in action. Age at death: 25.

Supplementary information: Son of Mrs E. Gorbey, of 9 The Terrace, Tranmore, Co. Waterford, and the late Mr J.W. Gorbey. From De Ruvigny's Roll of Honour:

Gorbey, Frances Rueben. Corporal, Number 8930, 1st Battalion, Royal Irish Regiment. Son of John W Gorbey, Constable (retired), Royal Irish Constabulary, now of 92 Main Street, Carrick-on-Suir, by his wife, Ellie, daughter of I. Huddy. Born in Villierstown, Waterford, 13 November 1889. Joined the 1st Battalion, Royal Irish Regiment at

Francis Rueben Gorbey.

Dublin, 22 March, 1906. Promoted Corporal, 15 February 1915. Served with the Expeditionary Force in France and Flanders. Killed in action at Hooge, near Ypres, 23 April 1915. Buried in the grounds of the Chateau at Hooge. He distinguished himself at Ypres, 15 February, 1915 by bringing in wounded under fire and blowing up an enemy mine. Two of his brothers, one in the Irish Guards and one a Corporal in the 7th Dragoon Guards, serving with the Expeditionary Force. Corporal F.R. Gorbey, had not met the latter brother for eight years, but a few days before he was killed they met during an action. A comrade wrote that; "A braver soldier or truer comrade never lived. He died as a brave man, with a smile on his face, and was mourned by his Regiment, as a true comrade. "His comrade placed a cross over his grave giving full particulars of how he died. His brother-in-Law, Company Sergeant-Major Charles Abbott, 1st Royal Irish Regiment, was also killed in action in May, 1915.

From the *Waterford News,* July 1917:

CARRICK-ON-SUIR FAMILY'S MILITARY RECORD
Company-Sergeant-Major T.J. Gorbey, of the 13th Middlesex Regiment, has won the D.C.M. Prior to becoming attached to the Middlesex Regiment he was in the 7th Dragoon Guards, and he has seen

action since the very beginning of the war. His brother, the late Corporal F. R. Gorbey, Royal Irish Regiment, also won the D.C.M., and was killed in action. A third brother, Pte. R.S. Gorbey, Irish Guards, was awarded the, Military Medal in September, 1916. All the above-named soldiers are sons of the late Mr J. W. Gorbey Carrick-on-Suir. On the reverse of his medal index card it says; –Hon Sec Nat Fed of ??? demob sailors and soldiers makes application o behalf of Mrs Gorbey, got 1915 star due to her late husband 23 July 1919.

See **ABBOTT, Charles Thomas**. He has no known grave but is listed on Panel 33 on the Ypres (Menin Gate) Memorial in Belgium.

GORMAN, Peter: Rank: Private. Regiment or Service: Welsh Regiment. Unit: 2nd Battalion. Date of death: 26 July 1916. Service No: 1763. Born in Waterford. Enlisted in Merthyr Tydfil while living in Kilshellan, Tipperary. Killed in action. He has no known grave but is listed on Pier 7 A and Face 10 A on the Thiepval Memorial in France

GOUGH, J. Michael: Rank: Sailor. Regiment or Service: Mercantile Marine. Unit: SS *Shimosa* (Liverpool). She was torpedoed and sunk by a German Submarine 220 miles off the West coast of Ireland. Age at death: 26. Date of death: 30 July 1917.

Supplementary information: Son of Alice Gough (*née* Power), of 21 Hennessy Road, Waterford, and the late James Gough. Born at Lisnakill, Butlerstown, Co. Waterford. He has no known grave but is listed on the Tower Hill Memorial in the UK.

GOUGH, Michael: Rank: Private. Regiment or Service: Irish Guards. Unit: 1st Battalion. Date of death: 27 September 1918. Service No: 11431. Born in Carrigerea, Co. Waterford. Enlisted in Merthyr, Glamorganshire while living in

Carrigerea, Co. Waterford. Killed in action. He is buried beside Wexfordman Private William Lacey who died on the same day and in the same unit. Grave or Memorial Reference: I.B.6. Cemetery: Sanders Keep Military Cemetery, Graincourt-Les-Havrincourt in France.

GOUGH, William: Rank: Private. Regiment or Service: Irish Guards. Unit: 1st Battalion. Date of death: 26 September 1916. Service No: 8459. Born in Ferrybank, Co. Waterford. Enlisted in Waterford. Killed in action. Grave or Memorial Reference: IV.H.48. Cemetery: Heilly Station Cemetery, Mericourt-L'Abbe in France.

GOULDING, Michael Joseph O'Neill: Rank: Able Seaman. Regiment or Service: Royal Naval Volunteer Reserve. Unit: HMS *Pembroke*. Age at death: 34. Date of death: 22 February 1919. Service No: London Z/7014.

Supplementary information: Son of Michael and Ellen O'Neill Goulding, of Hazeldene, London Road, Hertford, Herts. Husband of Bryde O'Neill Goulding (*née* Gough), of 21 Great George's Street, Waterford. Grave or Memorial Reference: Naval. R.C.6.272. Cemetery: Gillingham (Woodlands) Cemetery, UK.

GRANT, Edward: Rank: Gunner. Regiment or Service: Royal Horse Artillery and Royal Field Artillery. Date of death: 15 August 1917. Service No: 101149. Born in Waterford. Enlisted in Waterford. Died of wounds. From the *Waterford News*, August 1917:

ANOTHER YOUNG CITY MAN KILLED.

The list of Waterford victims of the great was is unfortunately, becoming longer day by day. This week we have to chronicle with regret the name of another young city man who has made the supreme sacrifice. This is Gunner E. Grant, R.F.A., nephew of the Messrs Wall, Thomas's Hill. Deceased, who was 22 years of age, joined the army about two years ago, and had seen much fighting, he having been previously wounded. On the 20th inst., he was dangerously wounded in France and he died in hospital on 23rd inst. Much sympathy is felt with his friends locally.

Grave or Memorial Reference: Special Memorial 2. Cemetery: Menin Road South Military Cemetery in Belgium.

GRANT, John: Rank: Refrigerator Greaser. Regiment or Service: Mercantile Marine. Unit: SS *Ausonia* (Liverpool). Steamship *Austinia* was torpedoed without warning and sunk by gunfire 620 miles W by S (true) from Fastnet. Age at death: 55. Date of death: 30 May 1918.

Supplementary information: Son of John Grant, and the late Bridget Grant. Husband of Mary Grant (*née* Walsh), of 13 The Glen, Waterford. Born in Waterford. He has no known grave but is listed on the Tower Hill Memorial in the UK.

GRANT, Keirnan. Rank: Cattleman. Regiment or Service: Mercantile Marine. Unit: SS *Coningbeg* (Glasgow). Torpedoed by German Submarine U-62. There were no survivors. U-62 surrendered in November 1918. Age at death: 17. Date of death: 18 December 1917.

Supplementary information: Son of Margaret Grant, of 3 Blake's Lane, Waterford, and the late Kiernan Grant. He has no known grave but is listed on the Tower Hill Memorial in the UK. He is also listed on the Formby-Coningbeg Memorial, Adelphi Quay in Waterford City.

GRANT, Maurice: Rank: Private. Regiment or Service: Northumberland Fusiliers. Unit: 26th Battalion (Tyneside Irish). Age at death: 32. Date of death: 1 July 1916. Service No: 26/240. Born in Waterford. Enlisted in Newcastle-on-Tyne. Killed in action.

Supplementary information: Husband of Mrs Rankin (formerly Grant), of 21 Baird Avenue, East Howdon, Northumberland. He has no known grave but is listed on Pier and Face 10B 11B and 12B on the Thiepval Memorial in France.

GRANT, Michael: Rank: Private. Regiment or Service: Royal Irish Regiment. Unit: 2nd Battalion. Date of death: 26 May 1915. Service No: 6732. Born in Butlerstown, Co. Waterford. Enlisted in Dublin while living in Liverpool. Died of wounds. Grave or Memorial Reference: I.A.37. Cemetery: Longuenesse (St Omer) Souvenir Cemetery in France.

GRANT, Patrick: Rank: Private. Regiment or Service: Irish Guards. Unit: 2nd Battalion. Date of death: 15 September 1916. Service No: 7482. Born in Ballybricken, Co. Waterford. Enlisted in Waterford. Killed in action. He has no known grave but is listed on Pier and Face 7D on the Thiepval Memorial in France.

GRANT, Richard: Rank: Private. Regiment or Service: East Lancashire Regiment. Unit: 1st Battalion. Age at death: 29. Date of death: 3 November 1914. Service No: 8798. Born in Trinity Without, Waterford. Enlisted in Waterford. Killed in action.

Supplementary information: Son of Richard and Catherine Grant, of 3 St Ignatius Street, Waterford. Grave or Memorial Reference: 5 and 6 on the Ploegsteert Memorial in Belgium.

GRAY, John: Rank: Driver. Regiment or Service: Royal Field Artillery. Unit: 8th Reserve Battery. Secondary Regiment: Labour Corps Secondary. Unit: transferred to (390180) 78th Coy. Age at death: 35. Date of death: 30 January 1920. Service No: 213138.

Supplementary information: Son of William and Mary Gray, of Waterford. Husband of Catherine Gray, of 1 Codrington Street, Liverpool. Grave or Memorial Reference: Screen Wall 1914/18 (RD. 278). Cemetery: Liverpool (Ford) Roman Catholic Cemetery in Liverpool.

GREEN, James: Rank: Private. Regiment or Service: Royal Irish Regiment. Unit: 2nd Battalion. Age at death: 29. Date of death: 19 October 1914. Service No: 4072. Born in Trinity

Without, Co. Waterford. Enlisted in Tipperary while living in Waterford. Killed in action.

Supplementary information: Brother of Mrs Mary Driscoll, of 5 Tanyard Arch, Waterford. He has no known grave but is listed on Panels 11 and 12 on the Le Touret Memorial in France.

GREEN, Thomas: Rank: Private. Regiment or Service: Royal Irish Regiment. Unit: 2nd Battalion. Age at death: 27. Date of death: 21 March 1918. Service No: 6430. Born in Ballybricken, Co. Waterford. Enlisted in Clonmel, County Tipperary while living in Waterford. Killed in action.

Supplementary information: Son of Michael Green, Tanyards Arch, Waterford. Grave or Memorial Reference: British. A.3. Cemetery: Ribemont Communal Cemetery Extension, Aisne in France.

GREY, Edward: Rank: Private. Regiment or Service: Irish Guards. Unit: 1st Battalion. Age at death: 22. Date of death: 12 September 1914. Service No: 4283. Born in Tallow, Co. Waterford. Enlisted in Fermoy, Co. Cork. Killed in action.

Supplementary information: Son of John and Ellen Grey, of Barrack St Tallow, Co. Waterford. He has no known grave but is listed on the La-Ferte-Sous-Jouarre Memorial in France.

GRIFFIN, Michael: Rank: Private. Regiment or Service: Royal Irish Regiment. Unit: 2nd Battalion. Age at death: 33. Date of death: 19 October 1914. Service No: 6212. Born in Tramore, Co. Waterford. Enlisted in Waterford while living in Tramore. Killed in action.

Supplementary information: Son of Joseph and Bridget Griffin, of Priest Road, Tramore. Husband of Sarah Griffin, of Upper Crobally, Tramore, Co. Waterford. Grave or Memorial Reference: 11 and 12 on the Le Touret Memorial in France.

GRIFFIN, Richard: Rank: Gunner. Royal Horse Artillery and Royal Field Artillery. Unit: 111th Battery, 24th Brigade. Age at death: 22. Date of death: 17 October 1918. Service No: 100418. Born in Kilmore, Tallow, Co. Waterford. Enlisted in Cork Killed in action.

Supplementary information: Son of Michael and Johanna Griffin. He has no known grave but is listed on Panel 3 and 4 on the Vis-En-Artois Memorial in France. Memorial.

GRIFFIN, Thomas: Rank: Able Seaman. Regiment or Service: Mercantile Marine. Unit: SS *Coningbeg* (Glasgow). Torpedoed by German Submarine U-62. There were no survivors. U-62 surrendered in November 1918. Age at death: 42. Date of death: 18 December 1917.

Supplementary information: Son of Ellen Grimn [*sic*], and Patrick Griffin. Husband of Agnes Griffin (*née* Jennings), of 20 Doyle Street, Waterford. He has no known grave but is listed on the Tower Hill Memorial in the UK. He is also listed (under **GRIFFEN**) on the Formby-Coningbeg Memorial, Adelphi Quay in Waterford City.

GUERINS, John: Rank: Private. Regiment or Service: Royal Munster Fusiliers. Unit: Depot. Age at death: 46. Date of death: 23 March 1915. Service No: 5189. Born in Cappoquin, Co. Waterford. Enlisted in Tralee while living in Dungarvan, Co. Waterford. Died at Home.

Supplementary information: Husband of Bridget Guerins, of Strand Street, Dungarvan. Grave or Memorial Reference: In the middle of the right section. Cemetery: Tralee Military Cemetery, Co. Kerry.

GUEST, FREDERICK. Rank: Rifleman. Regiment or Service: Rifle Brigade. Unit: 1st Battalion. Age at death: 19. Date of death: 28 April 1915. Service No: Z/805. Born in Cappoquin, Co. Waterford. Enlisted in Manchester while living in Manchester. Killed in action.

Supplementary information: Son of John Thomas and Sarah Ann Guest, of 1114 Eleventh Street, Trafford Park. Husband of Alice Guest, of 930 Ninth Street, Trafford Park, Manchester. He has no known grave but is listed on Panel 46-48 and 50 on the Ypres (Menin Gate) Memorial in Belgium.

GUIRY, John: Rank: Private. Regiment or Service: Royal Dublin Fusiliers. Unit: 2nd Battalion. Date of death: 1 July 1916. Service No: 21189. Born in Strabally, Waterford. Enlisted in Waterford. Killed in action. He has no known grave but is listed on Pier and face 15 A and 16 C on the Thiepval Memorial in France.

H

HACKETT, Henry Robert Theodore:
Rank: Second Lieutenant. Regiment or
Service: Royal Dublin Fusiliers. Unit: 1st
Battalion. Age at death: 19. Date of death: 2
November 1915. Killed in action.

Supplementary information: Youngest son
of the Revd H.M.M. Hackett, Vicar of St
Peter's, Belsize Park, London, and of Anna
Jane Hackett. He is listed on the Bishop Foy
School Memorial located in Christ Church
Cathedral (Church of Ireland), Henrietta
Street, Waterford. Born 12 May 1896 in
Hampstead, London. Father was Henry
Monck-Mason Hackett, born 1 March 1849
in Shankhill, Dublin. Mother was Anna Jane
Kennedy, born 23 April 1858 in India. From
'Our Heroes', 1916:

> Second Lieutenant H.R.S [*sic*].Hackett, 1st
> Battalion, Royal Irish [*sic*] Fusiliers, who
> was killed in action in the Dardanelles on
> November 2nd last, was the youngest son of
> the Very Rev. H.M.M. Hackett, lately dean
> of Waterford, but now Vicar of St Peter's,
> Belsize Park, Hampshire.

From the *Waterford News*, 1915:

A GALLANT FAMILY.
The Very Reverend Dr. Hackett, formerly
Protestant Dean of Waterford, has three
sons in the Army, and a fourth son is a
Chaplain to the forces. Dr Hackett's young-
est son is in the Royal Dublin Fusiliers.

From the *Waterford News*, November 1915:

LIEUTENANT HACKETT.
Lieutenant H.R.T. Hackett, Royal
Dublin Fusiliers, and youngest son of the
Reverend Dr H, M.M. Hackett, late Dean
of Waterford, has been killed in action at
the Dardanelles. The fighting in which
he fell took place on the 2nd inst. The late

Lieutenant Hackett, who was only 19 years
of age, passed into Sandhurst in October,
1914, and early in the present year he
received a commission in the Royal Dublin
Fusiliers, being for some time stationed at
Cork before going on active service. The
deceased young officer was well known in
Waterford, and his death at the beginning
of what was a promising career will occasion much sorrow amongst all who knew
him personally and also very sincere sympathy for his bereaved parents and the other
members of the family in their great loss.

Before entering Sandhurst Lieutenant
Hackett was educated in Templegrove,
Eastbourne, and afterwards in the Campbell
College, Belfast, where for three years he was
a member of the Officers Training Corps.
All of his four brothers are now serving
their country – the eldest as Chaplain to the
Forces in Boulogne, the second as Captain
in the 6th Gurkha Rifles, the third, in the
Canadian force, and the fourth in the Army
Service Corps.

Grave or Memorial Reference: II.G.1.
Cemetery: Azmak Cemetery, Suvla, Turkey.

HACKETT, James: Rank: Corporal and
Acting Corporal. Regiment or Service: Royal
army Medical Corps. Unit: Attached to the
1st Battalion The Queens (Royal West Surrey
Regiment). Date of death: 23 April 1917. Service
No: 2051. He won the Military Medal and is
listed in the *London Gazette*. Born in Waterford.
Enlisted in Dublin. Residence Cappoquin.
Killed in action. Grave or Memorial Reference:
Bay 10. Memorial: Arras Memorial in France.

HACKETT, William: Rank: Private.
Regiment or Service: Royal Irish Regiment.
Unit: 6th Battalion. Date of death: 9 September

1916. Service No: 9806. Born in Lismore, Co. Waterford. Enlisted in Cappoquin, Co. Waterford. Killed in action. He has no known grave but is listed on Pier and Face 3 A on the Thiepval Memorial in France.

HAIGH, John Caleb: Rank: Second Lieutenant. Regiment or Service: Royal Dublin Fusiliers. Unit: 3rd Battalion. Secondary Regiment: Royal Irish Rifles Secondary. Unit: Attached to 1st Battalion. Age at death: 28. Date of death: 2 October 1918. Killed in action.

Supplementary information: Son of late J. Haigh, of Kilmeaden, Waterford. Husband of Elsie Haigh, of 40 Ormiston Road, Greenwich, London.

TO JOIN THE ROYAL FUSILIERS.

During the week Mr Jack Brophy, C.R. son of Mrs Brophy, Lombard Street, Waterford to join the Sportsmen's Battalion of the Royal Fusiliers, at present stationed in London. A number of his friends assembled at the station previous to his departure by the Rosslare express to wish him good luck. Amongst other Waterford men who have joined the same Regiment is Mr John Haig [sic], who was attached to the clerical staff of Messrs Henry Denny and Sons, Penrose Lane, and who was assistant organist at Christ Church Cathedral.

Public Records Office, Kew, Kent, File ref: WO339/106992 200239:

Haigh, John Caleb, 2nd Lieutenant. Born 29-03-1890 at Kilmeaden, the only child of Joseph and Mary Jane Haigh of Kilmeaden, Waterford. The 1911 Census states that his father, born in England, was blind and his mother, born in Co. Cork, was a sub-postmistress. John's occupation was stated as an organist. Educated at Bishop Foy High School, Waterford. Enlisted as Pte 2859 in 24th R. Fusiliers at Waterford, 21. 1. 1915. Clerk, single, height 5 foot 9 inches, weight 123 pounds, chest 33–35 inches, Church of Ireland, vision

6/24 and 6/24, but a note stated that he had very good sight 'with glasses'. Next of kin mother.

Admitted Gidea Park Camp, 4 to 8 May 1915, with measles. Transferred to 33rd Divisional Cyclist Corps 30 July 1915. Transferred back to 24th Royal Fusiliers 14 October 1915. Home service 28 January 1915 to 14 November 1915. To BEF 15 November 1915. To hospital 'in the field' 4 March 1916, rejoining his unit 10 March 1916. Admitted Casualty Clearing Station 18 October 1916 with varicose ulcer right leg. Embarked Boulogne–England on the St David, 20 October. Admitted to the Italian Hospital, Queen Square, London, the next day and remained there until 21 November. Transferred to 4th London General Hospital until 25 January 1917. Posted 6th R. Fusiliers 30 April 1917.

Applied for a commission, 20 April 1917, requesting infantry, preferably 13th R. Fusiliers. Single. Father noted as deceased and had been manager of a Woolen Business. To No. 13 Officer Cadet Battalion at Newmarket, 8 September 1917. Discharged to a commission in 3rd RDF, 17 December-1917. Home service 21 October 1916 to 17 February 1917. Reposted to 1st RIR 25 April 1918. Wounded 11 September 1918. Killed in action 2. 10. 1918. A War Office telegram was sent to 'Mrs Haigh', 6 October, at Kilmeaden. Another note says 'we have no record of this officer's body having been recovered. ' Estate to wife Elsie, address then shown as 40 Ormiston Road, Greenwich, London SE10. There was some confusion here – the WO didn't seem to know whether they were dealing with the mother or the widow. A register form dated 8 October 1918 shows next of kin as 'Mrs Elsie Haigh (wife), Kilmeaden, Co. Waterford.' A War Office letter to her dated 12 February 1919, notified that Haigh was buried about 500 yards south-south-west of Panemolen, north of Gheluwe, east-south-east of Ypres.

The grave was marked with an inscribed wooden cross. A further letter, 20 August 1920, informed her that the body had been exhumed and moved to Dadizeele New British Cemetery, Moorslede, West-Vlaanderen, V.B.1.

Grave or Memorial Reference: V.B.1. Cemetery: Dadizeele New British Cemetery in Belgium. He is also listed on the Bishop Foy School Memorial in the Church of Ireland Cathedral, Henrietta Street, Waterford City.

HALES, William: Rank: Private. Regiment or Service: Canadian Infantry (Central Ontario Regiment). Unit: 19th Battalion. Age at death: 24. Date of death: 10 November 1918 Service No: 124752. Data from attestation papers:

What is your present address? 164 Baltimore West, Detroit, Michigan, USA.

In what Town, Township or Parish, and in what Country were you born? Waterford, Ireland.

What is the name of your next of kin? Bridget Hales.

What is the address of your next of kin? Brown Street, Portlaw, Waterford, Ireland.

What is the relationship of your next of kin? Mother.

What is the date of your birth? 12 June 1895.

What is your trade or calling? Labourer.

Are you married? No.

Do you now belong to the Active Militia? Yes. If so, state particulars of former service?. 2 months, 21st Guard Company, Windsor.

Apparent age: 18 years.

Height: 5 Ft, 10 ½. Ins.

Girth when fully expanded: 39 Ins

Range of expansion: 4Ins

April 21st-1916.

Supplementary information: Son of William and Bridget Hales, of Brown Street, Portlaw, Co. Waterford. Grave or Memorial Reference: X.A.41. Cemetery: Mons (Bergen) Communal Cemetery in Belgium.

HALLY, John: Rank: Able Seaman. Regiment or Service: Royal Naval Volunteer Reserve. Unit: Hawke Battalion. R.N. Div. Age at death: 26. Date of death: 13 November 1916. Service No: Tyneside Z/1176.

Supplementary information: Son of Patrick and Margaret Hally, of Fairbrook, Kilmeaden, Co. Waterford. He has no known grave but is listed on Pier and Face 1A of the Thiepval Memorial in France.

HALPIN, Patrick: Rank: Private. Regiment or Service: Royal Irish Regiment. Unit: 1st Battalion. Date of death: 9 March 1915. Service No: 10336. Born in Trinity Without, Waterford. Enlisted in Waterford. Died. Grave or Memorial Reference: III.A.27. Cemetery: Lille Southern Cemetery, Nord in France.

HALPIN, William: Rank: Private. Regiment or Service: Royal Irish Fusiliers. Unit: 1st Battalion. Age at death: 35. Date of death: 25 August 1916. Service No: 16203. Previously he was with the Royal Irish Regiment where his number was 1190. Born in Waterford. Enlisted in Waterford. Died of wounds.

Supplementary information: Brother of James Halpin, of 8 Buttermilk Lane, Waterford. Grave or Memorial Reference: IX.D.1A. Cemetery: Lijssenthoek Military Cemetery in Belgium.

HAMILTON, Henry Edward Redmond: Rank: Captain. Regiment or Service: Canadian Engineers. Unit: 3rd Battalion, Canadian Railway Troops. Date of death: 19 May 1917. Born: 6 June 1880. Next of kin listed as Margaret Farron Hamilton (Wife), 63 Douglas Lodge, Vancouver, British Columbia. Born in Waterford. Enlisted in Vancouver, British Columbia on 11 September 1916 while living in 63 Douglas Lodge, Vancouver. Occupation on enlistment: Civil Engineer. Age at enlistment: 36. He had prior military experience with the 72nd Seaforth Highlanders of Canada. Completed his Officers' Declaration Paper in September 1916 for the

239th Battalion C.E.F. Killed in action by shell-fire. From a Canadian Newspaper:

CAPTAIN HAMILTON DEAD IN FRANCE.
Vancouver, B. C., May 28. Word has been received here of the death in France of Captain H. E. Hamilton, of the railway Construction Corporation. He was a Civil Engineer, and was connected with the construction of the Grand Trunk Pacific Railway. He was a cousin of John Redmond, the Irish leader.

Grave or Memorial Reference: X.B.2. Cemetery: Villers Station Cemetery in France.

HANAN, George: Rank: Private. Regiment or Service: Royal Dublin Fusiliers Unit: A Company, 10th Battalion. Age at death: 39. Date of death: 13 November 1916. Service No: 25223. Born in Stradbally Waterford. Enlisted in Dublin. Killed in action.
Supplementary information: Son of the Ven. Archdeacon Denis Hanan, D.D. and Mrs Louisa Hanan. Formerly served in Ceylon Planters' Rifle Corps. Grave or Memorial Reference: IV.A.29. Cemetery: Ancre British Cemetery, Beaumont-Hamel in France.

HANNAN/HANNON, John: Rank: Private. Regiment or Service: Royal Irish Regiment. Unit: 6th Battalion. Age at death: 28. Date of death: 3 May 1916. Service No: 2270 (Soldiers died in the Great War), 6/2270 (The Commonwealth War Graves Commission). Enlisted in Dungarvan, Co. Waterford. Killed in action.
Supplementary information: Son of Patrick and Bridget Hannan, of Youghal Road, Dungarvan, Co. Waterford. From the *Waterford News*, May 1916:

KILLED ON THE BATTLEFIELD.
Among those returned as having been killed on the battlefield are the names of the following Dungarvan men: Messrs Hannon, O'Connor, and Flynn. Hannon

was a son of a respected employee of the Urban District Council, a man who for years possessed the confidence of the council in all their outdoor works, and to him and his family the people of Dungarvan offer their sympathy. Flynn is from Ballinacourty, a most promising young man. He was the son of a well-known resident of the pretty village, and a man who did a hero's part at the time of the wreck of the "Moresby" in Dungarvan harbour. The poor man has received the condolence of all the neighbours, and he has, too, the widespread sympathy of the populace.

Neither Flynn nor O'Connor appear in any of the army war dead databases of April and May 1916. Grave or Memorial Reference: I.H.5. Cemetery: Dud Corner Cemetery, Loos in France.

HANNIGAN, John: Rank: Private Regiment or Service: Australian Infantry, A.I.F. Unit: 16th Battalion. Date of death: 12 December 1916. Service No: 67. Enlisted 8 September 1914 in Freemantle. Hospitalised 20 August 1915 with a gun shot (he later told doctors it was a shell burst) injury to the right lung in Gallipoli and was taken out of the area with a 'weak chest'. Sent by Hospital Ship to College Hospital in Chelsea, England with Bronchial Catarrh. Two months later he was diagnosed with Tuberculosis of the chest and discharged. Lettergram dated 16 December 1916:

BASE RECORDS.
DEFENCE MELBOURNE.
Lettergram number thirty eight eighty John Hannigan die of phthisis at number eighth Australia General Hospital on twelfth instant stop he was originally number sixty seven of sixteenth battalion and returned to Australia on thirteenth December nineteen fifteen stop was discharged on pension on fourteenth July last stop please inform next of kin father T Hannigan Tramore Co. Waterford Ireland religion Roman Catholic. 2.15pm.

March. 10 1925

Dear Sir Recivesed your letter refferring to 1914 and 15 Star which My Son John Hannigan ex Private 6716 Battalion is entitiled To my address is the same. I am still waiting for naturely entiteled to me your respectfully, Thomas Hannigan Main st Tramore Co Waterford Ireland

John Hannigan.

Data from attestation papers:

In or near what Parish or Town were you born? Tramore, Waterford.

Are you a natural born British subject or a Naturalised British subject? British.

What is your age? 25 years 3 months, 1889.

What is your trade or calling? Ships Fireman.

Are you married? No.

Who is your next of kin? Minnie Hannigan, Tramore, Waterford.

Have you ever been convicted by the Civil Power? No.

Age: 26 years, 3 months.

Height 5 feet, 8 inches.

Weight, 133 lbs.

Chest measurement: 34-36 inches.

Complexion, dark.

Eyes: brown.

Hair: brown.

Religious denomination: R.C.

His father applied for a pension but was refused as he had 'adequate means of support'

From the *West Australia* 14 December 1915:

Hannigan The friends of the late Private John Hannigan, of the 16th Battalion, A.I.F. are respectfully invited to follow his remains to the place of internment. The Roman Catholic portion of the Fremantle Cemetery. The military Cortege will leave Messrs Arthur E Davies and Co's Private Montuary, Freemantle, This (Thursday) Morning the 14th inst, at 10 o/c.

FUNERAL OF A GALLIPOLI SOLDIER.

Private John Hannigan, late stretcher bearer of the 16th battalion, A.I.F., died on the ___ at the No 8 Australian Hospital, Fremantle in his thirty first year. At the memorable landing and through the campaign on the Gallipoli Peninsula owing to the good work and bravery of the stretcher bearers the section of our army has cover itself with glory, and the bravery of the deceased was most conspicuous and recognised by all members of his Battalion, it was quite a common occurrence for his to deny himself necessities so as to give them to a wounded comrade. A wreath which was sent by the returned soldiers of the 16th battalion bears the following inscription: "In memory of the bravest and best of the Battalion." Private Hannigan, who was shot through the lungs, was returned to Fremantle, but from the first it was recognised that he could not live very long. Fortunately he was able to go about and his happy and cheerful ___ endeared him to all who made his acquaintance. The long military cortege headed by the firing party and band arrived from Messrs Arthur E Davies and Co's private mortuary on Thursday, and proceeded to the local Roman Catholic cemetery, where the remains were interred. At the conclusion of the service which was conducted by the Rev Father J Callan, O.M.I, three volleys were fired and the 'Last Post' sounded by the bugler. The pall and coffin bearers were sergeant James, Lance-Corporal Vanteh, Privates Woodall, Swindells and Joare (16th Battalion), and Vincent (11th Battalion), all returned soldiers. The firing party, which was supplied from the details camp, Karrabatts was under Sergeant Wood of the Returned Soldiers Guard. The Blackboy Hill Band was in charge of the Bandmaster Halvarsen. The mourners were numerous returned soldiers of the 11th and 16th Battalions. The ___ was under the supervision of Colonel L.L. Tetney.

Grave or Memorial Reference: R.C.CC.613. Cemetery: Fremantle cemetery, Australia.

HANNIGAN, Patrick: Rank: Sergeant and Acting Sergeant. Regiment or Service: Connaught Rangers. Unit: 2nd Battalion. Age at death: 24. Date of death: 3 November 1914. Service No: 9095. Born in Waterford. Enlisted in Waterford while living in Waterford. Died of wounds.

Supplementary information: Son of James and Bridget Hannigan, of 11 Spring Gardens Alley, Waterford. From the *Waterford News*, 1915:

WATERFORD SOLDIER WOUNDED IN THE DARDANELLES.

Mr James Hannigan, of Spring Garden Alley, Waterford, has just received from the Defence Department of the Australian Commonwealth a letter stating that his son, Nicholas Hannigan of the 1st Battalion of the Australian Imperial Forces was wounded in action at the Dardanelles.

Nicholas Hannigan left Maidstone, Kent, about three years ago for Australia, and he returned to Europe with the Expeditionary Force which was ordered to the Dardanelles. A younger brother (Patrick) was killed at Ypres on November 3rd.

Mr James Hannigan has indeed had his full share of trouble for the past six months. His eldest daughter, a nun at Chittagong, died on March 19th.

From the *Waterford News*, 1914:

WATERFORD SOLDIER KILLED IN ACTION.

Mr J Hannigan, of Spring Gardens, was informed by the War Office yesterday that his son, Corporal Patrick Hannigan, Connaught Rangers, died on November 3rd of wounds received on the battlefield. The late Corporal Hannigan joined the Connaught Rangers eight years ago. Another son of Mr Hannigan who is in the Field Artillery was severely wounded and is at present in Leicester Hospital.

Grave or Memorial Reference: II.A.29. Cemetery: Ypres Town Cemetery Extension in Belgium.

HANNIGAN, Robert: Rank: Gunner. Regiment or Service: Royal Field Artillery. Unit: 14th Battery. 4th Brigade. Date of death: 18 July 1916. Service No: 5652. Born in Waterford and enlisted there also. Died in Mesopotamia.

Supplementary information: Husband of Annie Hannigan, of Town Wall, Carrick-on-Suir, Co. Tipperary. Grave or Memorial Reference: VII.C.7. Cemetery: Amara War Cemetery in Iraq.

HANRAHAN, J.: Rank: Private. Regiment or Service: Machine Gun Corps (Infantry). Date of death: 2 July 1920. Service No: 49045 Grave or Memorial Reference: F.A.16. Cemetery: Ballynaneashagh (St Otteran's) Catholic Cemetery, Co. Waterford.

HARE, Herbert Patrick: Rank: Lieutenant. Regiment or Service: Australian Field Artillery. Unit: 3rd Brigade. Age at death: 39. Date of death: 8 August 1916. Enlisted in Mount Morgan, Queensland, 24 August 1914. Died of wounds received the previous day (right arm) at the 3rd Casualty Clearing Station in France. Son of Henry and Maria Hare. Husband of E. Gladys Hare, of 14 Upper Arthur Street, Hobart,

Tasmania. Native of Hobart, Tasmania. Rose through the ranks to gain his commission to Lieutenant on 20 September 1916. Data from attestation papers:

In or near what Parish or Town were you born? Waterford, Ireland.

Are you a natural born British subject or a Naturalised British subject? Yes.

What is your age? 33 years 3 months.

What is your trade or calling? Minister.

Are you, or have you been an Apprentice? If so where, to whom, and for what period? Yes, Euguicot(?) 3 years.

Are you married? Yes.

Who is your next of kin? Eloise Gladys Hare (wife).

Do you now belong to, or have you ever served in, His Majesty's Army, the Marines, the Militia, the Militia Reserve, the Territorial Reserve, Royal Navy or Colonial Forces?, If so, state which, and if not now serving, state cause of discharge Southern Tasmanian Artillery, 3 years. Southern Tasmanian Infantry, D Company 2 years, Chaplain (Queensland) 1 yr 6 months.

Have you stated the whole, if any, of your previous service? Yes.

Age: 33 years, 3 months. Height: 6 feet, ½ inches. Weight: 13st 11 lbs. Chest measurement: 38 ½ -41 ½ inches. Complexion: dark. Eyes: brown. Hair: black curly Religious denomination: Methodist.

Copy of Will; -

'I leave and bequeath all I posess wheresoever and whatsoever to my wife Eloise Gladys Hare "Derwent View", Lansdowne Crescent, Hobart, Tasmania, and direct that a trunk and suitcase containing only personal belongings shall be sent to my wife, the said trunk and case being at Thos, Cook's, London. H.L.H. H.V. H.
April 17th 1916. H. P Hare
Lieutenant First Australian Artillery Brigade.

Two pensions were successfully applied for. The first by his wife, Eloise Gladys Hare who received a pension of £3 10s per fortnight from 19 October 1916 and the second by his adopted daughter Mildred Hope Sands who received a pension of 20s per fortnight from 19 October 1916 through her guardian, Eloise Gladys Hare. His brother Sergeant Major Harry Hare received two distinguished service orders. It also says that he was born in Hobart, Tasmania.

Grave or Memorial Reference: I.B.60. Cemetery: Puchevillers British Cemetery in France.

HARNEY, James: Rank: Able Seaman. Regiment or Service: Mercantile Marine. Unit: SS *Gretaston* (Glasgow). Sunk in the Atlantic possibly by a submarine, twenty-nine lives lost. Age at death: 28. Date of death: 11 April 1917.

Supplementary information: Son of Michael and Bridget Harney. Husband of Mary Ann Dooley (formerly Harney, *née* Sheridan), of 15 Earle Place, Cardiff. Born at Passage East, Co. Waterford. He has no known grave but is listed on the Tower Hill Memorial in the UK.

HARNEY, John: Rank: Sapper. Regiment or Service: Royal Engineers. Unit: 156th Field Coy. Age at death: 31. Date of death: 23 March 1918. Service No: 35968. Previously he was with the Royal Dublin Fusiliers where his number was 27952. Mentioned in Despatches. Born in Ballybricken, Co. Waterford. Enlisted in Waterford. Died of wounds.

Supplementary information: Husband of the late Ellen Harney (*née* Nolan), of Crobally, Tramore, Co. Waterford. Grave or Memorial Reference: I.E.13. Cemetery: Roye New British Cemetery in France.

HARRINGTON, John: Rank: Corporal. Regiment or Service: Royal Irish Regiment. Unit: 2nd Battalion. Age at death: 41. Date of death: 9 May 1915. Service No: 7131. Born in Trinity Without, Waterford. Enlisted in Waterford. Killed in action.

Supplementary information: Son of Michael Harrington, of Ballybrucken, Waterford.

Husband of Mary Harrington, of 12 Harrington's Lane, Waterford. From the *Waterford News*, 1914:

LATE VOLUNTEER INSTRUCTOR WOUNDED.

Intimation has reached his wife that Private John Harrington, of the Royal Irish Regiment, who up to the time of his departure for the war was an instructor of the Waterford Volunteers, was wounded at the battle of Mons. He is expected to arrive in England shortly.

He has no known grave but is listed on Panel 33 on the Ypres (Menin Gate) Memorial in Belgium.

HARRIS, James: Rank: Sergeant. Regiment or Service: Irish Guards. Unit: 1ˢᵗ Battalion. Age at death: 21. Date of death: 18 May 1915. Service No: 4185. Born in Dungarvan, Co. Waterford. Enlisted in Cork. Killed in action.

Supplementary information: Son of William and Catherine Harris, of 49 Poleberry, Waterford. From the *Waterford News*, January 1915:

James Harris.

Mrs Harris, of 45 Poleberry, Waterford, has received some interesting letters from her sons, Sergeant Benjamin Harris, Royal Irish Regiment and Sergeant James Harris of the Irish Guards (Second Division), both of whom went out with the Expeditionary Force at the outbreak of the war. The first-named has been a prisoner of war in Germany for some time, and the later is still fighting at the front with the Irish Guards.

Sergeant Harris, of the Guards, in the course of his letters, mentions the names of several Waterfordmen whom he met at the front. Constable Shortall, of Ferrybank, who also went out with the Irish Guards at the commencement of the war, was, he said, "The first man of ours to be wounded, he was hit on the left knee with the cap of a shell." In the course of another letter he states that he met Richard Harrison, of the Irish Guards, son of Sergeant-at-Mace Harrison, and Mr Jack Mitchell, son of Mrs Mitchell, Bath Street, who was well-known in rugby and association football circles in Waterford previous to joining the army. The latter has been given a commission as Second Lieutenant. In one of his letters, Sergeant Harris states: "I have seen some of the British papers, and they give a very good idea of what is going on. Thanks very much for the parcels of cigarettes and coffee, which I received all right. The coffee is the very thing I want out here, so you might send me an occasional tin when you think of it. It is very handy when you are in the trenches. Whatever chance we have of getting hot water, we have no chance of getting tea. I was speaking to Jack Mitchell yesterday. He is a Sergeant now (has since been promoted Second Lieutenant) and is in our division. We were talking for a long time all about Waterford. I suppose you read in the papers that we had a bit of a hard time. We lost a lot of men. The Germans charged us one day. They came in batches of about fifty, we cut up about twelve batches of them before we retired, and when we retired they got their artillery on us and shelled us, dropping about thirty shells a minute. It was something terrible to see the men getting killed and wounded, but I was one of the lucky birds." In another letter he states: "We are busy keeping those blokes on the move. We are in a position now seven days. We are opposed by about 3, 000 Germans, but we are giving them hell. The place about us is like the Park on a hot day with all the fellows lying about dead. "

In the last letter which Mrs Harris received from her son James, which is dated 17th January, he stated that he is in hospital having his teeth attended to, but otherwise is well, 'Mrs Harris has also allowed us to see some postcards and letters which she received from her son Benjamin, a Sergeant in the Royal Irish Regiment, who was taken prisoner by the Germans and is at present in a prison camp in Germany. In a postcard dated 12-10-1914, he wrote; "We are allowed to receive parcels weighing up to 10lbs, and I want you to send me some cigarettes, books, and a pack of cards. They would be a God-send." This postcard was addressed from "English Camp, Sennelager, via Paderborn, Germany." In another post-card dated 5th January, 1915, and addresses from "No 5 Kompagnie, Gifangenenlager, Germany," he states that he got the clothing and other parcels sent on the 28 November. "You will see by my address that I am after shifting from Sennelager. This is a nice place. I met several chaps who live opposite us, by the name of Sullivan. Don't be afraid to send me anything, as they generally arrive safe. I met a lot of my platoon here who were supposed to be killed, and I saw my name in a newspaper as unofficially missing." In another letter he stated that, on the whole, they were being fairly well treated, and in one dated 5th January, he stated:- "I received a parcel which you sent on the 9-12-14. The contents were plum pudding, 2 boxes of cocoa, 1 of coffee and sweets. The parcel was minus cigarettes. Any parcels you sent to the other camp will arrive in due course. This is a nice place; we have very good weather, better I believe, than they have at the front. When did you hear from Jim? Some of his Regiment (Irish Guards) are here. "

From the *Waterford News*, 1915:

TO THE EDITOR OF *WATERFORD NEWS*.
Dear Sir,
So many strange things happen in war time that one learns to take them as they come, but, although I've had lots of sur-prises since I left Dublin in August last, nothing really surprised me more than to find a copy of the *Waterford News* of 29th January in a tiny shop about four miles from here about ten days ago.

I was out exercising a newly-arrived horse that afternoon, and when return-ing to camp I dismounted at a shop in the village mentioned to purchase some matches. I saw some papers on the counter of the shop, and there I found the "News" amongst the French papers.

Needless to say I pounced on it at once and told the lady of the shop of the pecu-liar coincidence. She was just as pleased as I, and gave me the paper as a souve-nir. From what I could gather from her, it seems to have been left there by some troopers who passed through the day before. By the description the lady gave me, I think the Regiment must have been the Connaught Rangers. I can assure you I was extremely grateful to my unknown friend who so kindly left me latest home news for me.

I was very glad to see the letters of Sergeant Harris in the "News". I quite agree with what he says about the stay-at-homes who are too busy looking after their own pleasure to be able to give us a hand.

I can't boast of having seen as much as Sergeant Harris, but what I have seen is quite enough to make one resolve to see the thing through to a successful finish, no matter what the cost or how long it takes to do it.

Ever since August last both Sergeant Harris and I have been trying to see each other, but although we've often been near enough, we've never met. Still, I am of a very optimistic nature, so will still keep an eye out for him.

I forget to mention that I am in the Special Service Squadron of the South Irish Horse that came out from home on 17th August last. We have been employed as escort to the General of the 1st Army Corps since the beginning, and were only 12 miles from Mons when the retreat began.

We have had our hardships, just the same as all the other troops, and at Ypres, in October-November, we were kept at it night and day as dispatch riders.

None of the Irish Army Corps were sorry when the French army took over our positions during the middle of November and left us get back to Hazebrouck for a rest and a rest of clothing, etc.

Like all the cavalry, we are now having a rather easy time of it, but once the Germans are on the run it won't be the fault of the cavalry brigades, both English, French, and Indian if they are not kept on the move.

Pardon me for having occupied so much of your paper, but I thought the incident of the paper one which might interest you.

Yours truly.

J. W. Flynn.

See also under **GEARY, Patrick:** Grave or Memorial Reference: 4 on the Le Touret Memorial in France.

HARRISON, John F.: Rank: Sergeant. Regiment or Service: Leinster Regiment. Unit: 7th Battalion. Age at death: 25. Date of death: 09 September 1916. Service No: 2760. Born in Ballybricken, Co. Waterford. Enlisted in Waterford while living in Waterford. Killed in action.

Supplementary information: Son of John and Margaret Harrison, of 24 Ballybricken, Waterford. From the The *Waterford News*, September 1916:

THE ROLL OF HONOUR;

Several letters have been received in Waterford from soldiers at the front annoucing the death of Sergeant John Harrison, Leinster Regiment, son of Sergeant-at-Mace Harrison. Sergeant Harrison was quite a young man. He was in the South Irish Horse for some years, and during the special recruiting campaign in Waterford in March, 1915, he joined the cadet corps of the Leinster Regiment. He has been for some time at the front, and, although his death is not officially announced, there appears to be little doubt but that he has been killed, as the writer of one of the letters referred to stated that poor Jack Harrison was killed alongside of him, and that he only lived a short time after being struck. Amongst all who knew John Harrison he was very popular, and his death will be generally regretted. Deep sympathy will also be felt with his widow, father mother and other relatives in their bereavement.

From the *Munster Express*, 23 September 1916:

SERGEANT-AT-MACE'S SON
REPORTED KILLED.

Mr John Harrison, Sergeant-at-Mace of the Waterford Corporation, has received a letter from a soldier in France stating that his son, Sergeant John Harrison, of the Leinster Regiment has been killed in the recent big push in the Somme. Sergeant Harrison, who was 25 years of age, joined the 7th Leinster's last year. He was a popular and respected young Waterford man, the utmost sympathy is extended to his bereaved parents. In a letter written by a comrade by whose side he fell, the writer stated that out of his Regiment, the 7th Leinster's, only 100 men were left, and that the writer was the only Waterford man remaining.

He is also mentioned in the attached to **HARRIS, James:** Sergeant. He has no known grave but is listed on Pier and Face 16 C of the Thiepval Memorial in France.

HART, John: Rank: Seaman. Regiment or Service: Royal Naval Reserve. Unit: HMS *Clan McNaughton*. Age at death: 40. Date of death: 3 February 1915. Service No: 1383D.

Supplementary information: Son of Patrick and Margaret Hart, of Tramore. Husband of Nellie Hart, of Patrick Street, Tramore, Waterford. Grave or Memorial Reference: 8 on the Plymouth Naval Memorial, UK.

HART, Patrick: Rank: Private. Regiment or Service: Royal Irish Fusiliers. Unit: 7/8th Battalion. Date of death: 27 July 1917. Service No: 16536. Formerly he was with the Royal Irish Regiment where his number was 1500. Born in Waterford. Born in Waterford. Killed in action. Grave or Memorial Reference: V.A.29. Cemetery: Vlamertinghe New Military Cemetery in Belgium.

HARTE, James: Rank: Fireman and Trimmer. Regiment or Service: Mercantile Marine. Unit: SS *Treveal* (St Ives). Age at death: 36. Date of death: 4 February 1918. Steamship *Treveal* was wrecked off the coast of Dorset with the loss of thirty-six of her crew.

Supplementary information: Son of Elizabeth Harte, of 2 Smith's Place, Waterford, and the late William Harte. He has no known grave but is listed on the Tower Hill Memorial in the UK.

HARTERY, Michael: Rank: Private. Regiment or Service: Royal Irish Regiment. Unit: 2nd Battalion. Age at death: 23. Date of death: 5 July 1916. Service No: 7963. Born in Ballybricken, Co. Waterford. Enlisted in Waterford while living in Waterford. Killed in action.

Supplementary information: Son of Edward and Margaret Hartery, of 11 Convent Hill, Waterford. The *Waterford News*, July 1916:

The casualty lists during the past few days include many Waterford men. Private M. Hartery, who has been wounded, was well known in local sporting circles. He joined the Cadet Corps of the Royal Irish Regiment at the time of the special recruiting campaign here. A comrade of his wrote home stating that he had been killed but his relatives were much relieved at subsequently receiving official notification that he had been wounded and was in hospital.

From the *Waterford News*, August 1916:

WATERFORD MEN IN THE CASUALTY LIST.
It is feared that Private M Hartery, Cadet Corps, Royal Irish Regiment, has been killed. His mother received a notification that he had been wounded and was in hospital, the particular hospital not being named. A pal of his wrote home, however, some time ago stating that he had been killed, and yesterday his mother received a letter from Private Hennessy, Waterford, who stated that he was present at his burial.

The following is a letter which Mrs Hartery, Mayor's Walk, mother of Private Hartery referred to above, has received from the Reverend W. Fitzmaurice, Chaplain to the Forces:

2nd Battalion, the Royal Irish Regiment.
B.E.F., France.
Dear Mrs Hartery,
I am sorry to keep you so long without a reply to your letter, for I have so many to answer and must take them in rotation. Yes, it is true that your son was killed. I myself found his body after the fight, and we buried him together with others of his comrades near the spot where he was killed. We put up a cross with his name on it, and the grave will be cared for. The Graves Registration Commission will be able to tell you all about the locality of the grave after the war, as it has been reported to them, and they are charged with the care of it. Your son was killed on the morning of July 5th. Whether he was

killed instantly, I cannot say, as I was not near him at the time, but some distance behind. From the position in which I found him, and from his nearness to the enemy (he was only a few yards from the wood he was attacking) I should think he was killed almost instantly. Anyhow, he was a good lad and went to his duties, and a few minutes before he was killed he received the General Absolution from me together with the rest of his platoon, so you have nothing to be anxious about on that score. I offer you my sincerest sympathy in your loss. He has been remembered several times already in the Holy Sacrifice of the Mass, which I have offered up for those who were killed in the battle.

Yours sincerely.

W. Fitzmaurice, SJ., C.F.

A report on the court case where John Lannigan was charged with murder of Private William Hartery can be found in the *Waterford News* of February 1915. He was a member of the Volunteer Corps and may be a relative. Grave or Memorial Reference: IV.H. 8. Cemetery: Danzig Alley British Cemetery, Mametz in France.

HARTLEY, John: (Listed as **HARTLEY, James** in Soldiers died in the Great War and Ireland Memorial Records) Rank: Private. Regiment or Service: Welsh Regiment. Unit: 1st Battalion. Age at death: 44. Date of death: 18 February 1915. Service No: 1988 (Soldiers died in the Great War), 1998 (The Commonwealth War Graves Commission). Born in Ferrybank, Co. Waterford. Enlisted in Carmarthen while living in Liverpool. Died of wounds.

Supplementary information: Son of Edward and Ellen Hardey. Grave or Memorial Reference: C.13. Cemetery: Ramparts Cemetery, Lille Gate, Ieper in Belgium.

HARTLEY, Nicholas: Rank: Boatswain (Bosun). Regiment or Service: Mercantile

Marine. Unit: SS *Queen* (London). Sunk by German submarine U-52 off Cape Villano. Age at death: 51. Date of death: 28 June 1918.

Supplementary information: Son of the late Edward and Ellen Hartley. Husband of Margaret Hartley (*née* Moloney), of 62 Mayors Walk, Waterford. Born in Waterford. He has no known grave but is listed on the Tower Hill Memorial in the UK.

HARTLEY, Patrick: Rank: Gunner. Regiment or Service: Royal Horse Artillery and Royal Field Artillery. Unit: B Battery, 54th Brigade. Date of death: 22 May 1917. Service No: 76903. Enlisted in Waterford while living in Waterford. Died of wounds in Salonika. Grave or Memorial Reference: VII.D.3. Cemetery: Struma Military Cemetery in Greece.

HARTY, John: Rank: Private. Regiment or Service: Royal Irish Regiment. Unit: 2nd Battalion. Date of death: 7 February 1915. Service No: 4053. Born in St Patrick's, Waterford. Enlisted in Kilkenny. Killed in action. He has no known grave but is listed on Panel 33 on the Ypres (Menin Gate) Memorial in Belgium.

HASKER, Edward: Rank: Company Quartermaster Sergeant. Regiment or Service: Yorkshire Regiment. Unit: 'A' Coy. 11th Battalion. Age at death: 48. Date of death: 16 October 1915. Service No: 3677. Born in Sunderland. Enlisted in Richmond while living in Newcastle-on-Tyne. Died at home.

Supplementary information: Husband of Margaret Taylor (formerly Hasker), of Ballymacan, Dunmore East, Co. Waterford. Grave or Memorial Reference: E.C.414. Cemetery: Newcastle-Upon-Tyne (St Andrews and Jesmond) Cemetery, UK.

HASSEY, James: Rank: Private. Regiment or Service: Royal Dublin Fusiliers. Unit: 1st Battalion. Born in Waterford. Born in

Waterford. Age at death: 31. Date of death: 1 March 1917. Service No: 43118. Previously he was with the Royal Irish Regiment where his number was 9824. Killed in action.

Supplementary information: Son of Patrick Hassey. Husband of Johanna Hassey, of 7, Upper Yellow Road, Waterford. From the *Waterford News*, March 1917:

WATERFORD SOLDIERS KILLED.

The death took place, in action, on March 1st of Private James Hassey, R.D.F., son of Mrs Hassey, Upper Yellow Road. Deceased joined here fifteen months ago, and he leaves a wife and four young children. A comrade of deceased wrote to Mrs Hassey as follows;

1st Royal Dublin Fusiliers,

B.E.F., France.

March 25th, 1917.

Dear Mrs Hassey,

It is with the deepest regret that I write these few lines to let you know of the death of my friend and comrade, Mr Hassey, who, I am very sorry to say, was killed in action by my side on 1st March, 1917. For the past six months I had the pleasure of having Mr Hassey in my machine-gun section, and I am proud to say I always found his both a good soldier as well as a man. His death, you will be glad to know, was very peaceful. My home is in Clonmel, and I shortly anticipate going home on leave, and I greatly hope to be able to call on you and give you full details and particulars of him. Again offering you my greatest sympathy in your great loss. Believe me, sincerely yours.

L. -Cp. M. Boyle.

Grave or Memorial Reference: I.B.24. Cemetery: Honnechy British Cemetery in France.

HAVENS, Oliver: Rank: Private. Regiment or Service: The Buffs (East Kent Regiment). Unit: 3rd Battalion. Age at death: 39. Date of death: 27 November 1918. Service No: G/26056.

Supplementary information: Husband of A. Havens, of 9 Manson Place, Queen's Gate, London. Grave or Memorial Reference: Right of Church from entrance. Cemetery: Templemichael Church of Ireland Churchyard, Co. Waterford.

HAYDEN, Percy: Rank: Private. Regiment or Service: Scottish Rifles. Unit: 10th Battalion. Date of death: 24 September 1916. Service No: 40102. Born in Waterford. Enlisted in Glasgow. Died of wounds. He has no known grave but is commemorated on Pier and Face 4D. Memorial: Thiepval Memorial in France.

HAYDEN, William: Rank: Able Seaman. Regiment or Service: Mercantile Marine. Unit: SS *Lough Fisher* (Barrow). Shelled and sunk by a German submarine 12 miles southeast of Cork. Age at death: 17. Date of death: 30 March 1918.

Supplementary information: Son of Patrick and Mary Hayden (*née* McDonnell), of 35 Upper Ferrybank, Waterford. Born in Waterford. He has no known grave but is listed on the Tower Hill Memorial in the UK.

HAYES, John: Rank: Cattleman. Regiment or Service: Mercantile Marine. Unit: SS *Formby* (Glasgow). Age at death: 25. Date of death: 16 December 1917. The ship was lost with all hands and never located during a fierce storm.

Supplementary information: Son of James and Mary Hayes, of Lismore, Kilmeaden Road, Waterford. He has no known grave but is listed on the Tower Hill Memorial in the UK. He is also listed on the Formby-Coningbeg Memorial, Adelphi Quay in Waterford City.

HAYES, John: Rank: Private. Regiment or Service: Royal Irish Regiment. Unit: 2nd Battalion. Date of death: 8 May 1915. Service No: 10100. Born in Dungarvan, Co. Waterford. Enlisted in Waterford while living in Dungarvan, Co. Waterford. Died of wounds. Grave or Memorial Reference: II.A.107. Cemetery: Bailleul Communal Cemetery Extension (Nord) in France.

HAYES, Patrick: Rank: Private. Regiment or Service: South Wales Borderers. Unit: 2nd Battalion. Date of death: 25 September 1915. Service No: 19555. Born in Waterford. Enlisted in Brynmawr. Died in Gallipoli. Grave or Memorial Reference: E.EA.A.665. Cemetery: Addolorata Cemetery in Malta.

HAYES, Thomas: Rank: Private. Regiment or Service: Royal Irish Regiment. Unit: 2nd Battalion. Age at death: 19. Date of death: 8 May 1915. Service No: 6353. Born in Trinity Without, Waterford. Enlisted in Waterford. Killed in action.

Supplementary information: Son of Michael and Annie Hayes, of 25 Costelloe's Lane, Yellow Road, Waterford. He has no known grave but is listed on Panel 33 on the Ypres (Menin Gate) Memorial in Belgium.

HAYES, Timothy: Rank: Private. Regiment or Service: Royal Munster Fusiliers. Unit: 1st Battalion. Age at death: 36. Date of death: 28 August 1918. Service No: 8076. Born in Tipperary. Enlisted in Whitehall, Middlesex while living in Islington, Middlesex. Killed in action.

Supplementary information: Son of William and Julia Hayes, of 5 Baileys New Street Waterford. Grave or Memorial Reference: II.A.30. Cemetery: St Martin Calvaire British Cemetery, St Martin-Sur-Cojeu. Pas-de-Calais, France.

HEALY, Maurice M: Rank: Gunner. See **SHEEHAN, Michael:**

HEALY, John J.: Rank: Private. Regiment or Service: Irish Guards. Unit: 1st Battalion. Age at death: 25. Date of death: 18 May 1915.

Service No: 4852. Born in Terenure, Dublin. Enlisted in Dublin while living in Cracadan East, Co. Waterford. Killed in action.

Supplementary information: Son of Mrs Kate Healy, of Gracedieu East, Waterford. Grave or Memorial Reference: 4 on the Le Touret Memorial in France.

HEALY, Michael: Rank: Sergeant. Regiment or Service: Royal Munster Fusiliers. Unit: 2nd Battalion. Age at death: 25. Date of death: 2 March 1917. Service No: 5130. Born in Dungarvan, Co. Waterford. Enlisted in Swansea, Glamorganshire while living in Pontardawe, Glamorganshire. Died of wounds. Awards: A.M., D.C.M., M.M. and Bar.

Supplementary information: Son of Mrs Annie Healy, of Ballinamuck, Dungarvan, Co. Waterford. A War Office letter (68/Albert/109/A.G.10) records the following:

On 1st March, 1917, this non-commissioned officer, with a total disregard for his own personal safety and solely prompted by the desire to save his comrades, rushed to pick up a live bomb which had been thrown by a Private and which struck the parapet and rolled back into the trench near Lieutenant Roe and the Private. Sergeant Healy, fearing the party could not escape in time, made a most gallant attempt to seize and hurl the bomb from the trench. It exploded, however, and mortally wounded him. This was the last of Sergeant Healy's many acts of gallantry and devotion to duty. He was previously awarded the Distinguished Conduct Medal and the Military Medal and later a bar to his Military Medal.

From the *Waterford News.* September 1916:

AWARDED D.C.M. AND MILITARY MEDAL. Amongst the names of those recently published to whom awards have been made for conspicuous gallantry in the field appears that of Sergeant Michael Healy, Royal Munster Fusiliers. Sergeant Healy is son of Mr James Healy, of Ballinamuck, Dungarvan,

Co. Waterford, and for his great bravery while in action has been awarded the D.C.M., and the Military Medal. This gallant young man is now in hospital in Richmond recuperating from and illness contracted in the ntrenches His many friends compliment him on his courage in the hour of danger, and wish him a speedy recovery to health.

Grave or Memorial Reference: II.B.53. Cemetery: Bray Military Cemetery in the village of Bray-sur-Somme in France.

HEARN, John: Rank: Ordinary Seaman. Regiment or Service: Mercantile Marine. Unit: SS *Penvearn* (Falmouth). Torpedoed by a German submarine off the Irish coast. Age at death: 20. Date of death: 1 March 1918.

Supplementary information: Son of John and Margaret Hearn, of Passage East, Co. Waterford. He has no known grave but is listed on the Tower Hill Memorial in the UK.

HEARNE, George Henry: Rank: Gunner. Regiment or Service: Royal Garrison Artillery. Unit: 258th Siege Battery. Age at death: 19. Date of death: 28 October 1917. Service No: 139812. Born in Sabatha, India. Enlisted in Waterford. Died of wounds.

Supplementary information: Son of James Hearne, of R/5, Barrack Street, Waterford. Grave or Memorial Reference: III.M.1. Cemetery: White House Cemetery, St Jean-Les-Ypres in Belgium.

HEARNE, James: Rank: Private. Regiment or Service: Royal Irish Regiment. Unit: 2nd Battalion. Date of death: 27 March 1915. Service No: 9061. Born in Trinity Without, Waterford. Enlisted in Waterford. Killed in action. He has no known grave but is listed on Panel 4 on Ploegsteert Memorial in Belgium.

HEARNE, John: Rank: Private. Regiment or Service: Royal Irish Regiment. Unit: 2nd

Battalion. Date of death: 28 June 1916. Service No: 7549. Born in St John's, Waterford. Enlisted in Waterford. Died. He is buried beside Tipperaryman Lance Corporal Denis Jordan who was killed in action on the same day and in the same Battalion. Grave or Memorial Reference: II.B.1. Cemetery: Citadel New Military Cemetery, Fricourt in France.

HEARNE, John: Rank: Private. Regiment or Service: Royal Irish Regiment. Unit: 1st Battalion. Date of death: 25 April 1915. Service No: 6464. Born in Trinity Without, Waterford. Enlisted in Waterford. Died of wounds. From the *Waterford News*, May 1915:

DEATH OF A WATERFORD SOLDIER.
Pathetic Letter from a Belgian Priest.
Watou, near Poperinghe.
Belgium, 26th, April, 1915.

Dear Sir, Madam,
No man had a sadder task than I have, and that to write to the mother and father to say that their beloved son had given his life for his country. I desire you to accept my deepest sympathy in the great bereavement caused by the death of your beloved son; 6464 Hearne, Royal Irish Regiment. I know it will give you great consolation to hear that your loving son died in the "Grace of the Lord" and received the last Sacraments before leaving this world of sorrows.

On Sunday afternoon, 25th April, at 3 o'clock, I found your dead son wounded at the chest in the Field Ambulance of Poperinghe. He was quite conscious and asked me to make his Confession, which he was able to do. He received also the Holy Sacrament of Extreme Unction. Then he asked me to write to his dear mother and father, what I promised him to do. I left the room for paying a visit to the next one. At a sudden, your dear son was dying. The orderly called me in. I just came in time to receive his last words; God, Ireland, Father Mother … "He died in my hands, and in your name I closed the eyes of your dear son. It was 3.45P.M. Your beloved son had a happy death, dying with the grace of the Lord in his soul, and doing his duty in the service of his country; and though your grief in you bereavement is great, what a consolation to feel your beloved son is now in Heaven

On Monday afternoon, 2 o'clock, his body was carried to the cemetery of Poperinghe. I myself blessed the place where he was buried and afterwards I buried him with all the ceremonies of the Roman Catholic Church.

The ambulance authorities, after they had been of an utmost kindness to you dear son, erected a cross on his grave, with his name, rank, and description.

I would repeat for you consolation the words of Cardinal Mercier, Belgian Bishop, in his last pastoral letter; "If I am asked what I think of the eternal salvation of a brave man, who has consciously given his life in defence of his country and honour ... I shall not hesitate to reply that without any doubt whatever Christ crowns his military valour, and that death, accepted in this Christian spirit, assures the safety of that man's soul.""

I again tender you my sympathy in your bereavement, and will continue to pray for you and your dear son.

Jerome Brutsaert.

R. E., Priest-Belian.

At home at Watou.

Grave or Memorial Reference: II.K.25. Cemetery: Poperinghe Old Military Cemetery in Belgium.

HENLEY, Peter: Rank: Rifleman. Regiment or Service: Royal Irish Rifles. Unit: 2nd Battalion. Date of death: 26 October 1916. Service No: 8630. Born in Tallow, Co. Waterford. Enlisted in Cardiff, Glam while living in Lismore, Co. Waterford. Killed in action. He has no known grave but is listed on Pier and Face 15 A and 15 B on the Thiepval Memorial in France.

HENNESSY, Edward: Rank: Winchman. Regiment or Service: Mercantile Marine. Unit: SS *Formby* (Glasgow). The ship was lost with all hands and never located during a fierce storm. Age at death: 32. Date of death: 16 December 1917.

Supplementary information: Son of the late James and Mary Hennessy. Husband of Mary Hennessy (*née* Culleton) of 3 Bank Lane, Waterford. Born at New Ross, Co. Wexford. Memorial: Tower Hill Memorial UK. He is also listed on the Formby-Coningbeg Memorial, Adelphi Quay in Waterford City.

HENNESSY/HENNESSEY, John: Rank: Private. Regiment or Service: Royal Munster Fusiliers. Unit: 2nd Battalion. Age at death: 29. Date of death: 10 November 1917. Service No: 7099. Born in Waterford. Enlisted in Dundee while living in Dundee. Killed in action.

Supplementary information: Son of Patrick and Mary Hennessy, of 32 Morrison's Road, Waterford. Grave or Memorial Reference: 143 to 144 on the Tyne Cot Memorial in Belgium.

HENNESSEY/HENNESSY, Michael: Rank: Private. Regiment or Service: Royal Irish Regiment. Unit: 2nd Battalion. Age at death: 23. Date of death: 3 December 1915. Service No: 5801. Born in St John's, Waterford. Enlisted in Waterford. Died at home.

Supplementary information: Son of Michael and Catherine Hennessy, of 5 Gas House Lane, Waterford. Grave or Memorial Reference: R.C. 828. Cemetery: Netley Military Cemetery, Hampshire, UK.

HENNESSY, Michael: Rank: Able Seaman. Regiment or Service: Mercantile Marine. Unit: SS *Lough Fisher* (Barrow). Shelled and sunk by a German submarine 12 miles S. E of Cork. Age at death: 20. Date of death: 30 March 1918.

Supplementary information: Son of John and Margaret Hennessy (*née* McNamara), of 7 Thomas Hill, Waterford. Born in Waterford.

He has no known grave but is listed on the Tower Hill Memorial in the UK.

HENNESSEY, Michael: Rank: Private. Regiment or Service: Royal Irish Regiment. Unit: 2nd Battalion. Date of death: 22 September 1914. Service No: 10502. Born in Trinity Without, Waterford. Enlisted in Waterford. Died of wounds. He has no known grave but is listed on the La-Ferte-Sous-Jouarre-Memorial in France.

HENNESSY, Patrick: Rank: Private. Regiment or Service: Royal Irish Regiment. Unit: 2nd Battalion. Age at death: 42. Date of death: 17 February 1917. Service No: 365. Born in Kilmacow, Co. Kilkenny. Enlisted in Cork while living in Ballyduff, Co. Waterford. Died.
Supplementary information: Son of James and Margaret Hennessy, of Co. Kilkenny. Husband of Bridget Hennessy, of Ballyduff S.O., Co. Waterford. Grave or Memorial Reference: XXI.G.12. Cemetery: Etaples Military Cemetery in France.

HENNESSY, Patrick: Rank: Carpenter. Regiment or Service: Mercantile Marine. Unit: SS *Coningbeg* (Glasgow). Date of death: 18 December 1917. Torpedoed by German Submarine U-62. There were no survivors.
Supplementary information: Son of the late Thomas and Agnes Hennessy. Husband of Mary Hennessy (*née* Kough), of 28 St Alphonsus Road, Waterford. Born in Waterford. He has no known grave but is listed on the Tower Hill Memorial in the UK. He is also listed on the Formby-Coningbeg Memorial, Adelphi Quay in Waterford City.

HERLIHY, Patrick: Rank: Corporal. Regiment or Service: Leinster Regiment. Unit: 'B' Company, 1st Battalion. Age at death: 35. Date of death: 14 February 1915. Service No: 7024. Born in Lismore, Co. Waterford. Enlisted in Fermoy, County Cork. Killed in action.

Supplementary information: Son of Mrs Mary Herlihy. From the *Waterford News*, 1915:

LISMORE MEN LOST.
Mrs Herlihy, New-Street, Lismore, has been notified that her son Patrick, a Sergeant in the 1st Battalion, Leinster Regiment, was killed in action on 14th February. Corporal Sweeney and Private James Doherty, both of the Royal Irish Regiment, and Patrick Walsh, of the Leinster's, all Lismore men, are reported missing.

He has no known grave but is listed on Panel 44 on the Ypres (Menin Gate) Memorial in Belgium.

HERON, M.: Rank: Able Seaman. Regiment or Service: Mercantile Marine Reserve. Unit: H.H.S. *Eaglet*. Date of death: 9 February 1920 Grave or Memorial Reference: West of entrance. Cemetery: Crooke Old Graveyard, Co. Waterford.

HICKEY, Edward: Rank: Private. Regiment or Service: Argyll and Sutherland Highlanders. Unit: 2nd Battalion. Age at death: 27. Date of death: 26 July 1916. Service No: 4-9763. Born in Waterford and enlisted in Glasgow. Died of wounds.
Supplementary information: Son of Ellen and Sgt. John Hickey, of Tipperary. Hhusband of Bridget Hickey, of 12 Portugal Street, Glasgow. Grave or Memorial Reference: A.38.1. Cemetery: St Sever Cemetery Extension, Rouen in France.

HICKEY, Patrick J.: Rank: Gunner. Regiment or Service: Royal Horse Artillery and Royal Field Artillery. Unit: 187th Brigade. Age at death: 24. Date of death: 11 March 1917. Service No: 49551 (Soldiers died in the Great War), 40551 (The Commonwealth War Graves Commission). Born in Lismore, Co. Waterford. Enlisted in London. Died at home.

Supplementary information: Son of Patrick and Mary Hickey, of Upper Bishopstown, Lismore. Grave or Memorial Reference: In the south-east corner. Cemetery: Lismore Old Catholic Cemetery, Co. Waterford.

HICKEY, Patrick: Rank: Private. Regiment or Service: Royal Munster Fusiliers. Unit: 1st Battalion. Date of death: 8 September 1916. Service No: 8495. Born in St Patrick's, Waterford. Enlisted in Clonmel, Co. Tipperary. Killed in action. From the *Munster Express*, 'Five sons in the Army. Mr Michael Hickey, of Garrycloyne, Glencairn, Lismore, a labourer, has five sons in the army–two in the Irish Guards, two in the Royal Garrison Artillery, and one in the Munster Fusiliers.' He has no known grave but is listed on Pier and Face 16C on the Thiepval Memorial in France.

HIGGINS, John: Rank: Private. Regiment or Service: Royal Irish Regiment. Unit: 2nd Battalion. Age at death: 35. Date of death: 7 June 1917. Service No: 4931. Born in St Patrick's, Waterford. Enlisted in Carrick-on-Suir, Co. Waterford. Killed in action.
Supplementary information: Son of Sarah and Michael Higgins, of 2 Evis Lane, Waterford. Husband of Margaret Higgins, of 28 Peter Street, Waterford. He has no known grave but is listed on Panel 33 on the Ypres (Menin Gate) Memorial in Belgium.

HINES, William John: Rank: Lance Corporal. Regiment or Service: Coldstream Guards. Date of death: 22 October 1914. Age at death: 24. Service No: 6639. Born in Waterford. Enlisted in Norwich while living in Harleston, Norfolk. Died of wounds.
Supplementary information: Son of Mrs Mary Ann Martin, of Mill Terrace, Joy's Green, Harleston, Norfolk. Grave or Memorial Reference: II.A.1. Cemetery: Poperinghe Communal Cemetery in Belgium.

HODGES, Eric Colpoys: Initials: Rank: Second Lieutenant Regiment or Service: Royal Irish Regiment Unit: 2nd Battalion. Age at death: 18. Date of death: 15 July 1916.
Supplementary information: Son of the Revd Richard J. Hodges, M.A. and Mrs M.J. Hodges, of Youghal, Co. Cork. I am not sure of the Waterford connection but he is listed on the Bishop Foy School Memorial located in Christ Church Cathedral (Church of Ireland), Henrietta Street, Waterford. Grave or Memorial Reference: I.E.13. Cemetery: Heilly Station Cemetery, Mericourt-L'Abbe in France.

HOGAN, Frank: Rank: Private. Regiment or Service: Irish Guards. Unit: 2nd Battalion. Service No: 15 September 1916. Service No: 7629. Born in Waterford. Enlisted in Waterford. Killed in action. From the *Waterford News*. October 1916:

WATERFORDMEN IN
THE CASUALTY LISTS.
In yesterday's casualty lists the name of Private F. Hogan, Waterford (7629). Irish Guards, appears amongst those killed, and also the name of Private T. Croke, R.I.R., Waterford (5233).

He has no known grave but is listed on Pier and Face 7D on the Thiepval Memorial in France.

HOGAN, Joseph: Rank: Stoker 2nd Class. Regiment or Service: Royal Navy. Unit: HMS *Defence*. Age at death: 21. Date of death: 31 May 1916. Service No: K/29031. HMS *Defence* was an armoured cruiser and was sent to the bottom by the Naval guns of a German battleship during the battle of Jutland. HMS *Defence's* magazine exploded when it was hit by a German shell. The magazine explosion triggered off other explosions which almost blew the ship apart and she went down with the entire crew of 903 men. There were no survivors. Five Waterford men died with this ship on that day.

Supplementary information: Son of Michael and Mary Hogan, of Knock, Dungarvan, Co. Waterford. Grave or Memorial Reference: 16 on the Plymouth Naval Memorial, UK.

HOGAN, Michael: Rank: Private. Regiment or Service: Irish Guards. Unit: 1st Battalion. Age at death: 23. Date of death: 4 September 1917. Service No: 11090. Born in Portlaw, Co. Waterford. Enlisted in Waterford. Killed in action

Supplementary information: Son of Mrs Mary Hogan, of Carrick Road, Portlaw, Co. Waterford. Grave or Memorial Reference: IV.F.6. Cemetery: Artillery Wood Cemetery in Belgium.

HOGAN, Patrick: Rank: Chief Stoker. Regiment or Service: Royal Navy. Unit: HMS *Endymion*. Date of death: 30 July 1918. Service No: 290394.

Supplementary information: Son of John Hogan, of Longueville, Ballinoe, Tallon, Co. Waterford. Grave or Memorial Reference: 1872. Cemetery: Mikra British Cemetery, Kalamaria in Greece.

HOGAN, William J.: Rank: Private. Regiment or Service: Leinster Regiment. Unit: 7th Battalion. Age at death: 24. Date of death: 20 July 1916. Service No: 2964. Born in Killossorty Co. Waterford. Enlisted in Dublin while living in Kingstown, Co. Dublin. Killed in action.

William J. Hogan. Courtesy of grand-nephew Paul Butler, Kilkenny

Supplementary information: Son of Martin Hogan, of Rock Mount, Kilmacthomas, Co. Waterford. Husband of Kate Kirwin (formerly Hogan) although he states that William Hogan was not married and Kate was, in fact, William's mother. Native of Kilrossanty, Kilmacthomas. Grave or Memorial Reference: I.C.1. Cemetery: Philosophe British Cemetery, Mazingarbe in France.

HOLDEN, D.: Rank: Able Seaman. Regiment or Service: Mercantile Marine. Unit: HMS *Salta*. Hospital Ship *Salta* hit a mine and sank. There were no wounded on board at the time. Age at death: 26. Date of death: 10 April 1917.

Supplementary information: Son of William and Elizabeth Holden, of Waterford. Grave or Memorial Reference: *Salta* Memorial. Cemetery: Ste. Marie Cemetery, Le Havre in France.

HOLDEN, Edward James: Rank: Private. Regiment or Service: Australian Infantry, A.I.F. Unit: 23rd Battalion. Date of death: 3 August 1916. Service No: 3848. Enlisted in Melbourne, Victoria on 20 September 1915. Died of wounds (shell wounds to abdomen and hip) at No 44 Casualty Clearing Station in France. Charged in May 1916 with making used of a forged pass. Awarded twenty-one days Field Punishment number 1. Buried by Revd E.J. Cullen on the day Private Holden died.

In or near what Parish or Town were you born? Waterford, Ireland.

Are you a natural born British subject or a Naturalised British subject? Natural Born British Subject.

What is your trade or calling? Railway Employee.

Are you married? Yes, Widowed.

Who is your next of kin? Miss Mavis M Holden (daughter) c/o Mr W McMahon, 25 Maitland Street, Geelong, W.

Have you ever been convicted by the Civil Power? No.

Age: 32 years, 11 months.

Height 5 feet, 4 inches.

Weight: 11. 2 lbs.

Chest measurement: 36-38 inches.

Complexion: fresh.

Eyes: blue. Hair: brown.

Religious denomination: RC.

(Uncle) William McMahon, Kenmore Lunatic Asylum, Goulburn, Victoria.

A pension was claimed on behalf of his daughter, Mavis Mary Holden, North Golburn by trustee William McMahon (Great Uncle) Joshua Street, North Golburn. Mavis was entitled to £1 per fortnight from November 1916, rising to £1. 10/- from October-1918.

25 Maitland Street.

Geelong West.

24-11-21.

Sir,

Re your letter dated 7th Nov 21 requiring information of the next of kin of the late No 3848 Pte E. J. Holden, 23rd Battalion. I beg to inform you that the only blood relation in Australia of the late soldier is a daughter living with me and of whom I am Guardian. He had no other relatives alive his wife (my sister) having died ten years ago.

I would be deeply grateful if you would forward war medals etc, as I am sure the child will value them highly.

I am, Faithfully yours.

W McMahon.

P. S. I beg to inform you that I have left Goulburn N. S. W. I am residing at the above address.

War medals etc were sent to his daughter.

18 McDonald Street.

Herne Hill.

Geelong. Vic.

22. 3-55.

Officer in Charge.

Base Records.

Canberra.

Dear Sir,

I am writing to see if you could give me any details regarding my late father. I would like to know if possible what part of Ireland he was from, as I would like to contact his people, for my children's sake. I was his only child and lost my mother when a baby and before father went to the war and have another source of finding out any details. My late mothers relatives who brought me up, although know all my details have refused to tell me. The Repatriation Dept in Melbourne advised me to write to you and I would receive all details, also if a will was left.

He served in the first world war, his diary reads, No 3848. Private Edward James Holden, Signaller, 9th reinforcements, 23rd Battalion. Thanking you.

I am Yours sincerely.

(Mrs) M Sheill.

Grave or Memorial Reference: II.C.61. Cemetery: Puchevillers British Cemetery in France.

HOLMAN, THOMAS Edward: Rank: Lance Sergeant. Regiment or Service: London Regiment (London Rifle Brigade). Unit: 1st/5th Battalion. Secondary Regiment: Middlesex Regiment Secondary. Unit: formerly 4th/7th Battalion. Age at death: 30. Date of death: 10 September 1916. Service No: 10783. Enlisted in Hornsey while living in New Southgate. Killed in action.

Supplementary information: Son of J.F. Holman (R.S.M.R.F.A.) and Annie Holman, of 22 Goring Road, Bowes Park, London. Husband of Emmeline Holman of 32 Oakleigh Road, New Southgate, London. Manager at Lismore Gas Works, Co. Waterford. Enlisted in July 1915. Also served in Egypt. From the *Waterford News* and the *Munster Express*, October 1916.

KILLED IN ACTION.

Private Thomas Holden, of the 7th Middlesex Regiment, has been killed in action. The deceased soldier was well and favourably known in Lismore, as he was manager of the local Gas Works. A more popular, courteous, or social companion one could not meet.

He has no known grave but is listed on Pier and Face 9D of the Thiepval Memorial in France.

HOLROYD Smyth, Charles Edward Ridley: Rank: Lieutenant Colonel. Regiment or Service: 3rd Dragoon Guards (Prince of Wales' Own) Secondary Regiment: Durham Light Infantry Secondary. Unit: Commanding 15th Battalion. Age at death: 36. Date of death: 23 September 1918. Awards: D.S.O., M.C.

Supplementary information: Son of Col. and Lady Harriette Holroyd Smyth. Husband of Nora M. Holroyd Smyth (*née* Layard), of Southwood Lodge, Boldre, Lymington, Hants. Served in the South African Campaign. Born at Ballynatray, Co. Waterford. From the *Waterford News*, 1916:

COUNTY WATERFORD OFFICER DECORATED
Captain Charles E. R. Holroyd-Smyth, 3rd Dragoon Guards has been men-

Charles Edward Ridley Holroyd Smyth. Image from from 'Durham Forces in the Field'. 1914-18 by Captain Wilfrid Miles.

tioned in despatches and awarded the Military Cross for conspicuous gallantry in action He is the second son of the late Colonel Holroyd-Smyth of Ballynatray, Co. Waterford. Captain Holroyd-Smyth served in the South African war. He is well-known Ireland as a fine rider and has won many point-to-points. A portrait of the gallant officer appears in to-day's " Irish Life. "

From 'British Infantry Division on the Western Front', p 176:

HOLROYD-SMYTH, CHARLES EDWARD RIDLEY (18??-1918)
Lieutenant-Colonel. Dragoon Guards, also attached to Durham Light Infantry. Acting GOC 64th Brigade after McCulloch was wounded, 24–28 August 1918. Died of wounds received near Epéhy, 23 September 1918. DSO; MC; MiD four times.

From a memorial on the wall of St Mary's church, Youghal:

'In loving memory of Charles Edward Ridley Holroyd-Smyth, Distinguished Service Order, Military Cross, Captain Prince of Wales Own 3rd Dragoon Guards, temporary Lt Col 15th Battalion Durham Light Infantry. Died 25th September 1918 from wounds received in action while leading his battalion in the attack on Villers Guislain. Age 36. Greater love hath no man than that a man laid down his life for his friends'.

From the *London Gazette*, 16 November 1914:

GENERAL RESERVE OF OFFICERS. CAVALRY.
The following notification is substituted for that which appeared in the Gazette o 1st September-1914. Charles Edward Ridely Holroyd-Smyth, late Lieutenant, 3rd (Prince of Wales) Dragoon Guards, to be Lieutenant. Dated 31st August-1914.

Grave or Memorial Reference: 4.O.5A. Cemetery: Lansdown Burial Ground in Bath, UK.

HOOLAHAN, John: Rank: Fireman and Trimmer. Regiment or Service: Mercantile Marine. Unit: SS *Royal Edward* (Toronto). Sunk by a torpedo from German submarine U-14. Age at death: 50. Date of death: 13 August 1915.

Supplementary information: Son of John and Ellen Hoolahan (*née* Conway), of Rockshire Lodge, Ferry Bank, Waterford. Born in Co. Waterford. He has no known grave but is listed on the Tower Hill Memorial in the UK.

HORAN, Jeremiah: Rank: Private. Regiment or Service: Royal Dublin Fusiliers. Unit: 2nd Battalion. Date of death: 1 July 1916. Service No: 12226. Born in Waterford. Enlisted in Waterford. Killed in action. Grave or Memorial Reference: I.D.19. Cemetery: Sucrerie Military Cemetery, Colinclamps in France.

HOREY, John: Rank: Private. Regiment or Service: Household Cavalry and Cavalry of the line including the Yeomanry and Imperial Camel Corps. Unit: 4 Dragoon Guards (Royal Irish). Age at death: 21. Date of death: 3 November 1914. Service No: 7834. Born in Fallow, Waterford. Enlisted in Athlone, Co. Westmeath while living in Birr, Co. Offaly. Killed in action.

Supplementary information: Son of Martin and Margaret Horey, of Whiteford, Birr, Co. Offaly. He has no known grave but is listed on Panel 3-5 on the Ypres (Menin Gate) Memorial in Belgium.

HORGAN, Daniel: Rank: Private. Regiment or Service: Leinster Regiment. Unit: 7th Battalion. Secondary Regiment: Royal Munster Fusiliers Secondary. Unit: Attached to 2nd Battalion. Age at death: 26. Date of death: 29 August 1916. Service No: 3287. Born in Balinameela, Co. Waterford.

Enlisted in Dungarvan while living in Cappoquin, Co. Waterford. Died of wounds.

Supplementary information: Son of William Patrick and Margaret Horgan (*née* Houlihan). Born at Ballintaylor, Cappoquin, Co. Waterford. Enlisted July 1915. Grave or Memorial Reference: B.24.51. Cemetery: ST. Sever Cemetery, Rouen in France.

HORRIGAN, Stephen: Rank: Private/ Acting Corporal. Regiment or Service: Royal Irish Regiment. Unit: 2nd Battalion. Age at death: 49. Date of death: 19 October 1914. Service No: 5981 (Soldiers died in the Great War), 5081 (The Commonwealth War Graves Commission). Born in Dungarvan, Co. Waterford. Enlisted in Dungarvan, Co. Waterford. Killed in action.

Supplementary information: Son of Mr and Mrs Tom Horrigan. Husband of Ellen Horrigan, of 31 Main Street, Dungarvan, Co. Waterford. He has no known grave but is listed on Panel 11 and 12 of the Le Touret Memorial in France.

HORSOM, George: Rank: Private. Regiment or Service: Royal Dublin Fusiliers. Unit: 1st Battalion. Date of death: 29 September 1918. Service No: 23634. Born in Ballinameela, Co. Waterford. Enlisted in Dungarvan, Co. Waterford. Killed in action. Grave or Memorial Reference: XVII.C.9. Cemetery: Hooge Crater Cemetery Zillebeke, Belgium.

HOWGATE, Peter: Rank: Lance Bombardier. Regiment or Service: Royal Garrison Artillery. Unit: 319th Siege Battery. Age at death: 26. Date of death: 4 October 1918. Service No: 139225. Born in Everton, Liverpool. Enlisted in Liverpool. Died of wounds.

Supplementary information: Son of W. Howgate, of 109 Everton Terrace, Liverpool. Husband of Josephine Howgate, of Boatstrand, Annestown, Co. Waterford. Grave or Memorial Reference: V.D.41. Cemetery: Tincourt New British Cemetery in France.

HOWLETT, Martin: Rank: Private. Regiment or Service: Irish Guards. Unit: 2nd Battalion. Age at death: 22. Date of death: 31 July 1917. Service No: 9142. Enlisted in Caterham in Surrey while living in Campile, Co. Waterford. Killed in action.

Supplementary information: Son of Martin and Catherine Howlett, of Grange, Campile, Waterford. From the *Waterford News*, August 1917, ' The parents of Private Martin Howlett, Grange, Arthurstown, of the Irish Guards, have received the news of the death of their son in the recent fighting in France.' Grave or Memorial Reference: He has no known grave but is listed on Panel 11 on the Ypres (Menin Gate) Memorial in Belgium.

HUGHES, Nicholas: Rank: Able Seaman. Regiment or Service: Mercantile Marine. Unit: SS *Coningbeg* (Glasgow). Torpedoed by German Submarine U-62. There were no survivors. U-62 surrendered in November 1918. Age at death: 27. Date of death: 18 December 1917.

Supplementary information: Son of Patrick Hughes and the late Anastasia Hughes. Husband of Elizabeth Hughes (*née* Ford), of 11 Roaches Street, Waterford. Born in Waterford. He has no known grave but is listed on the Tower Hill Memorial in the UK. He is also listed on the Formby-Coningbeg Memorial, Adelphi Quay in Waterford City.

HUGHES, Thomas Mathew: Rank: Private. Regiment or Service: British South African Police. Age at death: 34. Date of death: 9 November 1916. Service No: A/27.

Supplementary information: Son of William and Annie Hughes, of Annestown, Tramore, Co. Waterford. Husband of Annie Hughes, of Annestown, Tramore. Grave or Memorial Reference: E.8.67. Cemetery: Bulawayo (Athlone) Cemetery in Zimbabwe, South Africa.

HUMPHRIES, James: Rank: Private. Regiment or Service: Royal Scots (Lothian Regiment.) Unit: 2nd Battalion also listed as the 8th Battalion. Age at death: 20. Date of death: 27 September 1917. Service No: 325684. Formerly he was with the Notts and Derby Regiment where his number was 28662. Born in Waterford, Co. Munster. Enlisted in Dublin while living in Dublin. Died of wounds.

Supplementary information: Son of David and Susan Humphries, of 1 Alphonsus Avenue, Drumcondra Road., Dublin. Grave or Memorial Reference: VIII.F.19. Cemetery: Dozinghem Military Cemetery in Belgium.

HUNT, Ambrose Langley: Rank: Master. Regiment or Service: Mercantile Marine. Unit: *Burrsfield*. Age at death: 46. Date of death: 5 October 1915. *Burrsfield* was a collier, captured by German submarine U-33 and shelled and sunk 80 miles short of Matapan.

Supplementary information: Younger son of Ambrose Hunt, M.D. of Dungarvan, Co. Waterford. Husband of Catherine M. Hunt, of 6 Pump Court, Temple, London, late of Old Hill House, Westerham, Kent. Lieutenant, R.N.R, until 1908. From an article in 'Our Heroes':

…was in command of an Admiralty transport when attacked by an Austrian submarine in the Eastern Mediterranean, and while endeavouring to save her under fire was killed by shrapnel. The majority of the ship's company were rescued from the damaged boats, the ship, riddled with shell, being torpedoed and sunk by the submarine, which was afterwards accounted for by H.M.S. Chatham. Captain Hunt was the fourth son of the late Dr Ambrose Hunt, M.D., of Dungarvan, Waterford, and husband of Mrs Catherine M. Hunt, Old Mill House, Westerham, Kent.

He is also listed on a brass wall plaque memorial in St Mary's church, Tatsfield, Surrey, England; -

'In proud and loving memory of my dear husband Captain Ambrose Langley Hunt RNR who was killed at his post on October 5 1915 aged 46 while navigating Admiralty transport ship to Mudros Base during operations on Gallipoli 'One who never turned his back but marched breast forward' Hunt, Ambrose Langley Date of death: 5 October 19 15. Cause of death: War casualty. Rank/Occupation: Captain RNR. Organisation: Royal Naval Reserve.

He has no known grave but is listed on the Tower Hill Memorial in the UK.

HUNT, Edward: Rank: Fireman. Regiment or Service: Mercantile Marine. Unit: SS *Coningbeg* (Glasgow). Torpedoed by German Submarine U-62. There were no survivors. U-62 surrendered in November 1918. Age at death: 32. Date of death: 18 December 1917.
Supplementary information: Son of Edward and Mary Hunt. Husband of Mary Jane Hunt (*née* Murphy), of 14 St Alphonsus Road, Waterford. Born at Ballyhuckle, Waterford. He has no known grave but is listed on the Tower Hill Memorial in the UK. He is also listed on the Formby-Coningbeg Memorial, Adelphi Quay in Waterford City.

HUNT, George: Rank: Private. Regiment or Service: Royal Dublin Fusiliers. Unit: 1st Battalion. Age at death: 24. Date of death: 29 June 1915. Service No: 11151. Born in Fethard, Co. Waterford. Enlisted in Dublin while living in Salterton, Devon. Killed in action in Gallipoli.
Supplementary information: Son of George and Mary Hunt, of Jutland, Greenway, Budleigh Salterton, Devon. He has no known grave but is listed on Panel 190 to 196 on the Helles Memorial in Turkey.

HUNT, Thomas: Rank: Private. Regiment or Service: Royal Irish Regiment. Unit: 2nd Battalion. Age at death: 21. Date of death: 15 October 1914. Service No: 6153. Born in Trinity Without, Waterford. Enlisted in Waterford. Killed in action.
Supplementary information: Son of Martin and Johanna Hunt, of 5 Kneefe's Lane,

Waterford. I am not sure if he is the Thomas Hunt listed on the Graves and Co. Roll of Honour Memorial. Located are located in Christ Church Cathedral (Church of Ireland), Henrietta Street, Waterford. The memorial reads:

ROLL OF HONOUR
Office Staff and Employees of
Messrs. Graves and Co. Limited
Who served in the great war
1914-1918.

Grave or Memorial Reference: 11 and 12 on the Le Touret Memorial in France.

HUNT, William: Rank: Private. Regiment or Service: Royal Irish Regiment. Unit: 2nd Battalion. Age at death: 19. Date of death: 19 October 1914. Service No: 10750. Born in Ballybricken, Co. Waterford. Enlisted in Waterford. Killed in action.
Supplementary information: Son of Martin and Johanna Hunt, of 5 Kneefe's Lane, Waterford. Grave or Memorial Reference: 11 and 12 on the Le Touret Memorial in France.

HURLEY, James: Rank: Private. Regiment or Service: Royal Irish Regiment. Unit: 4th Battalion. Age at death: 37. Date of death: 20 December 1915. Service No: 4932. Born in St. John's, Waterford. Enlisted in Carrick-on-Suir, Co. Tipperary while living in Waterford. Died at home.
Supplementary information: Husband of Sarah Hurley, of 33 Costelloe's Lane, Waterford. Grave or Memorial Reference: In southeast part. Cemetery: Dungarvan (St Mary) Catholic Churchyard, Co. Waterford.

HURLEY, John: Rank: Able Seaman. Regiment or Service: Mercantile Marine. Unit: SS *Formby* (Glasgow). Age at death: 52. Date of death: 16 December 1917. The ship was lost with all hands and never located during a fierce storm.

Supplementary information: Son of John and Mary Hurley. Husband of Mary Anne Hurley (*née* Tobin), of Passage East, Co. Waterford. Born at Passage East. He has no known grave but is listed on the Tower Hill Memorial in the UK. He is also listed on the Formby-Coningbeg Memorial, Adelphi Quay in Waterford City.

HURLEY, Patrick: Rank: Gunner. Regiment or Service: Royal Horse Artillery and Royal Field Artillery. Unit: 132nd Battery. 1st Brigade. Date of death: 9 May 1915. Service No: 24543. Born in Waterford. Enlisted in Ferndale. Killed in action. Grave or Memorial Reference: Panel 5 and 9. Memorial: Ypres (Menin Gate) Memorial in Belgium.

HURLEY, Patrick: Rank: Private. Regiment or Service: Royal Munster Fusiliers. Unit: 2nd Battalion. Age at death: 18. Date of death: 4 August 1916. Service No: 5679 (Soldiers died in the Great War), 9/5679 (The Commonwealth War Graves Commission). Born in Dungarvan, Co. Waterford. Enlisted in Cork while living in Cappoquin Co. Waterford. Died of wounds at Home. Grave or Memorial Reference: In the north-east part. Cemetery: Whitechurch Church of Ireland Churchyard, Co. Waterford.

HYDE, John: Rank: Chief Stoker Regiment or Service: Royal Navy. Unit: HMS *Cornwall*. Date of death: 22 June 1918. Service No:277751. Born in Kinsalebeg, Co. Waterford.

Supplementary information: Son of Michael Hyde, of Ferry Point, Youghal. Husband of Catherine Hyde, of 4 Grattan Street, Youghal, Co. Cork. Grave or memorial Reference: Screen Wall (North). V.R.C. 1746. Cemetery: Liverpool (Anfield) Cemetery, Lancashire, UK.

HYLAND, Michael Joseph: Rank: Private. Regiment or Service: Royal West Surrey Regiment. Unit: 6th Battalion. Age at death: 21. Date of death: 3 July 1917. Service No: G/34. Born in Waterford. Enlisted in Croydon, Surrey while living in Dublin, Ireland. Killed in action.

Supplementary information: Son of Joseph and Elizabeth Hyland, of 17 McMahon Street, South Circular Road, Dublin. He has no known grave but is listed on Pier and Face 5D and 6D on the Thiepval Memorial in France.

HYNES, Edmund: Rank: Private. Regiment or Service: Australian Infantry, A.I.F. Unit: 25th Battalion. Enlisted 5 October 1915 in Toowoomba, Queensland. Date of death: 11 January 1918. Service No: 4461 Killed in action.

Supplementary information: Son of Thomas and Kate Hynes, of Ballybrack, Knockanore, Youghal, Co. Cork. Admitted with V.D. Lobar Pneumonia and sore feet to hospital.

In or near what Parish or Town were you born? Waterford.

Are you a natural born British subject or a Naturalised British subject? Natural Born.

What is your age? 26 years 2 months.

What is your trade or calling? Labourer.

Are you married? No.

Who is your next of kin? (father) Thomas Hynes, Castlereagh Street, Waterford, later changed to Ballybrack, Knockanure, Tallow, Co Waterford

Have you ever been convicted by the Civil Power? No.

Age: 26 years, 2 months.

Height: 5 feet, 11 inches.

Weight: 150 lbs.

Chest measurement: 39½ inches.

Complexion: fair. Eyes: blueish.

Hair: light.

Religious denomination: R.C.

Grave or Memorial Reference: A.47. Cemetery: Underhill Farm Cemetery in Belgium.

HYNES, Michael: Rank: Private/Lance Corporal. Regiment or Service: Royal Irish Regiment. Unit: 2nd Battalion. Age at death: 35. Date of death: 28 July 1917. Service No: 6771. Born in Conna, Co. Cork. Enlisted in Lismore, Co. Waterford while living in Tallow, Co. Waterford. Died of wounds.

Supplementary information: Son of Denis and Eliza Hynes. Husband of Mary Hynes, of Fenor South, Tramore, Co. Waterford. Native of Tallow, Co. Waterford. Grave or Memorial Reference: V.A. 31. Cemetery: Vlamertinghe New Military Cemetery in Belgium.

I

IVERS, Daniel: Rank: Private. Regiment or Service: Royal Irish Rifles. Unit unknown. Died in the local infirmary in January 1915. This Lismore man is not in any of the War Dead databases and seems to have been discharged with wounds at the time of his death. Age at death: 31. Mobilised in 1915, he received internal wounds and was sent home from a military hospital one week before his death. His reserve time ceased before his return to Lismore. Service No: unknown. Died of wounds. Cemetery: Affane Cemetery.

J

JACKMAN, Thomas: Rank: Private. Regiment or Service: Royal Munster Fusiliers. Unit: 1st Battalion. Age at death: 21. Date of death: 12 August 1915. Service No: 10555. Born in Trinity Within, Waterford. Enlisted in Waterford while living in Waterford. Killed in action in Gallipoli. Previously he was with the Lancers of the Line where his number was 5527.

Supplementary information: Son of Mrs Anastasia Jackman (*née* Kennedy), of Grace Dieu Road, Waterford. He has no known grave but is listed on Panel 185 to 190 on the Helles Memorial in Turkey.

JACKSON, Martin: Rank: Private. Regiment or Service: Royal Irish Regiment. Unit: 1st Battalion. Date of death: 14 February 1915. Service No: 6753. Born in Trinity Without, Waterford. Enlisted in Waterford. Killed in action. Has no known grave but is commemorated on Panel 33 on the Ypres (Menin Gate) Memorial in Belgium.

JACOBS, George Richard: Rank: Engineman. Regiment or Service: Royal Naval Reserve. Unit: H.M. Trawler *Bradford*. Date of death: 26 October 1916. Service No: 1239/S(Ch). Supplementary information: Husband of Nellie Jacobs, of 168 Patrick Street, Grimsby. The Trawler *Bradford* was lost in a gale off Cork. He is also listed in the Absent Voters list, Milton Regis-South Ward where his address is given as 25 Epps Road. He is on this list as he was stationed on HMS *Canterbury* at the time. Grave or Memorial Reference: In north-east part. Cemetery: Pulla Graveyard, Co. Waterford.

JAMES, John: Rank: Gunner. Regiment or Service: Australian Field Artillery. Unit: 'Y' 4th Battery. Enlisted 20 July 1915 in Liverpool, New South Wales. Date of death: 9 June 1917.

In or near what Parish or Town were you born? Waterford, Ireland.

Are you a natural born British subject or a Naturalised British subject? Yes, Natural Born.

What is your trade or calling? Labourer.

Are you married? No.

Who is your next of kin? Parents Deceased. (sister) Hanna Reid, "Dalry" Maroo Street, Oakleigh, Victoria. (eldest brother) Mr J Downey, c/o Mrs Reid at above address.

Have you ever been convicted by the Civil Power? No.

Have you ever been discharged from any part of His Majesty's Forces, with Ignominy, or as Incorrigible and Worthless, or on account of conviction of felony, or of a Sentence of Penal Servitude, or have you been dismissed with Disgrace from the Navy? No.

Have you stated the whole, if any, of your previous service? Yes.

Have you ever been rejected as unfit for his Majesty's Service? No. If so, on what grounds?

Age: 29 years, 11 months.

Height: 5 feet, 5 ½ inches.

Weight: 154 lbs. Chest measurement: 35-38 inches.

Complexion: ruddy.

Eyes: green. Hair: black. Religious denomination: R.C.

Admitted to hospital in Egypt with Cold on chest, Pleurodina, Enemesis, Gonorrhoea and N.Y.D.

20 September, 1921.

Dear Sir.

Appended hereunder is a copy of a communication forwarded to you on 5th January last, to which no reply has been received; -

"I am informed you are the eldest surviving brother of the late No, 913 Gunner J. James,

9th(?) Heavy and medium Trench Mortar Batteries, but in order that I may be in a position to properly dispose of his 1914-15 star, and other war medals etc., when available. I shall be much obliged if you will advise me whether the father and mother of the late soldier are still living, and if so, their present address, also if you will furnish me with an explanation as to the difference in the surnames of yourself and your brother."

As I am holding the war medals etc, pending receipt of your reply, I shall be glad if you give the matter your early attention.
Yours faithfully.
Major. Officer I/C Base Records.

Mr J Downey,
C/o Mrs W Reid.
Maroo Street
Oakleigh.V.
Maroo Street.
Oakleigh.
September 26 1921.
Dear Sir.
I am the eldest brother of the late Gunner J James, 913. His Father and Mother are both dead. My sister, Mrs Reid, Maroo Street, Oakleigh, reared him. Like myself, he was rejected for bad teeth but he went to Sydney and enlisted under the name of John James. I would like to have any star or medals of his and I would also like to know where he was killed. My Sister only got 'somewhere in France.'
Sincerely yours.
J Downey.
C/o Mrs Reid.
Maroo Street.
Oakleigh.

The officer in charge of Base Records seemed satisfied with this reply and the medals were later issued to Mr J. Downey. Died of gun shot wounds at the 9th Australian Field Ambulance Advanced Dressing Station. Service No: 913. Buried by Chaplain B.F. Wilson.

Grave or Memorial Reference: VI.A.5. Cemetery: Strand Military Cemetery in Belgium.

JEPHSON, John H.: Rank: Clerk 3rd Class. Regiment or Service: Royal Air Force. Date of death: 22 December 1918. Service No: 306542 Grave or Memorial Reference: 574. Cemetery: Waterford Catholic Cemetery, Co. Waterford.

JEWELL, Alfred Henry: Rank: Petty Officer. Regiment or Service: Royal Navy Unit: H.M. Submarine "E50". Age at Death: 28. Date of Death: 31 January 1918. Service No: 236249 also listed as O/N 236249 (Ch). Born in Waterford, 16 January 1890. Drafted to Submarine "E50" on DTBR. "E50" was lost at sea with the loss of all hands. Believed to have struck a mine in the area of the South Dogger Light Vessel. Husband of Mabel Dora Jewell, 31 Hillmarten Road, Camden Town, London. Grave or Memorial Reference: Panel 28. He has no known grave but is listed on the Chatham Naval Memorial In England. He is not listed in the 'Roll of Honour' for London.

JOHNSON, Frederick: Rank: Shoeing Smith. Regiment or Service: Household Cavalry and Cavalry of the line including the Yeomanry and Imperial Camel Corps. Unit: 6th Dragoons (Inniskillings). Date of death: 6 April 1915. Service No: 3935. Born in Clonmell. Enlisted in Nenagh while living in Clonmel. Died.

Supplementary information: Brother of Mr A. Johnson, 41 Barrack Street, Waterford. Grave or Memorial Reference: 1.A.75. Cemetery: Longuenesse (St Omer) Souvenir Cemetery in France.

JOHNSON, James: Rank: Private. Regiment or Service: Royal Irish Regiment. Unit: 2nd Battalion. Date of death: 21 August 1918. Age at death: 18. Service No: 6110. Formerly he was with the Leinster Regiment where his number was 4598. Born in Knockboy, Co. Waterford. Enlisted in Waterford while living in Tramore, Co. Waterford. Killed in action.

Supplementary information: Son of Mary Power (formerly Johnson), of Waterford Road, Tramore, Co. Waterford. He has no known grave but is listed on Panel 5 on the Vis-En-Artois Memorial in France. Memorial.

JOLLY, Andrew Gordon: Rank: Lance Corporal. Regiment or Service: Royal Sussex Regiment. Unit: 4th Battalion. Date of death: 29 July 1918. Age at death: 30. Service No: G/4782. Born in Duncannon Fort, Co. Waterford. Enlisted in London. Killed in action. British Expeditionary Force.

Supplementary information: Son of Andrew and Julia Jolly, of 'St Leonard's', 31 Beach Road., Southsea. Has no known grave but is listed on the Soissons Memorial in France.

JONES, Hugh M.: Rank: Lieutenant and Temporary Lieutenant. Regiment or Service: King's Liverpool Regiment. Unit: 19th Battalion. Age at death: 28. Date of death: 30 July 1916. Killed in action.

Supplementary information: Son of the late Capt. William Jones, of Bank Buildings, Youghal, Co. Cork. A Master Mariner of the Holt Line, Liverpool. From the *Munster Express*:

LOCAL OFFICER KILLED.

Lieutenant H. M. Jones, King's Liverpool Regiment, who has been killed in action, was a younger son of the late Mr William, Jones, Master Mariner, bank Buildings, Youghal, County Cork (late of the Pacific Steam Navigation Company, Liverpool), and a brother of Mr W. J. Jones, pharmaceutical chemist, 82 Quay, Waterford, and Mrs Justin Condon, Springfield House, Youghal. He was a Master Mariner by profession and a junior officer in the Holt Line, Liverpool, aged 26. Two of his brothers are serving in the army, one as a trooper in the Australian Light Horse and the other is an officer in the Transport service.

From the *Waterford News*, August 1916:

LETTER FROM CATHOLIC CHAPLAIN.

The following letter has been received by a brother of the late Lieutenant Hugh Meredith Jones, who was killed on the 30th ult; --

August 11.

Dear Mrs Jones,

Your note of inquiry about your brother, Lieutenant H. M. Jones, has been passed on to me in order that I may be able to give you as much information about his death as possible. I knew him very well, being the Catholic Chaplain of the Brigade he was in and attached to his battalion. On a number of occasions in the past six months we have even shared the same bed, and it will interest you to know that I am a brother of the Principal of Waterford Technical School, Mr O'Shaughnessy. And now about your poor brother. He had been eating his heart out to go "over the top," as the soldiers put it – to be in the first line of attack – and about July 20 he was informed that his desire was about to be fulfilled. His battalion, and his company in particular, were chosen out for special work in the front line, and a particularly difficult and dangerous bit of work was assigned to him and his platoon of 75 men, because he was acknowledged by men and officers alike to be the coolest and bravest officer in the Regiment. We were all expecting great things of him, and had it not been for his untimely end he would, I am sure, have covered himself with glory – but, then, God willed otherwise. He started out for the attack with great zeal and energy, and led his men on through the heavy mist, amidst falling shells and bursting bombs, right up to within a stone's throw of the German trenches, when the latter suddenly uncovered a number of cleverly hidden machine guns, and simply poured death into our ranks. Unfortunately your brother was one of the first victims. Whilst cheering and encouraging his men to the last assault he was hit in the breast by a machine gun bullet. It must have pierced his heart, for when he fell dead on the spot and lay where he fell. He died like a hero, his face

to the enemy and urging on his men to the attack, and he died in defence of one of the grandest and noblest causes in which men have ever fought. He died, too, I trust, in the grace of God for only a few days before he had received absolution along with all his Catholic comrades at my hands. You have every reason, therefore, to take consolation as far as it is possible in his death. For whilst his name will always be cherished here as that of a brave and noble soldier, his soul is now, or let us hope will soon be, enjoying the glorious vision of God in heaven–a vision that will be all the brighter, stronger, and clearer because he died a noble death, fulfilling that great example set us by Our Lord Himself in dying in defence of one's weaker brethren. "Greater love than this no man hath, that a man lay down his life for his friend." Whilst offering you this little consolation, please accept also my deepest sympathies, for I know how great will your grief be at his loss. His very virtues make his loss the greater. I shall remember him constantly in my Masses, and I hope you and your good people will say a little prayer occasionally for me and my brave soldiers, Yours faithfully.
R. V. O'Shaughnessy.
C. F., attached 18th(?) Brigade.
K. L. Regiment.

Grave or Memorial Reference: He has no known grave but is listed on Pier and Face 1D, 8B and 8C of the Thiepval Memorial in France.

JONES, Samuel: Rank: Rifleman. Regiment or Service: Royal Irish Rifles Unit: 2nd Battalion. Date of death: 7 June 1917. Service No: 9631. Born in Anglesea. Enlisted in Cork while living in Waterford. Killed in action. He has no known grave but is listed on Panel 40 on the Ypres (Menin Gate) Memorial in Belgium.

JONES, Thomas: Rank: Private. Regiment or Service: Royal Fusilier (City of London Regiment.) Unit: 12th Battalion. Age at death: 19. Date of death: 11 January 1917. Service No: 61991. Formerly he was with the 6th Cavalry Reserve Regiment where his number was 24038. Born in Dublin. Enlisted in Dublin while living in Waterford. Died of wounds.
Supplementary information: Son of James and Alicia Jones, of 29 City Quay, Dublin. From the *Waterford News*, April 1915:

> Messrs, Thomas B Jones and Gilbert T Athel, both members of the electrical staff of the Clyde Shipping Company, have joined the Second Sportsmen's Battalion of the Royal Fusiliers, and left last night by the Rosslare express en-route to report themselves at headquarters. The Clyde Shipping Company has generously agreed to keep open the positions of Messrs, Jones and Athel, and these they resume when their military services are no longer required. The company has also arranged to pay the difference between their army pay and allowances and their present salaries, so that they will not suffer financially by joining the forces of the Crown.

He has no known grave but is listed on the Green Dump Memorial in Ancre British Cemetery, Beaumont-Hamel in France.

JOY, James: Rank: Private. Regiment or Service: South Wales Borderers Unit: 1st Battalion. Age at death: 27. Date of death: 9 May 1915. Service No: 13064. Born in Carrickbog in Waterford and enlisted in Tonypandy in Wales. Killed in action.
Supplementary information: Brother of John Joy, of Friary Hill, Carrickbeg, Carrick-on-Suir, Co. Tipperary. Grave or Memorial Reference: Has no known grave but is commemorated on Panel 14 and 15. Memorial: Le Touret Memorial in France.

K

KAVANAGH, Thomas: Rank: Sergeant. Regiment or Service: Royal Flying Corps. Unit: 22nd Squadron. Date of death: 24 January 1918. Service No: 4357.

Supplementary information: Son of Mrs M.A. Kavanagh, (nurse) Chapel Street. Died from injuries received in France after a test of aeronautics. Joined the Royal Flying Corps in March 1915, after his brother Matthew, who is now home, being first wounded. Prior to enlistment he was employed as a carpenter on the G.S. and W. Railway. A letter received from him a week before his death stated that he expected to be home on leave about 10 February. He had been in France for the previous twelve months. Grave or Memorial Reference: VII.A14. Cemetery: Lapugnoy Military Cemetery in France.

KAVANAGH, William: Rank: Private. Regiment or Service: Manchester Regiment. Unit: 1st Battalion. Age at death: 24. Date of death: 8 March 1916. Service No: 2764. Born in Waterford. Enlisted in Dublin while living in Waterford. Killed in action in Mesopotamia.

Supplementary information: Son of Mrs Annie Kavanagh, of 2 Goats Lane, Lower Yellow Road, Waterford. Grave or Memorial Reference: 31 and 64 on the Basra Memorial in Iraq.

KEANE, James: Rank: Fireman. Regiment or Service: Mercantile Marine. Unit: SS *Coningbeg* (Glasgow). Torpedoed by German Submarine U-62. There were no survivors. U-62 surrendered in November 1918. Age at death: 28. Date of death: 18 December 1917.

Supplementary information: Son of William and Catherine Keane. Husband of Julia Keane (*née* McDonnell), of 14 Passage Road, Waterford. Born in Waterford. He has no known grave but is listed on the Tower Hill Memorial in the UK. He is also listed on the Formby-Coningbeg Memorial, Adelphi Quay in Waterford City.

KEANE, John: Rank: Trimmer. Regiment or Service: Mercantile Marine Reserve. Unit: HMS *Calgarian*. Sunk by 4 torpedoes from German submarine U-19 off Rathlin Island. Age at death: 17. Date of death: 1 March 1918. Service No: 906577.

Supplementary information: Son of John and Catherine Keane, of 110 Ballytruckle, Waterford. Grave or Memorial Reference: 31 on the Plymouth Naval Memorial, UK.

KEANE, Maurice: Rank: Private. Regiment or Service: Machine Gun Corps (Infantry). Unit: 38th Coy. Age at death: 34. Date of death: 25 October 1918. Service No: 31408. Born in Dungarvan, Co. Waterford. Enlisted in Waterford while living in Dungarvan. Died in Mesopotamia. Previously he was with the Royal Irish Regiment where his number was 5334.

Supplementary information: Son of Daniel and Bridget Keane of Abbeyside, Dungarvan, Co. Waterford. Grave or Memorial Reference: IV.E.5. Cemetery: Baghdad (North Gate) War Cemetery in Iraq.

KEANE, Patrick: Rank: Private. Regiment or Service: Royal Irish Regiment. Unit: 6th Battalion. Age at death: 23. Date of death: 29 November 1917. Service No: 7611. Born in St John S. Waterford. Enlisted in Waterford. Killed in action.

Supplementary information: Son of Mrs Julia Keane, of 16 Lower Yellow Road, Waterford. Grave or Memorial Reference: I.D.28. Cemetery: Croisilles Railway Cemetery in France.

KEANE, Thomas: Rank: Fireman. Regiment or Service: Mercantile Marine. Unit: SS (Barrow). Shelled and sunk by a German submarine 12 miles south-east of Cork. Age at death: 27. Date of death: 30 March 1918.

Supplementary information: Son of John and Brigid Keane (*née* Dunne), of 70 Mulgrave Road, Ferrybank, Waterford. Born in Waterford. He has no known grave but is listed on the Tower Hill Memorial in the UK.

KEANE, Timothy: Rank: Private. Regiment or Service: Royal Irish Regiment. Unit: 5th Battalion. Age at death: 22. Date of death: 4 November 1918. Service No: 370. Born in Ballybricken, Co. Waterford. Enlisted in Waterford. Killed in action.

Supplementary information: Son of Timothy and Ellen Keane, of 8 Castle Terrace, Waterford. Grave or Memorial Reference: I.A.40. Cemetery: Cross Roads Cemetery, Fontaine-Au-Bois in France.

KEARNEY, Arthur Joseph: Rank: Lieutenant. Regiment or Service: Royal Munster Fusiliers. Unit: 1st Battalion. Age at death: 23. Date of death: 9 September 1916. Killed in action.

Supplementary information: Elder son of William, J.P. and Mary Kearney, of Grace Dieu, Waterford. Husband of E. Kearney, of Rosebank Cottage, Tramore, Co. Waterford. From the *Waterford News*, June 1915:

HOME FROM THE FRONT.

Lieutenant A. J. Kearney (Connaught Rangers) who had been in the firing line for some time arrived home this week, having been accidentally wounded. Notwithstanding his trying experiences in the trenches Lieutenant Kearney is looking well, though suffering from the effects of a revolver shot accidentally discharged. Previous to receiving his commission Lieutenant Kearney devoted much of his time fowling and other outdoor games, and he contrasted his life in the camp in Flanders with the home associations by stating that instead of birds he had overhead aeroplanes and instead of flies, shells. He is staying at Windsor Place, Tramore.

From the *Waterford News*, September 1915:

LIEUTENANT KEARNEY.

We are glad to learn that the wound which Lieutenant A. J. Kearney received is not very serious. He was struck in the shoulder by a piece of shell and is at present in the 4th London Hospital, King's College, Denmark Hill, London.

The *Waterford News*, September 1916:

LOCAL WAR ITEMS
OTHER CASUALTIES
Lieutenant. A. J. Kearney, son of Mr Wm. Kearney, J.P. Gracedieu. is unofficially reported wounded and missing. Lieutenant T. J. Kennedy, Royal Inniskilling Fusiliers, reported killed in action on the 9th inst., was a son of Mr Samuel Kennedy, of Tyresson, Cookstown. Prior to joining the army Lieutenant Kennedy was editor, of the "Monaghan Standard" and formerly a member of the staff of the "Waterford Standard". Lance-Corporal W. Hassett, Royal Irish Rifles, son of the late Mr Thos. Hassett, Clonmel, and Mrs Hassett, Newtown, Waterford, has been wounded.

P. Power, Waterford - Royal Irish Rifles - killed.
D. Foley, Cappoquin - King's Liverpool Regiment - missing.
J. W. Watson, Waterford - Gunner, R. F. A. - wounded.
E. Flynn, Carrickbeg - Royal Irish Rifles - wounded.
M. Keane, Waterford - Inniskilling Fusiliers - wounded.
D. Fitzgerald, Lismore-King's Liverpool Regiment-wounded.
Lance-Corporal M. Butler, R. I. Rifles, of Waterford - killed.

From the *Waterford News*, 1915:

AT THE FRONT.

Lieutenant A. J. Kearney, (Royal Munsters), Gracedieu, Waterford, has been in the war zone for the past couple of weeks. Writing home this week he mentions that the Germans are trying all kinds of tricks to lead the British force into a cul-de-sac. Lieutenant Kearney went to the front with a batch of officers on the Munsters so as to keep the Regiment up to the requirements of war strength.

From the *Waterford News*, May 1915:

LIGHT-HEARTED WATERFORD OFFICER. LAUGHTER FROM THE TRENCHES.

The following letter has been received by Mr A. Farrell, Secretary of the Harbour Board, from a Waterford officer closely connected with the Agricultural Show. You cannot argue under shell-fire, said Mr Lloyd George at Manchester yesterday; but the writer of this letter find no difficulty in being surprisingly light-hearted under shell-fire.

Rifle Munster Fusiliers.
British Expeditionary Force, France.
31st May, 1915.
Dear Austin,
You ought to give a prize this year for the man obtaining the largest number of recruits at the Show. This is a lively place, but Hell must be indeed be a warm spot if it is worse than the trenches. Between shells, bombs, bullets, etc., we are getting an idea into our minds now that the place is dangerous.

I have not had the pleasure of meeting the Kaiser so far, but am living in hope of doing so some time. It is very pleasant to see how important the Germans think we are, as they waste a few hundred rounds on us if we lift our unfortunate heads an inch over the trench.
Best Love.
A.J.K.

From the *Waterford News*, October 1916:

WATERFORDMEN IN THE CASUALTY LISTS.

In Mondays lists the following names appeared in the list of killed: Lieutenant A. J. Kearney, Munsters, son of Mr William Kearney, J.P., Gracedieu, is now officially reported missing.

He has no known grave but is listed on Pier and Face 16 C of the Thiepval Memorial in France.

KEATING, Thomas: Rank: Able Seaman. Regiment or Service: Mercantile Marine. Unit: SS *Formby* (Glasgow). Age at death: 48. Date of death: 16 December 1917. The ship was lost with all hands and never located during a fierce storm.

Supplementary information: Son of the late John and Hannah Keating. Husband of Anastasia Keating (*née* O'Brien), of Passage East, Co. Waterford. Born at Passage East. He has no known grave but is listed on the Tower Hill Memorial in the UK. He is also listed on the Formby-Coningbeg Memorial, Adelphi Quay in Waterford City.

KEATING, Thomas Joseph: Rank: Captain. Regiment or Service: Royal Air Force. Unit: 63rd Squadron. Secondary Regiment: Royal Field Artillery Secondary. Age at death: 24. Date of death: 14 June 1918.

Supplementary information: Son of Patrick and Mary Keating, of Ballinamult, Co. Waterford. Grave or Memorial Reference: III.E.5. Cemetery: Baghdad (North Gate) War Cemetery in Iraq.

KEEFE, William: Rank: Private. Regiment or Service: The Queen's (Royal West Surrey Regiment). Unit: 7th Battalion. Age at death: 21. Date of death: 25 October 1916. Service No: 6802 and S/6802. Born in Lismore, Co. Waterford. Enlisted in London while living in Bermondsey, Surrey. Died of wounds.

Supplementary information: Son of Thos. and Mary Anne Keefe, of Lismore, Co. Waterford. Grave or Memorial Reference: III.F.3. Cemetery: Contay British Cemetery, Contay in France.

KEEFFE, John: Rank: Private. Regiment or Service: Royal Irish Regiment. Unit: 6th Battalion. Date of death: 3 September 1916. Service No: 11070. Ahenny, Co. Tipperary (Soldiers died in the Great War), Ahenny, Carrick-on-Suir, Co. Waterford (Irelands Memorial Records). Enlisted in Carrick-on-Suir while living in Ahenny. Killed in action. He has no known grave but is listed on Pier and Face 3A on the Thiepval Memorial in France.

KEHOE, Patrick: Rank: Rifleman. Kings Royal Rifle Corps. Unit: 11th Battalion. Date of death: 3 September 1916. Service No: R-15491. Born in Mullinahone. Enlisted in Fethard while living in Waterford. Killed in action. He has no known grave but is listed on Pier and Face 13A and 13B on the Thiepval Memorial in France

KEHOE, Richard: Rank: Fireman. Regiment or Service: Mercantile Marine. Unit: SS *Coningbeg* (Glasgow). Torpedoed by German Submarine U-62. There were no survivors. U-62 surrendered in November 1918. Age at death: 39. Date of death: 18 December 1917.

Supplementary information: Son of John Kehoe and the late Mary Kehoe. Husband of Johanna Kehoe (*née* Hanley), of 24 Johnstown, Waterford. Born in Waterford. He has no known grave but is listed on the Tower Hill Memorial in the UK. He is also listed on the Formby-Coningbeg Memorial, Adelphi Quay in Waterford City.

KEILEY/KIELY, Patrick: Rank: Gunner. Regiment or Service: Royal Horse Artillery and Royal Field Artillery. Unit: B Battery, 70th Brigade. Date of death: 10 May 1917. Service No: 119621. Born in Waterford. Enlisted in Waterford. Killed in action. Grave or Memorial Reference: I.E.13. Cemetery: Tilloy British Cemetery, Tilloy-Les-Mofflaines in France.

KELLY, Cyrus: Rank: Private. Regiment or Service: Australian Infantry, A.I.F. Unit: 17th Battalion. Date of death: 9 October 1917.

Service No: 5367. Enlisted on 1 February 1916 at Liverpool Camp. Killed in action. From his records:

In or near what Parish or Town were you born? Waterford.

Are you a natural born British subject or a Naturalised British subject? Natural Born British Subject.

What is your trade or calling? Hospital Attendant in the Paramatta Mental Hospital, N. S. W.

Are you married? No.

Who is your next of kin? Step-father, Charles Downey, Northesk, Lansdowne, Limerick.

Have you ever been convicted by the Civil Power? No.

Have you stated the whole, if any, of your previous service? Yes.

Age: 30 years, 10 months.

Height: 5 feet, 8 ½ inches.

Weight: 155lbs.

Chest measurement: 36 inches.

Complexion: fair.

Eyes: brown.

Hair: fair.

Religious denomination: Church of England.

His pension was applied for by his step-father, Charles F. Downey, Northesk, Limerick, Ireland (previously 5 Wellington Terrace, Limerick) and was later withdrawn. Address of the deceased prior to enlistment was given as, Mental Hospital, Parramatta, New South Wales. Private Kelly's personal effects were sent to his step-father who replied with a receipt. Written on the receipt was 'With grateful thanks to those who have taken so much trouble to send these few treasures, C Downey.' Dated 23 December 1917. His papers record the memorial plaque and scroll went sent to his step-father but it does not show that his medals were ever issued.

Grave or Memorial Reference: Has no known grave but is commemorated on Panel 7-17-23-25-27-29-31 on the Ypres (Menin Gate) Memorial in Belgium.

KELLY, J.: Rank: Private. Regiment or Service: Royal Irish Fusiliers. Date of death: 6 February 1919. Service No: 29634 Grave or Memorial Reference: B.K.149. Cemetery: Ballynaneashagh (St Otteran's) Catholic Cemetery, Co. Waterford.

KELLY, John: Rank: Private. Regiment or Service: Royal Army Service Corps. Unit: H.T. Age at death: 28. Date of death: 18 February 1919. Service No: T1/3908. Supplementary information: Son of William Kelly, of Helwick Ring, Dunganan. Grave or Memorial Reference: South-East of Church. Cemetery: Ringville Catholic Churchyard, Co. Waterford.

KELLY, Michael: Rank: Private. Regiment or Service: Royal Irish Regiment. Unit: 2nd Battalion. Age at death: 34. Date of death: 11 November 1918. Service No: 3814. Born in St Patrick's, Waterford. Enlisted in Tipperary while living in Waterford. Died of wounds.

Supplementary information: Son of John and Mary Kelly of Waterford. Grave or Memorial Reference: XVII.B.18. Cemetery: Cement House Cemetery in Belgium.

KELLY, Thomas: Rank: Private. Regiment or Service: Royal Army Service Corps and Army Service Corps. Date of death: 10 October 1918. Service No: SS/232. Born in Waterford. Enlisted in Aldershot while living in Aldershot. Died at Sea. The SS *Leinster* sank on this day. He may have been a passenger as he 'died at sea'. He has no known grave but is listed on the Hollybrook Memorial, Southampton, UK.

KEMP, Timothy: Rank: Corporal. Regiment or Service: Royal Munster Fusiliers. Unit: 8th Battalion. Date of death: 17 September 1916. Service No: 4983. Born in Lismore, Co. Waterford. Enlisted in Dungarvan, Co. Waterford while living in Lismore. Died of wounds. From the *Munster Express*:

LISMORE SOLDIER DIES OF WOUNDS.

The Relatives of Sergeant Thomas Kemp, Munster Fusiliers, a native of Lismore, have been informed that he Died of wounds received in action. He was a prominent member of the Lismore Dramatic Class and a noted figure on the concert platforms in the comic turns. He was also a fine footballer, belonging to the Ballinwilling football club.

From the *Munster Express*:

Corporal Tim Kemp, of the Munsters, and Private Joseph O'Brien, of the Welsh Regiment, at present home on leave, have also been wounded. A *Munster Express* snippet in September 9, 1916 says that Thomas was home on leave with Pte O'Brien and they were both wounded.

Grave or Memorial Reference: B.19.41. Cemetery: St Sever Cemetery Extension, Rouen in France.

KENNEALLY, Janes (Soldiers died in the Great War and the Commonwealth War Graves Commission) **KENNEALLY, James:** (Ireland's Memorial Records). Rank: Private. Regiment or Service: Royal Army Service Corps. Unit: 35th Div. Motor Transport Company. Date of death: 11 November 1918 (the day the war ended). Service No: T4/127073. Born in Waterford. Enlisted in Merthyr while living in Merthyr. Died. Grave or Memorial Reference: A.2. Cemetery: Kortrijk (St January) Communal Cemetery in Belgium.

KENNEDY, Edward: Rank: Private. Regiment or Service: Canadian Infantry (Eastern Ontario Regiment). Unit: 38th Battalion. Age at death: 24. Date of death: 18 November 1916. Service No: 410520. Data from attestation papers:

In what Town or parish and in what Country were you born? Waterford, Ireland.

What is the name of your next of kin? Mrs Mary Anne Kennedy (mother).

What is the address of your next of kin? 15 Roches Street, Waterford, Ireland.

What is the date of your birth? 2 October 1885. (30 years).

What is your trade or calling? Labourer.

Are you married? No.

Apparent age: 29 years, 5 months.

Height: 5 Ft 7½ Ins.

Girth when fully expanded: 37½ Ins.

Complexion: fair.

Eyes: blue.

Hair: brown.

Date: 29 March 1915.

Supplementary information: Son of Mary Anne Kennedy, of 15 Roches Street, Waterford. He has no known grave but is listed on the Vimy Memorial in France.

KENNEDY, George: Rank: Private. Regiment or Service: Royal Irish Regiment. Unit: 'C' Coy. 1st Battalion. Age at death: 25. Date of death: 3 November 1916. Service No: 7571. Born in Waterford. Enlisted in Waterford. Died of wounds in Salonika.

Supplementary information: Son of John and Fanny Kennedy, of Waterford. Husband of M. Kennedy, of 14 Johnstown Avenue, Waterford. Grave or Memorial Reference: II.D.12. Cemetery: Lahana Military Cemetery in Greece.

KENNEDY, J.: Rank: Ordinary Seaman. Regiment or Service: Mercantile Marine. Unit: SS *Adriatic* (Hull). Struck a mine and sank off the Isle of Man. Age at death: 17. Date of death: 31 October 1916.

Supplementary information: Son of Mrs Kennedy, of 8 Roches Street, Waterford. Born in Waterford. He has no known grave but is listed on the Tower Hill Memorial in the UK.

KENNEDY, Laurence: Rank: Rifleman. Regiment or Service: Royal Irish Rifles. Unit: 6th Battalion. He was previously with

the Royal Field Artillery where his number was 100327. Age at death: 18. Date of death: 27 October 1915. Service No: 7763. Born in Clonmel and enlisted in Clonmel while living in Kilganny Co. Waterford. Died in Gallipoli.

Supplementary information: Son of Martin and Mary Kennedy, of Upper Croan, Clonmel, Co. Tipperary. Grave or Memorial Reference: III.C.70. Cemetery: East Mudros Military Cemetery in Greece.

KENNEDY, Michael: Rank: Private. Regiment or Service: Royal Irish Fusiliers. Unit: 7th Battalion. Age at death: 27. Date of death: 8 March 1916. Service No: 17050. Previously he was with the Royal Irish Regiment where his number was 1200. Born in Waterford. Enlisted in Waterford. Killed in action.

Supplementary information: Son of John and Mary Kennedy, of 5 Little Michael Streett, Waterford. Grave or Memorial Reference: 124 on the Loos Memorial in France.

KENNEDY, Ronald Bayly Craven: Rank: Lieutenant. Regiment or Service: Royal Dublin Fusiliers. Date of death: 10 August 1917. Died. De Ruvigny's Roll of Honour:

...elder son of Edward de Vere Kennedy, of Westown, Straffan, County Kildare, late 5th Lancers, by his wife, Nelly, daughter of Sir John Carden, 4th Bart. Born at Woodhouse, Stradbally, County Waterford, 21 September 1895. Educated at Clifton College, and only left there on the outbreak of war. Was gazetted 2nd Lieutenant, The Royal Dublin Fusiliers, 23 September 1914, and promoted Lieutenant in 1915. Served with the Mediterranean Expeditionary Force at Gallipoli from 10 July 1915, as Machine Gun Officer. Took part in the landing at Suvla Bay 6 August, being mae temporart Captain early in September, owing to all the other officers being killed or wounded; was severely wounded on the 27th, and invalided home, proceeded to France in August-1916, as A. D. C. to Lieutenant General Sir Edward

Fanshawe, 5th Army Corps, where he served until December, when he was invalided home, and died at his home at Westown, 10 August 1917; from illness contracted.

Grave or Memorial Reference: Family plot in North-East part. Cemetery: Stradbally Church of Ireland Churchyard, County Waterford.

KENNEDY, Thomas: Rank: Shipwright, 2nd Class. Regiment or Service: Royal Navy. Unit: HMS *Formidable*. Age at death: 40. Date of death: 1 January 1915. Date of birth: 16 February 1874. Service No: 344024. Born in Ballytruckle, Co. Waterford. HMS *Formidable* was struck by a torpedo from German Submarine U-34. Twenty minutes later she developed a list of 20 degrees and the Captain ordered the crew to abandon ship. Darkness and a 30 foot swell made it difficult to get the boats into the water and some fell in to the sea upside down twenty-five minutes later the *Formidable* was struck again by a torpedo and after about an hour or so she looked like she would capsize.

The Captain and his terrier dog were calmly organising the crew to abandon ship when it capsized and turned over on many of the men in the water. 347 crew died including the Captain and his terrier. From the *Waterford News*, 1914:

WATERFORD MAN LOST ON THE *FORMIDABLE*.
Mr Thomas Kennedy, Ballytruckle.
Amongst the crew of HMS *Formidable*, which was sunk in the Channel on Friday morning, was Mr Thomas Kennedy, Ballytruckle, and a telegram from the Admiralty, received on Sunday, announced with regret that he was not amongst the list of those saved. The deceased was son of Mrs Kennedy, manor Street, and a brother of Mr J.J. Kennedy. He was apprenticed as a carpenter to Mr George Nolan, builder, and joined the Navy 14 years ago as a shipright. He served in Chinese and Australian waters and was transferred to the Formidable about two years ago. He was married, and leaves a widow and six children. Deep regret will be felt for his family and relatives in their bereavement.

He has no known grave but is listed on the Chatham Naval Memorial, UK.

KENNEDY, Thomas: Rank: Private. Regiment or Service: Royal Irish Regiment. Unit: 2nd Battalion. Age at death: 22. Date of death: 14 July 1916. Service No: 7596. Born in Waterford. Enlisted in Waterford. Killed in action.
Supplementary information: Son of Margaret Kennedy, of 3 Alexander Street Waterford, and the late Patrick Kennedy. He has no known grave but is listed on Pier and Face 3A of the Thiepval Memorial in France.

KENNEDY, William: Rank: Private. Regiment or Service: Royal Dublin Fusiliers. Unit: 2nd Battalion. Age at death: 35. Date of death: 26 April 1915. Service No: 17716. Born in Waterford. Enlisted in St Pancras, Middlesex while living in Waterford. Killed in action.
Supplementary information: Son of Murtagh and Elizabeth Sommers Kennedy. Grave or Memorial Reference: XXV.H.1. Cemetery: New Irish Farm Cemetery in Belgium.

KENNY, John Mary Joseph: Rank: Lieutenant. Regiment or Service: Royal Flying Corps. Unit: 21st Squadron. Secondary Regiment: Army Service Corps (Officers Died in the Great War gives his secondary units and the ASC and the RFC in two different listing for him). Killed in action. Age at death: 20. Date of death: 23 September 1916.
Supplementary information: Son of Mrs Kenny, of Belair, Tramore, Co. Waterford. From the *Waterford News*, November 1916:

YOUNG WATERFORD OFFICER KILLED IN ACTION.
News has been received by Mrs Kenny, "Belair" Tramore, from the Red Cross Society at Geneva, that her son, Lieutenant.

J. M. Kenny, Royal Flying Corps, was killed on the 23rd September, 1916, while engaging a hostile aeroplane. No confirmation has yet been received from the War Office.

From the December 1916 edition of *Flight*:

Lieutenant J. M. Kenny, R. F. C, (killed in action on September 3rd), was twenty years of age, and son of the late Patrick J. Kenny, solicitor, Waterford. He had a commission in the Army Service Corps in April, 1915, and, transferring to the Royal Flying Corps, was gazetted flying officer in the September following. He was promoted in May of this year.

Memorial: Arras Flying Services Memorial in Faubourg D'Amiens Cemetery, Arras in France.

KENNY, Richard: Rank: Corporal. Regiment or Service: Royal Irish Regiment. Unit: 6th Battalion. Age at death: 19. Date of death: 3 September 1916. Service No: 7498. Born in Ballybricken, Co. Waterford. Enlisted in Waterford while living in Tipperary. Killed in action.

Supplementary information: Son of Thomas and Ellen Kenny, of 5 Barker St, Waterford. He has no known grave but is listed on Pier and Face 3A of the Thiepval Memorial in France.

KENT, Walter: Rank: Private (Lance Corporal). Regiment or Service: Royal Irish Regiment. Unit: 2nd Battalion. Age at death: 36. Date of death: 4 July 1916. Service No: 4898. Born in Duncannon, Co. Wicklow. Enlisted in Carrigtwohill, Co. Cork. Killed in action. Supplementary information: Son of Mrs Mary Ellen Kent, of Duncannon, New Ross, Co. Waterford; husband of Alice Kent, of Main Street, Carrigtwohill, Co. Cork. He has no known grave but is listed on Pier and Face 3A on the Thiepval Memorial in France.

KEOHAN, Patrick Joseph: Rank: Wireless Telegraph Operator. Regiment or Service: Royal Naval Reserve. Unit: HMS *Hawke*. Age at death: 22. Date of death: 15 October 1914. Service No: WTS/149.

Supplementary information: Son of Edmond and Ellen Keohan, of 17 Main Street, Dungarvan, Co. Waterford. From the *Waterford News*, 1914:

DUNGARVAN LETTER.

The parents of Mr Patrick J Keohan, Main Street, who at first entertained the belief when hearing of the disaster to HMS Hawke that their son was not on board now appear to have lost hope of his being alive. Enquiries at the Admiralty Offices seem but to confuse matters, no definite information being available. They at first reported that he had been transferred as wireless operator to HMS Crescent and afterwards it would seem that there must have been a re-transfer back to the ill-fated Hawke on which he had served since he joined as wireless operator some months ago. His father some days ago after the disaster received a letter, dated 10th October, written on board the Hawke from poor "Paddie". The name by which he was known in Dungarvan where he was most popular amongst all his friends.

Grave or Memorial Reference: 5 on the Plymouth Naval Memorial, UK.

KEOHAN, Thomas: Rank: Seaman. Regiment or Service: Royal Naval Reserve. Unit: HMS *Goliath*. Age at death: 34. Date of death: 13 May 1915. Service No: 4299B. HMS *Goliath* was sunk by three torpedoes from German destroyer 'Muvanet-I-Milet', she blew up and capsized immediately taking 570 of her 750 crew including the Captain to a watery grave. Ten Waterford men died on the *Goliath* that day.

Supplementary information: Son of Laurence and Mary Keohan, of Newtown, Tramore. Husband of Dora Keohan, of Newtown, Tramore, Co. Waterford. Grave or Memorial Reference: 8 on the Plymouth Naval Memorial, UK.

KETT, William: Rank: Private. Regiment or Service: Royal Irish Fusiliers. Unit: 3rd Garrison Battalion. Date of death: 3 May 1917. Service No: 19510 (Soldiers died in the Great War), G/19510 (Commonwealth War Graves Commission). Formerly he was with the Royal Irish Regiment where his number was. 5759. Born in Clashmore, Co. Waterford. Enlisted in Lismore, Co. Waterford while living in Kinsalebeg, Co. Waterford. Died at Home.

Supplementary information: Husband of K. Kett, of Clashmore. Grave or Memorial Reference: Left of Church from entrance. Cemetery: Clashmore Old Church of Ireland Churchyard, Waterford.

KIELY, Edward: Rank: Private. Regiment or Service: Australian Infantry, A.I.F. Unit: 5th Battalion. Age at death: 43. Date of death: 10 May 1917. Enlisted 27 March 1916 in Brunswick, Victoria. Service No: 6303. Killed in action.

Supplementary information: Son of Patrick and Mary Kiely, of 73 Beavers Road., Northcote, Victoria. Born at Dungarvan, Co. Waterford.

In or near what Parish or Town were you born? Waterford, Ireland.

Are you a natural born British subject or a Naturalised British subject? Natural Born British Subject.

What is your age? 42 years 8 Months.

What is your trade or calling? Farm Manager.

Are you, or have you been an Apprentice? No. If so where, to whom, and for what period?

Are you married? Single.

Who is your next of kin? [Mother] Mary Kiely, 33 McCracken Avenue, Northcote, Victoria, changed later after her death to [father] to Patrick Kiely, 73 Beavis Road, Northcote, war medals to father.

Have you ever been convicted by the Civil Power? No.

Have you stated the whole, if any, of your previous service? Yes

Age: 42 years, 8 months.
Height: 5 feet, 7 ½ inches.
Weight: 140 lbs.
Chest measurement: 35-37 inches.
Complexion: florid.
Eyes: blue.
Hair: grey.
Religious denomination: R. C.

Pension of 14/- per fortnight was awarded to Mary Anne Kiely from 24 July 1917. Medals were issued to his father.

Grave or Memorial Reference: He has no known grave but is listed on the Villers-Bretonneux Memorial in France.

KIELY, James: Rank: Private. Regiment or Service: Royal Irish Regiment. Unit: 2nd Battalion. Age at death: 25. Date of death: 19 October 1914. Service No: 8186. Born in Trinity Without, Waterford. Enlisted in Waterford. Killed in action.

Supplementary information: Son of James and Elizabeth Kiely, of 3 Brown's Lane, Waterford. Grave or Memorial Reference: 11 and 12 on the Le Touret Memorial in France.

KIELY, James: Rank: Private. Regiment or Service: Leinster Regiment. Unit: 7th Battalion. Age at death: 21. Date of death: 27 June 1916. Service No: 3180. Born in Waterford. Enlisted in Waterford while living in Waterford. Killed in action.

Supplementary information: Son of Patrick and Margaret Kiely, of 3 Brown's Lane, Waterford. Grave or Memorial Reference: 127 on the Loos Memorial in France.

KIELY, John: Rank: Fireman. Regiment or Service: Mercantile Marine. Unit: SS *Formby* (Glasgow). Date of death: 16 December 1917. The ship was lost with all hands and never located during a fierce storm.

Supplementary information: Son of the late William and Margaret Kiely. Born in Waterford. He has no known grave but

"HALT! WHO GOES THERE"?
—— 'FRIEND'!
"ADVANCE FRIEND AND GIVE THE COUNTERSIGN
—— "'SUMMIT' FLOUR"
"PASS FRIEND ALL'S WELL!"
SUMMIT

It's rub-a-dub-dub but not at the tub;
  You mustn't shrink Khaki in washing.
To call of the drum a Million Men come—
  A Million Shirts Lux should be washing.

Tommy's Postscript

The Censor always allows the postscript which
so many letters from the front now contain :—

P.S. **Don't forget more Pears' Soap In
your next parcel.**

Pears' Soap

thoroughly cleanses and refreshes the skin and
gives a feeling of exhilaration

A frequent sight on French roads in these exciting times

Cheers all the way for the Brave Boys and Pears

Pears' Soap and our soldiers typify to the best British qualities, and the Boys are delighted, when a box of this famous soap reaches them from home, for

Pears' Soap

and the gallant fighters, both stand for reliability and efficiency

Ask your dealer for **"SUMMIT" FLOUR**, you will get the best Flour it is possible to manufacture—and the **PUREST.** Be on the safe side and **ASK** for **"SUMMIT."**

SOLD IN SIZES TO SUIT EVERYONE
14's, 28's, 56's, 98's, 112's, & 140-lbs.

If necessary, Write for Name of the Nearest Dealer to

JOSEPH RANK, Ltd.
11 BRUNSWICK ST., LIVERPOOL

is listed on the Tower Hill Memorial in the UK. He is also listed on the Formby-Coningbeg Memorial, Adelphi Quay in Waterford City.

KIELY, John: Rank: Private. Regiment or Service: Gloucestershire Regiment. Unit: 12th (Service) (Bristol) Battalion. Date of death: 5 October 1917. Service No: 33584. Formerly he was with the Royal Army Service Corps where his number was 186895. Born in Waterford. Enlisted in Liverpool while living in Waterford. Died of wounds.

Supplementary information: Son of Mr J. Kiely, of 49 Castle Street, Waterford. Grave or Memorial Reference: I.L.37. Cemetery: Godewaersvelde British Cemetery in France.

KIELY/KEILEY, Patrick: Rank: Gunner. Regiment or Service: Royal Horse Artillery and Royal Field Artillery. Unit: B Battery, 70th Brigade. Date of death: 10 May 1917. Service No: 119621. Born in Waterford. Enlisted in Waterford. Killed in action. Grave or Memorial Reference: I.E.13. Cemetery: Tilloy British Cemetery, Tilloy-Les-Mofflaines in France.

KIELY, Patrick: Rank: Private. Regiment or Service: Royal Dublin Fusiliers. Unit: 3rd Battalion. Secondary Regiment: Labour Corps Secondary. Unit: transferred to (398557) 948th Area Employment Coy. Date of death: 1 March 1919. Service No: 21560.

Supplementary information: Husband of Johanna Keily, of 9 Stephenson Street, Waterford. Grave or Memorial Reference: VIII.G.1. Cemetery: Les Baraques Military Cemetery, Sangatte in France.

KIELY, Patrick: Rank: Private. Regiment or Service: Royal Irish Regiment. Unit: 2nd Battalion. Date of death: 24 May 1915. Service No: 7099. Born in Dungarvan, Co. Waterford. Enlisted in Liverpool while living in Dungarvan. Killed in action. He

KIELY, Richard: Rank: Private. Regiment or Service: Royal Irish Regiment. Unit: 2nd Battalion. Date of death: 5 July 1916. Service No: 7491. Born in Cathedral, Waterford. Enlisted in Waterford. Killed in action. He has no known grave but is listed on Pier and Face 3A on the Thiepval Memorial in France.

KIELY, Thomas: Rank: Seaman. Regiment or Service: Royal Naval Reserve. Unit: HMS *Orbita*. Age at death: 32. Date of death: 7 December 1915. Service No: 2221C.

Supplementary information: Son of John and Anna Kiely, of Tramore, Co. Waterford. Husband of Catherine Pawer (formerly Kiely), of New Line Road, Tramore, Co. Waterford. Grave or Memorial Reference: 8 on the Plymouth Naval Memorial, UK.

KIELY, William: Rank: Private. Regiment or Service: Royal Army Medical Corps. Unit: Attached to the 15th General Hospital. Age at death: 53.Date of death: 23 December 1915. Service No: 71039. Born in Waterford. Enlisted in Waterford. Died in Egypt.

Supplementary information: Husband of Catherine Kiely, of Little Patrick Street, Waterford. Grave or Memorial Reference: C.105. Cemetery: Alexandria (Chatby) Military and War Memorial Cemetery in Egypt.

KING, Patrick: Rank: Private. Regiment or Service: Connaught Rangers. Unit: 5th Battalion. Date of death: 21 August 1915. Service No: 930. Born in Waterford. Enlisted in Waterford while living in Waterford. Killed in action in Gallipoli. Grave or Memorial Reference: Panel 181 to 183. Memorial: Helles Memorial in Turkey.

KINSELLA, James: Rank: Private. Regiment or Service: Royal Irish Regiment. Unit: 2nd Battalion. Date of death: 19 October 1914. Service No: 6073. Born in Trinity Without, Waterford. Enlisted in Waterford while living in Dungarvan, Co. Waterford. Killed in action. Grave or Memorial Reference: He has no known grave but is listed on Panels 11 and 12 on the Le Touret Memorial in France.

KINSELLA, William: Rank: Able Seaman. Regiment or Service: Mercantile Marine. Unit: SS *Royal Edward* (Toronto). Sunk by a torpedo from German submarine U-14. Age at death: 52. Date of death: 13 August 1915.
Supplementary information: Son of the late Michael and Margaret Kinsella (*née* Walsh). Husband of Mary Kinsella, of 16 Newtown Hill, Waterford. Born in Waterford. He has no known grave but is listed on the Tower Hill Memorial in the UK.

KIRBY, Michael: Rank: Private. Regiment or Service: Royal Irish Regiment. Unit: 2nd Battalion. Date of death: 22 January 1915. Service No: 6382. Born in Trinity Without, Waterford. Enlisted in Waterford. Died of wounds. Grave or Memorial Reference: VIII.J.5. Cemetery: Cabaret-Rouge British Cemetery, Souchez in France.

KIRWAN, John: Rank: Private. Regiment or Service: Welsh Regiment. Unit: 2nd Battalion. Date of death: 29 October 1914. Service No: 8848. Born in Tramore, Co. Waterford. Enlisted in Merthyr. Killed in action. Grave or Memorial Reference: Panel 23 and 24l on the Le Touret Memorial in France.

KIRWAN, M.: Rank: Private. Regiment or Service: Army Service Corps. Unit: 3rd Coy. Age at death: 21. Date of death: 1 June 1915. Service No: T/37202. He is not listed in Soldiers Died in the Great War and he is not listed with Irelands Memorial Records.

Supplementary information: Son of Michael and Margaret Kirwan, of Killerguile, Clonea, Carrick-on-Suir, Co. Waterford. Grave or Memorial Reference: Screen Wall. T."U"81. Cemetery: Bradford (Undercliffe) Cemetery, Bradford, UK.

KIRWAN/KIRWEN, William: Rank: Private. Regiment or Service: The King's (Liverpool Regiment). Unit: 13th Battalion. Age at death: 17. Date of death: 9 July 1917. Service No: 32425. Born in Waterford. Enlisted in Liverpool while living in Waterford. Died.
Supplementary information: Son of John and Margaret Kirwan, of 5 Well Lane, Waterford. Grave or Memorial Reference: I.D.5. Cemetery: Red Cross Corner Cemetery, Beugny in France.

KNIGHT, John: Rank: Rifleman. Regiment or Service: London Regiment. Unit: 9th (County of London) Battalion (Queen Victoria's Rifles.). Date of death: 13 August 1918. Service No: 393611. Enlisted in Tallow while living in Tallow. Formerly he was with the 9th London Regiment where his number was 8299. Enlisted in Tallow, while living in Tallow, Killed in action. He has no known grave but is commemorated on Panel 54 on the Ypres (Menin Gate) Memorial in Belgium.

KNOX, Stephen: Rank: Sergeant. Regiment or Service: Royal Irish Regiment. Unit: 2nd Battalion. Age at death: 23. Date of death: 17 September 1914. Service No: 9861. Born in Mooncoin, Co. Kilkenny (Soldiers died in the Great War). Mooncoin, Co. Waterford (Irelands Memorial Records). Enlisted in Waterford while living in Piltown, Co. Kilkenny. Died of wounds.
Supplementary information: Son of James and Anastasia Knox, of Tobernabrone, Piltown, Co. Kilkenny. He has no known grave but is listed on the La Ferté-sous-Jouarre Memorial in France.

L

LACEY, James: Rank: Private. Regiment or Service: Royal Dublin Fusiliers. Unit: 1st Battalion. Date of death: 12 December 1915. Service No: 20163. Formerly he was with the Royal Garrison Artillery where his number was 6393. Born in Dungarvan, Co. Waterford. Enlisted in Dungarvan, Co. Waterford. Killed in action. From the *Waterford News*, February 1917:

> LETTERS FROM THE FRONT.
>
> Driver James Lacey, who is with a battery of artillery "Somewhere in France," sends us some verses entitled "My Bivouac," which we hope to publish in a future issue, also some lines called "Victory" written in Egypt by Private Frank Henry Westley.

The above was published eight weeks after the death of Private Lacey. Grave or Memorial Reference: II.E.11. Cemetery: Twelve Tree Copse Cemetery in Turkey.

LACEY, Maurice: Rank: Private. Regiment or Service: Irish Guards. Unit: 1st Battalion. Age at death: 35. Date of death: 11 September 1917. Service No: 8498. Born in Cappagh, Co. Waterford. Enlisted in Newcastle-on-Tyne, Northumberland while living in Knockawn, Co. Waterford. Died of wounds.
Supplementary information: Son of John and Ellen Lacey, of Knockaun, Cappagh. Grave or Memorial Reference: VII.B.9. Cemetery: Dozinghem Military Cemetery in Belgium.

LAMBERT, Thomas: Rank: Sapper. Regiment or Service: Canadian Engineers. Unit: 4th Battalion. Age at death: 28. Date of death: 2 September 1918 Service No: 119.
Supplementary information: Son of Mr and Mrs Henry Lambert, of Waterford, Ireland. Data from attestation papers:

In what Town, Township or Parish, and in what Country were you born? Waterford, Ireland.

What is the name of your next of kin? Mary Lambert [sister].

What is the address of your next of kin? Box, 538, Gowganda, Ontario.

What is the date of your birth? 11 April 1892.

What is your trade or calling? Locomotive Fireman.

Are you married? No.

Do you now belong to the Active Militia? 6th Field Co.,

Do you understand the nature and terms of your engagement? Yes.

Are you willing to be attested to serve in the Canadian Over-Seas Expeditionary Force? Yes.

Apparent age: 22 years, 7 months.

Height: 5 Ft, 5 Ins.

Girth when fully expanded: 38, Ins.

Range of expansion 3 ½ Ins.

Complexion: fair.

Eyes: blue.

Hair: light brown.

Distinctive marks: 1 vaccination scar right arm.

Date: 29 November 1914.

Grave or Memorial Reference: III.C.3. Cemetery: Wancourt British Cemetery in France.

LANDERS, Thomas: Rank: Private. Regiment or Service: Royal Irish Regiment. Unit: 2nd Battalion. Date of death: 27 September 1918. Service No: 16255. Formerly he was with the Royal Dublin Fusiliers where his number was 30656. Born in Stradbally, Waterford. Enlisted in Dublin while living in Dungarvan, Co. Waterford. Killed in action. Grave or Memorial Reference: I.B19.

Cemetery: Moeuvres Communal Cemetery Extension, Nord in France.

LANNIGAN, Patrick Francis: Rank: Mate. Regiment or Service: Mercantile Marine. Unit: SS *Haulwen* (Cardiff). Age at death: 27. Date of death: 9 June 1917. The Steam Ship *Haulwen* was a 4,032grt, defensively armed British Merchant steamer. She was torpedoed without warning and sunk by German submarine U-43. 4 250 miles NW from the Fastnet, Ireland. *Haulwen* was on route from Montreal to Manchester. Four men died, two from Waterford. LANNIGAN, Patrcik Francis and BARRY, Michael.

Supplementary information: Son of William and Margaret Lannigan (*née* Power), of 27 Spring Gardens, Waterford. Born in Waterford. He has no known grave but is listed on the Tower Hill Memorial in the UK.

LANNON, John: Rank: Private. Regiment or Service: Royal Inniskilling Fusiliers. Unit: 7th/8th Battalion. Age at death: 24. Date of death: 21 March 1918. Service No: 26509. Previously he was with the Royal Munster Fusiliers where his number was 3588. Born in Kilmacthomas, Co. Waterford. Enlisted in Cork. Killed in action.

Supplementary information: Son of Patrick and Johanna Lannon, of Strand Street, Dungarvan, Co. Waterford. Grave or Memorial Reference: II.A.35. Cemetery: Templeux-Le-Guerard British Cemetery Extension in France.

LAPPIN, Joseph: Rank: Rifleman. Regiment or Service: London Regiment. Unit: 12th (County of London) Battalion (The Rangers.) Date of death: 9 September 1916. Age at death: 19. Service No: 2271. Born in Waterford. Enlisted in London while living in Stamford Hill. Killed in action.

Supplementary information: Son of Mr and Mrs J. Lappin, of 43 Hillside Road, Stamford Hill, London. I include the following for

your reference. From the National Roll of the Great War. 1914-1918 (for London, Section 2, p. 200):

LAPPIN, G., PRIVATE, R.A.M.C.
He volunteered in September 1914, and after a period of training was drafted to France. He took an active part in many important operations, during which he was engaged on transport duties. He was demobilised in March, 1919, and holds the General Service and Victory Medals. 43, Hillside Road, South Tottenham, N. 15.

Grave or Memorial Reference: Pier and Face 9C. Memorial: Thiepval Memorial in France.

LARKIN, Peter: Rank: Private. Regiment or Service: Irish Guards. Unit: 2nd Battalion. Age at death: 27. Date of death: 30 September 1915. Service No: 6842. Born in Waterford. Enlisted in Waterford. Killed in action.

Supplementary information: Son of Michael and Elizabeth Larkin, of 93 Manor Street, Waterford. Husband of May Larkin (*née* Lumley), of 13 Percy Terrace, Waterford. From the *Waterford News*, October 1916:

KILLED IN ACTION.
Mrs Larkin, 13 Percy Terraces, Waterford, has just received official notification that her husband, Private Peter Larkin, Irish Guards, was killed in action as far back as the 30th December [*sic*] last. Rumours that Private Larkin had been killed at the front reached Waterford shortly after that time, but as no official intimation of his death was received his relatives were hoping for the best, and thought that he might possibly have been wounded and taken prisoner. Time almost dispelled these hopes however, and the official intimation of his death, sent to his young widow, cannot be said to have come with any great surprise, but was none the less sorrowfully received.

Private Larkin was a collector for the gas company previous to joining the army, and was well known throughout the city. For his widow and mother (who reside at 93 Manor Street) much sympathy will be felt in their bereavement.

Grave or Memorial Reference: 9 and 10 on the Loos Memorial in France.

LAWLESS, Thomas: Rank: Private. Regiment or Service: Royal Irish Regiment. Unit: 2nd Battalion. Date of death: 19 October 1914. Service No: 6396. Born in Tramore, Co. Waterford. Enlisted in Enniscorthy while living in Tramore. Killed in action. Grave or Memorial Reference: Panel 11 and 12l on the Le Touret Memorial in France.

LAWLOR, Joseph: Rank: Private. Regiment or Service: Royal Dublin Fusiliers. Unit: 10th Battalion. Date of death: 18 November 1916. Service No: 26869. Born in Ballybricken, Co. Waterford. Enlisted in Cork. Killed in action. He has no known grave but is listed on Pier and Face 16C on the Thiepval Memorial in France.

LAWLOR, Morgan: Rank: Able Seaman. Regiment or Service: Mercantile Marine. Unit: SS *Lorca* (London). Lorca was torpedoed by German submarine U-49. Age at death: 43. Date of death: 15 November 1916. *Supplementary information:* Husband of Kate Lawlor, of 55 Upper Ferry Bank, Waterford. Born in Waterford. From the *Waterford News*, June 1917:

WATERFORD SEAMEN LOST.
Applications at City Sessions.
The deaths at sea of two Waterford sailors formed the subject of applications before County Court Judge Fitzgerald, K. C., at the City Quarter Sessions last Friday.
.... The second application was on behalf of Mrs Kate Lalor, 55 Upper Ferrybank,

whose husband, Morgan Lalor, was also lost on the SS *Lorca*. A sum of £300 which was due by the company, would be lodged in court, and his Honor directed that £50 be paid to the widow when the money would be lodged, the application to be reconsidered at next session.

He has no known grave but is listed on the Tower Hill Memorial in the UK.

LEAHY, Michael Andrew: Rank: Private. Regiment or Service: Royal Irish Regiment. Unit: 2nd Battalion. Age at death: 39. Date of death: 21 March 1918. Service No: 5644.
Supplementary information: Son of John and Mary E. Leahy (*née* Russell), of Caherconlish, Co. Limerick. Husband of Ellen Catherine Leahy, of 32 Brown Street, Portlaw, Co. Waterford. Grave or Memorial Reference: 30 and 31 on the Pozières Memorial in France.

LEAHY, Thomas: Rank: Private. Regiment or Service: Royal Dublin Fusiliers. Unit: 9th Battalion. Age at death: 20. Date of death: 16 August 1917. Service No: 25583. Born in Caherconlish, Co. Limerick. Enlisted in Cahir, Co. Tipperary. Killed in action.
Supplementary information: Son of John and Mary Leahy, of Lord George's Lane, Dungarvan, Co. Waterford. Grave or Memorial Reference: 144 to 145 on the Tyne Cot Memorial in Belgium.

LECKIE, John: Rank: Private. Regiment or Service: Royal Irish Regiment. Unit: 2nd Battalion. Date of death: 20 October 1915. Service No: 10051. Born in St Johns, Waterford. Enlisted in Clonmel, Co. Tipperary while living in Waterford. Killed in action. Grave or Memorial Reference: I.A.10. Cemetery: Auchonvillers Military Cemetery in France.

LEE, Thomas: Rank: Private. Regiment or Service: Royal Irish Regiment. Unit: 2nd Battalion. Date of death: 21 March 1918. Service No: 7495. Born in Ballybricken, Co. Waterford. Enlisted in Waterford. Killed in action.

Supplementary information: Son of Martin and Bridget Lee, of 21 Smith's Lane, Waterford. Grave or Memorial Reference: 30 and 31 on the Pozières Memorial in France.

LEMMON, John: Rank: Third Engineer. Regiment or Service: Mercantile Marine. Unit: SS *Formby* (Glasgow). Age at death: 21. Date of death: 18 December 1917. The ship was lost with all hands and never located during a fierce storm.

Supplementary information: Son of George and Mary Ann Lemmon, (*née* Murphy), of Kilmeadan, Co. Waterford. Born in Waterford. He has no known grave but is listed on the Tower Hill Memorial in the UK. He is also listed on the Formby-Coningbeg Memorial, Adelphi Quay in Waterford City.

LEMMON, William: Rank: Sergeant. Regiment or Service: Yorkshire Regiment. Unit: 6th Battalion. Age at death: 22. Date of death: 21 August 1918. Service No: 9350. Born in Waterford. Enlisted in Middlesborough. Died of wounds. Killed in action in Gallipoli.

Supplementary information: Son of Thomas and Mary Lemmon of 105 Grange Road East. Middlesbrough. Grave or Memorial Reference: Panel 55 to 58. Memorial: Helles Memorial in Turkey.

LENIHAN, Edward: Rank: Private. Regiment or Service: Irish Guards. Unit: 2nd Battalion. Date of death: 30 September 1915. Service No: 6820. Born in Ballyduff, Co. Waterford. Enlisted in Manchester. Killed in action. He has no known grave but is listed on Panel 9 and 10 on the Loos Memorial in France.

LENIHAN, Thos: Rank: Cook. Regiment or Service: Mercantile Marine. Unit: SS *Lough Fisher* (Barrow). Shelled and sunk by a German submarine 12 miles south-east of Cork. Age at death: 18. Date of death: 30 March 1918.

Supplementary information: Son of William and Anastasia Lenihan (*née* Croke), of 8 Anne Street, Waterford. Born in Waterford. He has no known grave but is listed on the Tower Hill Memorial in the UK.

LEWIS, Michael: Rank: Private. Regiment or Service: Irish Guards. Unit: 1st Battalion. Age at death: 25. Date of death: 14 July 1917. Service No: 10028. Born in Ballinameela, Co. Waterford. Enlisted in Dungarvan, Co. Waterford. Killed in action. He won the Military Medal and is listed in the *London Gazette*.

Supplementary information: Son of James and Mary Lewis, of Kilgreany, Cappagh, Co. Waterford. Grave or Memorial Reference: I.F.7. Cemetery: Bleuet Farm Cemetery in Belgium.

LEWIS, William J.: Rank: Private. Regiment or Service: Royal Irish Regiment. Unit: 2nd Battalion. Age at death: 26. Date of death: 24 August 1914. Service No: 7288. Born in Dungarvan, Co. Waterford. Enlisted in Dungarvan. Killed in action. Previously he was with the Irish Guards.

Supplementary information: Son of John and Mary Lewis, of Dungarvan. Husband of Mary Lewis, of Davis Street, Dungarvan, Co. Waterford. Grave or Memorial Reference: II.B.13. Cemetery: St Symphorien Military Cemetery in Belgium.

LINDSAY, George Lawrence: Rank: Chief Stoker. Regiment or Service: Royal Navy. Unit: HMS *Good Hope*. Age at death: 43. Date of death: 1 December 1914. Service No: 176607.

Supplementary information: Son of James and Mary Lindsay. Husband of Rosey

Lindsay, of 3 Fyning Street, Landport, Portsmouth. I am not sure of the Waterford connection but he is listed on the Waterford and District Roll of Honour. Located in Christ Church Cathedral (Church of Ireland), Henrietta Street, Waterford. He is also listed on the Jersey Roll of Honour. Grave or Memorial Reference: 3. He has no known grave but is listed on the Portsmouth Naval Memorial.

LINE, Eric Alfred Thiselton: Rank: Second Lieutenant. Regiment or Service: Army Service Corps. Unit: H. Q. 26th Div. Train. Age at death: 21. Date of death: 16 December 1916. Died.

Supplementary information: Son of The Archdeacon of Waterford and Mrs Line, of The Rectory, Dunmore East, Co. Waterford. Gazetted 2 April 1915. From De Ruvigny's Roll of Honour:

Line, Eric Alfred Thiselton, 2nd Lieutenant, Army Service Corps, son of the Venerable Henry Line, of Dunmore. Waterford, Archdeacon of Waterford, by his wife. Caroline, daughter of the Rev. Alfred Clayton Thiselton, Vicar of Berwick, Shrewsbury, and formerly Rector of Baggotrath Church, Dublin. Born Dublin, 17 August. 1895, educated. High School Waterford ; Monckton Combe, Bath and entered Cambridge College in 1914; was gazetted 2nd Lieutenant. 18 March 1915; served with the Salonika Army from Sept., and died 16 December. 1916 of typhoid fever, contracted while on active service. Buried in the English Cemetery outside Salonika. His Commanding Officer wrote: "I became devoted to your son. He was a fine specimen of a young British officer, and was of great assistance to me during a trying and difficult period which the company had to go through." And a brother officer wrote : "A genial companion, one of the best examples of a clean, upright Briton. A boy such as he was must indeed be a large part of your lives, and

that a blank would be left which never could be filled, " and another wrote : "He peculiarly endeared himself to us both by reason of his age, which brought to us a delightful freshness and renewed enthusiasm, but more particularly because the super-imposed sense of military responsibility and power of leadership, which, instead of destroying, only served to enhance his cheerful youthfulness, made him an invaluable officer; not only was he so appreciated by his commanding and brother officers, but lie won to the utmost the confidence of his N.C.O.'s and men." Another also wrote: "Everyone had a good word to say for him. It is very rarely that one can say that of an officer, and especially a junior officer, If ever a boy gave up his life through keenness and devotion to his work, he did. " "Always looking after the welfare of his men." "One of the finest characters it has ever been our privilege to know." He is in the London Gazette, 2nd April-1915.

From the *Waterford News*, December 1916:

DIED ON ACTIVE SERVICE.

We regret to announce the death of Second Lieutenant Eric Alfred Thiselton Line, son of Archdeacon Line and of Mrs Line, Dunmore. Deceased was a very young man and was well-known and very popular amongst his friends in this city and district. He was preparing for the Church at Cambridge. He joined the Cadet Corps there, and, having received his commission and gone through his training, he was sent to Salonika, where he contracted typhoid fever, from which he died on December 16th. The greatest sympathy is expended by all classes and creeds to Archdeacon Line and his wife and family in this sad bereavement.

Grave or Memorial Reference: 0.26. Cemetery: Salonika (Lembet Road) Military Cemetery in Greece. He is also listed on the Waterford and District Roll of Honour.

Located in Christ Church Cathedral (Church of Ireland), Henrietta Street, Waterford.

LIVINGSTON, Donald: Rank: First Mate. Regiment or Service: Mercantile Marine. Unit: SS *Coningbeg* (Glasgow). Date of death: 18 December 1917. Torpedoed by German Submarine U–62. There were no survivors.

Supplementary information: Son of Donald and Mary Livingston. Husband of Catherine Livingston (*née* Porter), of 'Bealton' 142 Gracedean Road, Waterford. Born at Glenelg, Skye. He has no known grave but is listed on the Tower Hill Memorial in the UK. He is also listed (as **LIVINGSTONE**) on the Formby-Coningbeg Memorial, Adelphi Quay in Waterford City.

LONERGAN, Edward: Rank: Private. Regiment or Service: Irish Guards. Unit: 1ˢᵗ Battalion. Date of death: 1 April 1915. Service No: 4853. Born in Fethard. Enlisted in Seaford in Lancashire while living in Waterford City. Killed in action. Grave or Memorial Reference: I.E.20. Cemetery: Guards Cemetery, Windy Corner, Cuinchy in France.

LONERGAN, James: Rank: Gunner. Regiment or Service: Royal Horse Artillery and Royal Field Artillery. Date of death: 28 June 1915. Service No: 76727. Born in Castle. Waterford. Enlisted in Clonmel. Died of wounds in Egypt. Grave or Memorial Reference: E.133. Cemetery: Alexandria (Chatby) Military and War Memorial Cemetery in Egypt.

LONERGAN, Thomas: Rank: Lance Corporal. Regiment or Service: Royal Irish Rifles. Unit: 1ˢᵗ Battalion. Date of death: 16 August 1917. Service No: 9487. Born in Waterford. Enlisted in Waterford. Killed in action. He has no known grave but is commemorated on Panel 138 to 140 and 162 to 162A and 163A. Memorial; Tyne Cot Memorial in Belgium.

LONG, Thomas: Rank: Private. Regiment or Service: Royal Irish Regiment. Unit: 1ˢᵗ Battalion. Date of death: 14 February 1915. Service No: 5907. Born in St John's, Waterford. Enlisted in Waterford. Killed in action. He has no known grave but is commemorated on Panel 33. Memorial; Ypres (Menin Gate) Memorial in Belgium.

LONG, Thomas: Rank: Private. Regiment or Service: Royal Irish Regiment. Unit: 2ⁿᵈ Battalion. Date of death: 3 September 1916. Service No: 6434. Born in Born in St John's, Waterford. Enlisted in Waterford. Killed in action. He has no known grave but is listed on Pier and Face 3A on the Thiepval Memorial in France.

LOVE, James Robert: Rank: Second Lieutenant. Regiment or Service: Royal Munster Fusiliers. Unit: 3ʳᵈ Battalion. Age at death: 21. Date of death: 18 August 1917. Killed in action.

Supplementary information: Son of the late James and Caroline R. Love (*née* Stevenson), of Ballykinsella, Tramore, Waterford. From the the *Waterford News*, September 1917:

YOUNG WATERFORD OFFICER KILLED IN ACTION.

We deeply regret to learn that Lieutenant. James Love, 1st Munsters, previously reported missing, is now reported killed.

The circumstances of his last engagement are tragic in the extreme. Another Waterford officer, Lieutenant. George Hand, had just been speaking to him behind the lines, when a trench party was about to be relieved, and a few hours later learned that he had not turned up at mess. This was on August 17th, and since that date until now no tidings were to be had as to Lieutenant Love's fate.

On Saturday morning his uncle, Mr Stephenson (Messrs. J. Thornton and Son) received official notification from his Regiment that his body was found and buried by the men of the 12th Highland Light Infantry, and his grave has been properly marked and identified. No definite particulars are to be had as to where he was found, but it is understood that it was where he was last seen, in the trenches near Ypres; he was at that time about three-quarters of a mile behind the first line trenches. The only thing that has been sent home belonging to him are his cheque book and his officer's advance book.

Lieutenant Love was engaged in the offices of Messrs. Graves and Co., Ltd., Waterford, for some years. He joined the army in January, 1915-the 23rd Battalion. Royal Fusiliers, with whom he went to France in November., 1915. He was wounded in April, 1916; returned to the front in July, 1916, when he was attached to the 20th Battalion, Royal Fusiliers. He went through a lot of the engagements on the Somme front in July, 1916, and following months, until October, when he was sent home to be trained for commissioned rank. He was attached to an Officers' Cadet Battalion.at Trinity College, Cambridge, where he received his training, after which he was commissioned to the 1st Battalion, Royal Munster Fusiliers. in March, 1917. In April last he went to France with his Battalion, and on 17th August was posted missing.

There is also an article about him in the *Munster Express*, 15 September 1917. Grave or Memorial Reference: 143 to 144 on the Tyne Cot Memorial in Belgium. He is also listed on the Bishop Foy School Memorial in the Church of Ireland Cathedral, Henrietta Street, Waterford City.

LOWE, JAMES William: Rank: Private. Regiment or Service: Durham Light Infantry. Unit: 'D' Coy. 2nd Battalion. Age at death: 32. Date of death: 26 February 1918. Service No: 9075 Awarded the D.C.M. and also mentioned in Despatches. Born in Pelton Fell, Chester-Le-Street, Co. Durham. Enlisted in Newcastle-on-Tyne while living in Chester-le-Street. Died.

Supplementary information: Son of John and Margaret Lowe, of Chester-le-Street, Co. Durham. Husband of Mary Anne Lowe, of Carbally Hill, Dunmore East, Co. Waterford. Grave or Memorial Reference: V.F.9B. Mont Huon Military Cemetery, Le-Treport in France.

LUCAS, Daniel: Rank: Private. Regiment or Service: Royal Irish Regiment. Unit: 2nd Battalion. Date of death: 12 April 1918. Service No: 5948. Born in Ferrybank, Co. Kilkenny (Soldiers died in the Great War). Ferrybank, Co. Waterford (Irelands Memorial Records). Enlisted in Waterford. Killed in action. Grave or Memorial Reference: I.B.37. Caemeteru, Le Cateau Military Cemetery in France.

LUDGATE, Michael: Rank: Private. Regiment or Service: South Staffordshire Regiment. Unit: 2/5th (T. F.) Battalion. Date of death: 10 December 1917. Service No: 40788. Formerly he was with the West Riding Regiment where his number was 10700. Born in Waterford. Enlisted in Stratford, Essex while living in London. Killed in action. Grave or Memorial Reference: I.C.9. Cemetery: Ribecourt British Cemetery in France. He is also commemorated on the Cahir War Memorial.

LUMLEY, Joseph: Rank: Master. Regiment or Service: Mercantile Marine. Unit: SS *Coningbeg* (Glasgow). Torpedoed by German Submarine U-62. There were no survivors. U-62 surrendered in November 1918. Age at death: 56. Date of death: 18 December 1917.

Supplementary information: Son of James and Elizabeth Lumley. Husband of Mary Elizabeth Lumley, of 13 Percy Terrace, Waterford. He has no known grave but is listed on the Tower Hill Memorial in the UK. He is also listed on the Formby-Coningbeg Memorial, Adelphi Quay in Waterford City.

LUMLEY, William: Rank: Second Engineer. Regiment or Service: Mercantile Marine. Unit: SS *Formby* (Glasgow). Age at death: 31. Date of death: 16 December 1917. The ship was lost with all hands and never located during a fierce storm.

Supplementary information: Son of Joseph and Mary Elizabeth Lumley. Husband of Josephine Lumley (*née* Power), of 26 Thomas Street, Waterford. Born in Waterford. He has no known grave but is listed on the Tower Hill Memorial in the UK. He is also listed on the Formby-Coningbeg Memorial, Adelphi Quay in Waterford City.

LYNCH, John: Rank: Private. Regiment or Service: Royal Irish Regiment. Unit: 2nd Battalion. Age at death: 20. Date of death: 24 May 1915. Service No: 6349. Born in Ballygunnermore, Co. Waterford. Enlisted in Waterford while living in Callaghane, Co. Waterford. Died of wounds.

Supplementary information: Son of Michael and Catherine Lynch, of Callaghane, Rossduff, Waterford. Grave or Memorial Reference: III.B.3. Cemetery: Vlamertinghe Military Cemetery in Belgium.

LYNCH, Michael: Rank: Lance Corporal. Regiment or Service: Royal Irish Regiment. Unit: 2nd Battalion. Age at death: 27. Date of death: 4 September 1916. Service No: 10192. Born in Trinity Without, Waterford. Enlisted in Clonmel, Co. Tipperary while living in Waterford. Died of wounds.

Supplementary information: Son of Michael and Norah Lynch, of 14 Blakes Lane, Waterford. Grave or Memorial Reference: Plot 2. Row B. Grave 14. Cemetery: Corbie Communal Cemetery Extension in France.

LYNCH, Patrick Stephen: Rank: Acting Captain and Captain. Regiment or Service: Leinster Regiment. Unit: 7th Battalion. Attached to 2nd Battalion. Age at death: 25. Date of death: 27 December 1916. He won the Military Cross and is listed in the *London Gazette*. Killed in action.

Supplementary information: Son of Michael and Bridget Lynch, of 31 St John's Hill, Waterford. From the *Waterford News*, June 1916:

HOME ON LEAVE.

The following officers are at present home on leave; --Captain P. Lynch, Leinster Regiment, who was wounded at the front; 2nd Lieutenant Norman, Tramore, Leinster Regiment, who was slightly wounded in the street fighting in Dublin during the rebellion, and Lieutenant R.B. Nolan, R.N.V.R.

From the Munster Express:

WATERFORD OFFICER WOUNDED.

Captain Patrick Lynch, 7th Leinster's (son of Mr Michael Lynch, manager, Messrs. Robertson, Leslie Ferguson and Co.), has been wounded in action in France. He was promoted from Lieutenancy to his present rank quite recently.

From the *The Irish on the Somme* (p. 133 and 134):

Another fine exploit standing to the credit of the Irish Brigade was that of Lieutenant Patrick Stephen Lynch of the Leinster's, who got the Military Cross "for conspicuous gallantry when successfully laying and firing a torpedo under the enemy's wire." It was an uncommon deed, and just as uncommon is the very remarkable tribute with which the official record ends; "His cool bravery is very marked and his influence over his men very great." The Brigadier-General, George Pereira, D.S.O., in a letter of congratulation to Lieutenant Lynch, dated July 1, 1916, says; "Your leading the attack along the parapet was splendid, but you must be more careful another time." Before the month was out Lieutenant Lynch got a bar to his Military Cross, in other words he had won the distinction twice over, an honour which, as General Hickie wrote to him, was well deserved, and likely to be very rare.

This young Waterford man – a fine type of the fearless and dashing Irish officer, made out of a civilian in two years – was promoted Captain in the Leinster's, and was killed on his birthday and the competition of his twenty-fifth year, December 27, 1916. The Battalion was plunged into grief by the loss of Captain Lynch. "'Paddy', the name we all knew him by from the C.O. down to the youngest sub was considered the most efficient officer in his Battalion, and he was certainly the most popular," writes Lieutenant H.W. Norman, an officer of the Captain's company. "Everybody mourns his death, and when the news got to his men they could not believe that such a brave and daring officer could be killed, but news was only too true; and when it was confirmed I saw many's an officer and man crying like children. He lost his life to save his men, who were in a trench that was being heavily shelled. He went up with a Sergeant, in spite of danger and certain death, to get them out, and on the way up a shell landed in the trench where they were, killing both instantly."

From the *Waterford News*, January 1917:

BRAVE YOUNG WATERFORD OFFICER'S DEATH.
Captain Lynch killed at the Front.
News reached the city on Saturday that Captain Patrick Lynch, only son of our esteemed fellow-citizen, Mr Michael Lynch (manager of Messrs Rebertson, Ledlie's Waterford establishment), had been killed at the front.

About two years ago the deceased joined the Cadet Corps of the 7th Leinster Regiment., and shortly afterwards got his commission.

He went to France with the 16th Division in December last, and was wounded, and promoted Captain. He was also awarded the Military Cross for bravery on the field. He was home here in August last recovering from the effects of his wounds, and in September he was recalled to the front.

A popular young officer, the deepest regret will be felt at his death, which occurred on the 27th inst. The late Captain Lynch received his early education at Waterpark, and was afterwards at Clonliffe College, Dublin, and at the National University, Dublin. He was a very brilliant young student, and won exhibitions in French and Italian as well as in English. After completing his education, he entered the National Park service, and was engaged in a branch of the Bank in the County Cork before joining the army. He spoke at a special recruiting meeting held here on the occasion of Michael O'Leary's visit, and made a stirring appeal for recruits. All who knew "Paddy" Lynch held him in high regard, and to his sorrowing parents much sympathy will be felt in their bereavement.

From the *Waterford News*, January 1917:

THE LATE CAPTAIN LYNCH.
We received just as we were going to press copies of interesting letters of condolence sent to the sorrowing parents of the late Captain P Lynch by the Colonel Commanding of the 2nd Leinster Regiment, Lieutenant Mathias, of the 3rd Leinsters and other officers. We are obliged to hold over the publication of these letters until tomorrow.

Grave or Memorial Reference: I.L.23. Cemetery: Maroc British Cemetery, Grenay in France.

LYNCH, Stephen: Rank: Private. Regiment or Service: Royal Irish Regiment. Unit: 6th Battalion. Date of death: 19 December 1917 (Soldiers died in the Great War), 19 February 1917 (The Commonwealth War Graves Commission). Service No: 8053. Born in USA. Enlisted in Waterford while living in Dunmore East, Co. Waterford. Killed in action. Grave or Memorial Reference: J9. Cemetery: Pond Farm Cemetery in Belgium.

LYONS, John: Rank: Rifles. Regiment or Service: Royal Irish Rifles Unit: 2nd Battalion. Date of death: 7 November 1914. Service No: 8675. Born in Dungarvan, Co. Waterford. Enlisted in Carlow while living in Mallow, Co. Cork. Killed in action. Has no known grave but is commemorated on Panel 40 on the Ypres (Menin Gate) Memorial in Belgium.

M

MACGEE/McGEE, Walter K.: Rank: Private. Regiment or Service: Seaforth Highlanders. Unit: 6th Battalion. Date of death: 10 January 1918. Service No: 285301. Formerly he was with the A & S H where his number was 4595. Born in Dungarvan, Co. Waterford. Enlisted in Piccadilly, London, Middlesex. Killed in action. Died of wounds. Grave or Memorial Reference: I.H.13. Cemetery: Red Cross Corner Cemetery, Beugny in France.

MACKLIN, R.: Rank: Private. Regiment or Service: Leinster Regiment. Unit: 7th Battalion. Age at death: 35. Date of death: 12 May 1916. Service No: 2453. He is not listed in Soldiers Died in the Great War and he is not listed with Irelands Memorial Records.

Supplementary information: Husband of Ellen Macklin of Lower Strand Street, Dungarvan, Co. Waterford. Grave or Memorial Reference: V.C.45. Cemetery: Bethune Town Cemetery in France.

MADDOCK/MADDOCKS, John: Rank: Lance Corporal. Regiment or Service: Royal Berkshire Regiment. Unit: 5th Battalion. Date of death: 17 March 1917. Service No: 14696. Born in Waterford. Enlisted in Smethwick, Staffordshire. Killed in action. Grave or Memorial Reference: III.G.28. Cemetery: Faubourg D'Amiens Cemetery, Arras in France.

MADDOCK, Patrick: Rank: Private. Regiment or Service: Royal Irish Regiment. Unit: 2nd Battalion. Age at death: 19. Date of death: 19 October 1914. Service No: 10692. Born in Dungarvan, Co. Waterford. Enlisted in Clonmel, Co. Tipperary. Killed in action.

Supplementary information: Son of the late Mr and Mrs John Maddock. He has no known grave but is listed on Panels 11 and 12 on the Le Touret Memorial in France.

MADIGAN, John: Rank: Gunner. Regiment or Service: Royal Garrison Artillery. Date of death: 23 June 1920. Service No: 275594 Grave or Memorial Reference: X.2.15. Cemetery: Ballygunner (St Mary) Catholic Churchyard, Co. Waterford.

MADIGAN, John: Rank: Private. Regiment or Service: Royal Irish Regiment. Unit: 2nd Battalion. Age at death: 31. Date of death: 21 August 1918. Service No: 10074. Born in Ballybricken, Co. Waterford. Enlisted in Waterford. Killed in action.

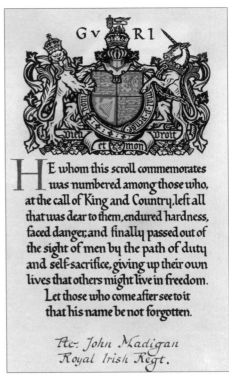

John Madigan.

Supplementary information: Son of Michael and Katherine Madigan, of Morrison's Road, Waterford. Husband of Mary Madigan of 2 Grace's Lane, Waterford. Grave or Memorial Reference: 5 on the Vis-En-Artois Memorial in France.

MAGUIRE, James: Rank: Private. Regiment or Service: Royal Munster Fusiliers. Unit: 2nd Battalion. Age at death: 21. Date of death: 9 May 1915. Service No: 10013. Born in Newtown, Co. Waterford. Enlisted in Waterford while living in Kilmacthomas, Co. Waterford. Killed in action.

Supplementary information: Son of Bridget Fitzgerald (formerly Maguire), of Barrack Street, Dungarvan, Co. Waterford. Grave or Memorial Reference 43 and 44 on the Le Touret Memorial in France.

MAHER, James: Rank: Private. Regiment or Service: Irish Guards. Unit: 1st Battalion. Date of death: 18 May 1915. Service No: 865. Born in Waterford. Enlisted in Waterford. Killed in action. He has no known grave but is listed on Panel 4 on the Le Touret Memorial in France.

MAHONEY, Michael: Rank: Private. Regiment or Service: Royal Irish Regiment. Unit: 2nd Battalion. Age at death: 19. Date of death: 9 May 1915. Service No: 6297. Born in Ballybricken, Co. Waterford. Enlisted in Waterford. Killed in action.

Supplementary information: Son of James and K. Mahoney, of 2 Thomas's Avenue, Waterford. From the the *Waterford News*, May 1917:

GALLANT BALLYBRICKEN MAN.

Private J. Mahoney, of Chapel Lane, Ballybricken, who joined the Regiment at the outbreak of the war has obtained a notification from Major-General Hickie, commanding the 16th Division, stating that he has read with pleasure the reports of the Regimental Commander regarding Private Mahoney's gallant conduct in the field during the year 1916, and that it has been ordered to enter his name in the record of the Irish Division.

Grave or Memorial Reference: He has no known grave but is listed on Panel 33 on the Ypres (Menin Gate) Memorial in Belgium.

MALCOLMSON, Hubert: Rank: Temporary Lieutenant and Adjutant. Regiment or Service: Royal Irish Regiment. Unit: 6th Battalion. Date of death: 16 September 1916. Died of wounds. From the *Waterford News*, September 1916:

LOCAL WAR ITEMS

Co. Waterford Officers Wounded.

Lieutenant. H. Malcomson, Royal Irish Regiment, wounded, was born at Portlaw, Co. Waterford, being son of Mr W. Malcomson, J.P. He graduated in 1912 at Cambridge with honours in mechnical sciences. He had been with Scott's Shipbuilding Company, Greenock, until the outbreak of war. He captained Pembroke College R.F.C. in 1911, and played for Greenock Wanderers.

Captain H.G. Newport, Leinster Regiment, younger son of Mr G.B. Newport, J.P., of Ballygallon, Inistioge, Co. Kilkenny, has been seriously wounded.

Second Lieutenant N.L. Bor, Connaught Rangers, wounded was born at Tramore, Co. Waterford, 22 years ago. He is a son of Mr E.N.C. Bor, Maryborough, a cousin of the late General J. N. Bor, of Lieutenant-Colonel Hobbs. and brother of Lieutenant T.H. Bor, R.N.R. He was a medical student at Trinity before entering the army. He played for the Wanderers, Dublin University Rugby Football Club, Clontarf Cricket Club, and Dublin University Swimming Club.

From the *Munster Express*:

DEATH OF CO. WATERFORD OFFICER.

Among Thursdays list of casualties the name of Second Lieutenant Malcomson, Royal Irish Regiment appeared, who

Died of wounds received in action. This young officer was born in Portlaw, and was the son of Mr W Malcomson, J. P. He was wounded in the attack on the Somme by the Irish Division, and his name appeared on the casualty list for September 16th. He graduated from Cambridge in 1912. In the previous year he captained the Pembroke College Rugby Club.

From the *Waterford News*, October 1916:

DEATH OF AN OFFICER.

Amongst this week's list of casualties we regret to find the name of Second Lieutenant Malcomson, Royal Irish Regiment, who Died of wounds receivd in action. This gallant young officer was born at Portlaw, and was the son of Mr W. Malcomson, J.P. He was wounded in the attack at the Somme by the Irish Division, and his name appeared in the casualty list for September 16th. He graduated at Cambridge in 1912. In the previous year he captained the Pembroke College Rugby Club.

Grave or Memorial Reference: Clonmel Friends Burial Ground. Grave location: In south west corner.

MALCOMSON, Llewellyn: Rank: Corporal. Regiment or Service: Royal Engineers. Unit: 2nd Battalion. Special Brigade. Age at death: 24. Date of death: 5 October 1916. Service No: 113329. Born in Portlaw, Co. Waterford. Enlisted in Westminister, Middlesex while living in Portlaw. Killed in action.
Supplementary information: Son of William and Adelina L. Malcomson, of Portlaw, Co. Waterford. B.A. of Cambridge University, (Emmanuel Coll.). His name first appeared on the casualty list for 6 September. Graduated from Cambridge in 1912. In the previous year he captained the Pembroke College Rugby Club. Grave or Memorial Reference: I.H.37. Cemetery: Philosophe British Cemetery, Mazingarbe in France.

MALONE, Michael: Rank: Private. Regiment or Service: Royal Irish Regiment. Unit: 2nd Battalion. Date of death: 19 October 1914. Service No: 5593. Born in St Patrick's, Waterford. Enlisted in Waterford. Killed in action. He has no known grave but is commemorated on Panel 11 and 12. Memorial: Le Touret Memorial in France.

MALONEY, Andrew: Rank: Lance Corporal. Regiment or Service: Royal Munster Fusiliers. Unit: 1st Battalion. Date of death: 12 April 1917. Service No: 6882. Born in Ballyhale, Co. Kilkenny. Enlisted in Waterford while living in Waterford. Died of wounds. Grave or Memorial Reference: I.C.37. Cemetery: Fosse No. 10 Communal Cemetery Extension, Sains-En-Gohelle in France.

MANAHAN/MANAGHAN, James: Rank: Private. Regiment or Service: Royal Irish Regiment. Unit: 2nd Battalion. Date of death: 16 November 1917. Service No: 7646. Born in St Patrick's, Waterford. Enlisted in Waterford while living in Dungarvan, Co. Waterford. Killed in action. From the *Waterford News* August 1916:

WATERFORD MEN IN THE CASUALTY LIST.

Amongst the names in yesterday's casualty lists and the following (wounded) from Waterford belonging to the R. I. Rifles. ; J Gough (9538), M Halahan (10331), F O'Brien (10199), and Lance-Corporal C.S. Roles (9786), Private P. O'Donnell, Waterford (7893), R.A.M.C., is given in the list as dead. Private Cullen, Leinster Regiment, whose parents reside at High Street, is wounded and in hospital. Private James Manahan, R. I. Regiment, has been wounded for the second time and is at home at present.

From the *Waterford News*, November 1917:

WATERFORD SOLDIER KILLED.

One more Waterford man has paid the toll that war extracts. The latest city victim is

Private James Manahan, son of Mr Con Manahan, Patrick Street, and brother of Mr C Managhan, poultry, fish, and game dealer, George's Street, and of Mr A Manahan, on of the leading vocalists and musicians at present in Dublin. During the great recruiting boom in March, 1915, Mr Manahan joined the Cadet Corps of the Royal Irish Regiment, and was only six weeks in training when he was sent to France. Prior to joining, he had three years of his apprenticeship served in the electrical department of Messrs, Peares motor works, Catherine Street. He was wounded three times in France, and it was but last month he was home on a short visit to his friends looking fit and well. Last week his sad end came. During his long period in the battle-line he had some exciting escapes. In one instance he was about to go "over the top" with a small party, when his officer sent him back on a message. Almost all the party were wiped out, the few who survived being more or less seriously wounded. Deceased, who was so respectably connected in the city, was an extremely popular, affable, and genial young man, and his death at a very early age is deeply regretted.

From the *Waterford News*, December 1917:

LATE PRIVATE J. MANAHAN.
Much sympathy has been extended to the young widow and friends of the late Private James Manahan, R. I. Regiment, Waterford, who fell in action recently. Writing to Mrs Manahan, his Captain, who encloses the deceased's beads and papers, expresses deep sympathy on his own behalf and on behalf of the other officers, the N.C.O.'s and men, and says—"He was a most popular N.C.O., liked by all, and we all feel his loss greatly. He was buried with all the rites of his church, beside his comrades, and a cross erected over his grave. " Private Manahan had received the parchment certificate of the 16th Irish Division for "gallant conduct and devotion to duty in the field" on the 7th June last.

Grave or Memorial Reference: II.A 6 Cemetery: Croiselles British Cemetery in France.

MANDERS, Richard Clive: See **VILLIERS-STUART, Desmond de la Poer**:

MANGAN, John: Rank: Stoker. Regiment or Service: Royal Naval Reserve. Unit: HMS *Queen Mary*. Age at death: 62. Date of death: 31 May 1916. Service No: 2172V.
Supplementary information: Son of Thomas and Catherine Lalor Mangan, of Lincoln Place, Dublin. Husband of Elizabeth Mangan (*née* Smyth), of 19 Waterford Street, Dublin. Grave or Memorial Reference: 23. Memorial, Portsmouth Naval Memorial, UK.

MANNING, CHRISTOPHER. Rank: Private. Regiment or Service: Welsh Regiment. Unit: 'C' Coy. 1st/6th Battalion. Age at death: 36. Date of death: 1 October 1915. Service No: 1663. Born in Kilkenny, Co. Kilkenny. Enlisted in Clydach, Glamorganshire. Killed in action.
Supplementary information: Son of Mrs Johanna Ryan, of Ballincur, Mooncoin. Waterford. Grave or Memorial Reference: 77 and 78 on the Loos Memorial in France.

MANNING, George Frederick: Rank: Volunteer. Listed in the *Munster Express* as George Frederick White-Manning, B.A., T.C.D., Kola Kola. Regiment or Service: Nyasaland Volunteer Reserve. Date of death: 9 September 1914. Killed in action leading a charge on German guns at Karonga, Nyasaland.
Supplementary information: Eldest son of Revd T. and Mrs White-Manning, Kilmacow Rectory. Grave or Memorial Reference: Grave 11. Cemetery: Karonga War cemetery, Malawi, Africa.

MANNING, James: Rank: Cattleman. Regiment or Service: Mercantile Marine. Unit: SS *Formby* (Glasgow). Age at death: 50.

Date of death: 16 December 1917. The ship was lost with all hands and never located during a fierce storm.

Supplementary information: Son of the late David and Mary Manning. Husband of Mary Manning (*née* Moran), of 41 Roanmore Terrace, Waterford. Born in Waterford. He has no known grave but is listed on the Tower Hill Memorial in the UK. He is also listed on the Formby-Coningbeg Memorial, Adelphi Quay in Waterford City.

MANNING, Patrick: Rank: Private. Regiment or Service: Welsh Regiment. Unit: 1-5th Battalion. Age at death: 24. Date of death: 3 November 1917. Service No: 240646. Born in Waterford. Enlisted in Pontypridd while living in Carrick-on-Suir, Co. Tipperary. Killed in action in Egypt.

Supplementary information: Son of Ellen Manning, of Rathgormack, Carrick-on-Suir, Co. Waterford. Grave or Memorial Reference: F.17. Cemetery: Beersheeba War Cemetery in Israel.

MANNING, Percy. (Listed as **MANNING, F** in the Commonwelath War Graves Commission) Rank: Private. Regiment or Service: Royal Irish Fusiliers. Unit: 1st Battalion. Date of death: 8 November 1914. Service No: 11248. Born in Waterford. Enlisted in Dublin. Died of wounds. From the *Waterford News*, 1915:

WATERFORDMAN KILLED IN ACTION.

We regret to learn that Mr Frederick Manning, third son of the late Mr Benjamin Manning, Waterford, has been killed in action fought near Bailleul. Young Mr Manning was only 17 years of age, and the greatest sympathy is felt for his mother, who is a daughter of Mr David Kenneally, Park View House. Deceased was nephew of the late Mr Michael Manning, formerly Town Clerk of Kingstown, and the late Mr T. P. Manning, Manager of the Arran Quay(Dublin) branch of the National Bank.

Grave or Memorial Reference: C. 23. Cemetery: Bailleul Communal Cemetery, (Nord). France.

MARKLE/MARKLEY, John: Rank: Private. Regiment or Service: Highland Light Infantry. Unit: 10th (Service) Battalion. Date of death: 25 September 1915. Service No: 943. Born in Dungaroon Waterford. Enlisted in Glasgow. Killed in action. Data from previous service: Name: John Markley. Estimated Birth Year: 1895. Age at Enlistment: 19. Birth Parish: Dungarvan. Birth County: Waterford. Document Year: 1914. Regimental Number: 13195. Attested short service three years 31 August 1914 Royal Scots discharged 11 September 1914 'not likely to become an efficient soldier; Address: 120 Thistle Street, Glasgow SS. Occupation on enlistment: Apprentice painter. Next of Kin: Mrs Mary Hogan or Markley, Address: 120 Thistle Street, Glasgow SS (mother). Age at death: 19 years 243 days. The GRO index of first World World War deaths has him listed as James Markley. He is listed on the Scottish War Memorial as **MARKLE**. He has no known grave but is listed on Panel 108 to 112 on the Loos Memorial in France.

MARRETT, Joseph: Rank: Guardsman. Regiment or Service: Guards Machine Gun Regiment. Unit: 4th Battalion. Age at death: 36. Date of death: 25 August 1918. Service No: 1884. Formerly he was with the Irish Guards where his number was 10907. Born in St. Patrick's, Waterford. Enlisted in Carrick-on-Suir, Co. Tipperary. Killed in action.

Supplementary information: Son of George Marrett. He has no known grave but is listed on Panel 30 of the Vis-En-Artois Memorial in France.

MARSHALL, Joseph: Rank: Private. Regiment or Service: Royal Irish Regiment. Unit: B Company, 2nd Battalion. Age at death: 18. Date of death: 16 September 1914. Service No: 10661(The Commonwealth War Graves Commission), 10861(Soldiers died in the Great War). Born in St Patrick's, Waterford. Enlisted in Liverpool while living in Waterford. Killed in action.

Supplementary information: Son of Joseph and Mary Marshall, of 6 New Street, Waterford. From the *Waterford News*, 1914:

WATERFORD SOLDIER
KILLED AT THE AISNE.

A letter addressed to Mr T. Marshall, Little Michael Street, was received from the Army Record Office, Cork, yesterday notifying the death of Private J. Marshall, Royal Irish Regiment, who was killed in action at the battle of the Aisne on the 16th ulto. The following message was also received with the letter: 'The King commands me to assure you of the true sympathy of his Majesty and the Queen in your sorrow. – Kitchener.'

Private Marshall was a prominent member of the Erin's Hope Prize Flute band, and after the lamentable death of the late conductor, Mr William Hodge, he was about to take over the conductorship of the band when he was called to active service. His brother, to whom the letter was addressed, had rejoined the Royal Irish from the reserve when the sad intelligence arrived.

He has no known grave but is listed on the La Ferté-sous-Jouarre Memorial in France.

MARTIN, Arthur James: Rank: Captain. Regiment or Service: Highland Light Infantry. Unit: 9th Battalion. Age at death: 39. Date of death: 15 May 1915. Killed.

Supplementary information: Son of Joseph and Tekla Martin, of Bristol. Husband of Jane Elizabeth Martin, of Woodview, Portlaw, Co. Waterford. Grave or Memorial Reference: I.A.26. Cemetery: Le Touret Military Cemetery, Richebourg-L'Avoue in France.

MARTIN, John: Rank: Lance Corporal. Regiment or Service: Royal Irish Fusiliers. Unit: 2nd Battalion. Age at death: 35. Date of death: 17 May 1915. Service No: 5754. Born in Clonmel and enlisted in Newry while living in Oldbridge Co. Waterford. Died of wounds.

Supplementary information: Husband of Annie Martin, of 13 Quin's Lane, Clonmel, Co. Tipperary. Grave or Memorial Reference: I.H.5A. Cemetery: Wimereux Communal Cemetery, Pas de Calais, France.

MARTIN, John: Rank: Lance Corporal. Regiment or Service: Royal Irish Fusiliers. Unit: 2nd Battalion. Age at death: 35. Date of death: 17 May 1915. Service No: 5754. Born in Clonmel and enlisted in Newry while living in Oldbridge Co. Waterford. Died of wounds.

Supplementary information: Husband of Annie Martin, of 13 Quin's Lane, Clonmel, Co. Tipperary. Grave or Memorial Reference: I.H.5A. Cemetery: Wimereux Communal Cemetery, Pas de Calais, France.

MARTIN, Redmond: Rank: Driver. Regiment or Service: Royal Horse Artillery and Royal Field Artillery. Unit: 4th Battery. Date of death: 29 July 1916. Service No: 101603. Born in Waterford. Enlisted in Waterford. Killed in action. Died in India.

Supplementary information: Buried in Agra Cantonment Cemetery. Grave or Memorial Reference: Face 4. Memorial: Madras 1914–1918 War Memorial, Chennai, India.

MASON, James: Rank: Able Seaman. Regiment or Service: Royal Navy. Unit: (RFR/DEV/B/3686). HMS *Goliath*. Age at death: 33. Date of death: 13 May 1915. Service No: 200152. HMS *Goliath* was sunk by three torpedoes from German destroyer *Muvanet-I-Milet*, she blew up and capsized immediately taking 570 of her 750 crew including the Captain to a watery grave. Ten Waterford men died on the *Goliath* that day.

Supplementary information: Son of Robert and Margaret Mason (*née* Power), of Passage East, Co. Waterford. Grave or Memorial Reference: 5 on the Plymouth Naval Memorial, UK.

MASON, Thomas: Rank: Corporal. Regiment or Service: Royal Irish Regiment. Unit: 1st Battalion. Age at death: 32. Date of death: 14 February 1915. Service No: 8358. Born in Cappoquin, Co. Waterford. Enlisted in Fermoy, Co. Cork while living in Cappoquin, Co. Waterford. Killed in action.

Supplementary information: Son of Richard and Kate Mason, of Main Street, Cappoquin, Co. Waterford. He has no known grave but is listed on Panel 33 on the Ypres (Menin Gate) Memorial in Belgium.

MAYE, John: Rank: Private. Regiment or Service: Irish Guards. Unit: 2nd Battalion. Date of death: 13 September 1918. Service No: 10064. Born in Kilmacthomas, Co. Waterford. Enlisted in Manchester while living in Kilmacthomas. Killed in action. He has no known grave but is listed on Panels 10 and 11 on the Tyne Cot Memorial in Belgium.

McAULIFFE, Frederick Charles: Rank: Lance Corporal. Regiment or Service: Royal Engineers. Unit: Guards Div. Signal Coy. Age at death: 25. Date of death: 27 August 1918. Service No: 198124. Previously he was with the Liverpool Regiment where his number was 2177. He won the Military Medal and is listed in the *London Gazette*. Born in Ballybricken, Co. Waterford. Enlisted in Liverpool. Killed in action.

Supplementary information: Son of John P. and E.M. McAuliffe, of Palace Square, Tramore, Co. Waterford:

SON OF MR AND MRS MCAULIFFE, POST OFFICE, TRAMORE.

'Sapper McAuliffe, in the face of intense enemy fire, kept a wireless station going for three days and three nights when all his comrades had become casualties. As a result he was able to send valuable information to headquarters. Two months after this remarkable example of courage and endurance he lost his life going over the top at St Leger, south of Arras. Before join-

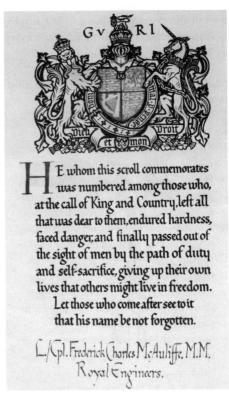

HE whom this scroll commemorates was numbered among those who, at the call of King and Country, left all that was dear to them, endured hardness, faced danger, and finally passed out of the sight of men by the path of duty and self-sacrifice, giving up their own lives that others might live in freedom. Let those who come after see to it that his name be not forgotten.

L./Cpl. Frederick Charles McAuliffe. M.M. Royal Engineers.

Frederick Charles Mc Auliffe.

ing the army he was in the Atlantic Cable Company in Liverpool. He joined voluntarily in August, 1914, the Irish Guards (Royal Engineers, Signalling Division) for four years, although he was practically of active service all the time, he never got a scratch, and it is one of the sad ironies of fate that just six weeks before the termination of hostilities he was killed "going over the top" on the 27th August, 1918.

Grave or Memorial Reference: II.D.13. Cemetery: Douchy-les-Ayette British Cemetery in France.

McBRIDE, Patrick: Rank: Fireman. Regiment or Service: Mercantile Marine. Unit: SS *Garmoyle* (Glasgow). Age at death: 28. Date of death: 10 July 1917.

Supplementary information: Born in Waterford. Grave or Memorial Reference: He has no known grave but is listed on the Tower Hill Memorial in the UK.

McCARTHY, Daniel: Rank: Corporal. Regiment or Service: Royal Garrison Artillery Secondary. Unit: attd. 'Y' 21st Trench Mortar Battery. Age at death: 45. Date of death: 26 June 1916. Service No: 6341 He was awarded the Miltary Medal and mentioned in the *London Gazette*. Born in Carrick-on-Suir and enlisted in Bury while living in Carrick Beg, Waterford. Killed in action.

Supplementary information: Son of Thomas and Kate McCarthy, of Ballyrichard Road, Carrick-on-Suir, Co. Tipperary. From the *Waterford News*, May 1917:

DEAD CARRICK SOLDIER'S BRAVERY REWARDED.

Mrs Catherine Lynch, Carrickbeg, Carrick-on-Suir, has received the military medal awarded "For Bravery in the Field" to her son, Corporal D McCarthy, who was killed just a year ago in action.

Grave or Memorial Reference: I.C.68. Cemetery: Norfolk Cemetery, Becordel-Becourt in France.

McCARTHY, Denis: Rank: Fireman. Regiment or Service: Mercantile Marine. Unit: SS *Lough Fisher* (Barrow). Shelled and sunk by a German submarine 12 miles south-east of Cork. Age at death: 34. Date of death: 30 March 1918.

Supplementary information: Son of Patrick and Bridget McCarthy (*née* Henessey), of 83 Gallows Hill, Waterford. Born in Waterford. He has no known grave but is listed on the Tower Hill Memorial in the UK.

McCARTHY, Edward: Rank: Private. Regiment or Service: Royal Irish Regiment. Unit: Depot. Age at death: 48. Born St Mary's, Dungarvan, Co. Waterford. Enlisted in Dungarvan. Died at home. Date of death: 20 January 1915. Service No: 7096.

Supplementary information: Husband of Mary McCarthy of 4 Davis Street, Dungarvan. Cemetery, Clonmel, St Patrick's Cemetery. Grave location: EA. 115.

McCARTHY, John: Rank: Private. Regiment or Service: Leinster Regiment. Unit: 1st Battalion. Date of death: 12 August 1915. Service No: 8518. Born in Waterford.

Supplementary information: This man is a bit of a mystery. He is not in Soldiers died in the Great War. Irelands Memorial Records are unsure of his year of death. The only additional information it has is that he was born in Waterford and was killed in action in 1914 or 1915 in Belgium. Note he is buried in France. His Victory Medal and 1915 Star were purchased from a USA Collector in 2009. Grave or Memorial Reference: II.A.10. Cemetery: Brewery Orchard Cemetery, Bois-Grenier, Nord in France.

McCARTHY, John: Rank: Fireman. Regiment or Service: Mercantile Marine. Unit: SS *Coningbeg* (Glasgow). Torpedoed by German Submarine U-62. There were no survivors. U-62 surrendered in November 1918. Age at death: 50. Date of death: 18 December 1917.

Supplementary information: Son of Richard and Bridget McCarthy. Husband of Hannah McCarthy (*née* O'Keefe), of 47 Lower Yellow Road, Waterford, Co. Waterford. Born in Waterford. He has no known grave but is listed on the Tower Hill Memorial in the UK. He is also listed on the Formby-Coningbeg Memorial, Adelphi Quay in Waterford City.

McCARTHY, Michael: Rank: Fireman. Regiment or Service: Mercantile Marine. Unit: SS *Coningbeg* (Glasgow). Torpedoed by German Submarine U-62. There were no survivors. U-62 surrendered in November 1918. Age at death: 50. Date of death: 18 December 1917.

Supplementary information: Son of Richard and Bridget McCarthy. Husband of Ellen

John McCarthy. The image is courtesy of Damien Cawley showing his two remaining medals. The War medal was missing. A quick look at his medal index card, listed under 2518 (not 8518) shows he entered the French theatre of war on 19 December 1914.

McCarthy (*née* McGrath), of 1 Stephen Street, Waterford. Born in Waterford. He has no known grave but is listed on the Tower Hill Memorial in the UK. He is also listed on the Formby-Coningbeg Memorial, Adelphi Quay in Waterford City.

McCARTHY, Michael: Rank: Private. Regiment or Service: Royal Irish Regiment. Unit: 3rd Battalion. Age at death: 29. Date of death: 4 May 1915. Service No: 87. Born in St Patrick's, Waterford. Enlisted in Waterford. Died at Home.

Supplementary information: Husband of Anne McCarthy. Grave or Memorial Reference: Brookwood (United Kingdom 1914-18) Memorial: 30 miles from London.

McCARTHY, Thomas: Rank: Private/ Lance Corporal. Regiment or Service: Royal Irish Regiment. Unit: 2nd Battalion. Date of death: 1 May 1915. Service No: 6187. Born in Trinity Without, Waterford. Enlisted in Waterford. Killed in action. He has no known grave but is listed on Panel 33 on the Ypres (Menin Gate) Memorial in Belgium.

McCARTHY, William: Rank: Air Mechanic 3rd Class. Regiment or Service: Royal Air Force. Age at death: 44. Date of death: 24 November 1918. Service No: 285603.

Supplementary information: Husband of Bridget McCarthy, of 6 St Lawrence Terrace, Lower Grange, Waterford. Grave or Memorial Reference: C.F. 15. Cemetery: Ballynaneashagh (St Otteran's) Catholic Cemetery in Co. Waterford.

McCARTHY, William: Rank: Private. Regiment or Service: Worcestershire Regiment. Unit: 3rd Battalion. Age at death: 35. Date of death: 7 November 1914. Service No: 7296. Born in Waterford. Enlisted in Monmouth while living in Waterford. Killed in action.

Supplementary information: Son of Mrs Johanna McCarthy, of Knockrour, Stradbally, Waterford. He has no known grave but is listed on Panel 34 on the Ypres (Menin Gate) Memorial in Belgium.

McCLEAN/McLEAN, George: Rank: Gunner. Regiment or Service: Royal Horse Artillery and Royal Field Artillery. Unit: 74th Brigade. Date of death: 23 December 1916. Service No: 41411. Born in Salterbridge, Waterford. Enlisted in Belfast. Died. Grave or Memorial Reference: A.34. Cemetery: Allonville Communal Cemetery in France.

McCLEAN/McLEAN, John: Rank: Rifleman. Regiment or Service: Royal Irish Rifles. Unit: 2nd Battalion. Date of death: 23 March 1918. Service No: 19987. Born in Cappoquin, Co. Waterford. Enlisted in Kildare while living in Blackrock, Co. Dublin Killed in action. He has no known grave but is listed on Panel 74 to 76 on the Pozières Memorial in France.

McCONNELL, Samuel: Rank: Private. Regiment or Service: Royal Irish Fusiliers. Unit: 1st Battalion. Age at death: 21. Date of death: 1 October 1918. Service No: 42391. Previously he was with the Royal Irish Rifles where his number was 22529. Born in Waterford. Enlisted in Waterford. Killed in action.

Supplementary information: Son of John and Margaret McConnell, of 5 King's Terrace, Waterford. Grave or Memorial Reference: III.D.10. Cemetery: Dadizeele New British Cemetery in Belgium.

McCORMACK, Michael: Rank; Private. Number 9902, 3rd Battalion, Royal Irish Regiment. Born in Holycross. Enlisted in Clonmel while living in Holycross (other records say Waterford). Also listed as Cormack, Michael. Age at death: 19. Date of Death: Thursday, 20 January 1916. Son of William and Brigid McCormack of Holycross. Buried in Holycross Abbey and moved during renovations to the left of the path in the graveyard. Official records say he died at home but oral tradition indicate his remains were brought home for burial.

McCOY, Arthur: Rank: Private. Regiment or Service: Irish Guards. Unit: 2nd Battalion. Date of death: 27 November 1917. Service No: 11436. Born in Waterford. Enlisted in Whitehall, Middlesex while living in Islington, Middlesex. Killed in action. Grave or Memorial Reference: Panel 2 and 3. Memorial: Cambrai Memorial, Louveral in France.

McDONALD, C.: Rank: Sailor. Regiment or Service: Mercantile Marine. Unit: SS *Ludgate* (London). Age at death: 41. Date of death: 26 July 1917.

Supplementary information: Husband of Mrs McDonald, of 22, Tatton Street, Salford. Born in Waterford. He has no known grave but is listed on the Tower Hill Memorial in the UK.

McDONALD, James: Rank: Private. Regiment or Service: Royal Irish Regiment. Unit: 2nd Battalion. Age at death: 35. Date of death: 25 May 1915. Service No: 8189. Born in Kilrush, Co. Wexford. Enlisted in Wexford while living in Ferrybank, Co. Kilkenny. Died of wounds.

Supplementary information: Husband of Mary Anne McDonald of Glasshouse, Ferrybank, Waterford. Grave or Memorial Reference: I.F.75. Cemetery: Bailleul Communal Cemetery Extension (Nord) in France.

McENIRY, David Bishop Mary: Rank: Gunner. Regiment or Service: Royal Garrison Artillery. Unit: 61st Trench Mortar Battery. Age at death: 33. Service No: 7637. Born in Clonmel. Enlisted in St Paul's Churchyard in Middlesex while living in Clonmel. Killed in action.

Supplementary information: Son of Dr David McEniry and Mrs Mary McEniry, of Ballymacarbry, Co. Waterford. From the *Waterford News*, April 1916:

BALLYMACARBERY DOCTOR'S SON KILLED IN ACTION.

Dr McEniry, Ballymacarbry, has received a notification from the war office that his second son, David B McNeiry, was killed in the trenches in France, on the 1st inst. The deceased, who was 34 years of age, served with the 3rd Dragoon Guards before the war, and had been on active service from the outbreak of hostilities. He was a very fine type of young fellow, and an athlete of no mean repute. While serving in India he held the middle-weight championship of the Central Provinces, and was a good foot runner and jumper. "Bishop," as he was familiarly known, was a very great favourite with all who knew him, and the news of his death has been received with genuine sorrow in the district. His death is a trying blow to his father and mother, especially the latter, whose favourite he was. A full measure of sympathy goes out to the afflicted parents from a people who have just cause to share in any trouble that comes to Dr McEniry. His eldest son, John McEniry, served with the Imperial Light Horse in the South African War, and lost his life in an attempt to carry despatches through the Boer lines at Waggon Hill.

Grave or Memorial Reference: I.M.15. Cemetery: Spoilbank Cemetery in Belgium.

McEVOY, Patrick: Rank: Private. Regiment or Service: Royal Irish Regiment. Unit: 2nd Battalion. Date of death: 14 September 1914. Service No: 9216. Born in Geashall, Co. Offaly. Enlisted in Tullamore while living in Ballymacarberry, Co. Waterford. Died of wounds. Grave or Memorial Reference: Plot 38, 1914-18, Row A Grave 4. Cemetery: Le Mans West Cemetery in France.

McGARRY, Francis: Rank: Corporal. Regiment or Service: Connaught Rangers. Unit: 5th Battalion. Date of death: 31 August 1915. Service No: 377. Born in Dungarven, Co. Waterford. Enlisted in Clitheroe while living in Newcastle, Satffordshire. Died in Gallipoli. He has no known grave but is listed on Panel 181 to 183 on the Helles Memorial in Turkey.

McGILLICUDDY, David: Rank: Private. Regiment or Service: Connaught Rangers. Unit: 2nd Battalion. Date of death: 14 November 1914. Service No: 8212. Born in Waterford. Enlisted in Waterford while living in Waterford. Died of wounds. Grave or Memorial Reference: III.C.30. Cemetery: Boulogne Eastern Cemetery, Pas de Calais in France.

McGILLICUDDY/McGILLICUDY, Patrick: Rank: Rifleman. Regiment or Service: Royal Irish Rifles. Unit: 1st Battalion. Date of death: 30 April 1916. Service No: 10072. Born in Waterford. Enlisted in Waterford. Died of wounds. Grave or Memorial Reference: E.3. Cemetery: Villiers-Bocage Communal Cemetery Extension in France.

McGOWAN, William: Rank: Second Lieutenant. Regiment or Service: Leinster Regiment. Unit: 7th Battalion. Date of death: 9 September 1917. From the *Waterford News*, September 1916:

CADETS PROMOTION.

Sergeant W. McGowan, D.C.M., son of Mr M. McGowan, Vice-President, North Leitrim Executive, U.I.L., has been promoted Lieutenant. Lieutenant McGowan was employed at Messrs Hearne's drapery establishment in this city for some years, and in March, 1915, during the special recruiting campaign in Waterford, he joined the Cadet Corps of the 7th Leinster's, together with others of the staff of the same firm. Lieutenant McGowan received the D.C.M. and promotion at the same time for bravery in the field.

Grave or Memorial Reference: He has no known grave but is listed on Pier and Face 16 C of the Thiepval Memorial in France.

McGRATH, CHRISTOPHER. Rank: Lance Corporal. Regiment or Service: Royal Irish Regiment. Unit: 2nd Battalion. Age at death: 19. Date of death: 14 July 1916. Service No: 7652. Born in St John's, Waterford. Enlisted in Waterford. Killed in action.

Supplementary information: Son of Maurice and Bridget McGrath, of 21 Castle Street, Waterford. From the *Munster Express*, July 1917:

WATERFORD MAN KILLED IN ACTION.

After being kept in suspense for twelve months as to the whereabouts of Lnace Corporal Christopher McGrath of the 2nd Battalion, Royal Irish Regiment, 7652, second eldest son of Mr and Mrs Maurice McGrath of 21 Castle Street, Waterford, news has now been officially received by them that he was killed in action in 1916 in France. The deceased, who was only 20 years of age, joined the army in March, 1915, and was attached to D Company of the 2nd R.I. Regiment and went to France in July of the same year. He was a great favourite as a quiet and good-natured disposition made for him many friends. He was brother of Corporal P McGrath who saw service at the Dardanelles and Gallipoli, where he got wounded. After spending a few weeks sick leave at his native city he was called away to his Regiment at the time of the Dublin rebel-

lion and was commended for the heroic work he performed there in saving his officer. "Christy" McGrath, as he was familiarly known, saw many engagements and was at first reported as "missing" and subsequently as "wounded", but within the past few weeks the official communication states he was killed in action. With the relatives of this plucky "Urbs Intacta" man we offer our sympathy. Lance-Corporal McGrath was brother of Miss Mary McGrath of Waterloo House, Mallow.

Grave or Memorial Reference: He has no known grave but is listed on Pier and Face 3A of the Thiepval Memorial in France.

McGRATH, Denis: Rank: Private. Regiment or Service: Irish Guards Unit: 1st Battalion. Date of death: 11 September 1916. Age at death: 28. Service No: 9560. Born in Dungarvan, Co. Waterford. Enlisted in Dungarvan, Co. Waterford. Killed in action.

Supplementary information: Son of Denis and Catherine McGrath. From the *Munster Express*:

A DUNGARVAN MAN KILLED IN ACTION.

The news has come to Dungarvan that Denis McGrath, a young man of the town, has been killed in action in France. The news was sent by a chaplain, Father Browne, who said that he was just close at the time when the young soldier was struck by the bursting of a shell, and killed almost instantly, but he had time to administer absolution before he died, and Father Browne speaks of the high esteem in which the deceased was held by all in the battalion. The poor fellow, who has died in action, volunteered about twelve months ago, and went through various battles. His afflicted mother, brother and friends in Dungarvan are the recipients of the sincere sympathy of numbers of friends. Some photographs found in the pocket of the deceased were sent home by the chaplain, and one was that of his old chum, in the character of

"Myles" in the "Colleen Bawn" play, which was produced here recently by the amateur dramatic corps.

He has no known grave but is listed on Pier and Face 7D on the Thiepval Memorial in France.

McGRATH, Edward: Rank: Acting Corporal. Regiment or Service: Corps of Royal Engineers. Unit: 98th Field Company, Royal Engineers. Unit: 98th Field Company. Age at death: 21. Date of death: 16 June 1917. Service No: 103695. He won the Military Medal and is listed in the *London Gazette*. Born in Aglish, Co. Waterford. Enlisted in Dungarvan, Co. Waterford. while living in Aglish, Co. Waterford. Killed in action.

Supplementary information: Son of the late John McGrath. He has no known grave but is listed in Bay 9 on the Arras Memorial in France.

McGRATH, John: Rank: Private. Regiment or Service: Machine Gun Corps. Unit: Infantry, 170th Company. Date of death: 16 August 1917. Age at death: 20. Service No: 8271. Formerly he was with the Royal Inniskilling Fusiliers where his number was 26385. Born in Waterford. Enlisted in Waterford. Killed in action. From the the *Waterford News* and the *Munster Express*, November 1917:

WATERFORD SOLDIER KILLED.
Driver John McGrath, Machine Gun Corps, whose people reside at 4 Mall Lane, Waterford, and who was reported missing on 16th August last, is now reported killed in France. The sad intelligence is contained in a letter from his Chaplain, Rev. F. Donohoe, S.J., who writes that the deceased, with a party carrying ammunition and water to the front line, successfully got through the barrage to his destination, but was lost on the return journey, for his mule returned riderless. "He was an excellent man," writes the Chaplain, "and was behaving with the

utmost gallantry. His officer sends his sincerest condolence and sympathy." The deceased soldier joined two years ago, and had been in France about twelve months. He was previously employed at O'Mara's, Bridge Street, was a member of the National Volunteers, and was a very popular young man.

Grave or Memorial Reference: Has no known grave but is commemorated on Panel 154 to 159 and 163A. Memorial: Tyne Cot Memorial in Belgium.

McGRATH, J.: Rank: Private. Regiment or Service: Royal Irish Regiment. Unit: 2nd Battalion. Age at death: 42. Date of death: 22 February 1920. Service No: 6787.

Supplementary information: Husband of Elizabeth McGrath, of 28 Peter Street, Waterford. Grave or Memorial Reference: C (Lower). B. 17. Cemetery: Ballynaneashagh (St Otteran's) Catholic Cemetery in Co. Waterford.

McGRATH, John: Rank: Cattleman. Regiment or Service: Mercantile Marine. Unit: SS *Formby* (Glasgow). Age at death: 31. Date of death: 16 December 1917. The ship was lost with all hands and never located during a fierce storm.

Supplementary information: Son of Catherine and the late Michael McGrath. Husband of Margaret McGrath (*née* Flynn), of 83 Lower Yellow Road, Waterford. Born in Waterford. He has no known grave but is listed on the Tower Hill Memorial in the UK. He is also listed on the Formby-Coningbeg Memorial, Adelphi Quay in Waterford City.

McGRATH, John: Rank: Private. Regiment or Service: Royal Irish Regiment. Unit: 2nd Battalion. Age at death: 20. Date of death: 19 October 1914. Service No: 5925. Born in Trinity Without, Waterford. Enlisted in Waterford. Killed in action.

Supplementary information: Son of William and Mary McGrath, of 5 Newport's Lane,

Waterford. Grave or Memorial Reference: 11 and 12 on the Le Touret Memorial in France.

McGRATH, John: Rank: Sergeant. Regiment or Service: Rifle Brigade Unit: 16th Battalion. Date of death: 3 September 1916. Service No: P/601. Born in Kilmacow, Co. Waterford. Enlisted in St Pancras, Middlesex while living in Kilmacow Co. Waterford. Killed in action. He has no known grave but is listed on Pier and Face 16B and 16C on the Thiepval Memorial in France.

McGRATH, John: Rank: Driver. Regiment or Service: Australian Field Artillery. Unit: 11th Brigade. H.Q. Date of death: 30 December 1916. Service No: 1997. Born in Dungarvan, Waterford. Enlisted in Victoria, Melbourne, on 9 July 1915. Killed in action. Data from his records:

In or near what Parish or Town were you born? Dungarvan, Waterford, Ireland.

Are you a natural born British subject or a Naturalised British subject? Natural born.

What is your age? 28.

What is your trade or calling? Gardener.

Are you married? No, parents deceased, medals etc to eldest brother. L. McGrath. Working Mans Club, Melbourne, Vic.

Heght: 5 feet, 9 inches.

Weight: 11st 7 lbs.

Chest measurement: 36½ –37½ inches.

Complexion: resh.

Eyes: blue.

Hair: Black.

Religious denomination: RC.

A letter from his brother dated July 1922, written from Mildura:

To: Officer in Charge.

In reply to yours dated 27th October, 1921. I beg to state I only received it this morning as I was away from Wildura. I must inform you that his mother died years ago and also that I am sole next-of-kin. I am also his oldest brother (all of which I am

after letting your Department known for about the twentieth time).

Yours etc.

Laurence McGrath.

John's pension was claimed by Laurence McGrath, 212 Dryburgh Street, N Melbourne. It was rejected-'claimant was not dependant on the deceased soldier for the 12 months prior to enlistment'. It was also claimed by his sister Mary, Ballinacourty, Cappagh, and was also rejected due to 'no proof of dependence'. However Mary did get his Death plaque and scroll.

Personal effects (Cap comforter, Tie and Fly Net) were delivered to Mary McGrath, Ballinacourty, Cappagh, Waterford on 06-04-1917.

He has no known grave but is listed on the Villers-Bretonneux Memorial in France.

McGRATH, Michael: Rank: Sergeant. Regiment or Service: Connaught Rangers. Unit: 6th Battalion. Date of death: 9 December 1916. Service No: 7060. Born in Fourmilewater, Co. Waterford. Enlisted in Dublin while living in Bandon, Co. Cork. Killed in action.

Supplementary information: Husband of Mrs M. McGrath, of 3 New Buildings, Watergate Street Bandon, Co. Cork. Grave or Memorial Reference: G.16. Cemetery: Pond Farm Cemetery in Belgium,

McGRATH, Michael: Rank: Private. Regiment or Service: Cheshire Regiment. Unit: 8th Battalion. Age at death: 24. Date of death: 13 August 1915. Service No: 10648. Born in Cappoquin, Co. Waterford. Enlisted in Chester while living in Cappoquin, Co. Waterford. Died of wounds in Egypt.

Supplementary information: Son of Patrick and Annie McGrath, of Mount Rivers, Cappoquin, Co. Waterford. Grave or Memorial Reference: L. 41. Cemetery: Alexandria (Chatby) Military and War Memorial Cemetery in Egypt.

McGRATH, Thomas: Rank: Leading Seaman. Regiment or Service: Royal Naval Reserve. Unit: HM Trawler *Robert Smith*. Age at death: 30. Date of death: 20 July 1917. Service No: 41578 Awards: D.S.M.

Supplementary information: Son of John and Mary McGrath, of 3 Phillip Street, Waterford. Husband of Annie McGrath, of 19 Waterside, Waterford. From the the *Waterford News*, November 1917:

BRAVE WATERFORD SEAMAN
HONOURED BY THE KING.

The distinguished Service Medal was awarded by His Majesty to Leading Seaman Thomas McGrath, R. N. R., of the Auxiliary Patrol Service, on 27th June, 1917, for exceptionally good work in that hazardous and vitally important branch of naval war operations. As this brave man lost his life in the performance of duty three weeks after the award was gazetted, he was unable to receive the coveted decoration. In compliance with His Majesty's wishes, and in accordance with instructions from the Admiral Commanding-in-Chief, Lieutenant-Commander R. C. Carew, Royal Navy (Divisional Coast-watching Officer, Irish Southern District) has presented the decoration to the widow of the deceased seaman who resides at Waterside, Waterford, and has one son aged 7 years. Mrs McGrath has also received a personal letter from Vice-Admiral Sir Lewis Baly, K.C.B., C.V.O., Commander-inChief on the Coast of Ireland Station. The deepest sympathy of the inhabitants of Waterford will be felt with the young widow in the loss of her husband.

Grave or Memorial Reference: 23 on the Plymouth Naval Memorial, UK.

McGRATH, William: Rank: Private. Regiment or Service: Royal Irish Regiment. Unit: 2nd Battalion. Age at death: 44. Date of death: 23 April 1916. Service No: 6577. Born in St Patrick's, Waterford. Enlisted in Waterford. Killed in action.

Supplementary information: Son of James and Mrs A.S. McGrath, of 13 Peter Street, Waterford. Served in the South African Campaign. Grave or Memorial Reference: I.B.13. Cemetery: Foncquevillers Military Cemetery in France.

McGRATH, William: Rank: Private. Regiment or Service: Royal Irish Regiment. Unit: 2nd Battalion. Date of death: 23 October 1914. Service No: 6154. Born in St. Patrick's, Waterford. Enlisted in Waterford. Killed in action. From the *Waterford News*, 1914: 'Mrs McGrath, of Peter Street, Waterford, has also been notified by the war office of the death of her son, William at the front. Deceased was an apprentice at O'Keeffe's stone works and went out about the same time as young O'Reilly.' Grave or Memorial Reference: I.B.22. Cemetery: Bethune Town Cemetery in France.

McGREAL (Also listed under **McGRECIL**), **Patrick:** Rank: Private. Regiment or Service: Royal Inniskilling Fusiliers. Unit: 8th Battalion. Date of death: 29 April 1915 (1916 on the CWGC). Age at death: 20. Service No: 21135. Born in Waterford. Enlisted in London while living in Waterford. Died of wounds.

Supplementary information: Son of John and Kate McGreal, of 44 Galtee Terrace, Castle Street, Waterford. He has no known grave but is listed on Panel 60 on the Loos Memorial in France.

McGUINN, MICHAEL John: Rank: Corporal. Regiment or Service: Household Cavalry and Cavalry of the line including the Yeomanry and Imperial Camel Corps. Unit: 3rd Dragoon Guards. Age at death: 31. Date of death: 18 May 1915. Service No: 5096. Born in Duncarrow Waterford. Enlisted in Chester while living in Bristol. Died of wounds.

Supplementary information: Son of Michael John and Mary McGuinn, of North Dungarvan, Co. Waterford. Husband of Mabel McGuinn, of 7 Park Avenue, Victoria

Park, Bristol. Grave or Memorial Reference: VIII.D.21. Cemetery: Boulogne Eastern Cemetery in France.

McGUINNESS, Simon: Rank: Private. Regiment or Service: Connaught Rangers. Unit: 6th Battalion. Age at death: 29. Date of death: 26 May 1916. Service No: 9204. Born in Waterford. Enlisted in Waterford while living in Waterford. Died.

Supplementary information: Son of Simon and Bridget McGuinness, of 32 Peter Street, Waterford. Grave or Memorial Reference: II.H.8. Cemetery: Dud Corner Cemetery, Loos in France.

McGUIRE, William: Rank: Private. Regiment or Service: Royal Munster Fusiliers. Unit: 2nd Battalion. Date of death: 14 March 1917. Service No: 4394. Born in Ballybricken, Co. Waterford. Enlisted in Waterford while living in Waterford. Killed in action. From the *Waterford News*, April 1917:

KILLED IN ACTION.

Mrs McGuire, 89 Lower Yellow Road, Waterford, has received official notification from the War Office that her son, Private William McGuire, who joined the 2nd Royal Munster Fusiliers eighteen months ago, was killed on 14th March. He fell in action, and was laid to rest in the British cemetery at Belloy. Lieutenant. F.G. Hayes has written to Mrs McGuire saying that by his Majesty's command he forwards a message of sympathy from the King and Queen.

From the *Waterford News*, April 1917:

OFFICERS TOUCHING TRIBUTE TO FALLEN SOLDIER.

Major Laurence Roche, 8th Royal Munster Fusiliers, has written a touching tribute to the memory of No 4394 Pte W. McGuire, 8th R.M.F. He writes from the Curragh to this soldier's relations at 89,

Lower Yellow Road, Waterford, as follows: "I saw in the papers to-day (18th inst) of the death in action of Private McGuire, and now hasten to offer to you my sincerest and deepest sympathy on the death of a gallant soldier. He was in my old D Company during our training in Ireland and England in 1915, and I was by his side when he was wounded at Loos in France in 1916. He was a brave fellow, a great favourite in the Battalion, and a credit to the 47th Irish Brigade."

Grave or Memorial Reference: I.BB.7. Cemetery: Fouquescourt British Cemetery in France.

McKENNA, MICHAEL Joseph: Rank: Private. Regiment or Service: South African Infantry. Unit: 3rd Regiment. Age at death: 23. Date of death: 10 April 1917 Service No: 8174.

Supplementary information: Son of Margaret McKenna, of Waterford. From the *Waterford News*, April 1917:

A DOUBLE BEREAVEMENT.

Much sympathy will be felt for Mrs McKenna, Summerhill Terrace, Waterford, who has received notification from the War Office that her son, Private James McKenna, attached to the Transport Corps, has died in hospital in France. Only last week Mrs McKenna received the intelligence that her youngest son, Michael, of the South African Infantry, was killed in action on the 10th April. Mrs McKenna has the sincere sympathy of the community in her double bereavement.

A James McKenna with a Waterford or Transport Corps connection can not be found in the War Dead databases. Grave or Memorial Reference: I.D.3. Cemetery: St Nicholas British Cemetery in France.

McKEON/McKEONE, John Henry:
Rank: Sergeant. Regiment or Service: Cheshire Regiment. Unit: 16th Battalion. Age at death: 35. Date of death: 22 April 1917. Service No: W/405. Born in Waterford. Enlisted in Port Sunlight, Cheshire while living in Rock Ferry, Cheshire. Killed in action.

Supplementary information: Son of William and Eleanor McKeone, of Waterford. Husband of Annie McKeone, of 31 Brunswick Street, Roch Ferry, Cheshire. Grave or Memorial Reference: III.E.13. Cemetery: Chapelle British Cemetery, Holnon, in France.

McLOUGHLIN/McLOUGHTEN, Henry: Rank: Sergeant. Regiment or Service: Middlesex Regiment. Unit: 16th Battalion. Date of death: 1 July 1916. Service No: P.S. 1682. Born in Waterford. Enlisted in Cockspur Street, Middlesex while living in Tottenham, Middlesex. Killed in action. Sergeant McLoughlin (SDGW) McLoughten (CWGC and IMR) is on the Overseas deaths list (as McLoughlin) but as yet the Commonwealth Wargraves Commission has not listed him in their databases. His name will be put forward by the 'In from the Cold' project and will have a grave reference sometime in the future. His death certificate is available from the British General Register Office under I. 69. 149 for 1916.

McNAMARA. ?: Rank: Private. Regiment or Service: Royal Irish Regiment. Unit: 18th Battalion. The only information I have on this man is contained in the below. He is not in any of the War Dead databases and may have died after discharge. From the *Waterford News*, March 1916, 'Military Funeral. The funeral took place yesterday with full military honours, to St Mary's, Ballygunner, of Private McNamara, of the 18th Royal Irish Regiment, who died from an illness consequent upon wounds received in action. The military band played the Dead March in Saul along the route.'

MEAGHER, Dominic: Rank: Private. Regiment or Service: Cheshire Regiment. Unit: 9th Battalion. Date of death: 14 November 1915. Service No: 12444. Born in Waterford. Enlisted in Birkinhead. Killed in action. Grave or Memorial Reference: III. B. 18. Cemetery, Le Touret Military Cemetery, Richebourg-L'Avoue in France.

MEANEY, Michael: Rank: Private. Regiment or Service: Royal Warwickshire Regiment. Unit: 9th Battalion. Age at death: 38. Date of death: 5 January 1916. Service No: 12504. Born in Bally Bricken, Co. Waterford. Enlisted in Waterford. Killed in action in Gallipoli. Previously he was with the Royal Garrison Artillery where his number was 46108.

Supplementary information: Son of Michael and Elizabeth Meaney, of Doyle Street, Waterford. Husband of Mrs Matthew Ryan (formerly Meaney), of 1 Goat's Lane, Waterford. He has no known grave but is listed on Panel 35 to 37 on the Helles Memorial in Turkey.

MEANEY, Thomas: Rank: Cattleman. Regiment or Service: Mercantile Marine. Unit: SS *Coningbe* (Glasgow). Torpedoed by German Submarine U-62. There were no survivors. U-62 surrendered in November 1918. Age at death: 46. Date of death: 18 December 1917.

Supplementary information: Son of Lawrence and Bridget Meaney. Husband of Kate Meaney. Born in Waterford. He has no known grave but is listed on the Tower Hill Memorial in the UK. He is also listed on the Formby-Coningbeg Memorial, Adelphi Quay in Waterford City.

MEEHAN, James: Rank: Private. Regiment or Service: Royal Dublin Fusiliers. Unit: 2nd Battalion. Age at death: 20. Date of death: 16 August 1917. Service No: 9138 He won the Military Medal and is listed in the *London Gazette*.

Supplementary information: Husband of Mrs Mary Meehan, of 19 Waterford Street, Dublin. Grave or Memorial Reference: 144 to 145 on the Tyne Cot Memorial in Belgium

MEEHAN, Thomas: Rank: Rifleman. Regiment or Service: London Regiment (Post Office Rifles). Unit: 2nd/8th Battalion. Age at death: 20. Date of death: 30 October 1917. Service No: 372700. Born in Dublin. Enlisted in Dublin. Killed in action.

Supplementary information: Son of Mary and Matthew Meehan, of 16 Thomas Street, Dungarvan, Co. Waterford. Grave or Memorial Reference: 150 to 151 on the Tyne Cot Memorial in Belgium.

MERRIGAN, John: Rank: Private. Regiment or Service: Household Cavalry and Cavalry of the line including the Yeomanry and Imperial Camel Corps. Unit: 4th (Queens Own) Hussars. Date of death: 8 November 1918. Service No: 45177. Born in Modelligo, Waterford. Enlisted in Mallow while living in Cappoquin, Co. Waterford. Died. Grave or Memorial Reference: S.III.U.15. Cemetery: St Sever Cemetery Extension, Rouen in France.

MEYLER, Edward: Rank: Cattleman. Regiment or Service: Mercantile Marine. Unit: SS *Coningbeg* (Glasgow). Torpedoed by German Submarine U-62. There were no survivors. U-62 surrendered in November 1918. Age at death: 55. Date of death: 18 December 1917.

Supplementary information: Son of Philip and Catherine Meyler. Husband of Catherine Burke Meyler (*née* Walsh), of 10 Lower Grange, Waterford. Born at Passage East, Co. Waterford. He has no known grave but is listed on the Tower Hill Memorial in the UK. He is also listed on the Formby-Coningbeg Memorial, Adelphi Quay in Waterford City.

MINARDS, Charles. Rank: Master. Regiment or Service: Mercantile Marine. Unit: *Formby.* Age at death: 62. Date of death: 16 December 1917. The ship was lost with all hands and never located during a fierce storm.

Supplementary information: Son of Richard and Mary Minards, of Plymouth. Husband of Margaret Minards, of 56 St Declan's Place, Newtown, Waterford. He has no known grave but is listed on the Tower Hill Memorial in the UK. He is also listed on the Formby-Coningbeg Memorial, Adelphi Quay in Waterford City.

MOIR, John: Rank: First Engineer. Regiment or Service: Mercantile Marine. Unit: SS *Formby* (Glasgow). Age at death: 51. Date of death: 16 December 1917. The ship was lost with all hands and never located during a fierce storm.

Supplementary information: Son of Sarah and the late James Moir. Husband of Lydia Oliver Moir (*née* McKeown), of 42 Lower Newtown, Waterford. Born in Waterford. He has no known grave but is listed on the Tower Hill Memorial in the UK. He is also listed on the Formby-Coningbeg Memorial, Adelphi Quay in Waterford City.

MOIR, John Hnery: Rank: Fourth Engineer Officer. Regiment or Service: Mercantile Marine. Unit: SS *Stuart Prince* (Newcastle). Age at death: 21. Date of death: 22 March 1917.

Supplementary information: Son of John and Johanna Moir, of, 42, Lower Newtown, Waterford. He has no known grave but is listed on the Tower Hill Memorial in the UK.

MOLLOY, James: Rank: Private. Regiment or Service: Royal Scots Fusiliers. Unit: 1st Battalion. Date of death: 6 September 1917. Service No: 14308. Born in Tramore, Co. Waterford. He no known grave but is commemorated on Panel 60t to 61 on the Memorial: Tyne Cot Memorial in Belgium.

MOLONEY, John: Rank: Private. Regiment or Service: Royal Irish Regiment. Unit: 2nd Battalion. Age at death: 32. Date of death: 24 May 1915. Service No: 10302. Born in St Patrick's, Waterford. Enlisted in Waterford. Died of wounds.

Supplementary information: Son of the late John and Margaret Moloney (*née* Power), of Waterford. Grave or Memorial Reference: XXVII.A.3. Cemetery: New Irish Farm Cemetery in Belgium.

MOONEY, Richard: Rank: Lance Corporal. Regiment or Service: Royal Dublin Fusiliers. Unit: 2nd Battalion. Age at death: 30. Date of death: 16 August 1917. Service No: 40035. Born in Fess, Co. Waterford. Enlisted in Ponrypridd while living in Kilmacthomas, Co. Waterford. Killed in action. Previously he was with the Royal Welsh Fusiliers where his number was 16312.

Supplementary information: Son of John and Ellen Mooney, of Rathmaiden, Kilmacthomas. Grave or Memorial Reference: 144 to 145 on the Tyne Cot Memorial in Belgium

Henry Moore. Courtesy of Maria Stenson.

MOONEY, William: Rank: Private. Regiment or Service: Royal Irish Regiment. Unit: 1st Battalion. Age at death: 19. Date of death: 2 May 1915. Service No: 9860. Born in Portlaw, Co. Waterford. Enlisted in Waterford while living in Portlaw. Killed in action.

Supplementary information: Son of Mathew Mooney, of Portlaw. He has no known grave but is listed on Panel 33 on the Ypres (Menin Gate) Memorial in Belgium.

MOORE, Henry: Rank: Lance Corporal. Regiment or Service: Royal Irish Rifles. Unit: 'B' Coy. 2nd Battalion. Age at death: 20. Date of death: 21 September 1914. Service No: 9966. Born in Waterford. Enlisted in Waterford. Killed in action. Henry Moore has three living nephews, Michael and Harry Halligan, Waterford, Eddie Halligan, Wales, and two living nieces, Mrs Kitty Patey, London and Mrs May Greene, Boston, USA.

Supplementary information: Son of Henry and Ellen Moore, of 62 Mount Sion Avenue, Waterford. He has no known grave but is listed on the La-Ferte-Sous-Jouarre Memorial in France.

MOORE, John: Rank: Private. Regiment or Service: Connaught Rangers. Unit: 5th Battalion. Date of death: 19 August 1915. Service No: 4458. Previously he was with the Royal Irish Regiment where his number was 321. Born in Clonea, Carrick-on-Suir, Co. Waterford. Enlisted in Clonmel while living in Clonmel. Killed in action in Gallipoli. He has no known grave but is listed on Panel 181 to 183 on the Helles Memorial in Turkey.

MOORE, John: Rank: Rifleman. Regiment or Service: Royal Irish Rifles. Unit: 2nd

Battalion. Age at death: 20. Date of death: 9 July 1916. Service No: 8016. Born in Waterford. Enlisted in Waterford. Killed in action.

Supplementary information: Son of Mrs E. Moore, of 16 Waterside, Waterford. From the *Waterford News*, March 1917, 'Waterford Soldiers Killed. The news has also been received of the death of Private John Moore (R.I. Rifles). 16 Waterside. Deceased was killed last July, but his death has only now been notified.' He has no known grave but is listed on Pier and Face 15A and 15B of the Thiepval Memorial in France.

MORAN, James: Rank: Private. Regiment or Service: Royal Irish Regiment. Unit: 2nd Battalion. Age at death: 21. Date of death: 14 July 1916. Service No: 7489. Born in St Patrick's, Waterford. Enlisted in Waterford. Killed in action.

Supplementary information: Son of William and Mary Moran, of 1 Jenkin's Lane, Waterford. He has no known grave but is listed on Pier and Face 3A of the Thiepval Memorial in France.

MORAN, James: Rank: Private. Regiment or Service: Connaught Rangers. Unit: 5th Battalion. Age at death: 35. Date of death: 21 August 1915. Service No: 4460. Born in Dungarvan, Co. Waterford. Enlisted in Waterford while living in Dungarvan. Killed in action in Gallipoli. Previously he was with the Royal Irish Regiment where his number was 220. He was mistakenly reported 'killed in action' during the Battle of Mons when he was, in fact, a prisoner of war in Lemburg, Germany.

Supplementary information: Son of James and Mary Moran, of Mitchel Street, Dungarvan, Co. Waterford. He has no known grave but is listed on Panel 181 to 183 on the Helles Memorial in Turkey.

MORAN, James: (Alias) Rank: Private. See **COMERFORD, James:**

MORAN, John: Rank: Private. Regiment or Service: Connaught Rangers Unit: 2nd Battalion. Date of death: 28 May 1916. Service No: 8458. Born in Dungarvan, Co. Waterford. Enlisted in Dungarvan while living in Dungarvan. Died of wounds. Grave or Memorial Reference: III.M.8. Cemetery: Niederzwehren Cemetery in Germany.

MORAN, Michael: Rank: Private. Regiment or Service: Royal Irish Regiment. Unit: 2nd Battalion. Date of death: 19 October 1914. Service No: 5873. Born in St Patrick's, Waterford. Enlisted in Waterford. Killed in action. He has no known grave but is listed on Panel 11 and 12 on the Le Touret Memorial in France.

MORAN, Thomas: Rank: Private. Regiment or Service: Royal Munster Fusiliers. Unit: 1st Battalion. Date of death: 20 November 1917. Service No: 18022. Formerly with the Royal Inniskilling Fusiliers where his number was 16551. Born in Waterford. Enlisted in Liverpool while living in Waterford. Killed in action. Grave or Memorial Reference: I.C.18. Cemetery: Croiselles Railway Cemetery in France.

MORAN, Thomas: Rank: Private. Regiment or Service: East Lancashire Regiment. Unit: 2nd Battalion. Age at death: 26. Date of death: 12 March 1915. Service No: 8761. Born in Waterford. Enlisted in Waterford while living in Ballynaboola, Co. Waterford. Killed in action.

Supplementary information: Son of Patrick and Kate Moran, of Ballynaboola, Halfway House, Co. Waterford. From the *Waterford News*, August 1915:

WATERFORD SOLDIER WRITES FROM HIS 'DUG-OUT'.
Somewhere in France, August 8th.
To the Editor of *Waterford News*
Dear Sir,
I am sending you this letter to ask if you would be kind enough to print it in your

paper in hopes that someone in Waterford may know something about my brother whose number is 8761 (F Moran.) He was in this Regiment (2nd East Lancashire). He served nine years in this Regiment, six of which he served in India and Africa. He finished his time with the colours eighteen months before the war broke out. During that time he lived with me in New York, up to the outbreak of the war. We came home to join the reserve. My brother was wounded in the earlier part of the war during the fighting round the Dunes, and was sent home on *sick* furlough returning out here again on January 17th. At the time of his return I was in hospital myself and wounded. I myself was home on furlough in Waterford for a short time. I returned back here in April to find that my brother had been missing since March 14th, which was the last day of Neuve Chapelle. We both belonged to the same company, but still I am not able to find anything about his whereabouts. Some of the fellows told me when I came out here that my brother got wounded in the left shoulder and he left them to go to the dressing station, but he has not been heard of since that time. It is my belief that he got too close to the German lines going out to get his wound dressed, and either got killed by a shell or taken prisoner. He has been reported in several papers killed, but he may still be in the land of the living. At least we all hope so out here for he was well liked by all in our Regiment. Well, I am back again myself and hope to stay here until the end of the game. There are a good many Waterford men in our Regiment who send their regards to all the people in Waterford. There are very few of our Battalion left now for we got a pretty bad cutting up at the battle of Augres Ridge on May 9th by loosing six hundred officers and men. We have been having luck with us since that battle, having very few losses.

I have now said enough, and so will jump into my dug-out and say good-night.

Will you kindly send me the paper that this is printed in to this address.
Pte M Moran.
2ns East Lancashire Regiment.
Expeditionary Force, France.
(Private Moran encloses us a photo of his missing brother. We are unable to reproduce this portrait in our paper as it is almost faded.
–Ed. W. N.)

Private F. Moran survived the war. Grave or Memorial Reference: Panel 8 on the Le Touret Memorial in France.

MORONEY, Michael: Rank: Carpenter. Regiment or Service: Mercantile Marine. Unit: SS *Mavisbrook* (Glasgow). Age at death: 19. Date of death: 17 May 1918.

Supplementary information: Son of Michael and Catherine Moroney (*née* Cahill), of Loughmore, Dungarvan, Co. Waterford. He has no known grave but is listed on the Tower Hill Memorial in the UK.

MORONEY, William: Rank: Private. Regiment or Service: Royal Irish Regiment. Unit: 2nd Battalion. Age at death: 23. Date of death: 28 May 1915. Service No: 5778. Born in Trinity Without, Waterford. Enlisted in Waterford. Died of wounds. Image on p. 194 is a picture of his headstone in a First World War frame.

Supplementary information: Son of Mrs M. Moroney, of 19 Morrison's Road, Waterford. Grave or Memorial Reference: II.A.8. Cemetery: Hazebrouck Communal Cemetery, Nord, in France.

MORRIS, Arthur Russell:. Rank; Private. Regiment or Service: Princess Patricia's Canadian Light Infantry (Eastern Ontario Regiment). Age at death: 22. Date of death: 8 May 1915. Service No: 51344.

Supplementary information: Son of J.R. Russel and Annie F. Morris. Killed in action. From the *Enniscorthy Guardian*:

William Moroney.

Private Arthur Russel Morris of Princess Patricia's Canadian Light Infantry, has been killed in action. He was son of Mr Joseph R Morris, Somerville, Wexford and was only 21 years of age.

Having spent 2 ½ years in Canada, at the outbreak of the war he resigned a good position in the bank there and joined the colours. On the completion of his training in England he left Southampton for France on the 29th of April, and was killed on the 8th of May.

I am not sure of the Waterford connection but he is listed on the Bishop Foy School Memorial located in Christ Church Cathedral (Church of Ireland), Henrietta Street, Waterford. Grave or Memorial Reference: Grave or Memorial Reference: Panel 10. Memorial: Ypres (Menin Gate) Memorial in Belgium.

MORRIS, Michael F S.: Rank: Private. Regiment or Service: Leinster Regiment. Unit: 7th Battalion. Age at death: 36. Date of death: 11 May 1916. Service No: 5356. Previously he was with the Connaught Rangers where his number was 3819. Born in Kilkenny. Enlisted in Clonmel while living in Clonmel. Killed in action.

Supplementary information: Son of Mr and Mrs Samuel Morris, of Newrath House, Waterford. From De Ruvigny's Roll of Honour:

Morris, Michael, F.S, Lance Corporal, Connuaght Rangers. Son of Samuel Morris, Merchant and Shipowner, Nationalist M.P. for South Kilkenny 1894-1900, J. P, by his wife, Catherine, younger daughter of the late James Feehan, County Kilkenny. Born at Airmount, Clonmel. Educated at Clongowes Wood College, subsequently became a Gentleman Farmer. Enlisted after the outbreak of war. Served with the Expeditionary Force in France and Flanders and was killed in action at Loos, 11 May, 1916 by an aerial grenade while on sentry duty. His Commanding Officer wrote; "I knew him quite well as a fine soldier and a brave fellow, who promised great things, and it was with deep regret that I learned of his death."

From the *Munster Express*:

WATERFORD GENTLEMAN KILLED IN ACTION.

Sincere sympathy is felt with Mr Samuel Morris, J.P., Newrath House, on having heard the sad news that his son, Mr Michael F. Morris, has lost his life on the battle front in France. The deceased, who was only 30 years of age, was a private in the 7th Leinster's, and he was not a month in France when he was killed on the 11th of May. He was a splendid type of manhood, standing six feet, and he was a great favourite in Waterford. Mr Morris has two other sons serving in the Army, one of them a Lieutenant in the Leinster's. The blow is a heavy one on our respected townsman, coming so soon after his recent bereavement. Office and

Michael Morris.

High Mass for the repose of the soul of the deceased took place to-day (Friday) at 11 o'clock at the Chapel of Ease, Ferrybank, at which a large number of priests attended.

Grave or Memorial Reference: I.B.4. Cemetery: Philosophe British Cemetery, Mazingarbe in France.

MORRISSEY, James: Rank: Cook. Regiment or Service: Mercantile Marine. Unit: SS *Formby* (Glasgow). Age at death: 47. Date of death: 16 December 1917. The ship was lost with all hands and never located during a fierce storm.

Supplementary information: Son of the late Walter and Ann Morrissey. Husband of Mary Bridget Morrissey (*née* O'Neill), of 14 Parliament Street, Waterford. Born at Tramore, Co. Waterford. He has no known grave but is listed on the Tower Hill Memorial in the UK. He is also listed on the Formby-Coningbeg Memorial, Adelphi Quay in Waterford City.

MORRISSEY, James: Rank: Private. Regiment or Service: Irish Guards. Unit: 3rd Battalion. Date of death: 2 June 1918. Service No: 10438. Born in Castlequarter, Co. Waterford. Enlisted in Clonmel, County Tipperary. Died at Home.

Supplementary information: Son of Mrs M. Morrissey, of Castlequarter, Ballymacarbry, Co. Waterford. Grave or Memorial Reference: About centre of Graveyard. Cemetery: Kilcreggane Graveyard in Co. Waterford.

MORRISSEY, Martin: Rank: Mate. Regiment or Service: Mercantile Marine. Unit: SS *Lough Fisher* (Barrow). Shelled and sunk by a German submarine 12 miles south-east of Cork. Age at death: 51. Date of death: 30 March 1918.

Supplementary information: Son of Thomas and Mary Anne Morrissey. Husband of Mary Morrissey (*née* Hartery), of 15 O'Brien Street, Waterford. Born in Waterford. He has no known grave but is listed on the Tower Hill Memorial in the UK.

MORRISSEY, Martin: Rank: Private. Regiment or Service: Royal Irish Regiment. Unit: 2nd Battalion. Age at death: 36. Date of death: 20 October 1914. Service No: 8191. Born in Dungarvan, Co. Waterford. Enlisted in Waterford. Killed in action.

Supplementary information: Son of Nicholas and Ellen Morrissey, of 56 O'Connell Street, Dungarvan, Co. Waterford. From the *Waterford News*, 1914:

LETTERS FROM THE FRONT.

Letters are being received in town from soldiers who are at the front. One was received during the week from Private Hegarty who is in Plymouth Hospital. He reports that when he was leaving the firing line he saw a number of Dungarvan boys there in good form and unwounded. In fact he mentions one young fellow named Riordan from Shandon, whom his parents having heard from some unofficial source, believed to have been killed, that he was well and hearty. Another young man from the town, Martin Morrissey, son of Mr Nicholas Morrissey, shoemaker, Blackpool, the same writer says in great trim, although he was in the firing line at the battle of Mons, and has several times been in engagements.

From the *Waterford News*, 1914:

MISSING.

The townspeople regretted to learn that Martin Morrissey, son of Mr Martin Morrissey, shoemaker, Blackpool, was this week reported among the missing. He also belongs to the Royal Irish Regiment. Up to the time of his being missed a few days ago he had been in the firing line almost constantly since the beginning of the war. He had been in numerous engagements and had escaped without a scratch. He was a well known footballer in this district and was a prominent member of the Shandon Rovers in their best days.

Grave or Memorial Reference: 11 and 12 on the Le Touret Memorial in France.

MORRISSEY, Michael: Rank: Private. Regiment or Service: South Lancashire Regiment. Unit: 8th Battalion. Age at death: 26. Date of death: 19 November 1915. Service No: 14300. Born in Waterford. Enlisted in Waterford. Killed in action.

Supplementary information: Son of Michael and Elizabeth Morrissey, of 9 Butcher's Lane, Barrack Street Waterford. From the *Waterford News.* December 1915:

WATERFORD SOLDIER'S FUNERAL.
Mr Redmond Present.
The following letter has been received my Mrs Morrissey, of Butchers Lane, whose son Michael was killed in action in France.

Pte W Thompson, 8th Battalion.
South Lancs Regiment, A Company, 14288.
Machine Gun Section, B.E.F.
France, November 24, 1915.
Dear Mrs Morrissey,
On behalf of all the men and myself of A Company, I write these few lines to express our deepest sympathy with you in the loss of your rear son Michael, who was killed in action on November 19th. We hope it will be a little consolation to know he was respected by everyone of us, and he has a very good character. He died a hero, fighting for the old country, and I am also pleased to tell you that he received Holy Communion with me a fortnight previous to being killed, and he had a very nice

funeral; the priest was present and read the prayers for eh dead over him before he was laid in his grace[sic]. It will also be a consolation to you to know that Mr John Redmond was present and saw your son before we buried him. Myself and all the boys of A Company hope you will bear your great loss with a brave heart–the sincere wish of us all his comrades
Yours sincerely.
Pte W Thompson.

Grave or Memorial Reference: IV.B.4. Cemetery, Rifle House Cemetery in Belgium.

MORRISSEY, Michael: Rank: Private. Regiment or Service: Australian Infantry, A.I.F. Unit: 6th Battalion. Age at death: 37. Date of death: 6 May 1915. Service No: 626. Died of wounds (gunshot wound to the head) received in action on board H.M.T. Dongala and buried at sea. Enlisted 24 August 1914 in Melbourne, Victoria.

Supplementary information: Son of John and Mary Morrissey, of 9 Hennessy Road, Waterford. From his attestation papers:

In or near what Parish or Town were you born? St John's, Waterford, Ireland.
Are you a natural born British subject or a Naturalised British subject? Yes.
What is your trade or calling? Labourer.
Are you, or have you been an Apprentice? If so where, to whom, and for
Who is your next of kin? [father] John Morrissey, Convent Hill, Waterford.
Do you now belong to, or have you ever served in, His Majesty's Army, the Marines, the Militia, the Militia Reserve, the Territorial Reserve, Royal Navy or Colonial Forces?, If so, state which, and if not now serving, state cause of discharge Royal Irish Regiment, 18 ½ years (Discharge seen)
Have you stated the whole, if any, of your previous service? Yes.
Age: 37 years, 6 months.
Height 5 feet, 6 inches.

Weight, 10st.

Chest measurement: 34 inches.

Complexion, medium.

Eyes: grey.

Hair: brown.

Religious denomination: R.C.

Last will and testament; –

I, No 626, Pte M Morrissey. In the event of my death I give the whole of my effects tp Mrs M Burkett, 265, High Street, Aldershot Co, Hants, England.

Signed No 626, M Morrissey, Private.

A Company, 6th A. I. E. F.

Date 20 April 1915.

His father was awarded a pension of £1 per week. However in a letter to the base records he mentions he was given a pension of 4 shillings per week. A later addition to his pension records show that he was awarded a pension of £10-8-0 per Annum, and at another time a pension of 10/- per fortnight. Pay and deferred pay to a total of £30/14/6 was made available for disposal in accordance with his will.

From the *Waterford News*, May 1915:

Died of wounds. Private Michael Morrissey, son of Mr Morrissey, Convent Hill, Waterford, has Died of wounds received at the Dardanelles on the 12th May. He served twenty years in the Royal Irish Regiment, and went to Melbourne about 18 months before the outbreak of the war.

He joined the 6th Battalion of the Australian contingent and received mortal wounds in the Dardanelles operations.

Grave or Memorial Reference: 27. Memorial: Lone Pine Memorial, Memorial in Gallipoli.

MORRISSEY, Patrick: Rank: Sergeant. Regiment or Service: Royal Irish Regiment. Unit: 2nd Battalion. Age at death: 26. Date of death: 8 December 1915. Service No: 9078. Born in Trinity Without, Waterford. Enlisted in Clonmel, Co. Tipperary while living in Liverpool. Killed in action.

Supplementary information: Son of the late Patrick and Mary Ellen Morrissey, of Waterford. From the *Waterford News*, January 1916:

WATERFORD SOLDIER KILLED AT THE FRONT.

Mrs Mary E Morrissey, 17 Dundee Street, Liverpool, has been notified of the death of her son, Sergeant P. J. Morrissey, Royal Irish Regiment. The deceased was born and reared in Barrack Street, Waterford, and spent some time in America, having previously served in the army. He came home from the States at the commencement of the war to rejoin his Regiment, and he had been in France since December, 1914.

Captain Tighe, B Company, wrote Mrs Morrissey as follows–" I regret to inform you that your son, Sergeant Morrissey, met his death in the trenches on 8th December, 1915, about 12, 45 p. m. He was killed by a bullet from a German sniper. His death was much regretted by his comrades as he was a most excellent N. C. O. and a brave soldier.

Grave or Memorial Reference: I.A.5. Cemetery: Auchonvillers Military Cemetery in France.

MORRISSEY, Thomas: Rank: Private. Regiment or Service: Royal Irish Regiment. Unit: 6th Battalion. Age at death: 29. Date of death: 15 March 1918. Service No: 4/3125 (Commonwealth War Graves Commission), 3125 (Soldiers died in the Great War). Born in Slieverue, Co. Kilkenny. Enlisted in Waterford. Died.

Supplementary information: Son of Ellen Morrissey, of Waterford. Grave or Memorial Reference: III.G.25. Cemetery: Abbeville Communal Cemetery Extension in France.

MOYLAN, Michael: Rank: Able Seaman. Regiment or Service: Royal Navy. Unit: HMS *Centurion*. Age at death: 28. Date of death: 23

August 1916. Service No: 238143 (Dev) Grave or Memorial Reference: Adjoining West boundary of ruin. Cemetery: Ardmore (Old Abbey) Graveyard, Co. Waterford.

MULCAHY, James: Rank: Able Seaman. Regiment or Service: Mercantile Marine. Unit: HMHS *Llandovery Castle* (London). Age at death: 37. Date of death: 27 June 1918.

Supplementary information: Son of the late Capt. John and Margaret Mulcahy (*née* Crotty). Born at Abbeyside, Co. Waterford. He has no known grave but is listed on the Tower Hill Memorial in the UK.

MULCAHY, Maurice: Rank: Private. Regiment or Service: Royal Irish Regiment. Unit: 1st Battalion. Age at death: 32. Date of death: 23 December 1918. Service No: 9854.

Supplementary information: Son of William and Mary Mulcahy, of Knockroe Colligan, Dungarvan, Co. Waterford. Grave or Memorial Reference: C.140. Cemetery: Alexandria (Hadra) War Memorial Cemetery in Egypt.

MULCAHY, Michael: Rank: Stoker 1st Class. Regiment or Service Royal Navy. Unit: HMS *Indefatigable*. Date of death: 31 May 1916. Age at death: 40. Service No:283299. Born in Ardmore, Co. Waterford.

Supplementary information: Son of John and Ellen Mulcahy, of Curragh, Ardmore, Youghal, Co. Cork. Grave or Memorial Reference:16. He has no known grave but is listed on the Playmouth Naval Memorial, Devon, U.K.

MULCAHY, William: Rank: Private. Regiment or Service: Royal Irish Regiment. Unit: 6th Battalion. Date of death: 30 April 1916. Service No: 1534. Born in St John's, Waterford. Enlisted in Waterford. Killed in action. He is listed on the Graves and Co. Roll of Honour Memorial. Located are located in Christ Church Cathedral (Church of Ireland), Henrietta Street, Waterford. The memorial reads:

ROLL OF HONOUR
Office Staff and Employees of Messrs. Graves and Co. Limited
Who served in the great war 1914-1918.

Grave or Memorial Reference: I.K.2. Cemetery: Dud Corner Cemetery, Loos in France.

MULCAHY, William: Rank: Gunner. Regiment or Service: Royal Garrison Artillery. Unit: 102nd Siege Battery. Date of death: 29 May 1916. Service No: 27358. Born in Lismore, Co. Waterford. Enlisted in Dungarvan, Co. Waterford while living in Lismore. Died of wounds. From the *Munster Express*:

THE WAR.
News has been received at Lismore that Gunner William Mulcahy, of the R. G. A., son of Mrs M Mulcahy, Main Street, was killed in action. He was wounded in the abdomen and died three hours after admission to hospital.

Grave or Memorial Reference: I.C.3. Cemetery: Doullens Communal Cemetery Extension, No 1 in France.

MULLINS, Edward: Rank: Unknown. Regiment or Service: Unknown. The only information I have on this soldier is contained in the below. He is not in any of the War Dead databases. From the *Waterford News* and the *Munster Express*, August 1915:

SOLDIER'S SUDDEN DEATH IN THE CITY.
A young soldier named Edward Mullins, living with his mother at Ballybricken, died at his home under somewhat tragic circumstances at his home early on Tuesday. Deceased had been I hospital as England for some time and was invalided home. He had been in the city only a few days and since his arrival had been under the care of Dr White. Between 1 and 2 o'clock he got a seizure in the house. Medical and spiritual aid were immediately requisitioned. The priest

arrived and administered the last Sacraments, but when the doctor came he pronounced life to be extinct. An inquest will not probably be held, as Dr White had attended Mullins as late as the previous evening.

MURDOCH, Hugh: Rank: Rifleman. Regiment or Service: The King's (Liverpool Regiment). Unit: 'B' Coy. 6th Battalion. Age at death: 28. Date of death: 1 July 1916. Service No: 2344. Enlisted in Liverpool while living in Tue Brook, Liverpool. Killed in action.

Supplementary information: Son of Hugh and Isabella Moody Murdoch, of 19, Rudgrave Square, Egremont, Wallasay. Born in Waterford. Grave or Memorial Reference: B. 8. Cemetery: Beaumetz-Les-Loges Communal Cemetery in France.

MURPHY, Edward: Rank: Private. Regiment or Service: Leinster Regiment. Unit: 1st Battalion. Date of death: 14 February 1915. Service No: 8910 (Soldiers died in the Great War) 8919 (The Commonwealth War Graves Commission). Born in Waterford. Enlisted in Cork. Killed in action. Grave or Memorial Reference: Has no known grave but is commemorated on Panel 44. Memorial; Ypres (Menin Gate) Memorial in Belgium.

MURPHY, George: Rank: Private. Regiment or Service: Kings Liverpool Regiment. Unit: 11th Battalion. Date of death: 20 July 1915. Service No: 12384. Born in Ross, Co. Wexford. Enlisted in Seaforth in Lancashire while living in Waterford, Ireland. Died of wounds. Grave or Memorial Reference: III.B.8A. From the *Echo*, 1915:

New Ross still continues to contribute to the roll of victims claimed in the last year, the latest casualties announced being Private George Murphy, a native of Bewley Street, who had been previously in the army and had been working in Wales before hostilities commenced.

Grave or Memorial Reference: III.B.8A. Cemetery: Lijssenthoek Military Cemetery in Belgium.

MURPHY, James: Rank: Private. Regiment or Service: Irish Guards. Unit: 2nd Battalion. Age at death: 26. Date of death: 18 October 1915. Service No: 4985. Born in Chereadel, Co. Waterford. Enlisted in while living in Waterford. Killed in action.

Supplementary information: Son of Patrick and Mary Murphy, of 39 The Glen, Waterford. Grave or Memorial Reference: I.H.9. Cemetery: Vermelles British Cemetery in France.

MURPHY, James: Rank: Corporal. Regiment or Service: Royal Engineers. Unit: 2nd Field Coy. Age at death: 35. Date of death: 12 October 1918. Service No: 13988. Born Kiltealy, Co. Waterford. Enlisted in Lixnaw, Co. Kerry. Killed in action.

Supplementary information: Son of James and Annie Murphy of New Ross, Co. Wexford. Husband of Ellie Murphy of Kilflynn, Co. Kerry. From the *Enniscorthy Guardian*, June 1915:

INTERESTING LETTER FROM THE FRONT. Writing home to his parents at New Ross last week from the front, James Murphy of the Royal Engineers, and son of Mr James Murphy, Neville Street, New Ross, gives very interesting details. He has been at the front since the war commenced and has gone through several battles, having miraculous escapes on several occasions. Previous to joining the Royal Engineers he was a prison warder and his great mechanical knowledge quickly attracted the attention of the authorities of his Regiment and he was offered promotion in a comparatively short time., The following is part of his letter:

"Dear Parents-Even though many miles from you and on the battlefield, I don't forget you and never will. Distance or circumstance will never make me forget the affection I owe my parents, whose prayers are being offered each day for my welfare along with the prayers of my dear and beloved wife. I write to my dear wife every day to keep her in good spirits, and with a devoted love to her as my wife, and with God;s help when the war is over we will all meet again, and I have made up my mind to spend my holidays with ye all, particularly as those holidays shall be the most enjoyable ones of my life, and away from the continuous roaring of weapons and spattering of shells, all of which I may say is second nature to me now. But give me peace, that beautiful peace that should always reign and which would be a blessing-one of the greatest blessings that ever came during our time from Almighty God. I attend Benediction every night since I have been out here, and go to Holy Communion every Sunday. Conscription is not far off in my opinion, and it is time to pull a lot of the slackers out of their feather beds. I am sure the poor class have well contributed their position, and, dear parents, you can say that you have contributed one son who is in the thick of the fight. Germany will be beaten if it was to take us years to do it, and there shall be no surrender to the Kaiser and his outlaws. I can tell you straight he will get something this month that he has not got since the beginning of the war, and he will get something twice as hot in July and treble as hot in October, or maybe sooner, and before the New Year I am sure peace will shine o'er the earth again, and in my opinion the Kaiser will then be fast on his way back to where he came from (dust). May God send peace soon and dispose of the Kaiser as He wishes. We are not the Kaisers judge, and it is a good job he is not ours either. As the French man says, he is no bonn (no good). The writer gives some further interesting passages, and winds up by saying that he is in the best of health, and hopes to meet his parents, wife and child and his brothers and sisters when the war is over."

Grave or Memorial Reference: II.A.2. Cemetery: Level Crossing Cemetery, Fampoux in France.

MURPHY, James: Rank: Private. Regiment or Service: East Lancashire Regiment. Unit: 1st Battalion. Date of death: 1 July 1916. Service No: 19419. He won the Military Medal Lancashire Fusiliers where his number was 6705. Born in Waterford. Enlisted in Bury in Lancashire while living in Waterford. Killed in action. He has no known grave but is listed on Pier and Face 6C on the Thiepval Memorial in France.

MURPHY, John: Rank: Private. Regiment or Service: Irish Guards. Unit: 1st Battalion. Date of death: 1 November 1914. Service No: 4364. Born in Waterford. Enlisted in Dublin. Killed in action. Grave or Memorial Reference: Has no known grave but is commemorated on Panel 11. Memorial: Ypres (Menin Gate) Memorial in Belgium.

MURPHY, John: Rank: Private. Regiment or Service: Royal Irish Regiment. Unit: 2nd Battalion. Date of death: 24 May 1915. Service No: 5074. Born in Trinity Without, Waterford. Enlisted in Waterford. Killed in action. He has no known grave but is listed on Panel 44 on the Ypres (Menin Gate) Memorial in Belgium.

MURPHY, John: Rank: Private/Lance Corporal. Regiment or Service: Royal Irish Regiment. Unit: 6th Battalion. Date of death: 3 August 1917. Service No: 1555. Born in St Patrick's, Waterford. Enlisted in Waterford. Killed in action. Grave or Memorial Reference: Enclosure No 4. XI. A.5. Cemetery: Bedford House Cemetery in Belgium.

MURPHY, John: Rank: Shoeing Smith. Regiment or Service: Royal Field Artillery. Unit: 184th Brigade. Age at death: 46. Date of death: 13 November 1915. Service No: 53034.

Born in Ballybricken, Co. Waterford. Enlisted in Liverpool. Died at Home.

Supplementary information: Husband of Johanna Murphy, of 9 Castle Street, Waterford. Grave or Memorial Reference: G.381. Cemetery: Guildford (Stoke) Old Cemetery, UK.

MURPHY, Maurice: Rank: Sapper. Regiment or Service: Royal Engineers. Unit: 5th Field Coy. Age at death: 26. Date of death: 3 November 1916. Service No: 28313. Born in Waterford. Enlisted in Waterford. Killed in action.

Supplementary information: Son of Patrick and Mary Anne Murphy, of Passage Road, Waterford. From the *Waterford News*, November 1916:

WATERFORD PLUMBER KILLED AT THE FRONT.

We regret to learn of the death of a young Waterford soldier, in the person of Private M. Murphy, of the Royal Engineers. Deceased was a plumber by trade, and was employed by Mr Robert Costelloe up to the time of the outbreak of the war, when he joined the Royal Engineers. He had been in France for a considerable time, and came home a few weeks ago to attend the funeral of his mother, who resided at Lower Newtown. Three days or so after going back to France he met his death. It appears that he was in a dug-out, and was just after writing a letter to his father, and was in the act of penning another, when a shell came along and killed him. The finished and unfinished letters were sent home to his father by his commanding officer. A fine type of young man, he was very popular with his friends in Waterford and with his comrades in the army. For his father much sympathy will be felt in his bereavement.

Grave or Memorial Reference: Plot 1. Row F. Grave 22. Cemetery: Bertrancourt Military Cemetery in France.

MURPHY, Michael: Rank: Private. Regiment or Service: Royal Irish Regiment. Unit: 6th Battalion. Age at death: 27. Date of death: 17 September 1916. Service No: 3582. Born in Trinity Without, Waterford. Enlisted in Tipperary while living in Waterford. Died of wounds.

Supplementary information: Son of Patrick and Mary Murphy, of Dunhill, Co. Waterford. Grave or Memorial Reference: Div. 3.F.10. Cemetery: Ste. Marie Cemetery, Le Havre in France.

MURPHY, Michael Joseph: Rank: Private. Regiment or Service: Irish Guards. Unit: 1st Battalion. Age at death: 24. Date of death: 8 March 1918. Service No: 10166. Born in Waterford. Enlisted in Dublin while living in Ballinhassing, County Cork. Died of wounds.

Supplementary information: Native of Waterford. Son of Martin and Johanna Murphy, of Post Office, Ballinhassig, Co. Cork. Volunteered after three years' service in R.I.C. Grave or Memorial Reference: VI.E.18. Cemetery: Duisans British Cemetery, Etrun in France.

MURPHY, Patrick: Rank: Private. Regiment or Service: Connaught Rangers. Unit: 1st Battalion. Age at death: 19. Date of death: 18 March 1915. Service No: 10884. Born in Lismore, Co. Waterford. Enlisted in in Cork while living in Lismore. Died of wounds.

Supplementary information: Son of Michael and Mary Murphy, of Glencairn, Co. Waterford. Grave or Memorial Reference: XXVII.A.16. Cemetery: Cabaret-Rouge British Cemetery, Souchez in France.

MURPHY, Patrick: Rank: Rifleman. Regiment or Service: City of London Regiment. Unit: 8th (City of London) Battalion, (Post Office Rifles.) Age at death: 36. Date of death: 20 September 1917. Service No: 371348. Born in Portarlington. Enlisted in Waterford while living in Waterford. Killed in action.

Supplementary information: Son of Michael and Mary Murphy, of 14 Gracefield Road., Portarlington, Queen's Co. Husband of Mary Kelly (formerly Murphy), of 3 Cassidy's Cottages, Kill, Monasterevan, Co. Kildare. He has no known grave but is listed on Panels 9-22 on the Ypres (Menin Gate) Memorial in Belgium.

MURPHY, Richard: Rank: Fireman. Regiment or Service: Mercantile Marine. Unit: SS *Formby* (Glasgow). Age at death: 43. Date of death: 16 December 1917. The ship was lost with all hands and never located during a fierce storm.

Supplementary information: Son of Mary and John Murphy. Husband of Elizabeth Murphy (*née* Carlin), of 53 Newport Lane, Waterford, Co. Waterford. Born in Waterford. He has no known grave but is listed on the Tower Hill Memorial in the UK. He is also listed on the Formby-Coningbeg Memorial, Adelphi Quay in Waterford City.

MURRAY, Denis: Rank: Trimmer. Regiment or Service: Mercantile Marine Reserve. Unit: HMS *Angora*. Date of death: 8 October 1915. Service No: 797586. From the *Waterford News*, October 1915:

WATERFORD SAILOR DROWNED.

Mr Patrick Murray, Green Street, has received notification from the Admiralty that his son, Denis, who was a trimmer on His Majesty's ship *Angora*, was found drowned at Sheerness on the 18th inst. The deceased, who had been only a couple of months in England, left Dublin fours years ago for Canada.

Grave or Memorial Reference: PP. 70. Cemetery: Sheerness (Isle of Sheppey) Cemetery in Kent, UK.

MURRAY, Edward: Rank: Private. Regiment or Service: Royal Irish Regiment. Unit: 2nd Battalion. Date of death: 10 October 1914. Service No: 5553. Born in Ballyduff, Co. Waterford. Enlisted in Waterford. Killed in action. He has no known grave but is listed on Panel 11 and 12. on the Le Touret Memorial in France.

MURRAY, John: Rank: Second Engineer. Regiment or Service: Mercantile Marine. Unit: SS *Southford* (Glasgow). Age at death: 38. Date of death: 25 February 1916.

Supplementary information: Son of Patrick and Rose Murray, of Glenariff, Waterford. Born at Red Bay. He has no known grave but is listed on the Tower Hill Memorial in the UK.

MURRAY, Thomas: Rank: Private. Regiment or Service: Royal Inniskilling Fusiliers. Unit: 1st Battalion. Date of death: 11 September 1915. Service No: 20303. Born in Waterford. Enlisted in Liverpool. Died at Sea. Has no known grave but is commemorated on Panel 97 to 101. Memorial: Helles Memorial in Turkey.

N

NASH, CHRISTOPHER. Rank: Private. Regiment or Service: Household Cavalry and Cavalry of the line including the Yeomanry and Imperial Camel Corps. Unit: 9th (Queen's Royal) Lancers, also listed as (Old) 7th Reserve Cavalry Regiment (9th and 21st lancers. Date of death: 7 January 1916. Service No: GS/4710. Born in Notting Hill in Middlesex. Enlisted in Hammersmith while living in Fulham, S.W. Died at home. From the *Waterford News*, January 1916:

MILITARY FUNERAL.

The remains of the late Private C Nash, 19th Lancers, a native of Notting Hill, Middlesex, who died suddenly at the Military Barracks, Waterford on last Friday, were interred in the Cemetery, John's Hill, on Tuesday with full military honours. The coffin borne on an open hearse, was wrapped in a Union Jack, and deceased's charger was led after the hearse. The hearse was preceded by a firing party and the band, which played the Dead March, and as followed by Lieutenant-Colonel Tristram, Lieutenant Henderson, and guard of soldiers. A volley was fired over the grave, and the "Last Post" sounded. The Very Reverend Dean Day and the Rev Mr Jackson conducted the burial service.

A SOLDIER'S SUDDEN DEATH.

An Inquest was held at the Military Barracks on Saturday by Dr George I. Mackesy, J.P., deputy Cororer, and a jury of which Mr R.C. Curtis was foreman touching the death of Christopher Nash, a private in the 9th Lancers, who died suddenly on Friday afternoon.

Dr Alex Stewart deposed – I did not see the deceased at the hospital yesterday; I was gone when he came; I have seen and examined the body to-day at the morgue; from what I saw and the evidence I have heard I am of the opinion that deceased was suffering from acute gastritis, and on getting up to go from his room he got a sudden attack of syncope and that is the cause of death. There were no external marks on the body.

The jury returned a verdict in accordance with the medical testimony.

Grave or Memorial Reference: 224. Cemetery: Waterford Catholic Cemetery, Co. Waterford.

NEALE, Thomas: Rank: Driver. See **O'NEILL, Thomas:**

NEILL, John: Rank: Gunner. Regiment or Service: Royal Garrison Artillery. Unit: 1st Trench Mortar Battery. Age at death: 23. Date of death: 30 August 1917. Service No: 3373. Born in Kilmacthomas, Co. Waterford. Enlisted in Waterford while living in Kilmacthomas. Died of wounds.

Supplementary information: Son of John and Mary O'Neill, of Ballybrack, Kilmacthomas. Grave or Memorial Reference: D.I. Cemetery: Adinkerke Military Cemetery in Belgium.

NEVIN, Jeremiah Patrick: Rank: Private. Regiment or Service: Royal Dublin Fusiliers. Unit: 10th Battalion. Age at death: 21. Date of death: 26 September 1917. Service No: 27508. Born in Waterford. Enlisted in Waterford. Died of wounds.

Supplementary information: Son of Thomas and Mary Nevin, of 13 St John's Avenue, Waterford. From the *Waterford News*, October 1917:

WATERFORD SOLDIER KILLED.

We regret to announce the death, from wounds received in action, on 27th of September last of Private Jerry Nevin, Dublin Fusiliers, son of Mr and Mrs T.

Nevin, 18 St John's Avenue, Waterford, at the early age of 20 years. Deceased who was a fine type of young man, joined the Army a little over a year ago, prior to which he was employed on the clerical staff of Messrs Wallace and Sons, the Quay. He was educated at the Mount Sion College, where he proved a brilliant student, and won many coveted prizes. Much sympathy is left for his sorrowing parents.

Grave or Memorial Reference: II.F.5. Cemetery: Bucquoy Road Cemetery, Ficheux in France

NEWELL, Charles Edward: Rank: Lieutenant. Regiment or Service: Royal Inniskilling Fusiliers. Unit: 8th Battailon. Age at death: 19. Date of death: 25 May 1916.

Supplementary information: Son of A.C. Newell (late R.M.) and K.M. Newell, of Romanesca, Sandycove, Kingstown, Co. Dublin. Born in Ballinasloe, Co. Galway. I am not sure of the Waterford connection but he is listed on the Bishop Foy School Memorial located in Christ Church Cathedral (Church of Ireland), Henrietta Street, Waterford. Grave or Memorial Reference: III.K.16. Cemetery: Bethune Town Cemetery in France.

NEWELL, Richard Alfred Aylmer: Rank: Private Regiment or Service: Canadian Infantry (Saskatchewan Regiment) Unit Text: 5th Battalion. Date of death: 9 September 1916 Service No: 440491. Data from enlistment documents:

Enlisted in Prince Albert, 7 May 1915.

In what Town, Township or Parish, and in what Country were you born? Kerry, Tyrlee [*sic*], Ireland.

What is the name of your next of kin? [mother], Mrs Catherine Mary Newell.

What is the address of your next of kin? 5 Mayville terrace, Dalkey, Co. Dublin.

What is the date of your birth? 29 March 1892.

What is your trade or calling? Farmer.

Are you married? No.

Are you willing to be vaccinated or re-vaccinated and inoculated? Yes.

Do you now belong to the Active Militia? 52nd P.A.V.

Do you understand the nature and terms of your engagement? Yes.

Are you willing to be attested to serve in the Canadian Over-Seas Expeditionary Force? Yes.

Apparent age: 23 years 3 months.

Height: 5 Ft11 Ins.

Girth when fully expanded: 38 Ins

Range of expansion: 2Ins

Complexion: fair.

Eyes: blue.

Hair: light brown.

I am not sure of the Waterford connection but he is listed on the Bishop Foy School Memorial located in Christ Church Cathedral (Church of Ireland), Henrietta Street, Waterford. Grave or Memorial Reference: III.M.31. Cemetery: Pozières British Cemetery, Ovillers-La Boisselle in France.

NICHOLSON, D: Rank: Unknown. The only reference I have to this man is contained in the *Munster Express* article of March 1915:

DEATH OF A WATERFORD VOLUNTEER.

The death occurred of Mr D. Nicholson on Friday last at his fathers residence, 32 Yellow Road, who was an active member of the Irish National Volunteers. His funeral took place on Monday to the Cemetery, John's Hill, and was attended by a large number of people. A firing party of the Volunteers preceded the bier, and a company marched behind. On the coffin were beautiful wreaths and deceased's Volunteer cap, belt and bandolier. The Very Rev. the Dean of Waterford and Rev. J. Jackson conducted the service at the graveside.

NICHOLSON, William: Rank: Private. Regiment or Service: Irish Guards. Unit: 2nd Battalion. Date of death: 13 September 1917. Service No: 7710. Born in Ballybricken, Co. Waterford. Enlisted in Waterford. Killed in action. He has no known grave but is listed on Panels 10 and 11 on the Tyne Cot Memorial in Belgium. Military Medal and is listed in the *London Gazette*.

NOLAN, David: Rank: Private. Regiment or Service: Royal Munster Fusiliers. Unit: 1st Battalion. Age at death: 28. Date of death: 16 May 1915. Service No: 8761. Born in Waterford. Enlisted in Mallow, Co. Cork while living in Mill Street, Co. Cork. Died of wounds in Gallipoli.

Supplementary information: Son of David and Margaret Nolan, of Oldcastletown, Kildorrery, Co. Cork. Has no known grave but is commemorated on Panel 185 to 190. Memorial: Helles Memorial in Turkey.

NOLAN, Edward: Rank: Corporal. Regiment or Service: Royal Dublin Fusiliers. Unit: 2nd Battalion. Age at death: 17. Date of death: 30 November 1917. Service No: 43040. Previously he was with the Royal Irish Regiment where his number was 4666. Born in Portlaw, Co. Waterford. Enlisted in Waterford while living in Portlaw. Died of wounds.

Supplementary information: Son of Mrs Mary Nolan, of Brown Street, Portlaw, Co. Waterford. Grave or Memorial Reference: H.5. Cemetery: St Leger British Cemetery in France.

NOLAN, Michael: Rank: Private. Regiment or Service: Northumberland Fusiliers. Unit: 1st/5th Battalion. Age at death: 23. Date of death: 4 September 1918. Service No: 62010. Born in Waterford. Enlisted in Waterford. Died.

Supplementary information: Son of Matt and Kate Nolan, of 11 Costelloe's Lane, Waterford. Grave or Memorial Reference: VIII.C.9. Cemetery: Berlin South-Western Cemetery in Germany.

NOLAN, Michael: Rank: Stoker 1st Class. Regiment or Service: Royal Navy. Unit: HMS *Redbreast*. Age at death: 21. Date of death: 15 July 1917. Service No: SS/115511. HMS *Redbreast* was torpedoed in the Eastern Mediterranean.

Supplementary information: Son of Mary Nolan, of 3 Railway Cottages, Tramore, Co. Waterford, and the late Martin Nolan. Grave or Memorial Reference: 26. Memorial, Portsmouth Naval Memorial, UK.

NOLAN, William: Rank: Leading Seaman. Regiment or Service: Royal Naval Reserve. Unit: SS *Euterpe*. Age at death: 28. Date of death: 1 March 1917. Service No: 2163A.

Supplementary information: Son of Richard and Bridget Nolan, of Cahir Fenor, Tramore, Co. Waterford. Grave or Memorial Reference: 23 on the Plymouth Naval Memorial, UK.

NOLAN, William Joseph: Rank: Sailor. Regiment or Service: Mercantile Marine. Unit: SS *Royal Edward* (Toronto). Sunk by a torpedo from German submarine U-14. Age at death: 39. Date of death: 13 August 1915.

Supplementary information: Son of George and Kate Nolan (*née* Swedmoor), of 8 St Alphonsus Road, Waterford. Born in Waterford. He has no known grave but is listed on the Tower Hill Memorial in the UK.

NOONAN, Michael: Rank: Private. Regiment or Service: Royal Irish Regiment. Unit: listed as 2nd Garrison Battalion and Depot. Age at death: 32. Date of death: 11 December 1917. Service No: 1605. Enlisted in Liverpool while living in Waterford. Died at home. Previously he was with the Royal Irish Fusiliers where his number was G/1287. Michael Moran has two entries in Soldiers died in the Great War, with the result that he is one of the few men ever to have been awarded two death plaques. He was stationed at the Depot Barracks in Clonmel.

Supplementary information: Husband of Mary Noonan, of 140 Barrack Street, Waterford.

Grave or Memorial Reference: Near south boundary. Cemetery: Regina Caeli Cemetery, Mooncoin, County Kilkenny.

NORRIS, John: Rank: Lance Corporal. Regiment or Service: South Wales Borderers. Unit: 6th Battalion. Date of death: 18 January 1917. Service No: 16943. Born in Waterford and enlisted in Tredegar while living in Clonmel. Died of wounds.

Supplementary information: Son of Thomas Norris, of Sillaheen, Ballymacarheny, Clonmell, Co. Tipperary. Grave or Memorial Reference: III.A.119. Cemetery: Bailleul Communal Cemetery Extension (Nord) in France.

NUGENT, Gerald William: Rank: Captain. Regiment or Service: General List, New Armies. Unit: Staff Headquarters, 29th Infantry Brigade, 10th Irish Division. Age at death: 28. Date of death: 10 August 1915. Killed in action

Supplementary information: Son of Sir John Nugent, 3rd Bart., and Lady Nugent, of 23 Rue du Lycee, Pau, B. Pyrennes, France. Husband of Norah Nugent, of 23 Rue Samonzet, Pau. From 'Our Heroes' 1916:

Captain Gerald William Nugent, Royal Irish Rifles and 29th Infantry Brigade, who has been killed in an action, was the second son of Sir John Nugent, Bart., of Cloncoskoraine, Co. Waterford. He was formerly in the Worcestershire Regiment, and was gazetted

temporary Captain in September, 1914, and Staff Captain in January of this year. Captain Nugent married Norah, daughter of the late Dr. W.H. Bagnell, and leaves one daughter.

He has no known grave but is listed on Panel 190 to 201 on the Helles Memorial in Turkey.

NUGENT, John: Rank: Private. Regiment or Service: Machine Gun Regiment. Unit: 30th Battalion. Date of death: 21 March 1918. Service No: 43299. Previously he was with the Royal Irish Regiment where his number was 11125. Born in Four Mile Water, Co. Tipperary. Enlisted in Clonmel while living in Ballymacarbury. Killed in action. Grave or Memorial Reference: I.H.23. Cemetery: Savy British Cemetery in France.

NUGENT, Maurice: Rank: Private. Regiment or Service: Royal Irish Regiment. Unit: 2nd Battalion. Age at death: 19. Date of death: 2 June 1916. Service No: 10798. Born in Ballymacarberry in Waterford and enlisted in Clonmel while living in Ballymacarberry. Died of wounds.

Supplementary information: Son of James and Johanna Nugent, of 4 Kickham Row, Clonmel, Co. Tipperary. Late of Ballymacarbery, Co. Waterford. Grave or Memorial Reference: Plot 1. Row A. Grave 20. Cemetery: Corbie Communal Cemetery Extension in France.

O

OAKSHOTT, William Albert Neville:
Rank: Lieutenant. Regiment or Service:
Royal Irish Rifles. Unit: 7th Battalion. Age
at death: 26. Date of death: 16 August 1917.
Killed in action.

Supplementary information: Son of James
Albert and Mary Townsend Oakshott, of The
Shrubberies, Monkstown, Co. Cork. He is listed
on the Waterford and District Roll of Honour
and on the Bishop Foy School Memorial.
Located in Christ Church Cathedral (Church
of Ireland), Henrietta Street, Waterford. St
Mary's church, Parish of Marmullane, Passage
West, Co. Cork. Gravestone: Also of their only
son Wm Albert Neville Oakshott Lieutenant 7th
Royal Irish Rifles. Killed in action near Ypres.
Place of burial is unknown St Mary's church,
Parish of Marmullane, Passage West, Co. Cork.
Memorial inside church: 'To the Glory of God
And in Loving Memory of Albert Neville
Oakshott Lieutenant, Royal Irish Rifles. Killed
in action east of Ypres, 16 August 1917 Aged
26 years Only son of James & Mary Oakshott
"Faithful unto Death" In Memory of Albert
Neville Oakshott Lieutenant, 7th Battalion,
Royal Irish Rifles who died on Thursday, 16
August 1917. Age 26. Son of James Albert and
Mary Townsend Oakshott of the Shrubberies,
Monkstown, Co. Cork.' From the *Waterford
News*, 1914:

COMMISSION FOR WATERFORD
GENTLEMAN.

Mr A. N. Oakshott, son of Dr Oakshott,
resident Medical Superintendent,
Waterford Lunatic Asylum, has received
a commission as 2nd Lieutenant in the 8th
Battalion, Royal Munster Fusiliers, and has
joined his Regiment at Fermoy.

He has no known grave but is commemorated on Panel 138 to 140 and 162 to 162A
and 163A. Memorial: Tyne Cot Memorial in
Belgium.

O'BEIRNE, Andrew: Rank: Second Engineer.
Regiment or Service: Mercantile Marine. Unit:
SS *Coningbeg* (Glasgow). Torpedoed by German
Submarine U-62. There were no survivors. U-62
surrendered in November 1918. Age at death: 31.
Date of death: 18 December 1917.

Supplementary information: Son of Mary
O'Beirne, of 9 Canada Street, Waterford. He
has no known grave but is listed on the Tower
Hill Memorial in the UK. He is also listed on
the Formby-Coningbeg Memorial, Adelphi
Quay in Waterford City.

O'BRIEN, Daniel: Rank: Stoker. Regiment
or Service: Royal Naval Reserve. Unit: HMS
Drake. Date of death: 26 October 1916. Service
No: 400V.

Supplementary information: Husband of Bridget
O'Brien, of Ballybricken, Co. Waterford. Grave
or Memorial Reference: Right of path between
entrance and Church. Cemetery: Slieverue
Catholic Churchyard, Co. Waterford.

O'BRIEN, James: Rank: Private. Regiment
or Service: Royal Irish Regiment. Unit: 1st
Battalion. Age at death: 24. Date of death: 25
June 1915. Service No: 10118. Born in Trinity
Without, Waterford. Enlisted in Waterford.
Killed in action.

Supplementary information: Son of James
and Mary O'Brien of Waterford. Husband of
Ellen O'Brien, of 74 St John's Road, Bootle,
Liverpool. Grave or Memorial Reference:
III.C.4. Cemetery: Houplines Communal
Cemetery Extension, France.

O'BRIEN, James: Rank: Private. Regiment
or Service: Irish Guards. Unit: 1st Battalion.
Age at death: 36. Date of death: 2 April 1918.
Service No: 11755. Born in Waterford. Enlisted
in Aldershot, Hants. Died of wounds.

Supplementary information: Son of James and Bridget O'Brien, of Co. Waterford. Grave or Memorial Reference: II.H.7. Cemetery: Gezaincourt Communal Cemetery Extension in France.

O'BRIEN, James: Rank: Private. Regiment or Service: York and Lancaster Regiment. Unit: 2nd Battalion. Age at death: 29. Date of death: 12 October 1916. Service No: 20794. Killed in action. Previously he was with the Hussars where his number was 13428. Born in Waterford. Enlisted in Tumble, Carmarthenshire while living in Waterford.

Supplementary information: Son of Patrick and Bridget O'Brien, of Kilcanavee, Kilmacthomas, Co. Waterford. The *Waterford News*, November 1916:

IN THE CASUALTY LISTS.

In the casualty lists this week the names of the following soldiers appeared: Pte. J. O'Brien, Waterford, York and Lancaster Regiment (20794), and Lee-Corporal G. Forbes, Sherwoods, Waterford, 13106.

From the *Waterford News*, December 1916:

A FINE GALLANT SOLDIER

Mrs O'Brien, of Kilcanavee, Kilmacthomas, has received news regarding her son's death at the front from the Captain of his company, who wrote as follows:

"Dear Mrs O'Brien,

I very much regret to say that your son, Private James O'Brien, was killed in an attack. He was hit in the ankle first, but continued to advance, and was afterwards his in the head. As we went to raise him up, his last words were; 'Tell my dear old, mother, father, brothers and sisters and the dear ones at home not to worry. I have fought and died for my country.' When we were relieved that night we buried him … I deeply regret the loss of such a fine and gallant soldier from my company. You will be proud to know he died a noble death,

doing his duty. Please accept my deepest sympathy in your very great losses. "

He has no known grave but is listed on Pier and Face 14A and 14B of the Thiepval Memorial in France.

O'BRIEN, John: Rank: Cattleman. Regiment or Service: Mercantile Marine. Unit: SS *Formby* (Glasgow). Date of death: 16 December 1917. The ship was lost with all hands and never located during a fierce storm.

Supplementary information: Son of the late Michael and Catherine O'Brien. Husband of Bridget O'Brien (*née* Reare), of 7 Sargint's Court, Waterford, Co. Waterford. Born in Waterford. He has no known grave but is listed on the Tower Hill Memorial in the UK. He is also listed on the Formby-Coningbeg Memorial, Adelphi Quay in Waterford City.

O'BRIEN, John: Rank: Gunner. Regiment or Service: Royal Field Artillery. Unit: 'C' Battery, 190th Brigade. Age at death: 30. Date of death: 24 October 1916. Service No: 6416. Born in Waterford. Enlisted in Waterford. Killed in action.

Supplementary information: Son of Geoffrey and Margaret O'Brien, of 25 Lower Grange, Ballytruckle, Waterford. He has no known grave but is listed on Pier and Face 1A and 8A of the Thiepval Memorial in France.

O'BRIEN, John: Rank: Rifleman. Regiment or Service: Royal Irish Rifles. Unit: 7th Battalion. Date of death: 7 September 1916. Service No: 4586. Born in Waterford. Enlisted in Waterford. Killed in action. From the *Waterford News*, September 1916:

ANOTHER WATERFORD OFFICER KILLED.

Mrs Mary O'Brien, Rockshire Road, Ferrybank, has received notification from the War Office, and also a message of sympathy from the King and Queen, on the death of her son, Rifleman J. O'Brien, 7th Battalion,

R.I. Rifles, who was killed in action He was son of Mr Laurence and Mrs Mary O'Brien, Rockshire Road, Ferrybank.

He has no known grave but is listed on Pier and Face 15 A and 15 B on the Thiepval Memorial in France.

O'BRIEN, John: Rank: Private. Rank: Gunner. Regiment or Service: Royal Horse Artillery and Royal Field Artillery. Unit: 'C' Battery, 190th Brigade. ge at death: 30. Date of death: 24 October 1916. A Service No: 6416. Born in Waterford. Enlisted in Waterford. Killed in action.

Supplementary information: Son of Geoffrey and Margaret O'Brien, of 25 Lower Grange, Ballytruckle, Waterford. He has no known grave but is listed on Pier and Face 1A and 8A on the Thiepval Memorial in France.

O'BRIEN, J. V.: Rank: Captain. Regiment or Service: Royal Army Medical Corps. Attached to the 5th Brigade. Date of death: 10 August 1916. Killed in action. From the *Waterford News*, March 1916:

HOME ON SHORT LEAVE.
Major O'Brien, son of Mr James V. O'Brien, J. P., of Aglish House, Co. Waterford, is home on short leave. He is staying with his parents at the family residence near Cappoquin.

From the *Waterford News*, 1915:

WATERFORD LETTERS FROM THE FRONT.
The following interesting letter has been received from Lieutenant O'Brien, who is at the front with his Regiment, the 2nd Battalion of the Leinster Regiment. Lieutenant O'Brien is a son of Mr J O'Brien, J.P., of Aglish House, Cappoquin.

27th December.
Dear Mother,
I hope my last letter reached you by Xmas. I spent Xmas Day in the trenches. It was a hard, frosty day, with a fog on all day. All the men got Xmas presents from Princess Mary's fund; the smokers got a pipe and tobacco, the others got little writing cases, etc. Each man also got a piece of plum pudding. Everyone was merry and bright. Our company's trenches were on the left of our lines, and in front of us were Prussians, who kept sniping at us all day, but we did not fire a shot. But in front of the company on our right there were Saxons and Bavarians, and on Xmas morning a few of them came out to bury about fifteen of their dead who had been lying for a few weeks between our trenches and theirs. Our chaps went out to help them, and soon all our men and all the Germans were out of the trenches and walking round talking to one another. Lots of them could speak English. One man, who used to be employed at Selfridge's, said the Russians were beaten a few weeks ago and that Ireland had declared war on England. These Bavarians and Saxons are evidently a very decent lot, quite different from the Prussians opposite my company. Their trenches were much the same as ours, but they were much more numerous. They were mostly young chaps, and said they had been there since October, with little rest. They were all Catholics. Whilst they were wandering round a hare got up between the lines, and Germans and British joined in the chase, but it escaped. A few of our chaps were in their trenches eating and drinking; but they sent out a patrol, armed with revolvers, to keep our men from going too near their trenches. All this happened a good distance on the my company. "They are d--- Prussians." The Bavarian said with a sneer. The Saxons and Bavarians don't seem to like the Prussians. On Xmas Eve the Prussians were playing a band behind their lines, and that night was very noisy—bugles, songs, shouts, etc., all night, and occasionally a shot from the Prussians. But on Xmas night not a shot was fired along the whole line. We thought the Prussians

might be preparing to attack us, and we had to keep well on the alert. Before it got dark on Xmas Day a German officer ordered all his men back to the trenches, and out chaps retired too. The Battalion on the right of ours were all out on Xmas Day and had a game of football with the Saxons and Bavarians. All this time you may not think possible, but it is absolutely true. One of our chaps took a few photos. I must try to get a print. A new officer came to this company last night when we got into billets; he is in my battalion and is a Canadian. These billets are near our former ones. I shall send you a postcard of the town we are in soon, and it will give you an idea of where we are … There are people living in these billets – a family of five, I think – and it is a sort of grocery shop, very clean, but three of us have to sleep in one room. However, it's a great thing to have a bed to lie on, and not to have to walk round in mud at all hours of the night. I had a very good dug-out in the last trenches, decorated with pictures, Xmas cards, etc. Yesterday I was looking at the German trenches with my glasses. I saw two Germans walking along carrying something between them. I fired, and one fell; the other ran away. I also saw a working party behind a hedge and made them stop work.

Well, I must close now. Good-bye for the present. By the way, could you send me a few candles every week; they are very difficult to get here, and if you could send the "Observer" or some paper with them I would be very grateful. They should be well packed and addressed.

Good-Bye.

J.J.

From the *Waterford News*, December 1915:

RAPID PROMOTION.

Captain J.J. O'Brien of the Leinster's Regiment, second son of Mr J.V. O'Brien of Aglish House, Cappoquin, has been promoted to the rank of Major, and has joined the 8th Battalion of the Royal Munster Fusiliers (16th Division). This is a remarkably quick promotion. Major O'Brien is only in his 23rd Year and is probably the youngest Major in the Service.

Grave or Memorial Reference: I.A.18. Cemetery: Gordon Dump Cemetery, Ovilliers-La-Boiselle in France.

O'BRIEN, Keirne: Rank: Private. Regiment or Service: Welsh Regiment. Unit: 1st Battalion. Date of death: 2 October 1915. Service No: 22575. Born in Waterford. Enlisted in Ammanford, Carmarthenshire while living in Mooncoin, Co. Waterford. Killed in action. He has no known grave but is listed on Panel 77 and 78 on the Loos Memorial in France.

O'BRIEN, Michael: Rank: Private. Regiment or Service: The King's (Liverpool Regiment). Unit: Supernumerary Coy. Age at death: 47. Date of death: 21 June 1915. He is not listed in Soldiers died in the Great War and he is not listed with Irelands Memorial Records. Supplementary Service No: 1427.

Supplementary information: Husband of Elizabeth Stack (formerly O'Brien). Born in Waterford. Grave or Memorial Reference: Screen Wall (AD. 1102). Cemetery: Liverpool (Ford) Roman Catholic Cemetery in Liverpool.

O'BRIEN, Michael: Rank: Private. Regiment or Service: Australian Infantry, A.I.F. Unit: 57th Battalion. Date of death: 15 October 1917 (CWGC but this may change soon, I have reported it). His records say he died in October 1918. Service No: 3578. Enlisted 16 August 1915 at Melbourne, Victoria. Died of wounds (gunshot to leg and hand) received in action at the 1st Australian general Hospital. Charges during service: gambling in that he played 'Crown and Anchor', absent from church parade, swimming parade and parade for checking equipment, while on active service conduct to the prejudice of good order and discipline, Using obscene language to his Superior Officer. While on active service drunkenness. While on active service absent with leave from place of parade. While on active service refusing to obey an order given by his Superior Officer in the execution of his office. While on active service being in town without a pass (twice). Despite all these charges he was mentioned in routine orders for Gallant services rendered, 31 October 1917. A congratulatory letter dated 29 January 1918 was sent to Miss I. Frane, Federal Hill, Swan Hill, Victoria, 'The Army Corps Commander wished to express his appreciation of the gallant services rendered by the under-mentioned soldier during the recent operations, No 5378 Pte M O'Brien.'

Will:

8 June 1917.

To C. C. 'B' Compnay.

I, the undersigned, do hereby certify that I do not wish to make a will.

No 3578.

Pte M. O'Brien

57th Battalion.

9th October-1919.

Dear Madam.

With reference to your report of the regrettable loss of the late No 3578. Private M O'Brien, 57th Battalion, I am now in receipt of advice that he was wounded on the 1st October, 1918 and admitted to 5th Australian Field Ambulance, suffering with gunshot wound legs, transferred to 53rd Casualty Clearing Station; transferred to No 2 Ambulance Train on 2nd October, 1918, thence to 1st Australian Central General Hospital, Rouen, on 3rd October, 1918, where he died as a result of his wounds (gunshot wound legs, amputation right thigh) on 15th October, 1918. He was buried in St Saver Cemetery Extension, Rouen, France.

The utmost care and attention is being devoted to the graves of our fallen soldiers, and photographs are being taken as soon as possible foe transmission to next-of-kin.

These additional details are furnished by direction, it being the policy of the department to forward all information received in connection with the deaths of members of the Australian Imperial Force.

Yours Faithfully.

Mrs I. L. Cramer.

Beveridge Street.

San Hill.

Victoria.

Major I/C Base records

Data from his attestation papers:

In or near what Parish or Town were you born? Waterford, Ireland.

Are you a natural born British subject or a Naturalised British subject? Natural Born British Subject.

What is your age? 25 years 8 months.

What is your trade or calling? Sailor.

Are you married? Married, Miss Ida L Ramon, Beveridge Street. Swan Hill.

Who is your next of kin? Father and mother dead.

Have you ever been convicted by the Civil Power? No.

Have you stated the whole, if any, of your previous service? Yes.

Height: 5 feet, 4 ½ inches.

Weight: 12st 13 lbs.

Chest measurement: 36-38 ½ inches.

Complexion, dark.

Eyes: grey.

Hair: brown.

Religious denomination: R. C.

Killed in action. Grave or Memorial Reference: S.II.F.21. Cemetery: St Sever Cemetery Extension, Rouen in France.

O'BRIEN, Patrick: Rank: Private. Regiment or Service: Royal Welsh Fusiliers. Unit: 2nd Battalion. Age at death: 18. Date of death: 13 August 1916. Service No: 24636. Born in Ballyguiry, Co. Waterford. Enlisted in Waterford, Co. Waterford. Killed in action.

Supplementary information: Son of Patrick and Mary O'Brien, of Ballyguiry, Dungarvan, Co. Waterford. Grave or Memorial Reference: II.B.8. Cemetery: Flatiron Copse Cemetery. Mametz in France.

O'BRIEN, Patrick: Rank: Rifleman. Regiment or Service: Royal Irish Rifles. Unit: 1st Battalion. Date of death: 16 August 1917. Service No: 8019. Born in Waterford. Enlisted in Waterford. Killed in action. He has no known grave but is listed on Panel 138 to 140 and 162 and 162A and 163A the Tyne Cot Memorial in Belgium.

O'BRIEN, Patrick Joseph: Rank: Corporal. Regiment or Service: Royal Garrison Artillery. Unit: 3rd Depot. Age at death: 47. Date of death: 30 December 1914. Service No: 4750. He is not listed in Soldiers Died in the Great War and he is not listed with Irelands Memorial Records.

Supplementary information: Son of Patrick and Margaret O'Brien, of Lismore. Husband of Mary O'Brien, of Chapel Street, Lismore, Co. Waterford. He had just returned from furlough and contracted pneumonia after getting wet. He died after a day or two. He was buried with full military honours in Plymouth, two bands being in attendance. In 1903 and during the Boer War he was a Sergeant in the Waterford Artillery and did service with the Battalion at Straddon Heights for nine months or so and won a medal for good conduct. From the *Waterford News*, January 1915:

CO WATERFORD VETERAN'S DEATH.

The death has taken place of Patrick O'Brien, a Corporal in the Royal Garrison Artillery, now stationed in Plymouth. Deceased was a native of Chapel Street, Lismore. During the Boer War deceased was Sergeant to the Waterford R. G. A. and did duty at Staddon Heights for nine months, and was awarded a medal for good conduct. Eight members of deceased's family are serving with the colours, as follows: Patrick O'Brien (son), attached to the R.G.A, Wm O'Brien (son), stoker HMS Monarch, Martin O'Brien (son) in the R.F.A. at the front, Cornelius O'Brien (brother) in the R.G.A, Walter Mansfield (nephew) in the R.G.A, Patrick James, and John Mansfield (nephews), all attached to the Leinster Regiment at the front, Patrick getting two fingers blown off lately in an engagement. Deceased was buried with full military honours at Plymouth.

Grave or Memorial Reference: R.C.C. 3354. Cemetery: Plymouth (Efford) Cemetery, UK.

O'BRIEN, Peter: Rank: Private. Regiment or Service: Irish Guards. Unit: 2nd Battalion. Age at death: 24. Date of death: 15 September 1916. Service No: 9338. Born in Fourmilewater, Co. Waterford. Enlisted in Clonmel, Co. Tipperary. Killed in action.

Supplementary information: Son of Patrick and Catherine O'Brien, of Fourmilewater, Ballymacarberry, Co. Waterford. He has no known grave but is listed on Pier and Face 7D of the Thiepval Memorial in France.

O'BRIEN, Richard: Rank: Unknown. Regiment or Service: Unknown. Unit: the barque, *Avanti Savoir*. The only information I have on this sailor is contained in the below. From the *Waterford News*, April 1915:

WATERFORD SAILOR DROWNED.

On Thursday last it was reported in the Press that the body of a Waterford sailor named Kennedy, had been washed ashore from the wreck of the barque Avanti Savoir, off the Shetlands. It now appears that though his discharge book had the name Kennedy on it, the man's real name was Richard O'Brien, and that he is son of Mr O'Brien, a Corporation employee, residing at John's Court, John Street. A kindly gentleman, residing at Sheld Reawick, Shetland, took the trouble of addressing a letter containing particulars, to "The relatives of Richard O'Brien, Seaman, John Street, Waterford" and through the instrumentality of Mr G Hynes, local Secretary of the Sailors ad Firemen's Union, the letter reached deceased's father. It appears that it is nine or ten years since the deceased has been in Waterford.

WRECK A MYSTERY.

In the course of his letter. Mr Moar states, "I was there when the wreckage came ashore, and am sorry to say the crew must all have been lost. Up to the present (the letter is dated 11th April) nine bodies have been recovered. It was on Tuesday morning that the body of Richard O'Brien was found. The name was found on the Union Book (Sailors and Fireman's Union) in his pocket. The bodies were interred in the churchyard, Weskerskeld, Sandsting, on Thursday. They were given a very decent burial, the people of the district doing everything possible. Over 200 men attended the funeral. How the barque went ashore is a mystery. There was a strong breeze blowing, but nothing to hurt a ship of her size unless she was disabled. It will likely remain a mystery. If this reaches any relative of Richard O'Brien, I am willing to tell them all I know."

O'BRIEN, Thomas: Rank: Private. Regiment or Service: Royal Irish Regiment. Unit: 6th Battalion. Age at death: 26. Date of death: 9 September 1916. Service No: 10155. Born in New Town, Co. Waterford. Enlisted in Kilkenny while living in New Town. Killed in action.
Supplementary information: Son of Mrs Margaret O'Brien. Grave or Memorial Reference: VI.A.5. Cemetery: Serre Road Cemetery No. 2 in France.

O'BRIEN, Thomas: Rank: Private. Regiment or Service: Royal Irish Regiment. Unit: 2nd Battalion. Date of death: 1 July 1916. Service No: 6067. Born in Stradbally Waterford. Enlisted in Waterford while living in Stradbally Co.

Waterford. Killed in action. Grave or Memorial Reference: K.24. Cemetery: Carnoy Military Cemetery in France.

O'BRIEN, Thomas Dominick: Rank: Boy 1st Class. Regiment or Service: Royal Navy. Unit: HMS *Viknor*. Age at death: 16. Date of death: 13 January 1915. Service No: J-28235. HMS *Viknor* was an armed Merchant Cruiser. She struck a sea mine off Tory Island and went down with all 295 crew. There were no survivors.
Supplementary information: Born in Waterford. Son of Thomas O'Brien, of Clonmel, Co. Tipperary. Grave or Memorial Reference: 8. He has no known grave but is listed on the Playmouth Naval Memorial. Devon, UK.

O'CALLAGHAN, Anne: Rank: Stewardess. Regiment or Service: Mercantile Marine. Unit: SS *Formby*. Age at death: 52. Date of death: 16 December 1917. The ship was lost with all hands and never located during a fierce storm.
Supplementary information: Daughter of John and Alice O'Callaghan, of 41 St Joseph's Terrace, Green Street, Waterford. Her body was washed up on the shore near Milford and she was identified by a badge of the Sacred Heart on the back of which she had written her name and address (St Joseph's Terrace, Waterford). Miss O'Callaghan's sister was Mrs E. Walshe of the Hotel, Kilmacthomas and her mother was eighty-six years old at this time. Her funeral and the disaster is chronicled in the *Munster Express* in the 19 January 1918 edition. Grave or Memorial Reference: East of middle path. Cemetery: Newtown (All Saints) Catholic Churchyard, Co. Waterford. He is also listed on the Formby-Coningbeg Memorial, Adelphi Quay in Waterford City.

O'CONNELL, Daniel: Rank: Cattleman. Regiment or Service: Mercantile Marine. Unit:

SS *Formby* (Glasgow). Age at death: 27. Date of death: 16 December 1917. The ship was lost with all hands and never located during a fierce storm.

Supplementary information: Son of the late Patrick and Catherine O'Connell. Husband of Elizabeth O'Connell (*née* Burke), of 5 Graces Lane, Waterford, Co. Waterford. Born in Waterford. He has no known grave but is listed on the Tower Hill Memorial in the UK. He is also listed on the Formby-Coningbeg Memorial, Adelphi Quay in Waterford City.

O'CONNELL, David: Rank: Stoker 2nd Class. Regiment or Service: Royal Navy. Unit: HMS *Vivid*. Age at death: 19. Date of death: 8 April 1916. Service No: K/31046.

Supplementary information: Son of Mrs Mary O'Connell, of Kilphilibeen, Ballynoe, Tallow, Co. Waterford. Grave or Memorial Reference: General T.7.33. Cemetery: Ford Park Cemetery (Formerly Plymouth Old Cemetery) (Pennycomequick) UK.

O'CONNOR, John: Rank: Private. Regiment or Service: Irish Guards. Unit: 2nd Battalion. Age at death: 20. Date of death: 22 October 1917. Service No: 7771. Born in Ballyduff, Co. Waterford. Enlisted in Dungarvan, Co. Waterford. Died of wounds.

Supplementary information: Son of Michael and Mary O'Connor, of Ballyduff, Co. Waterford. Grave or Memorial Reference: XXX.F.8. Cemetery: Etaples Military Cemetery in France.

O'CONNOR, Michael Joseph: Rank: Private. Regiment or Service: Royal Irish Regiment. Unit: 3rd Battalion. Age at death: 30. Born in Kilmackthomas, Co. Waterford. Enlisted in Waterford while living in Kilmackthomas. Died at home. Date of death: 27 September 1916. Service No: 8504.

Supplementary information: Son of William O'Connor. Husband of Margaret O'Connor of 135 East Main Street, Annadale, West

Lothian. Grave location: Plot 2. Cemetery: Templemore Catholic Cemetery.

O'CONNOR, Patrick: Rank: Private. Regiment or Service: Royal Munster Fusiliers. Unit: 2nd Battalion. Age at death: 23. Date of death: 4 October 1916. Service No: 6760. Born in Tramore, Co. Waterford. Enlisted in Partick, Glasgow while living in Glasgow. Died.

Supplementary information: Son of Michael and Ellen O'Connor. Born at Tramore, Co. Waterford. Grave or Memorial Reference: B.20.11. Cemetery: ST. Sever Cemetery, Rouen in France.

O'CONNOR, Patrick: Rank: Private. Regiment or Service: Royal Irish Regiment. Unit: 2nd Battalion. Date of death: 3 September 1916. Service No: 8798. Born in Dungarvan, Co. Waterford. Enlisted in Dungarvan, Co. Waterford. Killed in action. He has no known grave but is listed on Pier and Face 3A on the Thiepval Memorial in France.

ODELL, William: Rank: Captain. Regiment or Service: 123rd Outram's Rifles Secondary Regiment: 125th Napier's Rifles Secondary. Unit: attached. Age at death: 32. Date of death: 22 February 1917 Awarded the Military Cross while he was attached to the 125th Napier Rifles and is listed on the *London Gazette*, 6128, Supplement to the *London Gazette*, 23 June 1915.

Supplementary information: Son of the late Capt. W. Odell, of Ardmore, Co. Waterford. Husband of Evelyn Caroline Odell, of Carriglea, Lindenthorpe Road, Broadstairs, Kent. From De Ruvigny's Roll of Honour:

Odell, William, M. C. Captain, 123rd Outram's Rifles. Indian Army, only son of the late Capt. William Odell, of Ardmore. Co. Waterford, Royal Inniskiliing Fusiliers, by his wife, Emma. daughter, of the Late Simon Bagge. Born in Dublin. 30 April 1884: educated the Abbey.

Tipperary ; gazetted 2nd Lieutenant. The Manchester Regiment from the Militia 27 January 1904; promoted Lieutenant. 27 April 1900; transferred to the Connaught Rangers 4 May 1907, and to the Indian Army 4-February-1909, being promoted Capt. 27 January. 1913. Served with the Connaught Rangers in Singapore, Malta and India, until he joined the 123rd Outram's Rifles in February. 1909. Went to the Persian Gulf with the Mekran Field Force in April. 1911. Was employed on reconnaissance duty in Karenni, Burma, from Nov-1911, to May-1912, when he was thanked for his work in the Chief of Staff's letter to the G. O. C., Burma Division. Served with the Expeditionary Force in France and Flanders from December. 1914, attached to the 125th Napier Rifles. Was slightly wounded at Givenchy the same month. Proceeded to Egypt in December 1915. Served with the Indian Expeditionary Force in Mesopotamia from January 1916. Was severely wounded during bombing practice in the following August and was killed in action at Sanna-I-Yat 22-February-1917. Capt. Odell was mentioned in Despatches [London Gazette. 22 June 1915] by F.M. Sir John (now Lord) French, for gallant and distinguished service in the field, and was awarded the Military Cross (London Gazette, 23 June 1915). He married at St Mary's, The Boltons, London, S. W., 24th June, Evelyn Caroline, eldest daughter of Captain Ernest Foley, late Middlesex Regiment and had a son, Denis Edward, born 5 February 1915.

Grave or Memorial Reference: XVI.F.11. Cemetery: Amara War Cemetery in Iraq.

O'DONNELL, John Patrick: Rank: Private. Regiment or Service: Middlesex Regiment. Unit: 3rd Battalion. Date of death: 24 January 1915. Service No: G/5701. Born in Limerick. Enlisted in London. Killed in action. Has no known grave but is commemorated on Panel 34 on the Ypres (Menin Gate) Memorial in Belgium.

O'DONNELL, Patrick: Rank: Private. Regiment or Service: Royal Army Medical Corps. Unit: 21st Field Amb. Age at death: 22. Date of death: 18 July 1916. Service No: 7893. Born in Waterford. Enlisted in Waterford. Died of wounds.

Supplementary information: Son of Patrick and Margaret O'Donnell, of 9 New Lane, Waterford. From the *Waterford News*, August 1916:

WATERFORD SOLDIER'S DEATH.

The following letter has been received by Mrs O'Donnell, 9 New Lane, Waterford, in reference to the death of her son, Private P. O'Donnell, 1893 [sic]. R.A.M.C.

9th August, 1916.

Dear Mrs O'Donnell,

I regret to have to inform you that your son died on the 19th July from wounds received in action. He was hit in the head by a piece of a shell whilst doing his duty carrying back a wounded comrade on a stretcher. He was a splendid fellow, and as a tremendous favourite amongst all ranks in the Ambulance. He was always one of the first to volunteer for any hazardous duty, thereby setting a fine example to all ranks. Please accept, on behalf of the officers and men of the Ambulance, by sincerest sympathy in your very sad bereavement. Your son died at No 36 C.C.S., and is buried close to the hospital. He was wounded on the 15th July—

Yours faithfully.

W. Gordon Wright.

Major., R.A.M.C., A.C., 21st Field Ambulance.

Grave or Memorial Reference: II.D.38. Cemetery: Heilly Station Cemetery, Mericourt-L'Abbe in France.

O'DWYER, Pat: Rank: Trimmer. Regiment or Service: Mercantile Marine Reserve. Unit: HMS *Calgarian*. Age at death: 18. Date of death: 1 March 1918. Service No: 906583.

Supplementary information: Son of Laurence and Mary Ann O'Dwyer, of Crobally, Tramore, Co. Waterford. Grave or Memorial Reference: 31 on the Plymouth Naval Memorial, UK.

O'DWYER, Thomas: Rank: Private. Regiment or Service: Royal Irish Regiment. Unit: 1st Battalion. Age at death: 21. Date of death: 21 March 1915. Service No: 4567. Born in Carrickbeg, Co. Waterford. Enlisted in Waterford while living in Carrickbeg. Died of wounds.

Supplementary information: Son of Mary Maher, of Mass Road, Carrickbeg, Carrick-on-Suir. Grave or Memorial Reference: I.B.15. Cemetery: Etretat Churchyard, France.

O'FARRELL, Daniel: Rank: Private. Regiment or Service: Royal Munster Fusiliers. Unit: 8th Battalion. Age at death: 20. Service No: 5838. Born in Tramore, Co. Waterford. Enlisted in Limerick while living in Limerick. Killed in action. He has no known grave but is listed on Pier and Face 16C on the Thiepval Memorial in France.

O'FLYNN/O'FLYNNE, Patrick: Rank: Driver. Regiment or Service: Royal Horse Artillery and Royal Field Artillery. Unit: 35th Brigade. Ammunition Col. Age at death: 27. Date of death: 28 January 1915. Service No: 13878. Born in Waterford. Enlisted in Chatham in Kent. Died of wounds.

Supplementary information: Son of Michael and Alice O'Flynn, of 130, Victoria Street, Gillingham, Kent. Native of Cappoquin, Co. Waterford. Grave or Memorial Reference: C.1. Cemetery: Cemetery: Sailly-Sur-La-Lys Churchyard in France.

O'GORMAN, Eileen Mary: Rank: Sister. Regiment or Service: Territorial Force Nursing Service. Age at death: 42. Date of death: 20 November 1914.

Supplementary information: Daughter of Edward and Margaret O'Gorman, of John's Hill, Waterford. From the *Waterford News*, 1914:

WATERFORD NURSE BURIED WITH MILITARY HONOURS.

The death occurred this week at Bristol of Nurse Eileen Mary O'Gorman, daughter of Mr Patrick O'Gorman, land steward of the Waterford District Lunatic Asylum, who had been on nursing service – attached to the Royal Army Medical Corps – at the base hospital, Bristol. The high esteem and respect in which she late Nurse O'Gorman was held, and the regret felt at her demise, may well be judged from the following particulars, which are taken from the "Western Daily Press" of Tuesday last:

"Bristol has witnessed some solemn scenes in the streets of late. British and Belgian soldiers who have succumbed their wounds have been borne to their last resting-place attended by the ceremony which martial heroes are accorded, and yesterday there was the unique and impressive spectacle of a nurse, who up to Saturday was engaged in tending the wounded soldiers at Southmead, and who, by reason of her connection with the Royal Army Medical Corps, was buried with military honours. The death, after so short an illness, of Nurse Eileen Mary O'Gorman caused great regret at the hospital. Her home was at Waterford, but she was a matron at Ilkeston, Derbyshire, where she left to assist at the military base hospital at Bristol. As many as possible of the staff attended the service at the Pro-Cathedral, Clifton, at nine o'clock yesterday morning. The procession was headed by the band of the 6th Gloucester's, and eighteen men and six bearers of the 4th Gloucester's accompanied the gun carriage. Captain Nichols, who was in charge of the arrangements, preceded the gun carriage, and following it came the priests and a large number of officers. Then followed about fifty sisters and nurses, 30 members of the Field Ambulance, and a Red Cross detachment, including nurses. The coffin was covered by the Union Jack and flowers, and six non-commissioned officers acted as bearers. At the conclusion of the service at the Pro-Cathedral the procession was re-formed and proceeded to Arno's Vale, where, in the Catholic cemetery, the mortal remains of the nurse were laid to rest, and over the grave was heard "The Last Post." The flowers included a cross from father, mother, and sister; a wreath from the medical officers of Southmead; a harp from the matrons, sisters, and nursing staff of Southmead and Bristol base hospital; a wreath with the Red Cross from the N.C.O's and men of Southmead; a cross from friends at Gloucester; a cross from patients at Southmead."

From the *British Journal of Nursing*, 5 December 1914, p. 454:

It is our sad duty to record the death of Miss Eileen O'Gorman, the respected Matron of the Ilkeston Hospital, of whom it may well be said that she gave her life for her country. When war broke out she was called up as a member of the Territorial Force Nursing Service, and was stationed at the new Southmead Infirmary, Bristol, known as the Second Southern General Hospital. Recently she became ill and her case was diagnosed as appendicitis and acute peritonitis. An operation was performed, but proved unavailing. The death of Miss O'Gorman has caused much grief at Ilkeston, especially amongst the nursing staff.

Grave or Memorial Reference: LG.2.2. Cemetery: Bristol (Arnos Vale) Roman Catholic Cemetery, UK.

O'GORMAN, Thomas Christopher: Rank: Able Seaman. Regiment or Service:

Mercantile Marine. Unit: SS *Romeo* (Hull). Age at death: 22. Date of death: 3 March 1918.

Supplementary information: Son of Thomas and Rose Mary O'Gorman (*née* Kearney), of 19 O'Connell Street, Waterford. Born in Waterford. He has no known grave but is listed on the Tower Hill Memorial in the UK.

O'GRADY, William: Rank: Private. Regiment or Service: Royal Irish Regiment. Unit: 2nd Battalion. Date of death: 19 October 1914. Service No: 4931. Born in Trinity Without, Waterford. Enlisted in Tipperary while living in Waterford. Killed in action. From the *Waterford News*, February 1915:

A BET IN FRANCS.
To the Editor Weterford News.
British Expeditionary Force in the Field, 18th February, 1915.

Dear Sir - I have read a letter by one of my townsmen which appeared in your paper of the 12th inst., and I wish to put forward the suggestion that you might possibly be able to publish a list of the names of men from our city now serving at the front. I have seen such lists appear in English papers.

I have been in France from the beginning, have been in some "warm corners, " and have covered a good area of this country. I receive your paper regularly from home, and. needless to say, it is always welcome. I have met a few from the old country, and we can honestly say that the Irish Regiments have given a very good account of themselves.

By a curious coincidence, I was reading your paper one day, when I happened to be down at the base railway station, when one of the Munster Fusiliers, who had just arrived seriously wounded from the front, seeing the green 'un on the seat of the motor car, eagerly asked me if it contained the result of the Hurling Final. He said he had " a three franc bet" with a pal of his in the ambulance train. Is not this not a fine example of the cheerful and light-hearted Irish man?

Hoping you will consider my suggestion, as I am sure there are many families concerned who would be pleased to give their assistance in compiling the list.

M. David O'Grady, Corporal, Army Service Corps,

Mechnical Transport, B. E. F.

Grave or Memorial Reference: He has no known grave but is listed on the Le Touret Memorial in France on Panels 11 and 12 in France.

O'KEEFE, James: Rank: Stoker 1st Class. Regiment or Service: Royal Navy. Unit: HMS *Tornado*. Age at death: 22. Date of death: 23 December 1917. Service No: K/32657. Sunk when she struck a German sea-mine. The ship was only one year old.

Supplementary information: Son of John and Mary O'Keefe, of Newtown Cottage, Ballynoe, Tallow, Co. Waterford. Grave or Memorial Reference: 22 on the Plymouth Naval Memorial, UK.

O'KEEFE, John: Rank: Stoker 1st Class. Regiment or Service: Royal Navy. Unit: HMS *Bittern*. Age at death: 20. Date of death: 4 April 1918. Service No: K/32179. Sunk in collision with Steamship Kenilworth in fog off Portland Bill.

Supplementary information: Son of John and Mary O'Keeffe, of Newtown Cottage, Ballynoe, Tallow, Co. Waterford. Grave or Memorial Reference: 28 on the Plymouth Naval Memorial, UK.

O'KEEFFE, Michael: Rank: Sergeant. Regiment or Service: Irish Guards. Unit: 1st Battalion. Date of death: 26 July 1917. Age at death: 26. Service No: 3687. Born in Tallow, Co. Waterford. Enlisted in Cork while living in Westminster, Middlesex. Died of wounds.

Supplementary information: Husband of Nora O'Keeffe. Grave or Memorial Reference: I.H.7. Cemetery: Dozinghem Military Cemetery in Belgium.

O'KEEFFE, Thomas: Rank: Driver. Regiment or Service: Royal Field Artillery. Unit: 4th Div. Ammunition Col. Age at death: 26. Date of death: 29 August 1918. Service No: 74376. Born in Portlaw, Co. Waterford. Enlisted in Waterford. Killed in action.

Supplementary information: Son of Richard O'Keeffe and Catherine Londregan O'Keeffe, of 57 William Street, Portlaw. Grave or Memorial Reference: II.B.41. Cemetery: Tilloy British Cemetery, Tilloy-Les-Mofflaines in France.

O'KEEFE/O'KEEFFE, William: Rank: Private. Regiment or Service: Royal Irish Regiment. Unit: 3rd Battalion. Date of death: 4 November 1918. Age at death: 22. Service No: 5595. Born in Moneygran, Co. Waterford. Enlisted in Clonmel, Co. Tipperary while living in Cappoquin, Co. Waterford. Died at Home. Grave or Memorial Reference: Eight yards south east of the main path. Cemetery: Affane Old Church of Ireland Churchyard, Co. Waterford.

O'KEEFFE, William: Rank: Private. Regiment or Service: Leinster Regiment. Unit: 2nd Battalion. Date of death: 27 March 1918. Service No 3297:. Born in Ballybricken, Co. Waterford. Enlisted in Waterford while living in Waterford. Killed in action. Grave or Memorial Reference: VII.D.19. Cemetery: Tincourt New British Cemetery in France.

O'LEARY, Henry (Commonwealth War Graves Commission and Soldiers Died in the Great War), **O'LEARY, Harry:** (Irelands Memorial Records). Rank: Lance Corporal. Regiment or Service: Irish Guards. Unit: 1st Battalion. Service No: 5607. Born in

Macallagh, Co. Waterford. Enlisted in Dundalk, Co. Louth. Killed in action. He has no known grave but is listed on Pier and Face 7D on the Thiepval Memorial in France.

O'MALLEY, William Joseph: Rank: Second Lieutenant. Regiment or Service: Royal Horse Artillery and Royal Field Artillery. Unit: 'Y' 47th Trench Mortar Battery. Date of death: 9 April 1917. Killed in action. I am not sure of the Waterford connection however I include this officer for your consideration. From the *Waterford News*, April 1917:

YOUNG IRISH OFFICER'S FATE.

Last week we published a brief note about the death in action of Lieutenant O'Malley, only son of Mr William O'Malley, M. P. In the course of a letter to the Editor of this paper from Mr O'Malley we learn that the brave young officer was killed instantaneously. An enemy shell struck him as he was approaching his gun to trench mortar [sic]. Mass was said for him by special order of his commanding officer, and he was buried in a cemetery in the neighbourhood of Ypres where a cross marks his grave. Those who know Mr O'Malley and his kindly wife feel the deepest sympathy for them in their bereavement.

Grave or Memorial Reference: Enclosure No. 4I.H.13. Cemetery: Bedford House Cemetery in Belgium.

O'MEARA, James: Rank: Rifleman. Regiment or Service: Royal Irish Rifles. Unit: 7th Battalion. Age at death: 35. Date of death: 17 April 1916. Service No: 4499. Born in Waterford. Enlisted in Waterford. Died of wounds.

Supplementary information: Son of James O'Meara, of Waterford. Grave or Memorial Reference: I.H.136. Cemetery: Chocques Military Cemetery in France.

O'MEARA, Michael: Rank: Rifleman. Regiment or Service: Royal Irish Rifles. Unit: 2nd Battalion. Age at death: 31. Date of death: 31 October 1914. Service No: 6499. Born in Waterford. Enlisted in Waterford. Died of wounds.

Supplementary information: Son of Michael and Anne O'Meara, of Waterford. Husband of Margaret O'Meara, of 19, Peter's Lane, Waterford. From the *Waterford News*, 1914:

DIED FROM WOUNDS–WATERFORD
SOLDIER'S FATE.

The following letter was received by Mrs Mary O'Meara, 19, Peters Lane:

Record Office.
11th December, 1914.
Madam.

It is my painful duty to inform you that a report has this day been received from the War Office notifying the death of No 6499, Private Michael O'Meara, Royal Irish Rifles, which occurred at No 6 Clearing Hospital, Bethune, France, on the 31st of October, 1914, and I am to express to you the sympathy and regret of the Army Council at your loss. The cause of death was Died of wounds received in action.
I am, Madam, your obedient servant.
F. Law-Williams, Captain.
Mrs Mary O'Meara.

The following enclosure accompanied the letter:
"The King commands me to assure you of the true sympathy of His Majesty and the Queen in your sorrow. – Kitchener."

The deceased soldier was well known as a prominent member of the Waterford Battalion Irish National Volunteers, in which he took an active part since its inception. He was a Squad Commander of 'G' Company, and was up to the time of Mobilisation employed at Messrs Chapman Bros., O'Connell Street.

Grave or Memorial Reference: III.A.33. Cemetery: Bethune Town Cemetery in France.

O'NEILL, Cornelius: Rank: Private. Regiment or Service: Royal Irish Regiment. Unit: 6th Battalion. Date of death: 21 July 1916. Service No: 2008. Born in Portlaw, Co. Waterford. Enlisted in Portlaw. Killed in action. Grave or Memorial Reference: II.F.18. Cemetery: Dud Corner Cemetery, Loos in France.

O'NEILL, James: Rank: Private. Regiment or Service: Royal Irish Regiment. Unit: 2nd Battalion. Date of death: 24 May 1915. Service No: 6114. Born in Trinity Without, Waterford. Enlisted in Waterford. Died of wounds. Grave or Memorial Reference: XXVII.A.2. Cemetery: New Irish Farm Cemetery in Belgium.

O'NEILL, Richard: Rank: Rifleman. Regiment or Service: Royal Irish Rifles. Unit: 2nd Battalion. Age at death: 20. Date of death: 27 October 1914. Service No: 10216 (Commonwealth War Graves Commission), 10218, (Soldiers died in the Great War). Born in Tramore, Co. Waterford. Enlisted in Waterford. Killed in action.

Supplementary information: Son of Richard and Hannah O'Neill, of Churchtown, Carrick-on-Suir, Co. Waterford. From the *Waterford News*, 1914:

> Mrs O'Neill, Churchtown, near Carrick-on-Suir, has received a communication from the War Office informing her that her son, Private O'Neill, of the Royal Irish Rifles, was killed in action last month. The late Private O'Neill, who was only 20 years old, was very popular in his native district, where much sympathy is felt for his bereaved parents.

Grave or Memorial Reference: H 42 and 43 on the Le Touret Memorial in France.

O'NEILL, Robert: Rank: Private. Regiment or Service: Royal Inniskilling Fusiliers. Unit: 7th Battalion. Date of death: 21 March

1918. Service No: 26934. Born in St John's Waterford. Enlisted in Waterford while living in Dublin. Killed in action. He has no known grave but is commemorated on Panel 38 to 40. Memorial: Pozières Memorial in France.

O'NEILL, Thomas: Rank: Private. Regiment or Service: Irish Guards. Unit: 1st Battalion. Age at death: 28. Date of death: 10 December 1916. Service No: 9761. Born in Cappagh, Co. Waterford. Enlisted in Dungarvan. Killed in action.

Supplementary information: Son of Bridget O'Neill of Canty, Cappagh, Co. Waterford. Grave or Memorial Reference: I.D.10. Cemetery: Sailly-Saillisel British Cemetery in France.

O'NEILL, Thomas: Rank: Driver. Regiment or Service: Army Service Corps. Age at death: 30. Date of death: 14 October 1915. Service No: T4/043381. Born in Killishal, Co. Waterford. Enlisted in Duungarvan while living in Killishal. Died at Home.

Supplementary information: (Served as **NEALE, Thomas**). Son of Richard O'Neill of Coolenane, Cappagh, Co. Waterford. Grave or Memorial Reference: In south-east part. Cemetery: Affane Old Church of Ireland Churchyard, Co. Waterford.

O'NEILL, Thomas: Rank: Seaman. Regiment or Service: Mercantile Marine. Unit: SS *Coquet* (London). Age at death: 20. Date of death: 4 January 1916.

Supplementary information: Son of Martin Mary Ellen O'Neill of 9 New Street, Waterford. Grave or Memorial Reference: He has no known grave but is listed on the Tower Hill Memorial in the UK.

O'NEILL, Thomas: Rank: Private. Regiment or Service: Irish Guards. Unit: 2nd Battalion. Date of death: 3 December 1917. Service No: 10063. Born in Kilrosenty, Co.

Waterford. Enlisted in Manchester, Lancs, while living in Kilcomeragh Co. Waterford. Killed in action. Has no known grave but is commemorated on Panel 1 and 2. Memorial: Cambrai Memorial in Louveral in France.

O'NEILL, William: Rank: Private. Regiment or Service: King's Shropshire Light Infantry. Unit: 7th Battalion. Age at death: 24. Date of death: 27 January 1919. Service No: 35065.

Supplementary information: Son of Edward and Mary O'Neill, Mooncoin, Waterford, Ireland. Voluntary enlistment. Grave or Memorial Reference: XIII.B.16. Cemetery: Terlincthun British Cemetery, Wimille in France.

O'REGAN, Thomas: Rank: Private. Regiment or Service: Royal Dublin Fusiliers. Unit: 1st Battalion. Age at death: 22. Date of death: 7 August 1915. Service No: 19513. Joined the Dublin Fusiliers four months previous to his death. Also known as Thomas Regan. Born in Waterford. Enlisted in Waterford. Killed in action in Gallipoli. Son of Mr and Mrs D Regan, Ballybricken. Grave or Memorial Reference: VII.F.11. Cemetery: Twelve Tree Copse Cemetery in Turkey.

O'REILLY, Patrick Bernard: Rank: Lance Corporal. Regiment or Service: South Lancashire Regiment. Unit: 6th Battalion. Date of death: 10 August 1915. Age at death: 24. Service No: 10517. Born in Waterford. Enlisted in Liverpool. Killed in action in Gallipoli.

Supplementary information: Son of James and Mary O'Reilly, of 4 Madryn Street, Princes Park, Liverpool. He has no known grave but is listed on Panel 139 to 140 on the Helles Memorial in Turkey.

O'REILLY, William: Rank: Private. Regiment or Service: Royal Irish Regiment. Unit: 'C' Coy. 2nd Battalion. Age at death: 19.

Date of death: 30 October 1914. Service No: 6320. Born in Trinity Without, Waterford. Enlisted in Waterford. Killed in action.

Supplementary information: Son of Patrick and Julia O'Reilly, of 3 St John's Place, Waterford. From the *Waterford News*, 1914:

WATERFORD SOLDIERS KILLED.
One dies in German Hospital.
Impressive funeral scenes.
Mr P O'Reilly, John's Place, Waterford, has been notified by the War Office of the death of his son, William, which occurred, as a result of wounds received in action, in a German military hospital in Brussels. Young O; Reilly, who was only about 18 years of age, and had done one term of training the special reserve and was called up at the beginning of the war, and after a short time sent to the front with the Royal Irish Regiment. He was wounded and taken a prisoner by the Germans and died in the military hospital, Brussels, his funeral taking place on the 30th October. A Britisher who attended the funeral of O'Reilly wrote home to England describing the impressive event and giving particulars which led to the poor lad's identification. The following is the official notification which Mr O'Reilly received

Infantry Record Office.
Cork Station.
24th November, 1914
Sir—It is my painful duty to inform you that a report has this day been received from the War Office notifying the death of (no) 63209 (rank) private, (name) William O'Reilly, (Regiment) 3rd Royal Irish, which occurred at Brussels on the (not known) of ------, and I am to express to you the sympathy and regret of the Army Council at your loss. The cause of death was wounds received in action … I am, etc.,
Officer in charge of Records.
Mr O. O'Reilly, John's Place, Waterford.
Accompanying the above were the following:

War Office, London
20th November.

Sir–I am directed to enclose herewith a copy of a letter which has been received in this office giving information regarding the burial of a British soldier named O; Reilly, and to ask whether you are able to identify him from the particulars given, and if so to request you to inform the next-of-kin and to furnish this office with the information asked for on the enclosed form. I am, etc.

C. F. Walli-Viston.

The officer in charge of Records.

Cork.

The letter which the War Office forwarded to the officer in charge of records, Cork, was written by a person in Brussels who attended the deceased soldier's funeral and was as follows:

47 Rue Picard, Bruxelles,
November 1st, 1914.

Dear (incision),

I was told last Thursday that a British soldier had just Died of wounds at the military hospital here and was to be buried on Friday, the 30th, October. A few other Britishers (there are not many left in Brussels) besides myself considered it their duty to follow the coffin and pay their last respects to this gallant countryman.

At 3p.m. the funeral left the hospital, a Belgian soldier's funeral taking place at the same time. Large crowds of people lined the streets, from the hospital to Ste. Croix Church, where a Roman Catholic service took place; the church was too small to contain the mass of people; wreaths and garbs of flowers had been sent with suitable inscriptions, on tri-coloured ribbons with Union Jack. A short distance from the hospital the country flags had been spread over the coffins. From Ste. Croix Church the cortege went to the Ixelles Cemetery where at least 4,000 to 5,000 people had assembled. After a brief service by the British Catholic chaplain, Mr Buye, member of Parliament for Ostend and an Echevin of Ixelles at the same time, made a very moving speech in French, and then addressed the small British colony in English, saying a last "Adieu" to our soldiers, finishing his speech in Flemish, when he addressed the family of the Belgian soldier. I cannot put the words together to say the impression left by the ceremony and the scene I witnessed, but our soldier's family should know that he was buried with all the honours that could be given under existing circumstances, and that he is now resting in Ixelles cemetery by the side of his Belgian comrade-in-arms. I since made enquiries; the soldier's name is given by the German hospital staff as O'Reilly, but Mr Buye has given me further particulars as follows:

O'Reilly, No 6320, Roman Catholic, age about 20 years, Irish Royal Infantry Regiment (I. R. I. R.); the German authorities describe his Regiment as 1st Irish Infantry.

Possibly the War Office will only receive official news of the death of O'Reilly later, and you will like to inform them on receipt of this letter.

Yours, Sincerely

It might be mentioned that Mr O'Reilly has two other sons in the army, and one of them, who was locally known as 'Buck' Reilly, was wounded home from the front some time ago having been wounded in action.

Mrs McGrath, of Peter Street, Waterford, has also been notified by the war office of the death of her son, William at the front. Deceased was an apprentice at O'Keeffe's stone works and went out about the same time as young O'Reilly.

Grave or Memorial Reference: IV.D.11. Cemetery: Ixelles (Elsene) Communal Cemetery in Belgium.

ORGAN, Michael: Rank: Able Seaman. Regiment or Service: Mercantile Marine. Unit: SS *Dowlais* (Cardiff). Age at death: 31. Date of death: 3 December 1917.

Supplementary information: Son of Patrick Organ and Mary Organ, of Sarsfield Street, Abbeyside, Dungarvan, Co. Waterford. Born at Dungarvan. He has no known grave but is listed on the Tower Hill Memorial in the UK.

ORMOND, W.: Rank: Private 2nd Class. Regiment or Service: Royal Air Force. Unit: 18th Tent Detachment. Age at death: 33. Date of death: 29 December 1918. Service No: 286828.

Supplementary information: Husband of Mrs B. Ormond, of 32 Barrack Street, Waterford. Grave or Memorial Reference: S.IV.A.3. St Sever Cemetery Extension, Rouen in France.

O'ROURKE, James: Rank: Driver. Regiment or Service: Royal Horse Artillery and Royal Field Artillery. Unit: 112th Battery, 24th Brigade. Date of death: 9 November 1918. Service No: 36545. Born in Waterford. Enlisted in Waterford. Died of wounds. Grave or Memorial Reference: VII.N.12 A. Cemetery: Mont Huon Military Cemetery, Le-Treport in France.

O'ROURKE, John: Rank: Deck Hand. Regiment or Service: Royal Naval Reserve. Unit: H.M. Trawler *Strymon*. Age at death: 23. Date of death: 27 October 1917. Service No: 5559A. His residence is given as Boatstrand in *Waterford: Heroes, Poets and Villains.*

Supplementary information: Son of William and Margaret O'Rourke, of Dunabratton, Annestown, Co. Waterford. Grave or Memorial Reference: 24 on the Plymouth Naval Memorial, UK.

O'SHEA, James: Rank: Private. Regiment or Service: Royal Irish Regiment. Unit: 2nd Battalion. Age at death 25. Date of death: 29 October 1916. Service No: 8026. Born in Roscrea. Enlisted in Dungarvan Co. Waterford while living in Modeligo Co. Waterford. Killed in action.

Supplementary information: Husband of Mary Frances O'Shea of Modeligo. Grave or Memorial Reference: X.36. Cemetery: Kemmel Chateau Military Cametery.

O'SHEA, John: Rank: Gunner. Regiment or Service: Royal Horse Artillery and Royal Field Artillery. Unit: 81st Battery. Age at death: 24. Date of death: 20 December 1914. Service No: 52641. Born in Waterford. Enlisted in Stratford, London. Died of wounds.

Supplementary information: Stepson of Mrs Ada O'Shea, of 23, Morland Road, Walthamstow, London. Native of Waterford. Grave or Memorial Reference: III.B.27. Cemetery: Lillers Communal Cemetery in France.

O'SHEA, John: Rank: Lance Corporal. Regiment or Service: Royal Irish Regiment. Unit: 6th Battalion. Age at death: 32. Date of death: 7 June 1917. Service No: 4899. Born in Carrick-on-Suir, Co. Tipperary (Soldiers died in the Great War), Clishmuth, Carrick-on-Suir, Co. Waterford (Irelands Memorial Records) and enlisted in Wigan.

Supplementary information: Son of James and Margaret O'Shea, of Clasnasmuth, Ahenna, Carrick-on-Suir, Co. Tipperary. He has no known grave but is commemorated on Panel 33. Memorial: Ypres (Menin Gate) Memorial in Belgium.

O'SHEA, Joseph Bohan: Rank: Lance Corporal. Regiment or Service: Royal Engineers. Unit: 64th Field Coy. Age at death: 30. Date of death: 19 July 1916. Service No: 59553. Born in Waterford. Enlisted in Walthamstow, Essex. Killed in action.

Supplementary information: Son of Mr ad Mrs Joseph Bohan O'Shea, of 42 Grattan Terrace, Waterford. Husband of Mary Josephine O'Shea, of 42 Mount Sion Avenue, Waterford. Grave or Memorial Reference: III.L.10. Cemetery: Quarry Cemetery, Montauban in France.

O'SULLIVAN, James Eugene: Rank: Private. Regiment or Service: Machine Gun Corps (Infantry). Unit: 118th Coy. Age at death: 34. Date of death: 31 July 1917. Service No: 62946. Previously he was with the London Regiment where his number was 6669. Born in Waterford. Enlisted in London. Killed in action.

Supplementary information: Son of P.J. O'Sullivan. B.A. (Queen's College, Belfast) and Kate O'Sullivan of Waterford. He has no known grave but is listed on Panel 56 on the Ypres (Menin Gate) Memorial in Belgium.

OSWALD, Patrick: Rank: Private. Regiment or Service: Northumberland Fusiliers. Unit: 2nd Garrison Battalion. Date of death: 24 August 1918. Service No: 77357. Born in Waterford. Enlisted in Cardiff, Glams. Died in India. He has no known grave but is listed on Face 3 of the Kirkee 1914-18 Memorial in India.

O'TOOLE, James: Rank: Private. Regiment or Service: Royal Irish Fusiliers. Unit: 2nd Battalion. Date of death 14 March 1915. Service No: 10214. Born in Waterford. Enlisted in Carlow while living in Waterford. Killed in action. Has no known grave but is commemorated on Panel 42 on the Ypres (Menin Gate) Memorial in Belgium.

O'TOOLE, Thomas: Rank: Private. Regiment or Service: Household Cavalry and Cavalry of the line including the Yeomanry and Imperial Camel Corps. Unit: 2nd Dragoon Guards (Queens Bays.) Date of death: 31 October 1914. Service No: 6506. Born in St John's, Waterford. Enlisted in Waterford. Killed in action. Has no known grave but is commemorated on Panel 3. Memorial; Ypres (Menin Gate) Memorial in Belgium.

O'TOOLE, William: Rank: Bombardier. Regiment or Service: Royal Garrison Artillery. Unit: 50th Trench Mortar Battery. Date of death: 14 February 1916. Service No: 28603. Born in St. John's, Waterford. Enlisted in Waterford while living in Dungarvan, Co. Waterford. Killed in action. From the *Waterford News*, January 1916:

YET ANOTHER.

Bombardier W. O'Toole (28603), 32nd French [*sic*] Mortar Battery, B. E. F., France, writes—I belong to the city and have met some Waterford men out here. They are all enjoying the life, and we had a great chat together about the old place. The weather out here is cold and wet, but we all enjoy it (like young ducks) for we are content to know that our German cousins are situated just like ourselves. I am waiting anxiously to go back to the Urbs Intacta when this affair is over.

From the *Waterford News*, March 1916:

A FIGHTING FAMILY.

Bombardier O'Toole belonged to a fighting family. Two of his brothers were killed in the war, one on October, 1914, and the second in March, 1915. One of them belonged to the 2nd Dragoon Guards and the other to the Royal Irish Fusiliers. The deceased has another brother on active service in the navy. This is not a bad record for one family. Bombardier O'Toole had served in the R. F.A., and at the outbreak of the war got a transfer to an Irish Regiment. Sometime ago he was home on leave after being gassed. He was well known in Waterford and was very popular.

From the *Waterford News*, March 1916:

WATERFORD SOLDIER'S DEATH.

Mrs Annie Meyler, Castle Street, has received the following letter from the Officer Commanding 50 Trench Howitzer Battery R. F.A., with reference to the death of her brother, Bombardier – W. J. O'Toole – "It was with great regret that we learned that your brother was killed at St Aloi [*sic*] some days ago. He was a fine man and was at the time of his death under observation for a commission. Before his illness the way in which he stuck to his guns was one of my chief brags. This will be but little comfort to you in your loss which is ours also. He was buried near the village with two others who were killed at the same time. Death was instantaneous and took place during one of the counter-attacks following the loss of our trenches on the 14th and which were ultimately crowned with complete success. With what comfort I can offer. –I remain, etc., I. Williams. "

Has no known grave but is commemorated on Panel 9. Memorial: Ypres (Menin Gate) Memorial in Belgium.

OWEN, Arthur John: Rank: Battery Sergeant Major. Regiment or Service: Royal Field Artillery. Unit: H. Q. 42nd Brigade. Age at death: 38. Date of death: 26 October 1918. Service No: 17439 Awards: Twice Mentioned in Despatches. Born in Norwich, Norfolk. Enlisted in Great Yarmouth, Norfolk. Killed in action.

Supplementary information: Husband of Catherine Owen, of 90 Barrack Street, Waterford. Listed on the Langley War Memorial. Grave or Memorial Reference: I.A.3. Cemetery: Poix-Du-Nord Communal Cemetery Extension in France.

P

PAIMAL, Julian: Rank: Able Seaman. Regiment or Service: Mercantile Marine. Unit: SS *Pinewood* (London) Age at death: 32. Date of death: 17 February 1918.

Supplementary information: Son of Karl Paimal. Born in Estonia. Grave or Memorial Reference: East of church. Cemetery: Stradbally Church of Ireland Churchyard, Co. Waterford.

PALMER, Charles. Rank: Captain. Regiment or Service: King's Shropshire Light Infantry Age at death: 30. Date of death: 15 January 1916. Died. From 'Our Heroes':

> ...died in hospital in London as a result of wounds received in action about three months ago. Captain Palmer was a son of the late Mr Joseph W. Palmer, of Waterford, and a nephew of Miss Palmer, Mowbray Cottage, Tramore. He was educated at Waterford College, and subsequently at Liverpool College. He was subsequently appointed manager of important engineering works in China, but on the outbreak of the war he returned home to join the colours. He obtained his commission in the 5th King's Shropshire Light Infantry, and was promoted Captain in December last.

From the *Waterford News*, January 1916:

WATERFORD OFFICER'S DEATH.
Captain Charles Palmer.
We deeply regret to announce the death of Captain Charles Palmer, of the 6th Shropshire Light Infantry. The deceased was son of the late Mr Joseph W Palmer, formerly of Waterford, who died in Tramore about five years ago, and was nephew of Miss Palmer who at present resides at Mowbray Cottage, Tramore, and of the late Misses Firth, Lady Lane. The late Captain Palmer was a young man of about 30 years of age and was well known in this city. He was educated at Waterford College and by Mr O'Brien of Lady Lane, and subsequently at a Liverpool College. He went through a very successful course as a student and about nine years ago obtained an important appointment as manager of an engineering works in China. At the outbreak of war he relinquished his position and travelled home to England a distance of over 6, 000 miles to join the colours. He obtained a Lieutenancy in the 5th King's Shropshire Light Infantry and his abilities gained him rapid promotion, his appointment to a captain being gazetted on St Stephen's Day last. He went to the front about three months ago, and was wounded. He was sent home on short leave and although not feeling up to the mark he endeavoured to go back to the front again. His health completely broke down, however, and after a couple of days in a London Hospital he passed away ion Friday to the inexpressible regret of his relatives and intimate friends. The deceased's mother was formerly Miss Firth of Lady Lane, who died when he was quite young.

Those who knew "Charlie" Palmer recognised in him all the qualities which go to make a true gentleman. He was unassuming and generous and ever ready to oblige a friend. Of a bright and happy disposition he was the soul of good humour and he was most popular with all his acquaintances. The latter will join with us in tendering to his relatives sincere sympathy in their bereavement.

THE FUNERAL.
The remains of the late Captain Palmer who died in a London Hospital as a result of wounds received in France arrived here

on Wednesday by the Rosslare express, and were subsequently conveyed to Tramore and buried with military honours in the graveyard attached to the Church of the Holy Cross. The remains were accompanied to Portarlington Station by a party of soldiers and on arrival of the Rosslare express on Wednesday morning were met here by a detachment of military. The coffin was wrapped in a Union Jack and was borne to Tramore on an open hearse. The military including a firing party met the funeral on arrival in Tramore, and accompanied it to the church. A volley was fired over the grave and the "Last Post" sounded.

Grave or Memorial Reference: In southeast part. Cemetery: Tramore (Holy Cross) Catholic Churchyard, Co. Waterford.

PARKER, E.C.: Rank: Chief Officer. Regiment or Service: H.M. Coastguard. Date of death: 6 December 1919.

Supplementary information: Husband of Mrs Parker, of H.M. Coastguard Station, Helwick Head, Ring, Dungardan. Grave or Memorial Reference: G.A.17. Cemetery: Ballynaneashagh (St Otteran's) Catholic Cemetery in Co. Waterford.

PARKER, James Alexander: Rank: Lance Corporal. Regiment or Service: Royal Irish Rifles. Unit: 2nd Battalion. Age at death: 23. Date of death: 25 September 1915. Service No: 5197. Born in Templemichael, Co. Waterford. Enlisted in Cork. Killed in action.

Supplementary information: Son of John George and Mary Jane Parker, of 3 St Anthony's Villas, Friars Walk, Cork. He has no known grave but is listed on Panel 40 on the Ypres (Menin Gate) Memorial in Belgium.

PATCHELL, William Neville: Rank: Private. Regiment or Service: Royal Fusiliers (City of London Regiment.) Unit: 20th Battalion. Age at death: 25. Date of death:

16 July 1916. Service No: 5435. Born in Dungarvan, Co. Waterford. Enlisted in Belfast while living in Belfast. Killed in action.

Supplementary information: Son of William Anderson Patchell and Alice Louisa Patchell, of 45 Malone Avenue, Belfast. Educated at Portora Royal School, Enniskillen, Fermanagh. William Neville Patchell was listed as a member of the Peerage. He has no known grave but is listed on Pier and Face 8C 9A and 16A on the Thiepval Memorial in France.

PENDER, James: Rank: Rifleman. Regiment or Service: Royal Irish Rifles. Unit: 1st Battalion. ge at death: 21. Date of death: 2 July 1916. A Service No: 16130. Born in Kilkenny. Enlisted in Tonypandy, Glam while living in Ystrad, Glam. Died of wounds.

Supplementary information: Son of Michael and Bridget Pender, of Gauls Mills, Ferrybank, Waterford. Born at Kilmacow, Waterford. His brother Patrick also fell. Grave or Memorial Reference: Sp. Mem. Cemetery: Sanctuary Wood Cemetery, Ypres, Belgium.

PENDER, John: Rank: Private. Regiment or Service: Royal Irish Regiment. Unit: 1st Battalion. Date of death: 21 September 1918. Service No: 10445. Born in St Patrick's, Waterford. Enlisted in Clonmel, Co. Tipperary while living in Waterford. Killed in action in Palestine. Grave or Memorial Reference: J.39. Cemetery: Jerusalem War Cemetery, Israel.

PENDER, Patrick: Rank: Private. Regiment or Service: Royal Munster Fusiliers. Unit: 9th Battalion. Age at death: 26. Date of death: 01 May 1916. Service No: 3464. Born in Waterford. Enlisted in Tonpentre, South Wales while living in Tonpentre. Died of wounds at home.

Supplementary information: Son of Michael and Bridget Pender, of Gaul's Mills, Ferry Bank, Waterford. Native of Kilmacow, Co. Kilkenny. His brother James also fell. Grave or Memorial Reference: E.V.II. Cemetery: Dover (St James's) Cemetery, Kent, UK.

PENDER, Thomas: Rank: Cattleman. Regiment or Service: Mercantile Marine. Unit: SS *Coningbeg* (Glasgow). Torpedoed by German Submarine U-62. There were no survivors. U-62 surrendered in November 1918. Age at death: 37. Date of death: 18 December 1917.

Supplementary information: Son of Maurice and Bridget Pender, of 13 New Lane, Waterford. Born in Waterford. He has no known grave but is listed on the Tower Hill Memorial in the UK. He is also listed on the Formby-Coningbeg Memorial, Adelphi Quay in Waterford City.

PENROSE, John Samuel Sandford: Rank: Lieutenant Commander. Regiment or Service: Royal Navy. Unit: HMS *Bulwark*. Date of death: 26 November 1914. Age at death: 35. Gazetted, 3 January 1902.

Supplementary information: Son of Robert W.H. and Frances Alice Penrose Husband of Irene Hester Penrose. He is listed on the Waterford and District Roll of Honour. Located in Christ Church Cathedral (Church of Ireland), Henrietta Street, Waterford. Grave or Memorial Reference: 1. Portsmouth Naval Memorial, UK.

PERRY, Harry: Rank: Private. Regiment or Service: Wiltshire Regiment. Unit: 2nd Battalion. Age at death: 25. Date of death: 1 November 1914. Service No: 7714. Born in Derby. Enlisted in Woking, in Surrey while living in Wolverhampton, Staffordshire. Died of wounds.

Supplementary information: Son of James and Mary Donson, of 113 Whitecross Street, Derby. Husband of Annie Perry, of 28 Waterside, Waterford. Grave or Memorial Reference: II.A.23. Cemetery: Ypres Town Cemetery Extension in Belgium.

PERRY, Stanley Victor: Rank: Battery Sergeant Major. Regiment or Service: Canadian Field Artillery. Unit: 5th Brigade. Age at death: 29. Date of death: 20 April 1916. Service No: 87104.

Supplementary information: Son of Capt. and Mrs W.C. Perry. Husband of Sarah L. Perry, of Cove, Tramore, Waterford. Native of Old Charlton, London. Data from attestation papers:

In what Town, Township or Parish, and in what Country were you born? Woolwich, Kent.

What is the name of your next of kin? Mrs S V Perry.

What is the address of your next of kin? Tramore, Waterford, Ireland.

What is the relationship of your next of kin? Wife.

What is the date of your birth? 2 April 1886.

What is your trade or calling? Rancher.

Are you married? Yes.

Are you willing to be vaccinated or re-vaccinated? Yes.

Have you ever served in any Military Force? 10½ years Field Artillery.

Do you understand the nature and terms of your engagement? Yes.

Are you willing to be attested to serve in the Canadian Over-Seas Expeditionary Force? Yes.

Apparent age: 28 years 8 months.

Height: 5 Ft 10½ Ins.

Girth when fully expanded: 36½ Ins.

Range of expansion 3½ Ins.

Complexion: ruddy.

Eyes: blue.

Hair: brown.

Distinctive marks: none.

Date, 30 November: 1914.
Leithbridge Cenotaph;
Stanley Perry was born on April 2, 1880 in Kent, England to Mr and Mrs W. C. Perry. He was raised in England and as a young man, immigrated to Canada. He lived for a time with his wife, Sarah in Cranbrook, British Columbia. The couple later moved to the Lethbridge, Alberta area, where Stanley took up ranching. The Perry's were devout members of the Wesley Church in Lethbridge. Following

Stanley's enlistment, Sarah Perry and their only child took up residence in Ireland to wait out the war with her parents. On November 30, 1914, Stanley Perry enlisted with the 20th Battery 5th Brigade Canadian Field Artillery. He was one of the first Lethbridge area men to answer the call for service. Battery Sergeant Major Perry arrived in England on August 18, 1915 aboard the SS Metagama, and remained in England until embarking for France on January 15, 1916. He served in France and Belgium for 3 months with the men of the 5th Brigade CFA. On April 20, 1916, Battery Sergeant Major Perry was killed in action in Belgium. He was laid to rest at Dickebusch New Military Cemetery. Stanley Perry was awarded the British War Medal and Victory Medal. His wife, Sarah received the Memorial Cross and death plaque in honour of her husband.

Grave or Memorial Reference: J. 4. Cemetery: Dickiebusch New Military Cemetery in Belgium.

PETTIGREW, Douglas St George: Rank: Second Lieutenant. Regiment or Service: Sherwood Foresters (Notts and Derby Regiment). Unit: 14th Battalion. Attached to 17th Battalion. Age at death: 25. Date of death: 23 October 1917.

Supplementary information: Son of Robert William and Ella Pettigrew, of Penarth, Cardiff. Born Tramore, Co. Waterford. Severely wounded at Thiepval (Battle of the Somme), 7 October 1916. From De Ruvigny's Roll of Honour:

Pettigrew, Douglas St. George. 2nd Lieutenant, 14th, attached, 17th Battalion, The Sherwood Foresters (Nottinghamshire and Derbyshire Regiment), younger and only surviving son of Robert William Pettigrew, of Penarth, Cardiff, by his wife, Ella Elizabeth Leman, 2nd daughter of the late George Frederick Hare, of Limerick; and godson of the late William Pettigrew, of

Douglas St George Pettigrew. From De Ruvigny's Roll of Honour

Warrenpoint, County Down. Born at Tramore, Co. Waterford. 8-August-1892. Educated at Monkton Combe School, Bath, where he was a member of the O.T. C. Enlisted in the Public Schools Brigade, 15-Sept-1914. Gazetted 2nd Lieutenant, 14th Battalion. The Sherwood Foresters on 22 July 1916; severely wounded at Thiepval on 7 October 1916. Mortally wounded in action near Gheluvelt while leading his men on 22-October-1917. Died at No. 10 Casualty Clearing Station the following morning. D. St. G. Pettigrew came of a fighting stock, his great-great-grandfather having fought through the Peninsular War and at Waterloo. Volunteering immediately war was declared, he joined the Public Schools Brigade in the early days of Sept-1914. Went to France in Nov-1915, and as one of the Scouts of his Battalion, the 19th Royal Fusiliers (2nd Public Schools), took part in much patrol work between the trenches in Flanders during the winter of 1915-16. Being sent home for a commission in the spring of 1916. He was gazetted to the Sherwood Foresters in July. He went out again in September and was severely wounded in the fighting between the Ancre and the Somme outside Thiepval, in October-1916. After a complete recovery from his wounds at the end of seven months, he made his third and last journey to the front on 5 May 1917, and from that date was fighting on the stricken field of Ypres until he fell. All through the summer and into the autumn he had wonderful luck, never being hit. He came through the hard fighting which started on 20 Sept, (and in which the Sherwood's in a few days lost over fifty officers, killed and wounded) without a scratch, but the end came shortly afterwards. The Sherwood's were holding that part of the line known as the Tower Hamlets sector, and on Monday. 22 October. He and his Platoon were specially picked to take a couple of German "pill-boxes" on the side of the Ypres and Menin Road, between Hooge and Gheluvelt, west- north-west of the latter place. In leading the attack on which he was mortally wounded, and died at four o'clock the following morning (Tuesday, 23-October-1917). Buried in Lyssenthoek Military Cemetery. Poperinghe, in sure and certain hope of the Resurrection to eternal life, though our Lord Jesus Christ. He played the game. "In Flanders are the fields of fair renown." Only twenty- five, he was beloved by everybody. He had a genius for friendship, and had the affection and esteem of young and old, rich and poor together. His first Commanding Officer wrote:"I cannot tell you how grieved I was to hear he had been killed; he was one of those sure to be hit. the best always are." His Chaplain wrote: "He was one of the best loved Officers I have ever met, he was beloved, almost worshipped, by his men." His old Company Commander wrote "I was fortunate enough to have him in my company of the 19th Battalion. The Royal Fusiliers in France. He was in every way a splendid fellow, quite one of the best in A Coy, which I am proud to think contained a very large number of good fellows," and his servant : "He was idolized by his men, for he studied their every comfort, and always tried to better their condition, and cheer them. "He was very keen on flying (having been "up"). and was accepted for the Royal Flying Corps in August-1916, and would have been transferred to it that autumn, but for his going out to the front in September, the Sherwood's having been badly cut up in the fighting on the

Somme at that time. He put in again for it in the summer of 1917, and was expecting his transfer when he met his death. In the last letter he wrote home on Sunday, 21 October 1917, the day before he was mortally wounded, he said :"My application for the R.F.C. has gone past the Brigadier ; it has now been sent on to the division, so I am hoping to get my transfer any day now. " 'Dulce et decorum est pro patria mori.'

From the *Waterford News*, October 1917:

KILLED IN ACTION.
Second Lieutenant D. St. G. Pettigrew, Sherwood Foresters, reported killed, was a son of Mr and Mrs Pettigrew, formerly of Tramore, and a grandson of the late Mr W. Pettigrew. Warrenpoint.

Grave or Memorial Reference: XXII.B.17. Cemetery: Lijssenthoek Military Cemetery in Belgium.

PHELAN, Frank: Rank: Private. Regiment or Service: Northumberland Fusiliers. Unit: 26th Battalion (Tyneside Irish). Date of death: 1 July 1916. Age at death: 31. Service No: 26/550. Born in Waterford. Enlisted in Newcastle-on-Tyne. Killed in action.
Supplementary information: Husband of Ellen Coxon, (formerly Phelan), of 61 Norfolk Street, North Shields, Northumberland. Grave or Memorial Reference: 2.G.19. Cemetery: London Cemetery and Extension, Longueval in France.

PHELAN, James: Rank: Battery Sergeant Major. Regiment or Service: Royal Field Artillery. Unit: 113th Battery. 25th Brigade. Age at death: 35. Date of death: 19 July 1916. Service No: 29660. Born in Waterford. Enlisted in Liverpool, Lancashire. Died of wounds.
Supplementary information: Son of John and Alice Phelan, of Kilbarry, Waterford. Husband of E. Phelan, of Compass Hill, Kinsale, Co. Cork. From the *Waterford News*, August 1916:

DEATH OF KILBARRY SOLDIER.

We regret to announce the death in action of Battery Sergeant-Major J. Phelan, son of the late Mr John Phelan, Kilbarry. Sergeant-Major Phelan had been in the army for the past 17 years, and had been at the front since the beginning of hostilities. Before joining the army he was well-known in football circles in Waterford. His wife, who resides at Kinsale, County Cork, received the following letter from the Major of his battery; "It is with deep sympathy and regret I write about your husband. I did not know he had died from his wounds until we got back here a few days ago. He was hit, along with several others, by a shell. I bound up his wounds (head and face) and had him at once removed to the ambulance. We all thought that, although seriously wounded, it was not fatal. Your husband was a splendid type of battery Sergeant-Major, and although only a short time in my battery I had every confidence in him and was struck by his devotion to duty and the loyal support he gave me on all occasions. I miss him as a brave comrade and fine soldier very much. He would have risen to a high rank if he only had been spared. "

Grave or Memorial Reference: I.C.36. Cemetery: La Neuville British Cemetery, Corbie in France.

PHELAN, John: Rank: Private. Regiment or Service: Royal Irish Regiment. Unit: 1st Battalion. Age at death: 24. Date of death: 26 August 1919. Service No: 10565.

Supplementary information: Son of John Phelan, of 21 William Street, Portlaw, Co. Waterford. Grave or Memorial Reference: New. 679. Cemetery: Timperley (Christ Church) Churchyard, Cheshire, UK.

PHELAN, Michael: Rank: Able Seaman. Regiment or Service: Mercantile Marine. Unit: SS *Coningbeg* (Glasgow). Torpedoed by German Submarine U-62. There were no survivors. U-62 surrendered in November 1918. Age at death: 63. Date of death: 18 December 1917.

Supplementary information: Son of the late Michael and Catherine Phelan. Husband of the late Margaret Phelan. Born in Waterford. He has no known grave but is listed on the Tower Hill Memorial in the UK. He is also listed on the Formby-Coningbeg Memorial, Adelphi Quay in Waterford City.

PHELAN, Patrick: Rank: Private. Regiment or Service: Royal Irish Regiment. Unit: 2nd Battalion. Age at death: 32. Date of death: 19 October 1914. Service No: 8410. Born in Waterford. Enlisted in Liverpool while living in Kilmacthomas, Co. Waterford. Killed in action.

Supplementary information: Son of Mrs Mary Phelan, of Kilnagrange, Kilmacthomas, Co. Waterford. Grave or Memorial Reference: 11 and 12 on the Le Touret Memorial in France.

PHELAN, William: Rank: Private. Regiment or Service: Leinster Regiment. Unit: 7th Battalion. Date of death: 22 April 1916. Service No: 3298. Born in Waterford. Enlisted in Waterford. Died of wounds. Grave or Memorial Reference: I.D.11 Cemetery: Aire Communal Cemetery in France.

PIGOTT, William Gregory: Rank: Rifleman. Regiment or Service: Royal Irish Rifles. Unit: 15th Battalion. Age at death: 33. Date of death: 21 September 1918. Service No: 41200. Previously he was with the 4th Hussars where his number was 24620. Enlisted in Tralee, County Kerry while living in Portlaw. Killed in action.

Supplementary information: Son of George and the late May Pigott, of Kells, Co. Meath. Husband of Maria Alicia Pigott, of 3 William Street, Portlaw, Co. Waterford. Grave or Memorial Reference: In north-west part. Cemetery: Veldwezelt Communal Cemetery in Belgium.

PITTAWAY, Arthur: Rank: Private. Regiment or Service: Household Cavalry and Cavalry of the line including the Yeomanry and Imperial Camel Corps. Unit: Corps of Lancers, 5th (Royal Irish). Date of death: 23 March 1918. Service No: 6013. Born in Waterford. Enlisted in Waterford. Killed in action. He has no known grave but is listed on Panel 3 on the Pozières Memorial in France.

POOLE, Albert: Rank: Stoker 1st Class. Regiment or Service: Royal Navy. Unit: HMS *Tiger*. Date of death: 31 May 1916. Service No: K/23607. Born in Waterford. Died during the Battle of Jutland.

Supplementary information: Died on the first day of the Battle of Jutland. Grave or Memorial Reference: 16. Portsmouth Naval Memorial, UK.

POOLE, Walter Croker: Rank: Lieutenant. Regiment or Service: Royal Naval Volunteer Reserve. Unit: HM 'Mersey Examination Vessel No. 1.' Age at death: 65. Date of death: 28 December 1917.

Supplementary information: Son of William Crawford Poole (M.D., J.P.), of Glendysart House, Ardmore, Co. Waterford. Husband of Arabella Henrietta Poole, of 527 New Chester Road, Rock Ferry, Birkenhead. Captain in the Pacific Steamship Company for many years. Grave or Memorial Reference: 28. Memorial, Portsmouth Naval Memorial, UK. He is also listed on the Men of Christ Church Claughton, Christ Church, Merseyside, England.

POPE, Herbert (Bertie): Rank: Trooper. Regiment or Service: Australian Light Horse. Unit: 10th. Age at death: 20. Date of death: 7 August 1915. Service No: 631. Killed in action at Walker's Ridge, Gallipoli. Enlisted 19 October 1914 in Guildford, Western Australia. Killed in action. Data from attestation papers:

In or near what Parish or Town were you born? Waterford, Ireland.

Are you a natural born British subject or a Naturalised British subject? Yes.

What is your age? 22 years 6 months.

What is your trade or calling? Farmer.

Are you married? No.

Who is your next of kin? Mr Noel R Mullally, Dunedin.

Have you ever been convicted by the Civil Power? No.

Do you now belong to, or have you ever served in, His Majesty's Army, the Marines,

Have you stated the whole, if any, of your previous service? Yes

Age, 22 years, 6 months. Height 6 feet, ½ inches. Weight, 160 lbs. Chest measurement: 37-40 inches.

Complexion, dark.

Eyes: blue. Hair: dark.

Religious denomination: R. C.

Entered Gallipoli on 16 May 1915.

Supplementary information: Son of William Pope, of Waterford, Ireland. Mothers address: Mrs E/ Pope, C/o E. Harvey Esq, K. C., Lamb Building, Temple, London. Pension including money due (£38 plus £1 16s 9d per fortnight)) was awarded to Elizabeth Pope, Brook House, Pinner, Middlesex. Initially recorded as being buried at Shrapnel Terrace. Exhumed later (1922) and the means of identifying his grave in Shrapnel Terrace was his name on a tin plate that lay on top. From the *Waterford News*, September 1915:

WATERFORDMAN KILLED AT THE DARDANELLES.

We regret to learn of the death in action at the Dardanelles of Mr Bertie Pope, son of Mr William Pope, late of Belvedere, Waterford, and now residing in Canada. The news was received by a Waterford gentleman in a letter from a friend in London.

Young Mr Pope was only 21 years of age, and was of exceptionally fine physique, being 6 feet 4 inches high and proportionally built. The writer of the letter referred to stated that "he was the tallest and finest of all the fine Australians. "He went to Australia four or five years ago and was doing very well there, having a considerable farm of land. He joined the Australian Forces after the outbreak of war and was killed at the Dardanelles on the 7th August.

Mr Pope belonged to one of Waterford's oldest and most respected families. His father, Mr William Pope, was ver popular in this city, and his mother was a member of the Harney family who lived at Killotteran House.

Deceased was a nephew of the Hon. E.A. Harley, K.C., late Senator of the Australian Commonwealth, and now in active practice at the London Bar. Mr Harney, who formerly lived with his father and brothers and sisters at Killotteran House, was for some time at the Irish Bar, and was a well known member of it until he left Ireland for Australia. His career in Australia was exceptionally brilliant, and not only did he make a name for himself in the Commonwealth Parliament, but he rose to the highest position at the Bar, that of Attorney-General.

The news of young Mr Pope's death will be learned with regret in this, his native city.

He is also listed in De Ruvigny's Roll of Honour. Grave or Memorial Reference: II.C.5. Walker's Ridge Cemetery in Turkey.

POWELL, (Soldiers died in the Great War) **POWER,** (The Commonwealth War Graves Commission) **Edward:** Rank: Gunner. Regiment or Service: Royal Garrison Artillery Unit: 43rd Siege Battery. Date of death: 19 August 1917. Service No: 43060. Born in Waterford. Enlisted in Merthyr Tydvil, Glamorgan while living in Waterford. Died of wounds in Salonika. This man is listed under both Power and Powell.

Supplementary information: Husband of Catherine Power, of 218 Old Road., Gellyalog, Penydarren, Merthyr Tydvil. Grave or Memorial Reference: 1144. Cemetery: Salonika (Lembet Road) Military Cemetery in Greece.

POWER, Augustine: Rank: Private. Regiment or Service: Royal Irish Regiment. Unit: 2nd Battalion. Age at death: 23. Date of death: 24 May 1915. Service No: 10899. Born in Dungarvan, Co. Waterford. Enlisted in Dungarvan while living Waterford. Killed in action.

Supplementary information: Son of John and Mary Power, of David Street, Dungarvan, Co. Waterford. John Power had three sons who were killed in the war (*Waterford News*, November 1915). Grave or Memorial

Waterford News. 1914. Volunteers crossing the bridge at Waterford.

Reference: VI.B.3. Cemetery: Duhallow A.D.S. Cemetery in Belgium.

has no known grave but is listed on Panel 3 on the Pozières Memorial in France.

POWER, Christopher: Rank: Private. Regiment or Service: Royal Irish Regiment. Unit: 2nd Battalion. Age at death: 19. Date of death: 24 May 1915. Service No: 10953. Born in Trinity Without, Waterford. Enlisted in Waterford. Died of wounds.

Supplementary information: Son of Maurice and Kate Power, of 6 Gaffney's Place, Waterford. Grave or Memorial Reference: II.B.2. Cemetery: Hazebrouck Communal Cemetery, Nord, in France.

POWER, Christopher: Rank: Trimmer. Regiment or Service: Mercantile Marine. Unit: SS *Royal Edward* (Toronto). Sunk by a torpedo from German submarine U-14. Age at death: 17. Date of death: 13 August 1915.

Supplementary information: Born in Waterford. He has no known grave but is listed on the Tower Hill Memorial in the UK.

POWER, Christopher: Rank: Private. Regiment or Service: The Loyal North Lancashire Regiment. Unit: 1st/4th Battalion. Age at death: 25. Date of death: 21 July 1917. Service No: 202129. Born in Waterford. Enlisted in Horwich, Lancs, while living in Waterford. Killed in action.

Supplementary information: Son of Mr and Mrs Thomas Power, of 25 Lower Newtown, Waterford. Grave or Memorial Reference: I.H.8. Cemetery: Vlamertinghe New Military Cemetery in Belgium.

POWER, Daniel: Rank: Shoeing Smith. Regiment or Service: Household Cavalry and Cavalry of the line including the Yeomanry and Imperial Camel Corps. Unit: Corps of Lancers, 5th Lancers (Royal Irish). Date of death: 1 April 1918. Service No: 3780. Born in Waterford. Enlisted in Waterford. Died of wounds. Grave or Memorial Reference: He

POWER, David: Rank: Private. Regiment or Service: Machine Gun Corps. Unit: Infantry, 34th Company. Date of death: 10 June 1917. Age at death: 20. Service No: 43213. Formerly he was with the Royal Field Artillery where his number was 77185. Born in Waterford. Enlisted in March [*sic*] while living in Waterford. Killed in action.

Supplementary information: Son of John and Mary Power, of 45 Lower Grange, Waterford. He has no known grave but is listed on Panel 56 on the Ypres (Menin Gate) Memorial in Belgium.

POWER, David: Rank: Private. Regiment or Service: Australian Salvage Corps. Unit: 1st Coy. Age at death: 39. Date of death: 23 February 1917. Service No: 1057 Enlisted 17 September 1914 in Camperdown, Victoria. Died of disease. Son of John and Mary Power, of Waterford. Data from attestation papers:

In or near what Parish or Town were you born? Ballytruckle, (In another copy of this document it states 'Ballybricken') Waterford, Ireland.

Are you a natural born British subject or a Naturalised British subject? Yes.

What is your age? 24 years.

What is your trade or calling? Labourer.

Are you married? No.

Who is your next of kin? Kathleen Power, [sister] 18 St Johns Avenue (changed from Adelphi Terrace), Waterford.

Have you ever been convicted by the Civil Power? Yes

Do you now belong to, or have you ever served in, His Majesty's Army, the Marines, the Militia, the Militia Reserve, the Territorial Reserve, Royal Navy or Colonial Forces?, If so, state which, and if not now serving, state cause of discharge Yes, The King's Liverpool Regiment, Discharged, Time expired.

Have you stated the whole, if any, of your previous service? Yes.

Age: 34 years, months.

Height: 5 feet, 6 inches.

Weight: 140 lbs.

Chest measurement: inches.

Complexion: fresh.

Eyes: brown. Hair: dark brown.

Religious denomination: R. C.

Distinctive marks, Commencing rupture, 17 September 1914, rupture has been operated on and cured. Three parcels of personal effects were sent to Kathlene Power, Adelphi Terrace, Waterford, and one parcel to her at 18 John's Avenue Waterford.

Hospitalised twice, with a shrapnel wound to the mouth (St Andrews Hospital, Malta the Hospital ship to England), shrapnel wound to the left hand in Gallipoli, Bron Catarrh (in France) and died of lobar Pneumonia in No 1 Australian. General. Hospital, Rouen in France.

I include the below for your reference. He is the only Australian soldier to die in February-1917 with a Waterford connection. From the *Waterford News*, March 1917:

AUSTRALIAN SOLDIER'S DEATH.

Amongst many gallant Australian soldiers killed at the Dardanelles was Private Bertie Power, whose father, Mr Thomas Power, left Woodstown, near Waterford, for Australia many years ago. The late Private Power was a cousin of Mr Thomas Power, J. P., Callaghane, and a nephew of Mrs J. Hurley, Main Street, carrick-on-Suir, and of Mr Martin Power, J. P., Co. C., Ballygunntertemple, Waterford.

John Power had three sons who were killed in the war (*Waterford News*, November, 1915)

Grave or Memorial Reference: O. VI. J. 6. Cemetery: St Sever Cemetery Extension, Rouen in France.

POWER, Edward: Rank: Private. Regiment or Service: Royal Irish Regiment. Unit: 2nd Battalion. Date of death: 19 October 1914. Service No: 6061. Born in Stradbally Waterford. Enlisted in Kilmacthomas, Co. Waterford. Killed in action. He has no known grave but is listed on Panels 11 and 12 on the Le Touret Memorial in France.

POWER, Edward: Rank: Private. Regiment or Service: Royal Irish Regiment. Unit: 2nd Battalion. Date of death: 17 May 1915. Service No: 3028. Born in Slieverue, County Kilkenny. Enlisted in Tipperary while living in Waterford. Died of wounds at home.

Supplementary information: Son of Michael and Margaret Power, of 29 Peter Street, Waterford. Grave or Memorial Reference: D. 2477. Cemetery: Cambridge City Cemetery, UK.

POWER, Edward: See **POWELL, Edward:**

POWER, J. Rank: Private. Regiment or Service: Royal Marine Light Infantry. Unit: Plymouth Battalion. Royal Naval Division. Age at death: 23. Date of death: 4 March 1915. Service No: PLY/240(S).

Supplementary information: Son of Thomas Power, of Ballintlea, Mullinavat, Waterford. He has no known grave but is listed on Panel 2 to 7 on the Helles Memorial in Turkey.

POWER, James Aloysius: Rank: Able Seaman. Regiment or Service: Royal Navy. Unit: HMS *Nasturtium*. Age at death: 28. Date of death: 27 April 1916. Service No: SS/2237. Died when the HMS *Nasturtium* hit a sea-mine near Malta. He is listed in *The Fleet Annual and Naval Year Book*.

Supplementary information: Son of James and Margaret Power, of Waterford. From the *Waterford News*, May 1916:

WATERFORD NAVY MANS DEATH.

My James Power, 111 Gracedien Road, Waterford, has received a letter from the Admiralty informing him of the death of his third son, James, A Power. The communication is signed by the Accountant-General of the Navy, and runs as follows; "I regret to have to inform you that HMS ---was sunk by a mine on the night of the 27th-28th April, and that James Aloysius Power, A. B., official number SS2237, who was on board at the time, is reported to be missing. In these circumstances, it is feared that, in the absence of any evidence to the contrary, he must be regarded as having lost his life." Mr and Mrs Power have received a message of sympathy from the King and Queen on their bereavement. Deceased was well-known in this city. He was quite a young man, was educated at Mount Sion, and was very popular with all who knew him. He had been some years in the Navy.

Grave or Memorial Reference: 12 on the Plymouth Naval Memorial, UK.

POWER, James: Rank: Fireman and Trimmer. Regiment or Service: Mercantile Marine. Unit: SS *Constantia* (London). Age at death: 37. Date of death: 8 May 1918. Torpedoed off Scarborough by German Submarine U-21.

Supplementary information: Son of John Power, and the late Bridget Power (*née* Doran). Born in Waterford. He has no known grave but is listed on the Tower Hill Memorial in the UK.

POWER, James: Rank: Private. Regiment or Service: New Zealand Reinforcements. Unit: 40th. Occupation on Enlistment, driver. Date of death: 5 September 1918. Service No: 79406. Next of Kin: J. Power (father), Co. Waterford, Ireland. Died of disease at sea en route to England and buried at sea.

Supplementary information: Son of Mr and Mrs James Power, of Raheen, Kirmeaden, Co. Waterford, Ireland. Grave or Memorial Reference: He has no know grave but is listed on the Wellington Provincial Memorial, Wellington, New Zealand.

POWER, James: Rank: Private. Regiment or Service: Connaught Rangers. Unit: 1st Battalion. Date of death: 5 June 1916 (Soldiers died in the Great War), 5 May 1916 (The Commonwealth War Graves Commission and Irelands Memorial Records). Service No: 8085. Born in Waterford. Enlisted in Waterford while living in Waterford. Died in Mespotamia. Grave or Memorial Reference: XX.C.3. Cemetery: Amara War Cemetery in Iraq.

POWER, James: Rank: Private. Regiment or Service: Royal Irish Regiment. Unit: 2nd Battalion. Date of death: 20 October 1914. Service No: 6409. Born in Ballybricken, Co. Waterford. Enlisted in Waterford. Killed in action.

Supplementary information: Grave or Memorial Reference: Sainghin-En-Weppes German Cemetery Memorial. Cemetery: Sainghin-En-Weppes Communal Cemetery in France.

POWER, James: Rank: Private. Regiment or Service: Royal Irish Regiment. Unit: 1st Battalion. Age at death: 33. Date of death: 1 May 1915. Service No: 9185. Born in St James, Dublin. Enlisted in Waterford while living in Ballyduff, Co. Waterford. Killed in action.

Supplementary information: Son of Alice Power, of Ballyduff, Kilmeaden, Co. Waterford. He has no known grave but is listed on Panel 33 on the Ypres (Menin Gate) Memorial in Belgium.

POWER, John: Rank: Private. Regiment or Service: Irish Guards. Unit: 1st Battalion. Date of death: 27 September 1916. Service No: 10035. Born in Grenan, Co. Waterford. Enlisted in Waterford. Died of wounds.

Supplementary information: Son of Martin and Mary Power, of Ballyshunock, Newtown, Kilmacthomas, Co. Waterford. Grave or Memorial Reference: XI.C.16. Cemetery: Etaples Military Cemetery in France.

POWER, John: Rank: Private. Regiment or Service: Royal Irish Regiment. Unit: 2nd

Battalion. Age at death: 30. Date of death: 30 May 1915. Service No: 7602. Born in St Patrick's, Waterford. Enlisted in Waterford. Died of wounds at Home.

Supplementary information: Husband of Mrs K. Power, of 6 New Street, Waterford. Grave or Memorial Reference: II.G.2. Cemetery: Roeselare Communal Cemetery in Belgium.

POWER, John: Rank: Private. Regiment or Service: Royal Munster Fusiliers. Unit: 1st Battalion. Age at death: 23. Date of death: 2 September 1918. Service No: 10259. Born in Waterford. Enlisted in Cork. Killed in action.

Supplementary information: Son of Patrick and Bridget Power of Ballykerogue, Co. Wexford. Grave or Memorial Reference: E.23. Cemetery: Upton Wood Cemetery, Hendecourt-Les-Cagnicourt in France.

POWER, John: Rank: Sailor. Regiment or Service: Mercantile Marine. Unit: SS *Dowlais* (Cardiff). Age at death: 25. Date of death: 3 December 1917.

Supplementary information: Son of Patrick and Kate Power, of Home Rule Street, Abbeyside, Dungarvan, Co. Waterford. He has no known grave but is listed on the Tower Hill Memorial in the UK.

POWER, John: Rank: Private. Regiment or Service: Royal Fusiliers (City of London Regiment.) Unit: 4th Battalion. Date of death: 27 December 1915. Service No: G/14624, (Soldiers died in the Great War) and 14624 (The Commonwealth War Graves Commission). Born in Ballybricken. Enlisted in Nenagh while living in Waterford. Killed in action. Grave or Memorial Reference: A.6. Cemetery: Dickiebusch New Military Cemetery in Belgium.

POWER, John: Rank: Rifleman. Regiment or Service: Royal Irish Rifles. Unit: 1st Battalion. Date of death: 13 May 1915. Service

No: 5390. Born in Slieverue, Co. Waterford. Enlisted in Waterford. Died of wounds. Grave or Memorial Reference: I.C.20. Cemetery: Laventie Military Cemetery, La Gorgue, Nord in France.

POWER, John: Rank: Private. Regiment or Service: Royal Army Service Corps. Unit: Number 2 Remounts Company. Date of death: 10 April 1918. Service No: R/358421 (Soldiers died in the Great War), T/1358421 (Commonwealth Wargraves Commission). Born in Waterford. Enlisted in Waterford while living in Waterford. Died at Home. Grave or Memorial Reference: H.K.975. Cemetery: Thetford Cemetery in Norfolk, UK.

POWER, John: Rank: Private. Regiment or Service: Royal Irish Regiment. Unit: 2nd Battalion. Date of death: 14 July 1916. Service No: 4744. Born in St Patrick's, Waterford. Enlisted in Waterford. Killed in action. He has no known grave but is listed on Pier and Face 3A and 16C on the Thiepval Memorial in France.

POWER, John: Rank: Unknown. Regiment or Service: SS *Burmese Prince*. The only information I have on this sailor is contained in the below. From the *Waterford News*, 14 May 1915:

WATERFORD SAILOR BURIED AT SEA.
Mr John Mitchell, of No 1 Wilkinsin Street, Barnsley, writes to us stating that he was a shipmate of John Power, of Waterford, in the Steamship "Burmese Prince" and that Power died on board and was buried at sea on April 5th. Mr Mitchell says that he can give any of the dead sailors friends all details about him. He was about forty years of age, of dark complexion, and weighed about 11 stone.

POWER, Joseph: Rank: Private. Regiment or Service: Duke of Cornwall's Light Infantry. Unit: 6th Battalion. Date of death: 18 August

1916. Service No: 19150. Enlisted in Co. Waterford, while living in Galdy's Yard, Co. Waterford. Killed in action. He has no known grave but is listed on Pier and Face 6B on the Thiepval Memorial in France.

POWER, Martin: Rank: Private. Regiment or Service: Irish Guards. Unit: 1st Battalion. Date of death: 10 October 1917. Service No: 10362. Born in Carrickbeg, Co. Waterford. Enlisted in Carrick-on-Suir, County Tipperary. Killed in action.

Supplementary information: Son of Thomas Power. He has no known grave but is listed on Panels 10 and 11 on the Tyne Cot Memorial in Belgium.

POWER, Michael: Rank: Private. Regiment or Service: Royal Irish Regiment. Unit: 2nd Battalion. Date of death: 19 October 1914. Service No: 6291. Born in St Patrick's, Waterford. Enlisted in Waterford. Killed in action. He has no known grave but is listed on Panels 11 and 12 on the Le Touret Memorial in France

POWER, Michael: Rank: Donkeyman. Regiment or Service: Mercantile Marine. Unit: SS *Livington Court* (Liverpool). Age at death: 59. Date of death: 6 December 1917.

Supplementary information: Son of the late Lawrence, and Catherine Power. Born in Waterford. Grave or Memorial Reference: He has no known grave but is listed on the Tower Hill Memorial in the UK.

POWER, Michael: Rank: Private. Regiment or Service: Royal Irish Regiment. Unit: 2nd Battalion. Date of death: 27 October 1917. Service No: 1991. Born in St Patrick's, Waterford. Enlisted in Waterford. Died at Home.

Supplementary information: Son of Patrick Power, of 2 Little Patrick Street, Waterford. Grave or Memorial Reference: A. Ba. 99. Cemetery: Ballynaneashagh (St Otteran's) Catholic Cemetery in Co. Waterford.

POWER, Michael: Rank: Private. Regiment or Service: Irish Guards. Unit: 2nd Battalion. Age at death: 30. Date of death: 23 October 1915. Service No: 5824. Born in Dungarvan, Co. Waterford. Enlisted in Dungarvan. Died of wounds.

Supplementary information: Son of John and Mary Power, of Dungarvan. Husband of Margaret Power, of Patrick Street, Dungarvan, Co. Waterford. John Power had three sons who were killed in the war (*Waterford News*, November 1915). Grave or Memorial Reference: A.13.33. Cemetery: ST. Sever Cemetery, Rouen in France.

POWER, Michael: Rank: Private. Regiment or Service: Irish Guards. Unit: 1st Battalion. Date of death: 17 February 1915. Service No: 2260. Born in Stradbally Co. Waterford and enlisted in Waterford while living in Thurles.

Supplementary information: Husband of K. Power, of Quarry Street, Thurles, Co. Tipperary. From the *Waterford News*, 1915:

LETTER FROM IRISH GUARDS CHAPLAIN.
Mr W Power, c/o Mr T Conway, Broad Street, Waterford, has received a postcard, dated February 26th, from Private John Downes, of the Irish Guards (now in hospital) informing him of the death of his brother, Private Michael Power, of the Irish Guards, who was killed in action. The writer adds: "You may be after hearing it by now, as the priest wrote to his wife in Thurles and told her he was with him when he died. I was very sorry after him, as we were great chums. I myself am badly wounded."

The letter from the clergyman to deceased's wife was as follows:

Irish Guards,
B. E. F., France,
February 18th.
Dear Mrs Power—I am ever so sorry to have to tell you that your husband, Private M. Power, of the Irish Guards, was killed yesterday in the trenches. As I judged, he was not dead when I saw him. I gave him

Extreme Unction, so that ought to be a great consolation to you. As the brave men have had every opportunity of going to Confession and Communion, I am sure your husband availed himself of it. I shall remember him at my Mass, and ask God to give you strength and grace to bear this heavy cross. –I am, dear Mrs Power, yours sincerely.

John Gwynn, S. J.
Catholic Chaplain to the
Irish Guards.

Grave or Memorial Reference: II.D.5. Cemetery: Cuinchy Communal Cemetery in France.

POWER, Michael: Rank: Private. Regiment or Service: Wiltshire Regiment. Unit: 5th Battalion. Age at death: 26. Date of death: 5 April 1916. Service No: 20942. Born in Dunhill, Co. Waterford. Enlisted in Devizes, Wilts while living in Waterford. Killed in action in Mesopotamia.

Supplementary information: Son of Patrick and Kate Power, of Powersnock, Kilmeaden, Co. Waterford. Grave or Memorial Reference: 30 and 64 on the Basra Memorial in Iraq.

POWER, Michael: Rank: Private. Regiment or Service: Royal Irish Regiment. Unit: 2nd Battalion. Age at death: 20. Date of death: 24 May 1915. Service No: 6317. Born in Kill, Co. Waterford. Enlisted in Waterford while living in Bunmahon, Co. Waterford. Killed in action.

Supplementary information: Son of Robert and Ellen Power, of Ballinasisla, Bonmahon, Co. Waterford. He has no known grave but is listed on Panel 33 on the Ypres (Menin Gate) Memorial in Belgium.

POWER, Michael: Rank: Stoker 1st Class. Regiment or Service: Royal Navy. Unit: (RFR/DEV/IC/303). HMS *Goliath*. Age at death: 35. Date of death: 13 May 1915. Service No: SS/101956. HMS *Goliath* was sunk by

three torpedoes from German destroyer *Muvanet-I-Milet*, she blew up and capsized immediately taking 570 of her 750 crew including the Captain to a watery grave. Ten Waterford men died on the *Goliath* that day.

Supplementary information: Son of Michael and Hannah Power, of Convent Street, Tallow, Co. Waterford. Grave or Memorial Reference: 6 on the Plymouth Naval Memorial, UK.

POWER, Patrick: Rank: Private. Regiment or Service: Royal Irish Regiment. Unit: 6th Battalion. Date of death: 17 August 1918. Service No: 11269. Born in Ballinameela, Co. Waterford. Enlisted in Dungarvan, Co. Waterford. While living in Ballinameela, Co. Waterford. Killed in action. Grave or Memorial Reference: I.A.12. Cemetery: St Patrick's Cemetery, Loos in France.

POWER, Patrick: Rank: Private. Regiment or Service: Royal Dublin Fusiliers. Unit: 1st Battalion. Age at death: 45. Date of death: 22 December 1915. Service No: 23096. Born in Tramore, Co. Waterford. Enlisted in Northwick. Killed in action in Gallipoli.

Supplementary information: Son of Patrick and Helen Power, of Co. Waterford. Grave or Memorial Reference: II.E.8. Cemetery: Twelve Tree Copse Cemetery in Turkey.

POWER, Patrick: The only information I have on this sailor is contained in the below. He is not in any of the War Dead databases. *Waterford News,* January 1917:

Dungarvan Sailor Killed on board Ship.
The sad intelligence has come to hand of the death on board ship of a sailor from Abbeyside, Dungarvan, named Patrick Power. He was thirty-one years of age, and held the permanent position among the crew. It appears he was called to go on watch at five o'clock in the morning, when the ship was somewhere in the Bay of Biscay, bound for Truro, and walking along

the deck, it being quite dark, he fell into the hold to a depth of forty feet, and was killed instantly. The news was sent to the Rev. P. Byrne, P. P., Abbeyside, and conveyed to the poor mother, who is heart-broken, as the son was her chief mainstay, always sending her the greater portion of his wages. The remains were taken on shore to the nearest island and interred. The greatest sympathy is expended to the poor mother in her great affliction.

POWER, Paul: Rank: Private. Regiment or Service: Royal Irish Regiment. Unit: 2nd Battalion. Date of death: 3 September 1916. Service No: 7673. Born in Ballybricken, Co. Waterford. Enlisted in Waterford. Killed in action. Grave or Memorial Reference: XV.M.5. Cemetery: Delville Wood Cemetery, Longueval in France.

POWER, Pierce: Rank: Private. Regiment or Service: Leinster Regiment. Unit: 2nd Battalion. Age at death: 30. Date of death: 12 April 1917. Service No: 3524. Born in Waterford. Enlisted in Birr, King's County. Killed in action.

Supplementary information: Son of James and the late Mary Power, of 48 John Street, Waterford. From the *Waterford News* July 1916.

WATERFORD SOLDIER DESCRIBES THE GREAT ADVANCE.

Four of the Messrs Power, 48 John Street, are in the Army, two in Salonika and two in France. Miss D Power has received from one of her brothers, Mr Pierce Power, a very interesting letter describing how he was wounded in the opening stages of the great offensive, which began on Saturday, July 1st.

Netley Hospital.
Southampton.
8th July, 1916.
Dear Sister—Just a letter to inform you that I am in hospital in England, wounded. I was in the great advance and was wounded on Tuesday morning, 4th July, in the right side, but not dangerously, thank God. After a long and tedious voyage I arrived here this morning about 4, 30. We had a great and glorious victory over the Kaiser's dirty crew, They fought very hard for the first hour. It was at 7, 30 on Saturday morning it began. The Germans were taken rather by surprise, for at ten to eight their first line of trenches were taken, and a little later their second, and so on. They surrendered in drives that evening. The next morning the battlefield presented a horrible sight. It was covered with dead bodies, both Germans and British. In some cases they fought like tigers because they were dead locked in each others arms. Young Eustace was killed on Tuesday morning. Jack Hearne met a sad death on 29th June, poor fellow. Young Tobin, Waterside, was slightly wounded. If you only saw the positions we took from the Huns you would say we were marvellous men. I must say a special word of praise to the Gordon Highlanders. Everyone of them fought as though he had the strength of a lion. We knocked hell out of them with bombs. Village after village fell into our hands. It wasn't the poor girls or priests of Belgium they were up against this time. They'll remember the boys of the Old Brigade, I tell you. Some of them were on their knees begging for mercy. They got it, too, I don't think. It was the finest thing at all to go through their dug-outs the following day, They appeared to me to be a fresh Regiment from Belgium, because everyone of them had new clothes, new leggings, watches and jewellery galore. The contents of their pack consisted of three different classes of bread, white, brown and fancy. Their dug-outs were fitted out with beds of the latest German design, cold stores, etc. Their dug-outs were twenty four feet below the surface of the ground, and running down the right-hand side were electric bells. They had boxes of fruit, wine, beer, and maybe we didn't drink their health for them. They made up their minds to settle down forever in France, but they got a

nasty knock on Saturday. The only thing I regret is that I lost all my relics when I was wounded–in fact, everything, rifle and ammunition, everything I possessed.

One more word before I finish, Don't any of you in the house be the least bit worried about me as, thank God, except for my wound, I am otherwise in good health. I daresay I will be a month or five weeks here, and then twelve days on glorious furlough at home in the old country, Best love to Eileen, Leslie, Jack, Bill, Cissie, Jim and yourself, mother and father. Let me know if mother got the money yet. Write by return. Send no papers only local ones and Lloyd's. Good bye now– From your fond brother.

Pierce.

Cheer up!! I will soon be home.

Grave or Memorial Reference: I.B.12. Cemetery: Sucrerie Cemetery, Ablain-St-Nazaire in France.

POWER, Richard: Rank: Pioneer. Regiment or Service: Royal Engineers. Unit: 'K' Special Coy. Age at death: 30. Date of death: 20 September 1918. Service No: 192743. Previously he was with the Royal Field Artillery where his number was 79367. Born in Cappoquin, Co. Waterford. Enlisted in Dungarvan, Co. Waterford while living in Cappoquin, Co. Waterford. Killed in action.

Supplementary information: Son of Richard and Honora Power, of Main Street, Cappoquin, Co. Waterford. Grave or Memorial Reference: M.5. Cemetery: Ruyaulcourt Military Cemetery in France.

POWER, Robert: Rank: Rifleman. Regiment or Service: Royal Irish Rifles. Unit: 'C' Coy. 1st Battalion. Age at death: 16. Date of death: 1 July 1916. Service No: 8763. Born in Waterford. Enlisted in Waterford. Killed in action.

Supplementary information: Son of Patrick Power, of 2 Little Patrick Street, Waterford. Grave or Memorial Reference: VII.M.5. Cemetery: Ovillers Military Cemetery in France.

POWER, Stephen: Rank: Boy 1st Class. Regiment or Service: Royal Navy. Unit: HMS *Defence*. Age at death: 17. Date of death: 31 May 1916. Service No: J/31976. HMS *Defence* was an armoured cruiser and was sent to the bottom by the Naval guns of a German battleship during the battle of Jutland. HMS *Defence*'s magazine exploded when it was hit by a German shell. The magazine explosion triggered off other explosions which almost blew the ship apart and she went down with the entire crew of 903 men. There were no survivors. Five Waterford men died with this ship on that day.

Supplementary information: Son of Richard and Bridget Power, of 100 Doyles Street, Waterford. Grave or Memorial Reference: 13 on the Plymouth Naval Memorial, UK.

POWER, Thomas: Rank: Sergeant. Regiment or Service: Australian Infantry, A.I.F. Unit: 3rd Battalion. Age at death: 38. Date of death: 31 May 1918. Died of wounds (gunshot to right thigh, right foot, left knee and left leg) at the 13th Casualty Clearing Station. Hospitalised with shell shock for a month in July 1916 in France. Service No: 3183. Enlisted 10 August 1915 in Holdsworthy, New South Wales.

Supplementary information: Son of Robert and Hannah Power. Husband of Lena Power, of 83 Styles Street, Leichhardt, New South Wales. Native of Dungarvan. Data from attestation papers:

In or near what Parish or Town were you born? Abbeyside, Dungarvan, Waterford, Ireland.

Are you a natural born British subject or a Naturalised British subject? Yes.

What is your age? 32 years 9 months.

What is your trade or calling? Labourer.

Are you, or have you been an Apprentice? No.

Are you married? Yes,

Who is your next of kin? [wife], Lena Power, 83 Style Street, Reichardt, New South Wales. [died 1938].

Age: 32 years, 9 months.
Height: 5 feet, 7½ inches.
Weight, 140 lbs.
Chest measurement: 36 inches.
Complexion: fair.
Eyes: blue, good.
Hair: fair.
Religious denomination R. C.

Grave or Memorial Reference: III.B.4. Cemetery: Arneke British Cemetery in France.

POWER, Thomas: Rank: Boatswain (Bosun). Regiment or Service: Mercantile Marine. Unit: SS *Conargo* (London). Age at death: 29. Date of death: 31 March 1918.

Supplementary information: Son of Mary Anne Power and the late Thomas Power. Husband of Eileen Power (*née* Quinn), of 68 Manor Street, Waterford. Born in Waterford. He has no known grave but is listed on the Tower Hill Memorial in the UK.

POWER, Thomas: Rank: Private. Regiment or Service: Royal Irish Regiment. Unit: 2nd Battalion. Age at death: 22. Date of death: 27 May 1915. Service No: 6359. Born in Bohermore, Co. Galway. Enlisted in Dungarvan. Died of wounds.

Supplementary information: Son of Mrs Mary Power, of Strand Strand, Dungarvan, Co. Waterford. Grave or Memorial Reference: II.B.28. Cemetery: Hazebrouck Communal Cemetery, Nord, in France.

POWER, William: Rank: Corporal. Regiment or Service: Royal Irish Regiment. Unit: 2nd Battalion. Age at death: 30. Date of death: 8 May 1915. Service No: 6843. Born in Lismore, Co. Waterford. Enlisted in Lismore. Killed in action. His medal index card shows the he entered France on 15 January 1915. He was one of the chief instructors in the local Irish National Volunteers and his nickname was 'Toddy'.

Supplementary information: Son of Michael and Frances Power, of New Street, Lismore,

Co. Waterford. William Power and Edmond Nugent, both Lismore men, embarked for the war in September 1914 on a steamship from Rosslare Horbour, sent on their way by a fife and drum band. He was reported missing after the battle for hill 60. He has no known grave but is listed on Panel 33 on the Ypres (Menin Gate) Memorial in Belgium.

POWER, William: Rank: Seaman. Regiment or Service: Royal Naval Reserve. Unit: HMS *Goliath*. Age at death: 20. Date of death: 13 May 1915. Service No: 5200A. HMS *Goliath* was sunk by three torpedoes from German destroyer *Muvanet-I-Milet*, she blew up and capsized immediately taking 570 of her 750 crew including the Captain to a watery grave. Ten Waterford men died on the *Goliath* that day.

William Power, courtesy of Sinéad Motherway.

Supplementary information: Son of Michael and Johanna Power (*née* Nolan), of Westown, Tramore, Co. Waterford. Grave or Memorial Reference: 8 on the Plymouth Naval Memorial, UK.

POWER, William: Rank: Private. Regiment or Service: Royal Irish Regiment. Unit: 2nd Battalion. Age at death: 26. Date of death: 8 September 1914. Service No: 10897. Born in Dungarvan, Co. Waterford. Enlisted in Dungarvan, Co. Waterford. Killed in action. From the *Waterford News*, 1914:

KILLED IN ACTION.
The Town Clerk read a document from the military authorities enclosing £3 for Mrs Mary Power, Davis Street, whose son, William Power, Royal Irish , was killed in action. It was suggested to give the £3 in lump or in weekly instalments as considered best. It was agreed to give the £3 altogether to Mrs Power.

Grave or Memorial Reference: Orly-Sur-Morin Communal Cemetery in France.

POWER, William: Rank: Gunner. Regiment or Service: Royal Horse Artillery and Royal Field Artillery. Unit: 6th Reserve Brigade. Age at death: 43. Date of death: 2 June 1915. Service No: 5899. Born in Portlaw, Co. Waterford. Enlisted in Waterford. Died of wounds at Home.
Supplementary information: Husband of Catherine Power, of 7 Carrick Road, Portlaw. Grave or Memorial Reference: In the northeast part. Cemetery: Portlaw (St Patrick's) Catholic Churchyard, Co. Waterford.

POWER, William: Rank: Rifleman. Regiment or Service: Royal Irish Rifles. Unit: 7th Battalion. Date of death: 31 July 1916. Service No: 4572. Born in Waterford. Enlisted in Waterford. Killed in action. Grave or Memorial Reference: D.17. Cemetery: Bois-Carre Military Cemetery, Haisnes in France

POWER, William Joseph: Rank: Private. Regiment or Service: Royal Fusiliers. Unit: 9th Battalion. Age at death: 27. Date of death: 17 February 1917. Service No: 62354. Born in Bootle. Enlisted in Putney while living in Walthamstow. Died. Formerly he was with the 3rd City of London Yeomanry where his number was 3816.
Supplementary information: Only son of Ellen and the late William Power, of Co. Waterford, and Liverpool. Educated at Simmaries, 1906-1910. Grave or Memorial Reference: IV.B.10. Cemetery: Avesnes-Le-Comte Communal Cemetery Extension in France.

PRENDERGAST, Bartholomew: Rank: Driver. Regiment or Service: Royal Engineers. Unit: 23rd Field Coy. Age at death: 19. Date of death: 27 January 1915. Service No: 26205. Born in Tallow, Co. Waterford. Enlisted in Fermoy while living in Tallow. Killed in action.
Supplementary information: Son of James and Mary Prendergast, of Barrack Street, Tallow, Co. Waterford. Grave or Memorial Reference: 29. Cemetery: Beuvry Communal Cemetery in France.

PRENDERGAST, Cornelius: Rank: Gunner. Regiment or Service: Royal Garrison Artillery. Date of death: 18 March 1920. Service No: 40313. Supplementary information: Husband of Bridget Prendergast. Grave or Memorial Reference: Near right boundary from entrance. Cemetery: Tallow Catholic Churchyard, Co. Waterford.

PRENDERGAST, David: Rank: Private. Regiment or Service: Royal Irish Regiment. Unit: 2nd Battalion. Age at death: 19. Date of death; 27 September 1918. Service No: 6739. Born in Dungarvan, Co. Waterford. Enlisted in Dungarvan, Co. Waterford. Killed in action.
Supplementary information: Son of the late Mr and Mrs Michael Prendergast. He has no

known grave but is listed on Panel 5 on the Vis-En-Artois Memorial in France.

PRENDERGAST, James: Rank: Private. Regiment or Service: Leinster Regiment. Unit: 2nd Battalion. Date of death: 8 May 1918. Service No: 4492. Previously he was with the Royal Field Artillery where his number was 100205. Born in Waterford. Enlisted in Clonmel while living in Clonmel. Died of wounds. Grave or Memorial Reference: I.E. 35. Cemetery: Ebblinghem Military Cemetery in France.

PRENDERGAST, James Francis: Rank: Second Lieutenant. Regiment or Service: Royal Munster Fusiliers. Unit: 1st Battalion. Date of death: 27 July 1916. Killed in action.

Supplementary information: Son of Mr J.W. Prendergast, of Lismore, Co. Waterford. Grave or Memorial Reference: I.J.23. Cemetery: Philosophe British Cemetery, Mazingarbe in France.

PRENDERGAST, John: Rank: Private. Regiment or Service: Royal Munster Fusiliers. Unit: 6th Battalion. Date of death: 9 August 1915. Service No: 1066. Born in Dungarvan, Co. Waterford. Enlisted in Cardiff. Killed in action in Gallipoli. He has no known grave but is listed on Panel 185 to 190 on the Helles Memorial in Turkey.

PRENDERGAST, (The Revd) **Mathew/ Matthew Vincent:** Rank: Chaplain 4th Class. Regiment or Service: Army Chaplains' Department. Age at death: 37. Date of death: 16 September 1918.

Supplementary information: Son of Patrick Prendergast, of Ballysaggart, Lismore, Co. Waterford. Grave or Memorial Reference: M.179. Cemetery, Cairo War Memorial Cemetery in Egypt.

PRINCE, Patrick: Rank: Private. Regiment or Service: The King's (Liverpool Regiment). Unit: 20th Battalion. Age at death: 19. Date of death: 26 June 1916. Service No: 26568. Born in Waterford. Enlisted in Liverpool while living in Liverpool. Killed in action.

Supplementary information: Son of Michael and Catherine Prince, of 1 Robinson Lane, Waterford. Grave or Memorial Reference: II.L.26. Cemetery: Cerisy-Gailly Military Cemetery in France.

PURCELL, Simon: Rank: Able Seaman. Regiment or Service: Mercantile Marine. Unit: SS *Lough Fisher* (Barrow). Shelled and sunk by a German submarine 12 miles S.E. of Cork. Age at death: 45. Date of death: 30 March 1918.

Supplementary information: Son of Mary Purcell and the late Michael Purcell. Husband of Lucy Purcell (*née* Byrne), of 5 Jail Street, Waterford, Co. Waterford. Born at Bannon, Co. Wexford. He has no known grave but is listed on the Tower Hill Memorial in the UK.

PURCELL, William: Rank: Corporal. Regiment or Service: Royal Munster Fusiliers. Unit: 1st Battalion. Date of death: 1 May 1915. Service No: 7322. Born in Dungarvan, Co. Waterford. Enlisted in Cork. Killed in action in Gallipoli. Grave or Memorial Reference: He has no known grave but is listed on Panel 185 to 190 on the Helles Memorial in Turkey.

Q

QUANN, James: Rank: Lance Corporal. Regiment or Service: Manchester Regiment. Unit: 'C' Coy. 16th Battalion. Age at death: 21. Date of death: 28 September 1917. Service No: 27033. Born in Waterford. Enlisted in Manchester. Killed in action.

Supplementary information: Son of James and Bridget Quann, of 118 Taylorson Street, Salford, Manchester. Native of Waterford. Grave or Memorial Reference: C.5. Cemetery: Pond Farm Cemetery in Belgium.

QUIBELL, Albert: Rank: Private. Regiment or Service: Middlesex Regiment. Unit: 23rd Battalion. Date of death: 8 September 1918. Service No: G/60660 (Soldiers died in the Great War), 60660 (The Commonwealth War Graves Commission). Born in Waterford. Enlisted in West London. Killed in action. Grave or Memorial Reference: XXIV.D.26A. Cemetery: Lijssenthoek Military Cemetery in Belgium.

QUILTY, Bertie: Rank: Private. Regiment or Service: Royal Irish Regiment. Unit: 6th Battalion. Date of death: 11 May 1916. Service No: 2585. Born in St John's, Waterford. Enlisted in Waterford. Killed in action. Grave or Memorial Reference: I.G.15. Cemetery: Dud Corner Cemetery, Loos in France.

QUILTY, Patrick: Rank: Private. Regiment or Service: East Surrey Regiment. Unit: 1st Battalion. Age at death: 22. Date of death: 9 May 1917. Service No: 32515. Born in Waterford. Enlisted in Waterford. Died of wounds.

Supplementary information: Son of Andrew Quilty, of 14 Roches Street, Waterford. Grave or Memorial Reference: II.H.26. Cemetery: Aubigny Communal Cemetery Extension in France.

QUINLAN, John: Rank: Private. Regiment or Service: Royal Irish Regiment. Unit: 2nd Battalion. Date of death: 24 July 1916. Service No: 7726 (Soldiers died in the Great War), 3/7726 (Commonwealth War Graves Commission). Born in Carrowleigh, Co. Waterford. A short in the Waterford news states that Private Quinlan is a Lismore man and was in hospital wounded. Enlisted in Carrick-on-Suir-County Tipperary while living in Carrowleigh. Died of wounds. We have a bit of a mystery here as Private John Quinlan and Private Francis Blake, from Ennis, Co. Clare are both listed as occupiers of this grave. Grave or Memorial Reference: H. 1324A. Cemetery; Glasgow Western Necropolis, Scotland.

QUINLAN, Patrick: Rank: Cattleman. Regiment or Service: Mercantile Marine. Unit: SS *Coningbeg* (Glasgow). Torpedoed by German Submarine U-62. There were no survivors. U-62 surrendered in November 1918. Age at death: 55. Date of death: 18 December 1917.

Supplementary information: Son of the late Thomas and Margaret Quinlan. Husband of Elizabeth Quinlan (*née* Binstead), of 14 Canon Street, Waterford. Born in Waterford. He has no known grave but is listed on the Tower Hill Memorial in the UK. He is also listed on the Formby-Coningbeg Memorial, Adelphi Quay in Waterford City.

QUINLAN, Thomas: Rank: Seaman. Regiment or Service: Royal Naval Reserve. Unit: HMS *Laurentic*. Age at death: 34. Date of death: 25 January 1917. Service No: 2466C.

Supplementary information: Son of Nicholas and Anastatia Quinlan, of Ballymacaw, Dunmore East, Co. Waterford. Grave or Memorial Reference: 24 on the Plymouth Naval Memorial, UK.

QUINLISK, Michael: Rank: Private. Regiment or Service: Royal Irish Regiment. Unit: 2nd Battalion. Age at death: 17. Date of death: 15 October 1914. Service No: 10747. Born in St Bridgets Co. Wexford. Enlisted in Wexford. Killed in action.

Supplementary information: Son of Denis Joseph Quinlisk of 15 Lombard Street, Waterford and the late Alice Quinlisk. From the *Waterford News*:

A FAMILY OF FIGHTERS.
Wexford youth Killed in action.
Has brother held a prisoner of war.
Mr Denis Quinlisk, of Ram Street, Wexford, and ex-Sgt of the R. I. C. (mounted section) was notified by the War Office during the week that his son, Michael, who was a Private in the 2nd Battalion, 18th [*sic*] Royal Irish Regiment, had been killed in action on the 15th October. Mr Quinlisk received correspondence expressing the sympathy of the King, Queen and Lord Kitchener.

The deceased youth, who had been only about 18 months with the colours, was very popular in Wexford, and his end will be learned with sincere regret by a wide circle of friends. His elder brother, Timmy, of the same Regiment, who was promoted in their field to the rank of Corporal for personal bravery, was taken prisoner on the day prior to that on which he was to receive his promotion. Writing to his father from Hamelin, Hannover, Timothy says; –"I do not know if I can write to you in my usual coherent strain, for I don't know whether I am a prisoner of war or not, as I am bewildered by the sudden train of events. Anyhow I am now settled down fairly well, and am certainly in Germany. Mr Dear father–I have a most unwelcome and sad piece of news for you, for which I find very hard in committing to paper. Poor Michael was killed on the 16th October. Poor lad, he died a soldiers death.

I am heartbroken now, as I think of him lying alone on the battlefield. I was by his side as he breathed his last; he died very peacefully, with a prayer on his lips. May God have mercy on his soul. My God, it was terrible that day!. Nearly all the chaps that left Davenport with me are now buried in France. Dear Dad do not grieve too much over Michaels death, for someone had to go, and at last one of us is safe, but I would have been quite content to have been killed if I thought that Michael would be saved. We are well treated here and get enough to eat and drink, but I miss the cigarette very much. I was to be promoted still further the day after my capture, but when I return to Ireland after the war, I hope with God's help to wear the Sergeant's sash.

Don't fret too much on my account, and try not to think of poor Michael. Don't fret too much on my account, and try not to think of poor Michael. The Germans are very good shots with the rifle, although people may say they are not. "Another son of Mr Quinlisk's, a boy of 11 years, is a worthy chip off the old block, and as will be seen elsewhere in our columns, pluckily jumped over the quay to rescue a drowning child during the week. It may be of interest to learn that on the outbreak of war Mr Quinlisk wrote offering his services to the War Office, and was thanked by Sir Neville Chamberlain for his patriotic action. From another in the People, 1915; Lance Corporal, T. A. Quinlisk, Son of ex-Sergeant Denis Quinlisk, Wexford, is at present a prisoner of war in Gefangenlagers, Germany. Writing to his father this week he states; – "We got shifted from Limburg, In any case it was rather crowded there. How are you all getting on in dear old Wexford? Well I hope. We are still having very jolly weather here, but the nights are cold. What a difference in my daily life this September. Last September I was in the trenches, the cold, miserable trenches. I have become quite reconciled in my captivity, though as I look out over the barricade and see the vista of green fields studded here and there with peaceful-looking farm houses.

I find it hard to think that a horrible war is raging over the world. When do you think this war is going to end?". Lance Corporal Quinlisk, who is about 30 years of age, was in action for nearly a year in France. His brother, a Corporal, was killed in France some months ago.

From another article in the *People*, 1915:

Private Michael Quinlisk, son of Mr Quinlisk, Ram Street, Wexford was killed in action at La Basse on the 19th of October, 1914. His brother, Corporal Quinlisk, mention of whom is also made in this column, also fought in the same engagement. Deceased was twelve in the army before the commencement of hostilities. He was about 18 years of age. Other relatives of ex-Sergeant Quinlisk, at present in the service are his cousins, Sergeant Major Maher of the Army Service Corps and Mr Richard P Maher of the clerical department of the Naval Service.

THE PEOPLE

In a letter to his father, Ex-Sergeant Quinlisk, Ram Street, Wexford, Corporal Timothy Quinlisk, of the 8th Royal Irish Regiment, now at the front, states that his brother, Michael, who was killed a short time ago, went back to aid a comrade after the order to retreat had been given, and before he was able to get away he was fatally wounded.

Has no known grave but is commemorated on Panel 11 and 12. Memorial: Le Touret Memorial in France.

QUINN, John Henry: Rank: Lieutenant. Regiment or Service: Royal Field Artillery. Unit: 220th Brigade. Age at death: 23. Date of death: 11 August 1919.

Supplementary information: Son of Cdr. J. Quinn (Indian Ordnance Dept.) and Constance Quinn, of The Myrtles, Hounsdown, Southampton. Born in Waterford. Grave or Memorial Reference: VII.C.3. Cemetery: Baghdad (North Gate) War Cemetery in Iraq.

QUINN, Michael: Rank: Private. Regiment or Service: Royal Irish Regiment. Unit: 2nd Battalion. Date of death: 25 September 1914. Service No: 6172. Born in Trinity Without, Waterford. Enlisted in Waterford. Killed in action. Grave or Memorial Reference: XXVII. A.2. Cemetery: New Irish Farm Cemetery in Belgium.

QUINN, Thomas: Rank: Private. Regiment or Service: Royal Irish Fusiliers. Unit: 7th Battalion. Date of death: 2 May 1916. Service No: 16223. Formerly he was with the Royal Irish Regiment where his number was 385. Born in Waterford. Enlisted in Waterford. Died of wounds. Killed in action. Grave or Memorial Reference: He has no known grave but is listed on Panel 124 on the Loos Memorial in France.

R

RAHER, William: Rank: Stoker. Regiment or Service: Royal Naval Reserve. Unit: HMS *Vivid*. Date of death: 9 November 1918. Service No: 5991.

Supplementary information: Husband of B. Raher, of 77 Lower Yellow Road, Waterford. Grave or Memorial Reference: In northeast part. Cemetery: Tramore (Holy Cross) Catholic Churchyard, Co. Waterford.

RANDALL, Albert Arnaud: Rank: Able Seaman. Regiment or Service: Royal Navy. Unit: HMS *Tipperary*. Age at death: 19. Date of death: 1 June 1916. Service No: J/24830. HMS *Tipperary* was sunk during the Battle of Jutland.

Supplementary information: Son of Fred and Elizabeth Randall, of Protestant Hall, Catherine Street, Waterford. Grave or Memorial Reference: 13. Memorial, Portsmouth Naval Memorial, UK.

RAYMOND, Dan: Rank: Private. Regiment or Service: Wiltshire Regiment. Regiment. Unit: 1st Battalion. Date of death: 19 September 1918. Service No: 205771. Formerly he was with the Middlesex Regiment where his number was 4512. Born in Waterford. Enlisted in Southall in Middlesex while living in Birmingam. Died of wounds. Grave or Memorial Reference: IV.F.6. Cemetery: Abbeville Communal Cemetery Extension in France.

REARDON, William: Rank: Private. Regiment or Service: Royal Irish Regiment. Unit: 2nd Battalion. Date of death: 5 August 1917. Service No: 8204. Born in Dungarvan, Co. Waterford. Enlisted in Dungarvan, Co. Waterford. Died of wounds. Grave or Memorial Reference: XVII. B. 7A. Cemetery: Lijssenthoek Military Cemetary in Belgium.

REDMOND, Patrick: Rank: Private. Regiment or Service: Royal Dublin Fusiliers. Unit: 9th Battalion. Age at death: 21. Date of death: 9 September 1916. Service No: 8302. Born in Tyrone. Enlisted in Dublin while living in Portmarnock, County Dublin. Killed in action.

Supplementary information: Son of James and Annie Redmond, of Grace Dine, Waterford. He has no known grave but is listed on Pier and Face 16C of the Thiepval Memorial in France.

REGAN, Thomas: See **O'REGAN, Thomas:**

REYNOLDS, John Charles, Rank: Private. Hertfordshire Regiment. Unit: 1/1st Battalion. Date of death: 13 December 1915. Age at death: 20. Service No: 3074. Born in Waterford. Enlisted in Hereford. Died in Egypt.

Supplementary information: Son of Herbert and Eliza Reynolds, of The Bungalow, Dinedor, Hereford. Grave or Memorial Reference: B.50. Cemetery: Alexandria (Chatby) Military and War Memorial Cemetery in Egypt.

RING, JOHN Francis: Rank: Staff Sergeant. Regiment or Service: Royal Engineers. Age at death: 33. Date of death: 24 February 1921. Service No: 1851414.

Supplementary information: Long Service and Good Conduct Medal. Son of John Ring (late C.S.M,R.E.) and Margaret Ring, of 16 Wilkin Street, Waterford. Grave or Memorial Reference: O.D.28. Cemetery: Calcutta (Bhowanipore) Cemetery, Kilkata in India.

RIORDAN, Michael: Rank: Private. Regiment or Service: Leinster Regiment. Unit: 3rd Battalion. Date of death: 9 July

1915. Service No: 4288. Born in Tramore, Co. Waterford. Enlisted in Waterford while living in Tramore. Died at Home. Grave or Memorial Reference: In the north part. Cemetery: Youghal (North Abbey) County Cork.

ROBERTS, Sir Frederick Sleigh:
Rank: Field Marshal. Regiment or Service; Commands and Staff, General Staff and Colonel Commandant, Royal Artillery and Colonel in the Irish Guards. From 'Our Heroes':

> ...was wounded on June 4th at the Dardanelles and succumbed the following day. He joined Queen Victoria's Rifles at the outbreak of the war and afterwards received a commission in the 12th Worcestershire regiment. He was very quickly promoted to the rank of Captain and at the time of his death was attached to the 2nd Royal Fusiliers. He was the youngest son of the late James Robertson, Newtown Lodge, Waterford.

CWGC; Awards; VC, KG, KP, GCB, OM, GCSI, GCIE. Age at Death 82. Date of death 14 November 1914. 1st Earl of Kandahar, Pretoria and Waterford. Born at Cawnpore, India. Privy Counsellor. Son of the late Gen. Sir Abraham Roberts, G. C. B, and the late Lady Roberts; husband of the late Countess Roberts, C. I, R. R. C, of Englemere, Ascot, Berks. Educated at Eton, Sandhurst and Addiscombe. Commissioned to the Bengal Artillery (December, 1851); served throughout the Indian Mutiny 1857 (V. C.); and the Abyssinian (1867-68) and Lushai (1871-72) Expeditions. Also served in the Afghanistan Campaign (1878-80) and Commanded the Kabul-Kandahar Field Force August. -Sept, 1880. Commanded the Forces in Ireland (1895-99); Commander-in-Chief in the South African War (1899-1900). Commander-in-Chief in India (1885-93) and at Home (1901-04). Master Gunner of St. James' Park and Colonel-in-Chief of Overseas and Indian Forces in the United Kingdom during the Great War.

An extract from the *London Gazette*, 24 December 1858:

> On the 2nd January 1858 at Khodagunge, India, on following up the retreating enemy, Lieutenant Roberts saw in the distance two sepoys going away with a standard. He immediately gave chase, overtaking them just as they were about to enter a village. Although one of them fired at him the Lieutenant was not hit and he took possession of the standard, cutting down the man who was carrying it. He had also on the same day saved the life of a sowar who was being attacked by a sepoy. "His Mother was from Kilfeacle in Tipperary and he died of Pneumonia in St Omer in France on 14 November 1914 while visiting Indian Troops.

Buried in St Pauls Cathedral in London. He is also commemorated on the Cahir War Memorial.

ROBERTSON, Frank R.:
Rank: Captain. Regiment or Service: Worcestershire Regiment. Unit: 12th Battalion. Age at death: 29. Date of death: 25 June 1915. Died of wounds.

Supplementary information: Son of James and Lizzie Robertson, of Newton Lodge, Waterford. From the *Waterford News*, 1915:

CAPTAIN F ROBERTSON.

His numerous friends in Waterford will be pleased to learn that Captain Frank Robertson, who, as already announced, was wounded in the head during the operations at the Dardanelles, is improving. Captain Robertson is a brother of the Messrs. Robertson, the Quay (Robertson Brothers), and held an important position with Messrs Dent, Allcroft, and Co., London, the well-known glove manufacturers, until the outbreak of the War, when he got a commission in the 12th Worcestershire Regiment, being attached to the Royal Fusiliers. Of the six officers in his company who went to the Dardanelles four were killed and two (including him-self) wounded. Captain Robertson is at present in hospital in Alexandria, and his friends will join with us in wishing him a speedy recovery.

From the *Waterford News*, June 1915:

DEATH OF CAPTAIN FRANK ROBERTSON. We very much regret to have to record the death of this young Waterford officer, which took place at Deaconess Hospital, Alexandria, from wounds received in the Dardanelles operations. The late Captain Robertson came of one of Waterford's most respected families, being seventh son of the late Mr James Robertson, Newtown, and brother of Messrs, Robertson, The Quay. He was together with his brothers, con-nected with the firm of Robertson and Leslie, and about four years ago he left Waterford to take up an important posi-tion with the well-known firm of glove makers, Messrs Dent, Alcroft, and Co., London. Like his other brothers, Mr Frank Robertson was extremely popular with all who knew him. He was a thorough sports-man, being particularly keen on coursing, and he kept many good hounds from time to time which he entered at local meetings. His many excellent qualities endeared him to a large circle of friends who will learn with regret of his demise.

To his sorrowing brothers, sisters, and other relatives we tender our sincere sympathy.

There is a large on this officer's death in the *Munster Express*, July 1915. From the *Waterford News*, October 1915:

TWO WATERFORD OFFICERS BURIED IN ALEXANDRIA.
Over the grave of Captain Frank Robertson in Alexandria is a small cross bearing the words "Captain Robertson, of Newtown, Waterford," and giving the date of his death from wounds received in the Dardinelles. Immediately behind the words "Pasha

Sheehan, native of Waterford" and giving the date of his death also. It is an extraordinary coincidence that these two Waterfordmen should find their last resting place in the one grave ... conferred upon him. "Pasha Sheehan" was a brother of the famous Irish scholar, the Revd. Dr Michael Sheehan.

There is no person named SHEEHAN buried in this cemetery. Grave or Memorial Reference: J. 4. Cemetery: Alexandria (Chatby) Military and War Memorial Cemetery in Egypt. He is also listed on the Waterford and District Roll of Honour. Located in Christ Church Cathedral (Church of Ireland), Henrietta Street, Waterford.

ROBINSON, John: Rank: Gunner. Regiment or Service: Royal Garrison Artillery. Unit: Depot, M.H. Brigade. Age at death: 36. Date of death: 21 January 1919. Service No: 282281.
Supplementary information: Husband of Mary Robinson, of 18 Carrigeen Lane, Waterford. Grave or Memorial Reference: P.Ba.82. Cemetery: Ballynaneashagh (St Otteran's) Catholic Cemetery in Co. Waterford.

ROCHE, James: Rank: Private. Regiment or Service: Royal Munster Fusiliers. Unit: 8th Battalion. Age at death: 29. Date of death: 2 June 1916. Service No: 4791. Born in St Anne's, Cork Enlisted in Cork while living in Cork. Killed in action.
Supplementary information: Brother of Mrs M. Mernin, of 4 New Street, Waterford. Grave or Memorial Reference: 127 on the Loos Memorial in France.

ROCHE, Patrick: Rank: Private. Regiment or Service: Royal Irish Regiment. Unit: 6th Battalion. Date of death: 29 November 1917. Service No: 10533. Born in Trinity Without, Waterford. Enlisted in Waterford. Killed in action. Grave or Memorial Reference: I.D.30. Cemetery: Croisilles Railway Cemetery in France.

ROCHE, William: Rank: Private. Regiment or Service: Royal Irish Regiment. Unit: 2nd Battalion. Date of death: 23 August 1915. Service No: 6820. Born in Trinity Without, Waterford. Enlisted in Waterford. Killed in action. Grave or Memorial Reference: He has no known grave but is listed on the La-Ferte-Sous-Jouarre-Memorial in France.

ROGERS Patrick Joseph: Rank: Private. Regiment or Service: Australian Infantry, A.I.F. Unit: 25th Battalion. Date of death: 17 July 1918. Enlisted 4 March 1915 at Port Douglas, Queensland. Service No: 1992. Went sick with VD in Gallipoli and transferred to Hospitals in Mudros, Abbassia and Cairo then discharged after 3 months to re-join unit. Hospitalised with a gunshot wound to the eye and head in France, treated and discharged. Wounded again by a gas shell and transferred 'gassed, second occasion' to England. Treated and returned to France. Data from attestation papers:

What is your name? Patrick Joseph Rogers.

In or near what Parish or Town were you born? Crooke, Waterford, Ireland.

Are you a natural born British subject or a Naturalised British subject? Natural Born.

What is your age? 41 years.

Patrick Joseph Rogers.

What is your trade or calling? Draper.

Are you, or have you been an Apprentice? If so where, to whom, and for what period? Waterford, Reberta, for 4 years.

Are you married? No.

Who is your next of kin? [brother] Thomas Rogers. 38 South Parade, Waterford, Ireland.

Have you stated the whole, if any, of your previous service? Yes.

Have you ever been rejected as unfit for his Majesty's Service? No. If so, on what grounds?

Age: 41 years, 5 months.

Height: 5 feet, 6 inches.

Weight: 156 lbs.

Chest measurement: 37½ inches.

Complexion: dark.

Eyes: blue. Hair: brown.

Religious denomination: R. C.

Killed in instantaneously by shell fire and buried the same day.

Charged at various times with drunkenness and being absent.

Will.

In the event of my death I give £5 to my brother William and I give £5 to my brother John and I give £10 to my Step Mother, And I give the remaining part of my property to my brother Thomas.

Date, Sept-16-1917. Signed, Patrick Joseph Rogers.

Grave or Memorial Reference: III.L.13. Cemetery: Adelaide Cemetery, Villers-Bretonneux in France.

ROSS, John James: Rank: Private. Regiment or Service: Royal Scots (Lothian Regiment). Unit: 2nd Battalion. Date of death: 22 March 1915. Service No: 11208. Born in Waterford. Enlisted in Glencorse while living in Forest Hill London. Killed in action. Has no known grave but is commemorated on Panel 11 on the Ypres (Menin Gate) Memorial in Belgium.

RUSSELL, Martin: Rank: Guardsman. Regiment or Service: Grenadier Guards. Unit: 2nd Battalion. Date of death: 14 October 1915. Service No: 11481. Born in Aglish, Co. Waterford. Enlisted in Cardiff. Died of wounds. Grave or Memorial Reference: IV.F.17. Cemetery: Bethune Town Cemetery in France.

RUSSELL, Samuel: Rank: Sapper. Regiment or Service: Corps of Royal Engineers. Unit: 222nd Field Company, Royal Engineers. Age at death: 21. Date of death: 5 March 1917. Service No: 143369. Born in Waterford. Enlisted in Belfast while living in Mylor, Cornwall. Died of wounds.

Supplementary information: Son of Isaac Russell, of Church View, Holywood, Co. Down. Assistant Scoutmaster, 1st Holywood Troop. Grave or Memorial Reference: I.G.13. Cemetery: Hem Farm Military Cemetery, Hem-Monacu in France.

RUSSELL, Thomas: Rank: Private. Regiment or Service: Royal Munster Fusiliers. Unit: 8th Battalion. Date of death: 18 June 1916. Service No: 4792. Born in Newtown, Co. Waterford. Enlisted in Manchester while living in Kilmacthomas, Co. Waterford. Killed in action. Grave or Memorial Reference: I.F.2. Cemetery: St Patrick's Cemetery, Loos in France.

RUSSELL, Thomas: Rank: Private. Regiment or Service: Royal Guards. Date of death: 1 November 1914. Service No: 3944. Born in Waterford. Enlisted in Clonmel, Co. Tipperary. Killed in action. Has no known grave but is commemorated on Panel 11 on the Ypres (Menin Gate) Memorial in Belgium.

RUTH, Francis: Rank: Fireman. Regiment or Service: Mercantile Marine. Unit: SS *Memphian* (Liverpool). Age at death: 39. Date of death: 8 October 1917.

Supplementary information: Son of the late Cornelius and Mary Ann Ruth. Born at Waterford. He has no known grave but is listed on the Tower Hill Memorial in the UK.

RYAN, James: Rank: Pantry Steward. Regiment or Service: Mercantile Marine. Unit: SS *Falaba* (Liverpool). Age at death: 38. Date of death: 28 March 1915.

Supplementary information: Son of the late John and Annastia Ryan. Husband of Elizabeth Ryan (*née* Barnes), of 69 Sutcliffe Street, Liverpool. Born in Waterford. He has no known grave but is listed on the Tower Hill Memorial in the UK.

RYAN, John: Rank: Sergeant. Regiment or Service: Royal Engineers. Unit: 'Z' Special Coy. Age at death: 40. Date of death: 6 May 1917. Service No: 1836. Born in Ballybricken, Co. Waterford. Enlisted in Waterford while livening in Fermoy, Co. Cork. Killed in action.

Supplementary information: Son of James and Margaret Ryan of 13 Hennessey's Road, Waterford. Husband of Margaret Ryan, of 7 Kellehers Buildings, Ashburton, Cork. Grave or Memorial Reference: III.F.10. Cemetery: Beaulencourt British Cemetery, Ligny-Thilloy in France.

RYAN, John Anthony: Rank: Gunner. Regiment or Service: Royal Garrison Artillery. Unit: 'T' 34th Howitzer Battery. Age at death: 27. Date of death: 14 August 1915. Service No: 53237. Born in Waterford. Enlisted in Liverpool while living in Galway. Killed in action.

Supplementary information: Son of Michael and Bridget Ryan, of Dublin. Grave or Memorial Reference: IV.A.20. Cemetery: Talana Farm Cemetery in Belgium.

RYAN, Matthew: Rank: Able Seaman. Regiment or Service: Mercantile Marine.

Unit: SS *Jutland* (Cardiff). Age at death: 24. Date of death: 19 November 1917.

Supplementary information: Son of Lawrence and Bridget Ryan, of 4 Little Michael Street, Waterford. He has no known grave but is listed on the Tower Hill Memorial in the UK.

RYAN, Maurice: Rank: Private. Regiment or Service: Royal Dublin Fusiliers. Unit: 1st Battalion. Age at death: 23. Date of death: 15 August 1915. Service No: 19584. Born in Waterford. Enlisted in Waterford. Died of wounds in Gallilpoli.

Supplementary information: Son of Mrs Ryan, of 13 Hennessy Road, Waterford. Husband of Elizabeth O'Brien (formerly Ryan), of 125 Ballytruckle, Waterford. He has no known grave but is listed on Panel 190 to 196 on the Helles Memorial in Turkey.

RYAN, Maurice: Rank: Private. Regiment or Service: Leinster Regiment. Unit: 2nd Battalion also listed as 7th Battalion. Date of death: 28 March 1916. Service No: 2778. There are two listings for Maurice in Soldiers died in the Great War. One is in the 2nd battalion and the other in the 7th Battalion, all other details are the same. The Commonwealth War Graves Commission give his Battalion as the 8th. Born in Portlaw, Co. Waterford. Enlisted in Waterford while living in Waterford. Died of wounds. Grave or Memorial Reference: I.B.7 Cemetery: Philosophe British Cemetery, Mazingarbe in France.

RYAN, Michael: Rank: Private. Regiment or Service: Royal Irish Regiment. Unit: 6th Battalion. Age at death: 18. Date of death: 30 November 1917. Service No: 3640. Born in Lismore, Co. Waterford. Enlisted in Fermoy, Co. Cork. Killed in action.

Supplementary information: Son of John Ryan, of New Street, Lismore, Co. Waterford. Grave or Memorial Reference: I.E.14. Cemetery: Croisilles Railway Cemetery in France.

RYAN, Michael: Rank: Private. Regiment or Service: Royal Irish Regiment. Unit: 3rd Battalion. Age at death: 21. Date of death: 25 June 1916. Service No: 9912. Born in Nenagh. Enlisted in Limerick while living in Cloughjordan. Died of wounds.

Supplementary information: Son of John Ryan, New Street, Lismore, Co. Waterford. Grave or Memorial Reference: 30693. Cemetery: Limerick (St Lawrence's) Catholic Cemetery, County Limerick.

RYAN, Patrick: Rank: Private. Regiment or Service: Royal Irish Regiment. Unit: 2nd Battalion. Age at death: 38. Date of death: 23 August 1914. Service No: 4834. Born in Ballybricken, Co. Waterford. Enlisted in Waterford while living in Vale, Guernsey, Channel Islands. Killed in action.

Supplementary information: Husband of Evelyn Jane Ryan, of 1 Cliff Terrace, St Peter Port, Guernsey. He has no known grave but is listed on the La-Ferte-Sous-Jouarre-Memorial in France.

RYAN, Patrick: Thomas: Rank: Private. Regiment or Service: Royal Irish Fusiliers. Unit: 6th Battalion. Date of death: 15 August 1915. Service No: 13559. Born in Waterford. Enlisted in Cardiff, Glamorgam while living in Waterford. Killed in action in Gallipoli. Has no known grave but is commemorated on Panel 178 to 180. Memorial: Helles Memorial in Turkey.

RYAN, William: Rank: Gunner. Regiment or Service: Royal Garrison Artillery. Unit: 45th Battery, 29th Ammunition, Sub Park. Date of death: 10 February 1917. Service No: 7793. Born in Butlerstown, Co. Waterford. Enlisted in Dungarvan, Waterford. Died. Grave or Memorial Reference: III.B.38, Grove Town Cemetery, Meaulte in France.

RYAN, William: Rank: Lance Corporal. Regiment or Service: Household Cavalry and

Cavalry of the line including the Yeomanry and Imperial Camel Corps. Unit: 20th Hussars, C Squadron. Age at death: 21. Date of death: 29 August 1914. Service No: 5248. Born in St Mary's, Waterford. Enlisted in Cork while living in Cork. Died of wounds.

Supplementary information: Son of Patrick and Esther Ryan, of 14 Portland Place, Carlisle. Born at Carlow. Grave or Memorial Reference: In the south-west corner. Cemetery: Moy-De-L'Aisne Communal Cemetery, Aisne in France.

RYAN, William: Rank: Private. Regiment or Service: Royal Munster Fusiliers. Unit: 2nd Battalion. Date of death: 21 December 1914. Service No: 8352. Born in Cappoquin, Co. Waterford. Enlisted in Kinsale, Co. Cork while living in Birmingham. Killed in action. Grave or Memorial Reference: Private William Ryan, No:8352 has not yet been found by Commonwealth Wargraves Commission staff in their databases. His name has been put forward by the 'In from the Cold' project and, it is hoped, he will have a burial reference sometime in the future. This project is ongoing and endeavours to find unknown burial locations for soldiers sourced in other databases.

RYAN, William: Rank: Petty Officer Stoker. Regiment or Service: Royal Navy. Unit: HMS *Defence*. Age at death: 41. Date of death: 31 May 1916. Service No: 277112. HMS *Defence* was an armoured cruiser and was sent to the bottom by the Naval guns of a German battleship during the battle of Jutland. HMS *Defence*'s magazine exploded when it was hit by a German shell. The magazine explosion triggered off other explosions which almost blew the ship apart and she went down with the entire crew of 903 men. There were no survivors. Five Waterford men died with this ship on that day.

Supplementary information: Native of Ballymacaw, Dunmore East, Co. Waterford. Son of the late Martin and Margaret Ryan. Grave or Memorial Reference: 14 on the Plymouth Naval Memorial, UK.

S

SAGE, Joseph: Rank: Private. Regiment or Service: Australian Infantry, A.I.F. Unit: 28th Battalion. Date of death: 29 July 1916. Enlisted 19 May 1915 in Perth, Western Australia. Killed in action. Service No: 1036. Hospitalised at Anzac and Egypt with peritonitis, heart strain and N.Y.D. Reported missing 6 August 1916, changed after a Court of Enquiry to Killed in Action 4 January 1917.

What is your name? Joseph Sage.

In or near what Parish or Town were you born? Waterford, Ireland.

Are you a natural born British subject or a Naturalised British subject? Yes.

What is your age? 26 years.

What is your trade or calling? Grocer.

Are you, or have you been an Apprentice? No. If so where, to whom, and for what period?

Are you married? No.

Who is your next of kin? [father] Joseph Sage, Waterfod, Ireland.

Height: 5 feet, 9 ¾ inches.

Weight, 156 lbs.

Chest measurement: 36-38 inches.

Complexion, sallow.

Eyes: blue.

Hair: light brown.

Religious denomination: R.C.

He has no known grave but is listed on the Villers-Bretonneux Memorial in France.

SAMPSON, Hugh: Rank: Private. Regiment or Service: King's Liverpool Regiment. Unit: 17th Battalion. Date of death: 30 July 1917. Service No: 27579. Enlisted in Liverpool while living in Duncannon, Co. Waterford. Killed in action. Grave or Memorial Reference: IX.L.3. Cemetery: Serre Road Cemetery No 2 in France.

SANDERSON, Harry: Rank: Acting Bombardier. Regiment or Service: Royal Garrison Artillery. Unit: 13th Siege Battery. Age at death: 22. Date of death: 3 August 1917. Service No: 51086. Born in Waterfoot in Lancs. Enlisted in Bacup, Lancs while living in Waterford. Killed in action.

Supplementary information: Son of Fred and Mary Alice Sanderson, of 12 Wales Bank, Waterfoot, Manchester. Grave or Memorial Reference: III.G.II. Cemetery: Dickiebusch New Military Cemetery Extension in Belgium.

SCROWSTON, John Edward Briggs: Rank: Private. Regiment or Service: Household Cavalry and Cavalry of the line including the Yeomanry and Imperial Camel Corps. Unit: East Riding of Yorkshire Yeomanry. Unit: 2nd/1st Age at death: 20. Date of death: 2 November 1918. Born in South Cave, Yorks. Enlisted in Hull while living in Hull. Died at Home. Service No: 51139.

Supplementary information: Son of C.E. Scrowston, of 12 Gilbert Street, Hessle Road., Hull. Grave or Memorial Reference: 231. Cemetery: Waterford Catholic Cemetery, Co. Waterford.

SEALEY/SEALY, James: Rank: Lance Corporal. Regiment or Service: Royal Scots (Lothian Regiment.) Unit: 1st Battalion. Date of death: 30 September 1916. Service No: 11978. Born in Waterford. Enlisted in Edinburgh while living in Portlaw, Co. Waterford. Killed in action in Salonika. Grave or Memorial Reference: V.A.12. Cemetery: Struma Military Cemetery in Greece.

SHANAHAN, James: Rank: Private. Regiment or Service: Royal Irish Regiment. Unit: 2nd Battalion. Age at death: 49. Date of death: 21 September 1915. Service No: 7611. Born in Aglish, Co. Waterford. Enlisted in Dungarvan, Co. Waterford. while living in Ballingown Co. Waterford. Killed in action.

Supplementary information: Son of Thomas and Mary Shanahan, of Ballygown, Villierstown, Cappoquin, Co. Waterford. He has no known grave but is listed on Pier and Face 3A of the Thiepval Memorial in France.

SHANAHAN, John: Rank: Private. Regiment or Service: Royal Irish Regiment. Unit: 6th Battalion. Date of death: 25 July 1916. Service No: 7578 (Soldiers died in the Great War), 3/7578 (The Commonwealth War Graves Commission). Born in Aglish, Co. Waterford. Enlisted in Dungarvan, Co. Waterford. while living in Aglish. Killed in action. Grave or Memorial Reference: II.E.4. Cemetery: Dud Corner Cemetery, Loos in France

SHANAHAN, Patrick: Rank: Private. Regiment or Service: Royal Irish Regiment. Unit: 2nd Battalion. Date of death: 10 November 1918. Service No: 5568. Born in Carrickbeg, Co. Waterford. Enlisted in Carrick-on-Suir, County Tipperary while living in Carrickbeg. Killed in action.

Supplementary information: He won the Military Medal and is listed in the *London Gazette.* From the *Waterford News,* September 1917:

RECOMMENDATION FOR MILITARY MEDAL.

Mr D Shanahan, coach builder, Main Street, Carrick-on-Suir, has received the following letter from Adjutant. A. Charles Hall, 47 Trench Mortar Battery, France:

Sir,
Your letter to hand. I am directed to inform you that your son, Private Paddy Shanahan, will be granted leave very soon. You will be glad to hear that he performed an act of great gallantry three days ago, for which he has been recommended the Military Medal.

Grave or Memorial Reference: In the southeast part. Cemetery: Spiennes Communal Cemetery, Mons, Hainaut in Belgium.

SHANAHAN, William: Rank: Private. Regiment or Service: Irish Guards. Unit: 1st Battalion. Date of death: 1 November 1914. Service No: 642. Born in Newtown, Co. Waterford. Enlisted in Waterford. Killed in action.

Supplementary information: Son of William Shanahan, of Scrahan, Kilmacthomas, Co. Waterford. He has no known grave but is listed on Panel 11 on the Ypres (Menin Gate) Memorial in Belgium.

SHAW, Thomas: Rank: Private. Regiment or Service: Royal Irish Regiment. Unit: 4th Battalion. Date of death: 22 December 1916. Service No: 5406. Born in Waterford. Enlisted in Burry Port, Carmarthenshire while living in Waterford. Died at Home.

Supplementary information: Husband of Mrs Shaw, of 5 Brown's Lane, Waterford. Grave or Memorial Reference: S.Ba.52. Cemetery: Ballynaneashagh (St Otteran's) Catholic Cemetery in Co. Waterford.

SHEA, Patrick: Rank: Private. Regiment or Service: Royal Irish Regiment. Unit: 7th Battalion. Formerly he was with the South Irish Horse where his number was 1610. Date of death: 12 December 1917. Service No: 25772. Born in Ballinameale, Co. Waterford. Enlisted in Dublin while living in Loughbane, County Cork. Killed in action. Grave or Memorial Reference: II.H.27. Cemetery: Templeux-Le-Guerard British Cemetery in France.

SHEA, Thomas: Rank: Private. Regiment or Service: Royal Irish Regiment. Unit: 6th Battalion. Age at death: 33. Date of death: 25 July 1916. Service No: 5269 and 4/5269. Born in Tramore, Co. Waterford. Enlisted in Waterford while living in Tramore. Killed in action.

Supplementary information: Son of Daniel and Catherine Shea, of Carriglong, Tramore, Co. Waterford. Grave or Memorial Reference: II.F.19. Cemetery: Dud Corner Cemetery, Loos in France.

SHEEHAN, Denis: Rank: Private. Regiment or Service: Royal Irish Fusiliers. Unit: 9th Battalion. Date of death: 16 August 1917. Service No: 16199. Formerly he was with the Royal Irish Regiment where his number was 1279. Born in Waterford. Enlisted in Waterford. Killed in action. Grave or Memorial Reference: IV.C.6. Cemetery: New Irish Farm Cemetery in Belgium.

SHEEHAN, Jeremiah Joseph: Rank: Lance Corporal. Regiment or Service: Cheshire Regiment. Unit: 13th Battalion. Date of death: 15 May 1916. Service No: W/871. Born in Waterford. Enlisted in Portsunlight, Cheshire while living in Dungarvan, Co. Waterford. Killed in action.

Supplementary information: Husband of Catherine Sheehan. From the *Munster Express*:

KILLED IN ACTION.

Official news has been received in Dungarvan of the death of Jeremiah Sheehan who has been killed in action in France. He was about 26 years of age, and a young man of fine promise. He belonged to a most respectable family connected with this district, and volunteered for service on the outbreak of the war. He was the eldest son of Mrs Sheehan, now living at Killosera, Dungarvan. He was a fine type of Irish Manhood, brave almost to a fault, and held in high esteem by all who knew him. His sister, Margaret, who was in Belgium on the outbreak of hostilities, was interned for a time, but eventually got across the frontier to France, where she joined the Red Cross, and has done duty as a nurse in a military hospital ever since. From here the news of her fine brother's death came to Dungarvan, but it has been officially confirmed since, and at the Churches last Sunday prayers were asked for the repose of his soul. To the sorrowing widowed mother and members of the family the widest sympathy goes out on the loss of her affectionate son, who was deeply attached to the loved ones at home.

From the *Southern Star*:

Andrew Heffernan, a Kilmallock man, wrote to his wife before the battle in which he was killed as follows:

TRENCHES, 8TH MAY, 1915.
Dear Little Girl,
I believe your kind and welcome letters on the 6th and 7th, and was glad to se by them that you and the children were in good health, as I am at present, thank God. This will be the last letter for a long time, but do not be uneasy about me, for I will come out of this the same as I always did, with the help of God and his Blessed Mother. We have a frightful piece of work to do. As I said before it is the last letter for a while, and it may be the last ever, but if I fall in this big battle I will haunt the Kaiser for the rest of his life. If anything happens to me I know there is no fear of the children with you- but, little girl, I bind you to no promise, but mind the children. I could not tell you what it cost me to write this letter to you, if I go down this time the War Office will give you whatever is belonging to me, and will send you my watch or any little things I have. When you receive this letter I will be back in the thick of the fun; it is a glorious life only for you and the children, I would not ask for a better death. Goodbye, and may God bless you, little girl, and the children. Mind Eileen, for me whatever you do as she is a girl. Tell her father was asking for her, and kiss mamma for me. Good-bye once more. Love to you and the children. Remember, no matter what will happen, I died like a soldier and a man.
From your fond husband.
Andy.

John Hanly, wrote to Mrs Heffernan on the 15th May, and in the course of the letter said–Your husband died a glorious death. He received Holy Communion a couple of days before he was killed, so he was all right. Father Gleeson is to write to you if he is not done so before now. The night before the battle your husband told me that he wrote to you. Poor Jack Curtin also got wounded.

Sergeant George Renton wrote: I expect you have heard before this time that your husband has died fighting for his King and Country. I was one of the party who carried out and paid a soldier's compliment at the burial, and found this watch with a little note for you in your husband's possession. Your address was on a slip of paper in the back case of the watch which I am forwarding on to you. You have my deepest sympathy in your great loss. Still you have the comfort to know that he died doing his duty like a good soldier.

Lance-Corporal Sheehan, in a letter of sympathy, wrote:
But, thank God, he (deceased) was ready, for he had Confession and received Holy Communion the week before he went into the charge, and also that night before the battle. I saw him killed. I thought at first he was only wounded. I had to creep along the grass to come near him. I found him quite dead. I need not tell you the way I felt. My first impulse was to get his watch to send to you, as I promised, but as I reached him, there was another of my comrades wounded. He was shouting for me to help him, as it was my duty to do so, and when I went and dresses that man's wounds I nearly got killed myself, for they (the Germans) were firing at me all the time, but, thank God, I escaped this time. I expect you have heard from the priest, he is a Tipperary man, he is very good, like a father to us and his name in Father Gleeson. He does all in his power for us. He writes to the soldiers friends to tell

if anything happens to them. He is loved by us. He gives us the Blessed Sacrament as often as he can, and every night that we are out in the trenches he gives us Benediction of the Blessed Sacrament. We cannot expect better. I expect that Andy told you before about our beloved Priest.

Grave or Memorial Reference: L.N.3. Cemetery: Ecoivres Military Cemetery, Mont-St-Eloi in France.

SHEEHAN, John: Rank: Private. Regiment or Service: Royal Irish Regiment. Unit: 5th Battalion. Date of death: 16 August 1915. Service No: 54. Born in Faws, Co. Waterford. Enlisted in Merthyr. Killed in action in Gallipoli. He has no known grave but is listed on Panel 55 on the Helles Memorial in Turkey.

SHEEHAN, Michael: (This is an alias. The true name was **HEALY, Maurice M.**) Rank: Gunner. Regiment or Service: Royal Horse Artillery and Royal Field Artillery. D Battery, 122nd Brigade. Age at death: 25. Date of death: 6 May 1918. Service No: W/2151. Born in Waterford. Enlisted in Cardiff. Killed in action.
Supplementary information: (Served as Sheehen), Son of Patrick and Johanna Healy, of Charleville, Co. Cork. Grave or Memorial Reference: II.L.4. Cemetery: Poperinghe New Military Cemetery in Belgium.

SHEEHAN, Patrick: Rank: Private. Regiment or Service: Machine Gun Corps (Infantry) Age at death: 24. Date of death: 17 November 1919. Service No: 88773. Supplementary information: Son of Mrs Bridget Sheehan, of Ballyscanlon, Fenor. Grave or Memorial Reference: In south-west part. Cemetery: Fenor, Catholic Churchyard, Co. Waterford.

SHELTON, Edward Willington: Rank: Private. Regiment or Service: Canadian

Infantry (Central Ontario Regiment). Unit: 15th Battalion. Date of death: 16 June 1915. Service No: 77748. Data from enlistment documents:

Enlisted in Victoria, 10 November 1914.

In what Town, Township or Parish, and in what Country were you born? County Limerick, Ireland.

What is the name of your next of kin? Deane Shelton.

What is the address of your next of kin? Rossmore, Charleville, County Cork.

What is the date of your birth? August 15th-1890.

What is your trade or calling? Clerk.

Are you married? No.

Are you willing to be vaccinated or re-vaccinated and inoculated? Yes.

Do you now belong to the Active Militia? 102nd RMRA. A Co, Kamloops.

Do you understand the nature and terms of your engagement? Yes.

Are you willing to be attested to serve in the Canadian Over-Seas Expeditionary Force? Yes.

Apparent age: 24 years 2 months.

Height: 5 Ft 10½ Ins.

Girth when fully expanded...36. Ins.

Range of expansion 2 Ins.

Complexion: dark.

Eyes: brown.

Hair: brown.

I am not sure of the Waterford connection but he is listed on the Bishop Foy School Memorial located in Christ Church Cathedral (Church of Ireland), Henrietta Street, Waterford. Grave or Memorial Reference: A.8.37. Cemetery: St Sever Cemetery, Rouen in France.

SHEPHERD, Edward Holiburton Symers: Rank: Deck Hand. Regiment or Service: Royal Naval Reserve. Unit: HMS *Colleen*. Age at death: 27. Date of death: 25 November 1918. Service No: 13423DA.

Supplementary information: Son of Mrs Elizabeth Shepherd, of 38 Hotspur Street, Maryhill, Glasgow. Grave or Memorial Reference: 2053. Cemetery: Waterford Catholic Cemetery, Co. Waterford.

SHINE, Hugh Patrick: Rank: Second Lieutenant. Regiment or Service: Royal Irish Fusiliers. Unit: 1st Battalion. Date of death: 25 May 1915. Killed in action.

Supplementary information: Son of Col. J.M.F. Shine, C.B., of Abbeyside, Dungarvan, Co. Waterford, and the late Kathleen Mary Shine. There is a newspaper report of Lt Shine's death in the *Waterford News*, June 1915. He has no known grave but is listed on Panel 42 on the Ypres (Menin Gate) Memorial in Belgium.

SHINE, James Owen Williams: Rank: Captain. Regiment or Service: Royal Dublin Fusiliers. Unit: 2nd Battalion. Age at death: 26. Date of death: 16 August 1917 Awards: Mentioned in Despatches. Killed in action.

Supplementary information: Son of Col. J.M.F. and Kathleen Mary Shine, C.B., of Abbeyside, Dunganan [sic], Co. Waterford. Educated at Downside School and Sandhurst. From the *Waterford News*, August 1917:

CAPTAIN JAMES SHINE KILLED IN ACTION. Intelligence was received in Dungarvan last Saturday that Captain James Shine has been killed in action. He was eldest son of Colonel Shine, R.A.M.C., and was the last surviving son, two others having been killed in the present war. Captain Shine was a native of Dungarvan, and obtained a commission on the opening of hostilities, securing rapid promotion to the rank of Captain. Much sympathy is felt in this district with his mother and father, who are widely and influentially connected.

Grave or Memorial Reference: 144 to 145 on the Tyne Cot Memorial in Belgium.

SHINE, John Denys/Denis: Rank: Second Lieutenant. Regiment or Service: Royal Irish

Regiment. Unit: 1st Battalion. Attached to 2nd Battalion. Age at death: 19. Date of death: 25 August 1914. Died.

Supplementary information: Son of Col. J.M.F. and Kathleen Mary Shine, of Abbeyside, Dungarvan, Co. Waterford. His brother, Second Lieutenant. H.P. Shine, also fell. From the *Waterford News*, 1914:

> ...was with Lieutenant Shine's company when the latter was wounded. With regard to Lieutenant. Shine, his people, to whom it was first reported at Mons, now entertain little or no hope of his being alive. A letter from a private, which appeared in the Press a few days ago, mentioned that Mr Shine had died in hospital and was interred there.

Grave or Memorial Reference: IV.B.18. Cemetery: Mons (Bergen) Communal Cemetery in Belgium.

Thomas Charles Sturton Simmonds.

SIMMONDS, Thomas Charles Sturton: Rank: Private. Regiment or Service: The Queen's (Royal West Surrey Regiment). Unit: 'D' Coy. 11th Battalion. Age at death: 26. Date of death: 11 December 1916. Service No: G/11271. Born in Watford, Herts. Enlisted in Lamberth, Surrey while living in Thornton Heath, Surrey. Killed in action near 'The Spoilbank'.

Supplementary information: Son of William James and Catherine Simmonds. Husband of Florence Mabel Parnell (formerly Simmonds), of Sandridge Garage, Ascot, Berks. Native of Waterford. Grave or Memorial Reference: I.B.2. Cemetery: Spoilbank Cemetery in Belgium.

SINCLAIR, Gerald John: Rank: Captain. Regiment or Service: Black Watch (Royal Highlanders). Unit: 1st Battalion. Age at death: 21. Date of death: 18 April 1918. Killed in action.

Supplementary information: Nephew of Esther Sinclair, of Cheekpoint, Waterford. Grave or Memorial Reference: III.F.1. Cemetery: Vieille-Chapelle New British Cemetery, Lacouture in France.

SINNOTT, Michael: Rank: Private. Regiment or Service: Royal Irish Regiment. Unit: 2nd Battalion. Date of death: 14 July 1916. Service No: 7366. Born in Cappoquin, Co. Waterford. Enlisted in Waterford. Killed in action.

Supplementary information: Husband of Ellen Sinnott, of 81 Gracedieu Road, Waterford. He has no known grave but is listed on Pier and Face 3A of the Thiepval Memorial in France.

SLATTERY, John Martin: Rank: Private. Regiment or Service: South African Infantry. Unit: 2nd Regiment. Age at death: 50. Date of death: 17 July 1916 Service No: 3180. Killed in action at Delville Wood.

Supplementary information: Son of Thomas Slattery, of Baddy Gagin, Dungarvan, Co. Waterford. Son of Mr Thomas Slattery, Ballygregan. Emigrated to South Africa eighteen years ago. Volunteered for the South African Infantry and later drafted to France. He was nephew-in-law of Mr O'Hea, solicitor. From the *Munster Express*, 15 Apri 1916:

MR J. M. SLATTERY KILLED IN ACTION.
The sad news has come to us that Mr J. M. Slattery has been killed in action in France. He was the son of Mr Thomas Slattery, Ballygegan, a most respected farmer, living about two miles from Dungarvan. The poor young man had nearly reached his fortieth year. Some eighteen years ago he emigrated to South Africa, and held there, up to the time of the war, a most lucrative position. When the strife had gone on for a short

time he volunteered in the South African Infantry and saw a good deal of fighting in West Africa. When the successes were achieved in South Africa he was drafted to France and later on the firing line. There he was in many fierce engagements, but on July 17th last he was killed instantaneously. The bereaved father did not hear the sad news until quite recently and is naturally much affected. The deceased was nephew-in-law of Mr O'Hea, solicitor, who at one time, in the height of the agitation, held a seat in Parliament, and was a member of the Irish Party. It is to Mr O'Hea that Mr Thomas Slattery is indebted for the news of his son's death. In a South African paper the following notice of the sad event is given: "We announce in your issue of August 3rd, that Mr O'Hea had received a cable to say that his nephew, Mr J. M. Slattery, had been killed in action in France on 17th, July. He received a letter from captain C. R. Heenan, V.C., who wrote: "It is with the deepest regret that I write to you concerning the death of your nephew, Pte J. M. Slattery. It must be some consolation to you to know that he was killed instantaneously and therefore suffered no pain. He was a fine soldier, and is a great loss to my company. Please accept my heartfelt sympathy for you in your time of trouble." It takes the sting from grief to know that the soldier who died in the field of battle deserved such a handsome tribute as that paid to the memory of Mr O'Hea's nephew by Captain Heenan, V.C. Mr J.M. Slattery, who has unfortunately been killed, was a fine type of manhood, well known in this town and district for his fine and noble characteristics, and while in South Africa he was getting on very well and the recipient of a handsome salary. The news of his death has been heard of here with great sorrow, and the afflicted father has received very numerous messages of sympathy. The deceased was nephew also of Mr D.F. Slattery, solicitor, Dungarvan.

He has no known grave but is listed on Pier and Face 4 C on the Thiepval Memorial in France.

SMITH, Andrew Patrick: Rank: Lance Corporal. Regiment or Service: Leinster Regiment. Unit: 6th Battalion. Age at death: 22. Date of death: 11 August 1915. Service No: 3085. Born in Ballybricken, Co. Waterford. Enlisted in Galway. Killed in action in Gallipoli.

Supplementary information: Son of the late John George Smith, of 5 Consent Hill Terrace, Waterford. He has no known grave but is listed on 184 and 185. He has no known grave but is listed on Panel 190 to 196 on the Helles Memorial in Turkey.

SMITH, Ernest Frederick William: Rank: Second Lieutenant. Regiment or Service: Royal Flying Corps Secondary Regiment: Leinster Regiment Secondary. Unit: and 1st Battalion. Age at death, 20. Date of death: 27 December 1916. Died of wounds.

Supplementary information: Son of Ernest Palmer Smith and Annie Ryall (formerly Smith), of Camcor, Birr, King's Co. From the *King's County Chronicle,* January 1917:

Died on 21 December, 1916, of injuries received while flying in action, Sec-Lieutenant, Ernest F. W. Smith, 7th Leinster Regiment, attached, Royal Flying Corps, only son of the late Ernest Palmer Smith and Mrs Smith, Camcor, Kinnitty, and grandson of the late George W Smith, Dove Hill, Birr, aged 20.

King's County Chronicle, January 1917:

YOUNG AIRMAN KILLED IN FLYING ACTION.

Lieutenant Smith's Career
Pulpit References at Kinnitty.
Lieutenant Ernest Frederick William Smith, whose sad death in action occurred on the 28th of December, was educated at Bishop Foy's School, Waterford. He entered Trinity College before his seventeenth year. After passing his Little-Go(?), he joined the Medical School and passed the examinations of the first year with credit. He belonged to the O. T. C. of Trinity College

and at the outbreak of the war volunteered in the 7th Leinster's in September, 1914. He went to France with his Regiment in December, 1915, spending Christmas in the trenches. In May, 1916, his ankle was injured by the fall off a parapet after shelling and he had to return. He went out again in August to rejoin his Regiment and took part in the severe fighting in the battle of the Somme, where his Regiment greatly distinguished itself. He then received his orders for the Flying Corps, which he entered in September. He worked as an observation officer for some time and died from injuries received in a flying action. He was the only child of the late Ernest Palmer Smith, of Camcor, Kinnitty, and grandson of the late George William Smith, of Dove Hill. His widowed mother, Mrs Smith, of Camcor, has been the recipient of innumerable messages of sympathy in the loss of her gallant son, who was held in very high regard by everyone who knew him.

The Rector, Dr Montgomery Hitchcock, alluded to the death of this gallant young officer in his sermon on Sunday last. He said: " It was with great distress and genuine grief that we heard on Saturday of the death in action of Lieutenant Ernest Smith, of the Royal Flying Corps. He was a gallant and brave officer, of whom we all may be justly proud. He died in battle. He gave his life for his country. He could do no more. In the battle on the Somme he fought bravely with his Regiment–the 7th Leinster's. He then entered the Flying Corps, and was greatly interested in his work, for which he had a natural aptitude. From his youth he had always been keen on flying; and when he was given his chance he took it. His death removes a very promising airman, and a courageous and efficient officer at a time when such can ill be spared. Our hearts go out in sympathy to his poor widowed mother, who has lost her only hope, her only joy in life. May God comfort her and the friends who mourn his loss with her in a common grief. And may the memory and example of this youthful hero

encourage and inspire others to show a like enthusiasm for their country's cause. We are sure that the Lord who said 'weep not' to the widowed mother and gave her back her only son will restore to the bereaved mother in our midst her son, in His own good time and in a more real, spiritual and lasting hope. Many people have said 'don't cry' and many will say it so long as women may weep; but no one ever said it in such a way, giving the power to bear the blow with the sympathy that went forth from his soul, to heal the broken-hearted and comfort those that mourn. May those words, eternal in value and spirit, alleviate the sorrow that lies upon his mother's heart."

King's County Chronicle, January 1917:

LATE LIEUTENANT SMITH.
His fine Air Feats.
Commander's Letter.
How he met his death. In connection with the death in a flying action of the brilliant young King's County man. Lieutenant Smith (reported in our last issue) the following letter received by his relatives from the commander of his flying squadron give the additional particulars of the manner in which he met his death.

No 9 Squadron, R. F. C.
28th December, 1916.
Dear Mrs Smith.
I very much regret having to give you some very bad news. It is with feelings of the greatest sympathy that I have to inform you that your son, Ernest, was yesterday involved in an aeroplane smash which resulted in his death whilst in hospital last night. I got to the scene of the accident only a few minutes after it occurred when he was quite unconscious and did not regain consciousness before he died. A doctor attended him almost immediately and he was removed to hospital where he was operated on last night, but died shortly after. The bone of his skull was fractured in the fall, but it will console you to know

that he could have suffered no pain. I have only commanded the squadron for a short time and did not, therefore know your son at all well, but the day before his accident he distinguished himself in a flight with a hostile machine which attacked him, by bringing it down, a thing rarely done from the type of machine in which he was flying at the time.

All the officers speak of him as a most capable and promising officer, and from the result of his work I thoroughly endorse their opinion. At the time of his accident he was returning from a very successful photographic flight and the accident occurred just prior to landing on the aerodrome. He will be buried this afternoon at two p. m., when several of his brother officers and men will attend. Please accept my very deepest sympathy with you in your great bereavement. I am, yours sincerely

E. Edwards.

I am not sure of the Waterford connection but he is listed on the Bishop Foy School Memorial located in Christ Church Cathedral (Church of Ireland), Henrietta Street, Waterford.

Grave or Memorial Reference: VI.A.5. Cemetery: Heilly Station Cemetery, Mericourt-l'Abbe in France.

SMITH, Frederick James: Rank: Private. Regiment or Service: Hampshire Regiment. Unit: 2nd Battalion. Date of death: 12 October 1916. Service No: 16666. Formerly he was with the Royal Irish Regiment where his number was H/15120. Born in Waterford. Enlisted in Hull, Yorkshire. Killed in action. Grave or Memorial Reference: I.G.3. Cemetery: Poperinghe New Military Cemetery in Belgium.

SMITH, Frederick Patrick: Rank: Gunner. Regiment or Service: Royal Horse Artillery and Royal Field Artillery. Unit: B Battery, 210th Brigade. Date of death: 26 September 1917.

Age at death: 26. Service No: 150820. Born in Waterford. Enlisted in Luton, Beds. Died.

Supplementary information: Son of Patrick Frederick Smith. Husband of Elizabeth May Smith, of 5 Rosary Terrace, Rosary Road, Norwich. Grave or Memorial Reference: Cemetery: VII.D.32. Mendingham Military Cemetery in Belgium.

SMITH, Robert: Rank: Sapper. Regiment or Service: Corps of Royal Engineers. Unit: 406th Field Company, Royal Engineers. Age at death: 22. Date of death: 9 April 1917. Service No: 420355. Born in Duncannon, Co. Waterford. Enlisted in Paisley, Renfrewshire while living in Nitshill, Lanarkshire. Killed in action.

Supplementary information: Son of Thomas and Margaret Smith, of Victoria Road, Nitshill, Glasgow. Grave or Memorial Reference: I.A.10. Cemetery: St Nicholas British Cemetery in France.

SMITH, Thomas Emmanual: Rank: Second Lieutenant Regiment or Service: Royal Garrison Artillery. Unit: 263rd Siege Battery. Age at death: 19. Date of death: 23 April 1917. Supplementary information: Son of Capt. T. Smith (R.E.), of 19 Rue Doubreh, Cairo, Egypt. He is listed on the Bishop Foy School Memorial located in Christ Church Cathedral (Church of Ireland), Henrietta Street, Waterford. From the the *Waterford News*, May 1917:

YOUNG OFFICER KILLED.

Sec. -Lieutenant. T.E. Smith, Royal Garrison Artillery, son of Lieutenant. T. Smith, R.E. (who is at present in Egypt) and of Mrs Smith, the Laurels, Waterford, has been killed at the front. The sad news reached his mother on yesterday. Lieutenant. Smith was reported missing since the 23rd of last month.

Grave or Memorial Reference: VIII.E.40. Cemetery: Orchard Dump Cemetery, Arleux-En-Gohelle in France.

SOMERS, Patrick: Rank: Private. Regiment or Service: Royal Irish Regiment. Unit: 2nd Battalion. Date of death: 28 May 1916. Service No: 7622. Born in Waterford. Enlisted in Waterford. Died of wounds. Grave or Memorial Reference: I.C.20. Cemetery: Mericourt-l'Abbe Communal Cemetery Extenstion, Mericourt-l'Abbe in France.

SPARKES, Edward: Rank: Private. Regiment or Service: Nottinghamshire and Derbyshire Regiment. Unit: 16th Battalion. Date of death: 10 October 1916. Service No: 70088. Born in Fermoy, Waterford. Enlisted in St Pancras, Middlesex while living in Southall, Middlesex. Killed in action. He has no known grave but is listed on Pier and Face 10C, 10D, and 11 A on the Thiepval Memorial in France.

STAFFORD, John: Rank: Boatswain (Bosun). Regiment or Service: Mercantile Marine. Unit: SS *Lorca* (London). Lorca was torpedoed by German submarine U-49. Age at death: 38. Date of death: 15 November 1916.
Supplementary information: Husband of Mary Stafford, of 12 Mount Sion Avenue, Waterford. Born at: Bannow. From the *Waterford News*, June 1917:

WATERFORD SEAMEN LOST.

Applications at City Sessions.

The deaths at sea of two Waterford sailors formed the subject of applications before County Court Judge Fitzgerald, K. C., at the City Quarter Sessions las Friday.

Mr P.R. Buggy (instructed by the local branch of the Seamen's Union) applied on behalf of Mary Stafford, 10 Mount Sion Avenue, for the distribution of a sum of £300, paid into court by the owners of the SS *Lorca*, a London vessel, on which her husband, John Stafford, sailed as A. B. The steamer left Norfolk, Virginia, USA. on 29th October, 1916, for a United Kingdom part, under Admiralty orders, but has not since been heard of, and she had been declared lost at Lloyds. Stafford left a widow and four children, the eldest of whom, William, was his son by his first wife, and was, since last April, living at Bannow, County Wexford, with its grandmother. The widow and children, said Mr Buggy, would be entitled to a pension under the Admiralty scheme.

Mrs Mary Stafford corroborated those statements, and Mr Hill, Secretary of the local branch of the Seamen's Union, explained to his Honour the scheme of pensions provided by the admiralty.

Mr Keane appeared for Mrs M. Stafford, senior, mother of the deceased sailor, and his examination of her elicited the statement that it was the intention of the father of the boy now with her to give the son to her and take him away from his stepmother, and he said that the last time he returned from a voyage.

Mr Michael Murphy informed the court that the last witness was a respectable woman.

His Honor directed that £100 be allocated to the widow, and £200 evenly divided among the four children, He ordered £50 to be paid out of the widow's share at once, and impounded the children's share, with interest to accrue.

He has no known grave but is listed on the Tower Hill Memorial in the UK.

STAPLETON, Edward: Rank: Gunner. Regiment or Service: Royal Garrison Artillery. Unit: 117th Heavy Battery. Date of death: 22 April 1917. Service No: 3571. Born in Trinity Without, Waterford. Enlisted in Waterford. Died. From the the *Waterford News*, May 1917:

WATERFORD SOLDIER KILLED IN ACTION.

On Tuesday Mrs Kate Stapleton, 42 Upper Yellow Road, Waterford, received notification from the War Office that her husband, Gunner E. Stapleton, 117th Heavy Battery, Royal Garrison Artillery, was killed in action on the 22nd April last.

Grave or Memorial Reference: A. 44. Cemetery: Bapaume Australian Cemetery in France.

STAPLETON, Reginald: Rank: Private. Regiment or Service: King's (Liverpool Regiment.) Unit: 18th Battalion. Date of death: 24 July 1917. Service No: 11439. Born in Battersea, London. Enlisted in Waterford, while living in Waterford. Killed in action. Has no known grave but is commemorated on Panel 33. Memorial: Ypres (Menin Gate) Memorial in Belgium.

ST CLAIR Richard: Rank: Private. Regiment or Service: The King's (Liverpool Regiment). Unit: 11th Battalion. Date of death: 12 August 1915. Service No: 13050. Born in Waterford. Enlisted in Liverpool while living in. Dublin. Killed in action.

Supplementary information: Son of Thomas and Bridget St Clair. Born in Waterford. Grave or Memorial Reference: V.AA.2. Cemetery: Ypres Reservoir Cemetery in Belgium.

ST CLAIR, Robert: Rank: Private. Regiment or Service: Cheshire Regiment. Unit: 9th Battalion. Date of death: 3 September 1917. Service No: 33637. Formerly he was with the Liverpool Regiment where his number was 14047. Born in Waterford. Enlisted in Liverpool. Died of wounds. Grave or Memorial Reference: P.III.C.5A. Cemetery: St Sever Cemetery Extension, Rouen in France.

STEPHENS. Michael: Rank: Stoker 2nd Class. Regiment or Service: Royal Navy. Unit: Hood Battalion. Royal Naval Division. Age at death: 19. Date of death: 8 May 1915. Service No: K/21670.

Supplementary information: Son of Mr and Mrs Stephens, of Ozier Bank Terrace, Poleberry, Waterford. From the *Waterford News*, 1915:

KILLED IN THE DARDANELLES.

Mr William Stephens, Ozier Bank Terrace, Waterford, has been notified by the Admiralty that his son, Michael Stephens, has died at Alexandria as a result of wounds received in the Dardanelles. Deceased joined the navy about fifteen months ago and was in the force which was landed to fight the Turks in the battle for the Dardanelles. He was wounded on Thursday last and died on Friday. He was a young fellow, being only in his nineteenth year, and it is a melancholy coincidence that he received the fateful wounds on his birthday. He was a young man of fine physique, and was popular with a large number of friends in the city. Previous to joining the navy he was employed at Messrs Graves, and before that at the G.P.O

Grave or Memorial Reference: E.13. Cemetery: Lancashire Landing Cemetery in Turkey.

STEPHENS, William: Rank: Private. Regiment or Service: Royal Fusiliers (City of London Regiment.) Unit: 23rd Battalion. Date of death: 15 February 1917. Age at death: 19. Service No: G/61982. Born in Stradbally. Enlisted in Dungarvan while living in Stradbally. Killed in action.

Supplementary information: Son of William and Julia Stephens, of Stradbally, Co. Waterford. Grave or Memorial Reference: I.E.14. Cemetery, Ovillers Military Cemetery in France.

STONEY, Thomas Ramsay: Rank: Second Lieutenant (Adjt.). Regiment or Service: King's Own Scottish Borderers. Unit: 3rd Battalion. Attached to 6th Battalion. Age at death: 35. Date of death: 10 April 1918. Killed in action.

Supplementary information: Born at Dungarvan, Co. Waterford. Son of Maj. George Ormonde Stoney (K.O.S.B.) and Meylia Stoney. Husband of Dorothy Agnes Stoney, of Stokelake House, Chudleigh, Devon. Thomas is listed as a member of the Peerage. Grave or Memorial Reference: IV.A.19. Cemetery: La-Clytte Military Cemetery, in Belgium.

SULLIVAN, Daniel: Rank: Private. Regiment or Service: Household Cavalry and Cavalry of the line including the Yeomanry and Imperial Camel Corps. Unit: 2nd Reserve Regiment of Cavalry. Date of death: 19 December 1916 Service No: 29431. Born in Waterford. Enlisted in Liverpool while living in Liverpool. Died with the African Expeditionary Force. Grave or Memorial Reference: R.C.III.A.3. Cemetery: Mombasa (MBARAKI) Cemetery in Kenya.

SULLIVAN, James: Rank: Private. Regiment or Service: Royal Irish Regiment. Unit: 6th Battalion. Age at death: 30. Date of death: 31 August 1915. Service No: 109. Born in St John's, Waterford. Enlisted in Waterford. Killed in action in Gallipoli.

Supplementary information: Son of John and Ellen Sullivan, of Waterford. Grave or Memorial Reference: III.B.7. Cemetery: Lala Baba Cemetery in Turkey.

SULLIVAN, Jeremiah: Rank: Cattleman. Regiment or Service: Mercantile Marine. Unit: SS *Formby* (Glasgow). Age at death: 44. Date of death: 16 December 1917. The ship was lost with all hands and never located during a fierce storm.

Supplementary information: Son of the late James and Catherine Sullivan. Husband of Mary Sullivan (*née* Cummins) of Faithlegg, Halfway House, Waterford. Born at Cork. He has no known grave but is listed on the Tower Hill Memorial in the UK. He is also listed on the Formby-Coningbeg Memorial, Adelphi Quay in Waterford City.

SULLIVAN, John: Rank: Private. Regiment or Service: Royal Irish Regiment. Unit: 6th Battalion. Age at death: 34. Date of death: 21 August 1916. Service No: 3378. Born in St John's, Waterford. Enlisted in Waterford. Killed in action.

Supplementary information: Son of John and Nora Sullivan. Husband of Elizabeth Sullivan, of 30 Roches Street, Waterford. Born in Waterford. From the *Waterford News*, September 1916:

DEATH OF A GALLANT WATERFORD SOLDIER.

"We were very proud of him."

News have been received that Private Jack Sullivan, of Roche's Street, has been killed in France. He was a limeburner with Mr Spencer, and about two years ago got £5 and a Carnegie Certificate for saving the life of a young woman on the Waterside who, with a pony and trap, got into difficulties and over turned into the pill opposite the gas works.

Mrs Sullivan, the sorrowing wife of this gallant fellow, has received two letters, one from a comrade of her husband, and another from the officer in charge of his company. We reprint the letters below, and it will be seen from reading them that Private Sullivan was popular with his comrades and valued by his officers. The soldier writes:

Dear Madam—It is very hard to me have to break the sad news to you and your family of the death of your husband, John Sullivan. I am pleased to say he died a happy death, for he had the priest to anoint him. He died of wounds. I am sending a photo which I found in his pay-book. Your husband had been well looked after before his death by his comrades. He was buried in the cemetery of the Regiment.

Yours sincerely.

3655. Peter Keogh.

C Company, 6th R.I.R., France.

[Peter Keogh was a Kildare man and was KIA in September, 1917, Author].

The officer writes:

Dear Madam,

As I was the officer commanding the party in which your husband took part, I wish to offer you my deepest sympathy. When wounded your husband was well cared for by his comrades, and died in the hands of his priest. He did his duty most gallantly, and all were very proud of him. We mourn the loss of a brave comrade with deepest sympathy.

I am sincerely yours.

Arthur C. Pateman.

2nd Lieutenant. 'C' R. I. Regiment.

Grave or Memorial Reference: I.A.8. Cemetery: St Patrick's Cemetery, Loos in France.

SULLIVAN, John: Rank: Stoker 2nd Class. Regiment or Service: Royal Navy. Unit: HMS *Monmouth*. Age at death: 20. Date of death: 1 November 1914. On this day HMS *Monmouth* received an 8.2-inch shell from the SMS *Gneisenau* which almost blew her to pieces. She limped away and later that day was sent to the bottom by SS Nurnberg. There were no survivors. Service No: SS/115772.

Supplementary information: Son of John and Catherine Sullivan, of 15 St Ignatius Street, Waterford. Grave or Memorial Reference: 3 on the Plymouth Naval Memorial, UK.

SULLIVAN, John: Rank: Winchman. Regiment or Service: Mercantile Marine. Unit: SS *Coningbeg* (Glasgow). Torpedoed by German Submarine U-62. There were no survivors. U-62 surrendered in November 1918. Age at death: 57. Date of death: 18 December 1917.

Supplementary information: Son of the late James and Anne Sullivan. Husband of Margaret Sullivan (*née* Foran), of 16 Poleberry, Waterford. Born in Waterford. (Consider, **SULLIVAN, Patrick:** Rank: Fireman, Author). He has no known grave but is listed on the Tower Hill Memorial in the UK. He is also listed on the Formby-Coningbeg Memorial, Adelphi Quay in Waterford City.

SULLIVAN, John: Rank: Private. Regiment or Service: Irish Guards. Unit: 1st Battalion. Date of death: 28 July 1915. Service No: 3749. Born in Lismore, Co. Waterford. Enlisted in

Dublin while living in Belfast, Co. Antrim. Died of wounds. Grave or Memorial Reference: III.E.4. Cemetery: Niederzwehren Cemetery in Germany.

SULLIVAN, Martin: Rank: Fireman and Trimmer. Regiment or Service: Mercantile Marine. Unit: SS *Lodaner* (London). Age at death: 43. Date of death: 14 April 1918.

Supplementary information: Son of the late Cornelius and Mary Sullivan. Husband of Sarah Sullivan (*née* Brogan), of 401 St Vincent Street, Glasgow. Born in Waterford. He has no known grave but is listed on the Tower Hill Memorial in the UK.

SULLIVAN, Michael: Rank: Rifleman. Regiment or Service: London Regiment. Unit: 18th (County of London) Battalion (London Irish Rifles). Date of death: 4 May 1918. Service No: 592308. Born in Waterford. Enlisted in Piccadilly while living in London West. Killed in action in Egypt. Grave or Memorial Reference: K.5. Cemetery: Jerusalem War Cemetery, Israel.

SULLIVAN, Michael: Rank: Private. Regiment or Service: Royal Irish Regiment. Unit: 2nd Battalion. Age at death: 33. Date of death: 17 September 1914. Service No: 7225. Born in Portlaw, Co. Waterford. Enlisted in Carrick-on-Suir, Co. Tipperary while living in Portlaw. Died of wounds.

Supplementary information: Son of James and Honora Sullivan, of Queen Street, Portlaw, Co. Waterford. Grave or Memorial Reference: Plot 38. 1914-18 Row A. Grave 10. Cemetery: Le Mans West Cemetery in France.

SULLIVAN, Patrick: Rank: Fireman. Regiment or Service: Mercantile Marine. Unit: SS *Coningbeg* (Glasgow). The only information I have on this sailor is contained in the below. He is not in any of the War Dead databases. From the *Waterford News*, May 1915:

WATERFORD FIREMAN KILLED IN
LIVERPOOL.

A man named Patrick Sullivan, of
Ballytruckle, Waterford, a fireman on board
the SS *Coningbeg* owned by the Clyde
Shipping Company, fell into the Princess
Dry Dock at Liverpool on Sunday and died
on Monday from the effects of the injuries
received. Deceased was a young man. He
was unmarried and lived with his sister at
Ballytruckle. He had a brother working
aboard the *Coningbeg* also.

(Consider **SULLIVAN, John:** Rank:
Winchman. He may be the brother.)

SULLIVAN, Patrick: Rank: Private.
Regiment or Service: Royal Irish Regiment.
Unit: 2nd Battalion. Age at death: 40. Date of
death: 14 July 1916. Service No: 6831. Born
in Portlaw, Co. Waterford. Enlisted in Portlaw.
Died of wounds.

Supplementary information: Son of James and
Nora Sullivan. Husband of Bridget Sullivan. He
has no known grave but is listed on Pier and
Face 3A on the Thiepval Memorial in France.

SULLIVAN, Peter: Rank: Private. Regiment
or Service: Royal Irish Regiment. Unit: 5th
Battalion. Date of death: 16 August 1915. Service
No: 206. Born in Crooke, Co. Waterford. Resided
at Knockboy. Enlisted in Harverfordwest,
Pembrokeshire while living in Waterford. Killed
in action in Gallipoli. Killed at Suvla. He has no
known grave but is listed on Panel 55 on the
Helles Memorial in Turkey.

SULLIVAN, William: Rank: Private.
Regiment or Service: Machine Gun Corps
(Infantry). Unit: 51st Battalion. Age at death:
20. Date of death: 21 March 1918. Service
No: 43320. Previously he was with the Royal
Irish Regiment where his number was 7677.
Killed in action. Born in Waterford. Enlisted
in Waterford.

Supplementary information: Son of John and
Margaret Sullivan, of 16 Poleberry, Waterford.
Grave or Memorial Reference: Bay 10 on the
Arras Memorial in France.

SUTTON, John: Rank: Sapper. Regiment
or Service: Royal Engineers. (R.E.
Reinforcements). Age at death: 39. Date of
death: 5 July 1916. Service No: 140341. Born
in Manchester. Enlisted in Waterford. Died in
Mesopotamia.

Supplementary information: Husband of Ellen
Sutton, of 1 Robinson's Lane, Waterford. Grave
or Memorial Reference: V.Q.7. Cemetery:
Basra War Cemetery in Iraq.

SUTTON, Michael: Rank: Private.
Regiment or Service: Irish Guards. Unit: 2nd
Battalion. Date of death: 27 September 1915.
Service No: 7258. Born in Waterford. Enlisted
in Waterford. Killed in action. He has no
known grave but is listed on Panels 9 and 10
on the Loos Memorial in France.

SWEENEY, John: Rank: Stoker. Regiment
or Service: Royal Naval Reserve. Unit:
HMS *Vivid*. Age at death: 40. Date of
death: 1 September 1917. Service No: 5337.
Supplementary information: Husband of
Mary Anne Sweeney, of Main Street, Tramore.
Grave or Memorial Reference: Near north-
east corner. Cemetery: Corbally Catholic
Churchyard, Co. Waterford.

SWEENEY, Patrick: Rank: Private.
Regiment or Service: Royal Irish Regiment.
Unit: 2nd Battalion. Age at death: 40. Date of
death: 19 October 1914. Service No: 6645.
Born in Lismore, Co. Waterford. Enlisted in
Waterford while living in Lismore. Killed in
action.

Supplementary information: Son of Cornelius
Sweeney, and Mrs Sweeney. Husband of
Ellen Sweeney, of New Street, Lismore, Co.
Waterford. From the *Munster Express*, 'The

War. Corporal Patrick Sweeney, of the Royal Irish Regiment, a native of New Street, Lismore, was prayed for at Lismore R.C. Church on Sunday last.' Grave or Memorial Reference: IV.J.6. Cemetery: Bailleul Road East Cemetery, ST. Laurent-Blangy in France.

SWEENEY, Patrick: Rank: Seaman. Regiment or Service: Royal Naval Reserve. Unit: HMS *Goliath*. Age at death: 38. Date of death: 13 May 1915. Service No: 4776B. HMS *Goliath* was sunk by three torpedoes from German destroyer *Muvanet-I-Milet*, she blew up and capsized immediately taking 570 of her 750 crew including the Captain to a watery grave. Ten Waterford men died on the *Goliath* that day.

Supplementary information: Son of Michael and Mary Sweeney, of Ballymacaw, Dunmore East, Co. Waterford. Grave or Memorial Reference: 8 on the Plymouth Naval Memorial, UK.

SWEENY, William: Rank: Private. Regiment or Service: Black Watch. Unit: 1st Battalion. Date of death: 3 September 1916. Service No: S/4031. Born in Lismore, Co. Waterford. Enlisted in Glasgow, Lanarkshire Killed in action. He has no known grave but is listed on Pier and Face 10 A on the Thiepval Memorial in France.

SWIFT, James: Rank: Private. Regiment or Service: Royal Irish Regiment. Unit: 2nd Battalion. Age at death: 23. Date of death: 19 October 1914. Service No: 5971. Born in St John's, Waterford. Enlisted in Waterford. Killed in action

Supplementary information: Stepson of Mrs Mary Swift, of 3 Harterys Avenue, Johnstown, Waterford. Grave or Memorial Reference: 11 and 12 on the Le Touret Memorial in France.

SWIFT, John: Rank: Private. Regiment or Service: Royal Dublin Fusiliers. Unit: 2nd Battalion. Date of death: 18 October 1914. Service No: 7284. Born in Drogheda, Count Louth (Soldiers died in the Great War) Waterford (Irelands Memorial Records). Enlisted in Drogheda. Killed in action. Has no known grave but is commemorated on Panel 10 on the Ploegsteert Memorial in Belgium.

T

THOMPSON, J.: Rank: Private. Regiment or Service: Royal Irish Regiment. Unit: 2nd Battalion. Age at death: 27. Date of death: 6 September 1920. Service No: 10716.

Supplementary information: Son of Mrs Ellen Thompson, of 10 Walshe's Lane, Waterford. Grave or Memorial Reference: S.B.138. Cemetery: Ballynaneashagh (St Otteran's) Catholic Cemetery in Co. Waterford.

THOMPSON, Patrick: Rank: Gunner. Regiment or Service: Royal Field Artillery. Unit: 402nd Battery. Age at death: 32. Date of death: 5 June 1918. Service No: 101533. Born in Kilmacthomas. Enlisted in Carlow. Died of wounds.

Supplementary information: Son of Thomas Thompson, of Kilmacthomas, Co. Waterford. Grave or Memorial Reference: I.E.6. Cemetery: Longeau British Cemetery in France.

TOBIN, Francis: Rank: Private. Regiment or Service: Royal Munster Fusiliers Unit: 1st Battalion. Date of death: 12 December 1916. Service No: 6917. Born in Kilrossentry, Co. Waterford. Enlisted in Waterford while living in Kilrossenty, Co. Waterford. Died of wounds. Grave or Memorial Reference: IV.E.9. Cemetery: Dernancourt Communal Cemetery Extension in France.

TOBIN, John: Rank: Private. Regiment or Service: Royal Irish Regiment. Unit: 1st Battalion. Date of death: 18 March 1915. Service No: 7281. Born in Ring, Co. Waterford. Enlisted in Clonmel. Died of wounds. He has no known grave but is listed on Panel 55 on the Helles Memorial in Turkey.

TOOLE, Andrew Brown: Rank: Private. Regiment or Service: Queen's Own Cameron Highlanders. Unit: 7th Battalion. Date of death: 25 September 1915. Service No: S/13674. Born in Cowdenbeath, Fifeshire. Enlisted in Glasgow, Lanarkshire while living in Bonnachon, Co. Waterford. Killed in action. He has no known grave but is listed on Panel 119 and 124 on the Loos Memorial in France.

TOOLE, John: Rank: Sergeant. Regiment or Service: Royal Garrison Artillery. Unit: 109th Siege Battery. Date of death: 28 January 1917. Service No: 2108. Born in Waterford. Enlisted in Waterford. Died. From the *Waterford News*, February 1917:

DEATH OF A WATERFORD SOLDIER.

The death took place on Sunday evening in hospital at Rouen, France, of Quartermaster Sergant O'Toole [*sic*], Morrisson's Road, Waterford. Deceased had twenty three years service, and served in the South African War. The deceased was brother of Mr Nicholas O'Toole, at present employed in Messrs Hall's Stores, Ferrybank.

Grave or Memorial Reference: O.IV.F.2. Cemetery: St Sever Cemetery Extension, Rouen in France.

TREACY, Hugh: Rank: Steward. Regiment or Service: Mercantile Marine. Unit: SS *Coningbeg* (Glasgow). Torpedoed by German Submarine U-62. There were no survivors. U-62 surrendered in November 1918. Age at death: 46. Date of death: 18 December 1917.

Supplementary information: Son of the late John and Mary Treacy. Husband of Anne Treacy (*née* McCabe), of 44 Thomas Street, Waterford. Born in Waterford. He has no known grave but is listed on the Tower Hill Memorial in the UK. He is also listed on the Formby-Coningbeg Memorial, Adelphi Quay in Waterford City.

TROY, Donald Patrick: Rank: Sergeant. Regiment or Service: Army Service Corps. Unit: 3rd Div. Ammunition Park. Age at death: 25. Date of death: 6 October 1917. Service No: M/22977. Born in Malta. Enlisted in Dover while living in Dover. Killed in action.

Supplementary information: Son of James and Annie Troy, of Portlaw, Co. Waterford. Grave or Memorial Reference: I.K.22. Cemetery: Brandhoek New Military Cemetery No 3 in Belgium.

TUOHY, Michael: Rank: Donkeyman. Regiment or Service: Mercantile Marine. Unit: SS *Hazelwood* (Middlesbrough). Age at death: 54. Date of death: 19 October 1917.

Supplementary information: Husband of Margaret Tuohy (*née* Hickey), of 6 Mall Lane, Waterford. Born at Limerick. He has no known grave but is listed on the Tower Hill Memorial in the UK.

TYLER, George: Rank: Private. Regiment or Service: East Surrey Regiment. Unit: 13th Battalion. Date of death: 26 November 1917. Service No: 30597. Previously he was with the Middlesex Regiment where his number was 24178. Born in Clonmel, Waterford, Ireland. Enlisted in Shoreditch, Middlesex. He has no known grave but is listed on Panel 6 on the Cambrai Memorial in Louveral in France.

U

USSHER, Beverly: Rank: Captain. Regiment or Service: Leinster Regiment. Unit: Attached as Staff Captain to the 88th Brigade, 29th Division. Age at death: 35. Date of death: 19 June 1915. Killed in action.

Supplementary information: Son of the Revd Richard Ussher and Mary Ussher, of Westbury Vicarage, Brackley, Northants. Husband of Ethel. His brother Stephen also fell. From 'Our Heroes' 1916:

Beverly Ussher. From 'Our Heroes'.

Captain Beverly Ussher, Leinster Regiment, went out with the Mediterranean Expeditionary Force as Staff Captain and was killed at the Dardanelles. Captain Ussher was a son of the rev. R. Ussher, Vicar of Westbury, Brackley, Northampton. He was born in 1879, was educated at St Edward's School and Wadham College, Oxford, and in 1900 received a University commission in the Leinsters. For service in the South African War he received the Queen's Medal with four clasps. His brother, Captain Stephen Ussher, 129th Baluchis, was killed in action in France in December last.

Grave or Memorial Reference: II.C.8. Cemetery: Twelve Tree Copse Cemetery in Turkey.

USSHER, Stephen: Rank: Captain. Regiment or Service: Indian Army. Unit: 129th Duke of Connaught's Own Baluchis. Age at death: 32. Date of death: 16 December 1914.

Supplementary information: Son of the Revd Richard and Mary Ussher, of Westbury Vicarage, Brackley, Northants. From 'Our Heroes' 1916:

Captain Stephen Ussher, 129th Duke of Connaught's Own Baluchis, Indian Army, was killed at Givenchy on December 16th last. Captain Ussher came from an Irish family, his father, Rev. Richard Ussher, Vicar of Westbury, North Hants, being a native of Co. Waterford. Captain Ussher was educated at St. Edward's School, Oxford, and the Royal Military College, Sandhurst. He was first attached to the Buffs at Poona in 1902, and in 1904 received Captaincy in 1911 and served as Adjutant to the Regiment for four years.

Grave or Memorial Reference: 3. Cemetery: Beuvry Communal Cemetery in France.

V

VEALE, Martin: Rank: Private. Regiment or Service: The King's (Liverpool Regiment). Unit: 12th Battalion. Date of death: 11 October 1916. Service No: 38322. Born in Waterford. Enlisted in Seaforth, Lancashire while living in Bootle, Liverpool. Killed in action. Has no known grave but is commemorated on Pier and Face 1D 8B and 8C on the Thiepval Memorial in France.

VEALE, Michael: Rank: Stoker. Regiment or Service: Royal Naval Reserve. Unit: HMS *Hampshire*. Age at death: 35. Date of death: 5 June 1916. Service No: 6984S.

Supplementary information: Son of John and Margaret Veale, of Dungarvan, Co. Waterford. Husband of Mary Ellen Connor (formerly Veale), of 5 Pontyglasdwr Street, Swansea. Grave or Memorial Reference: 19 on the Plymouth Naval Memorial, UK.

VEALE, Michael: Rank: Petty Officer Stoker. Regiment or Service: Royal Navy. Unit: HMS *Vivid*. Date of death: 15 July 1915. Service No: 295061 (Dev) Grave or Memorial Reference: In south-west part. Cemetery: Dungarvan (Ballinroad) Catholic Graveyard, Co. Waterford.

VEALE, Thomas: Rank: Private. Regiment or Service: The King's (Liverpool Regiment). Unit: 13th Battalion. Age at death: 28. Date of death: 10 October 1918. Service No: 88774. Previously he was with the Royal Engineers where his number was 88774. Born in Kilgobnet, Waterford. Enlisted 'in the field' while living in Ballynelty, Dunjarvon. Killed in action.

Supplementary information: Son of William and Catherine Veale, of Ballyreeta, Dungarvan, Co. Waterford. Grave or Memorial Reference: C.9. Cemetery: Fornville Military Cemetery in France.

VILLIERS-STUART, Desmond De la Poer: Rank: Private Regiment or Service: Australian Infantry, A.I.F. Unit: 16th Battalion. Age at death: 20. Date of death: 7 August 1917. Service No: 7107. Enlisted in Blackboy Hill, Western Australia. Killed in action.

Supplementary information: (Served as Manders). Son of Capt. Gerald and Maud Hutcheson Villiers-Stuart, of Richmond, Cappoquin, Co. Waterford. Data from attestation papers:

What is your name? Richard Clive Manders.

In or near what Parish or Town were you born? Goring, Oxford, England. (The details on his original application ; -Born Columbus Ohio, USA,)

Are you a natural born British subject or a Naturalised British subject? British Subject.

What is your age? 23 years.

What is your trade or calling? Orchardist.

Are you, or have you been an Apprentice? No. If so where, to whom, and for what period?

Are you married? No.

Who is your next of kin? [father] Henry Philip Manders, Barrone County(, Goring, Oxford, England. The details on his original application.

Next of Kin, [father] Gerrald Villers Stuart, Richmond, Cappoquin, Waterford.

Impaired foot, operated.

Age: 21 years, 2 months.

Height 5 feet, 11 inches.

Weight: 160 lbs.

Chest measurement: 34½ inches.

Complexion, fair.

Eyes: dark.

Hair: dark.

Religious denomination: C of E.

Enlisted under the name of VILLIERS-STUART, DESMOND DE LA POER. Discharged from the AIF 06 March

1016, 'Not likely to become an efficient soldier'. After he was discharged he re-enlisted under the name of MANDERS, RICHARD CLIVE. Last will leaves all his personal effects to his friend Miss Isabel S Power, 21 Wesley Road, Rathgar, Dublin.

Grave or Memorial Reference: He has no known grave but is listed on Panel 7-17-23 -25-27-29-31 on the Ypres (Menin Gate) Memorial in Belgium.

W

WALKER, William Henry: Rank: Bombardier. Regiment or Service: Royal Garrison Artillery. Unit: 326th Siege Battery. Date of death: 31 August 1917. Service No: 37016. Born in Waterford. Enlisted in Devonport while living in Plymouth. Killed in action. Grave or Memorial Reference: I.K.6. Cemetery: Anzac Cemetery, Sailly-Sur-La-Lys in France.

WALL, Albert: Rank: Private. Regiment or Service: Royal Irish Fusiliers. Unit: 7th Battalion. Date of death: 29 April 1916. Service No: 16196. Formerly he was with the Royal Irish Regiment where his number was 504. Born in Waterford. Enlisted in Waterford. Died of wounds. He has no known grave but is listed on Panel 124 on the Loos Memorial in France.

WALL, Edward: Rank: Private. Regiment or Service: Royal Irish Regiment. Unit: 2nd Battalion. Date of death: 19 October 1914. Service No: 6156. Born in Dungarvan, Co. Waterford. Enlisted in Waterford while living in Dungarvan, Co. Waterford. Killed in action. Grave or Memorial Reference: He has no known grave but is listed on Panel 11 and 12 on the Le Touret Memorial in France.

WALL, James: Rank: Fireman. Regiment or Service: Mercantile Marine. Unit: SS *Coningbeg* (Glasgow). Torpedoed by German Submarine U-62. There were no survivors. U-62 surrendered in November 1918. Age at death: 42. Date of death: 18 December 1917.

Supplementary information: Son of the late James and Johanna Wall. Husband of Bridget Wall (*née* Roche), of 13 Grange Terrace, Waterford. Born at Slieverue Co. Kilkenny. He has no known grave but is listed on the Tower Hill Memorial in the UK. He is also listed on the Formby-Coningbeg Memorial, Adelphi Quay in Waterford City.

WALL, Mark: Rank: Private. Regiment or Service: Royal Irish Regiment. Unit: 'C' Coy. 5th Battalion. Age at death: 25. Date of death: 19 December 1917. Service No: 7565. Born in Slieverue, Co. Kilkenny. Enlisted in Waterford. Died at Home.

Supplementary information: Son of Thomas and Margaret Wall, of Hollow House, Abbey Lands, Ferry Bank, Waterford. From the *Munster Express*, January 1918:

WATERFORD SOLDIERS DEATH.

The death occurred at the 2nd Southern General Hospital, Bristol, on the 129th December, of Private Mark Wall, Royal Irish Regiment. The deceased, who was aged 26 years, was a native of Sallypark, Waterford, and joined the army in 1915. His service was unbroken by any term of sickness until July last when he underwent a surgical operation and from which point his health seems to have broken down. He was marked for home and arrived at Bristol on the 22nd November. His condition became worse, so much so that his parents were summoned ad he breathed his last in the presence of his mother and sister. He was interred with military honours at Arnos Vale Cemetery, Bristol.

Grave or Memorial Reference: Screen Wall. War Plot. C.9. Cemetery: Bristol (Arnos Vale) Roman Catholic Cemetery, UK.

WALL, Patrick: Rank: Fireman. Regiment or Service: Mercantile Marine. Unit: SS *Coningbeg* (Glasgow). Date of death: 18 December 1917. Torpedoed by German Submarine U-62. There were no survivors.

Supplementary information: Son of Catherine and Mark Wall. Husband of Mary Catherine Wall (*née* Connolly), of 94 Gracedieu Road, Waterford. Born in Co. Kilkenny. He has no known grave but is listed on the Tower Hill Memorial in the UK. He is also listed on the Formby-Coningbeg Memorial, Adelphi Quay in Waterford City.

WALLACE, Edward: Rank: Stoker 1st Class. Regiment or Service: Royal Navy. Unit: HMS *Defence*. Age at death: 22. Date of death: 31 May 1916. Service No: K/18630. HMS *Defence* was an armoured cruiser and was sent to the bottom by the Naval guns of a German battleship during the battle of Jutland. HMS *Defence's* magazine exploded when it was hit by a German shell. The magazine explosion triggered off other explosions which almost blew the ship apart and she went down with the entire crew of 903 men. There were no survivors. Five Waterford men died with this ship on that day.

Supplementary information: Son of Thomas and Ellen Wallace, of Sargents Court, Waterford. Grave or Memorial Reference: 16 on the Plymouth Naval Memorial, UK.

WALSH, Cornelius: Rank: Private. Regiment or Service: Royal Irish Regiment. Unit: 'B' Coy. 2nd Battalion. Age at death: 34. Date of death: 6 December 1918. Service No: 1670.

Supplementary information: Husband of Annie Walsh, of 15 Corrigeen Lane, Waterford. Grave or Memorial Reference: I.B.3. Cemetery: Belgrade Cemetery in Belgium.

WALSH, Daniel: Rank: Private. Regiment or Service: Royal Irish Regiment. Unit: 1st Garrison Battalion. Date of death: 1 June 1918. Service No: 4429. Formerly he was with the Royal Munster Fusiliers where his number was 1773. Born in Portlaw, Co. Waterford. Enlisted in Limerick while living in Listowel, Co. Kerry. Died of wounds in Egypt. Grave or Memorial Reference: H.79. Cemetery, Cairo War Memorial Cemetery in Egypt.

WALSH, Denis: Rank: Sergeant. Regiment or Service: Royal Irish Regiment. Unit: 2nd Battalion. Age at death: 39. Date of death: 23 August 1914. Service No: 4969. Born in Cappoquin, Co. Waterford. Enlisted in Dungarvan, Co. Waterford, while living in Lackeen, Co. Waterford. Killed in action.

Supplementary information: Son of Denis Walsh, of Affane, Cappoquin. Husband of Margaret Walsh (*née* Lenane), of The Green, Villierstown, Cappoquin, Co. Waterford. Grave or Memorial Reference: VI.A.47. Cemetery: St Symphorien Military Cemetery in Belgium.

WALSH, Edward: (Commonwealth War Graves Commission), **Edmond** (Soldiers died in the Great War). Rank: Private. Regiment or Service: Royal Irish Regiment. Unit: 2nd Battalion. Age at death: 36. Date of death: 14 June 1915. Service No: 7517. Born in Waterford. Enlisted in Waterford. Died of wounds.

Supplementary information: Son of Edward and Elizabeth Walsh, of 18 Peter Street, Waterford. Grave or Memorial Reference: I.E.114. Cemetery: Bailleul Communal Cemetery Extension (Nord) in France.

WALSH, Edward: Rank: Private. Regiment or Service: Royal Irish Regiment. Unit: 1st Battalion. Age at death: 25. Date of death: 24 April 1915. Service No: 9692. Born in Waterford. Enlisted in Waterford while living in Waterford. Killed in action. He has no known grave but is listed on Panel 11 on the Ypres (Menin Gate) Memorial in Belgium.

WALSH, E.: Rank: Able Seaman. Regiment or Service: Mercantile Marine. Unit: SS *Lux* (London). Age at death: 33. Date of death: 8 February 1917.

Supplementary information: Son of Ellen, and the late Patrick Walsh. Husband of Johanna Walsh (*née* Haven), of Cross Strand Street, Dungarvan, Co. Waterford. Born at

Courtmacherry, Co. Cork. He has no known grave but is listed on the Tower Hill Memorial in the UK.

WALSH, James: Rank: Seaman. Regiment or Service: Royal Naval Reserve. Unit: HMS *Goliath*. Age at death: 29. Date of death: 13 May 1915. Service No: 3852B. HMS *Goliath* was sunk by three torpedoes from German destroyer 'Muvanet-I-Milet', she blew up and capsized immediately taking 570 of her 750 crew including the Captain to a watery grave. Ten Waterford men died on the *Goliath* that day.

Supplementary information: Son of John and Julia Boston Walsh, of Passage East, Co. Waterford. Grave or Memorial Reference: 8 on the Plymouth Naval Memorial, UK.

WALSH, James: Rank: Private. Regiment or Service: Auckland Infantry Regiment, N.Z.E.F. Unit: 1st Battalion. Age at death: 37. Date of death: 7 June 1917. Service No: 19196. Occupation on Enlistment: Labourer. Killed in action.

Supplementary information: Son of James and Annie Walsh, of 1 Shee Terrace, Bath Street, Waterford, Ireland. Next of Kin, Mrs A. Walsh (mother), 1 Chase Terrace, Bath Street, Waterford. He has no known grave but is listed on Panel 33 on the Messines Ridge (N. Z.) Memorial in Belgium.

WALSH, James: Rank: Private. Regiment or Service: Royal Munster Fusiliers. Unit: 8th Battalion. Date of death: 5 September 1916. Service No: 4398. Born in Ballybricken, Co. Waterford. Enlisted in Waterford while living in Waterford. Died of wounds. (Consider Private John Walsh, No 4399, they may be brothers and joined up on the same day, Author). Grave or Memorial Reference: I.B.23. Cemetery: Dive Copse British Cemetery, Sailly-Le-Sec in France.

WALSH, John: Rank: Private. Regiment or Service: Royal Irish Regiment. Unit:

2nd Battalion. Date of death: 25 August 1918. Service No: 11094. Born in Waterford. Enlisted in Waterford. Killed in action. Grave or Memorial Reference: IV.B.38. Cemetery: Warlencourt British Cemetery in France.

WALSH, John: Rank: Private. Regiment or Service: Gloucestershire Regiment. Unit: 7th (Service) Battalion. Date of death: 21 April 1916. Service No: 15130. Born in Waterford. Enlisted in Pentre, Glam. Killed in action in Mesopotamia. He has no known grave but is listed on Panel 17 of the Basra Memorial in Iraq.

WALSH, John: Rank: Fireman. Regiment or Service: Mercantile Marine. Unit: SS *Formby* (Glasgow). Age at death: 41. Date of death: 16 December 1917. The ship was lost with all hands and never located during a fierce storm.

Supplementary information: Son of the late Patrick, and Catherine Walsh. Husband of Elizabeth Walsh (*née* Rogers, see **ROGERS, THOMAS MARTIN,** there may be a connecton), of Passage East, Co. Waterford. Born at Passage East. Co. Waterford. He has no known grave but is listed on the Tower Hill Memorial in the UK. He is also listed on the Formby-Coningbeg Memorial, Adelphi Quay in Waterford City.

WALSH, John: Rank: Private. Regiment or Service: Leinster Regiment. Unit: 2nd Battalion. Age at death: 32. Date of death: 15 May 1916. Service No: 5054. Born in Waterford. Enlisted in Cork while living in Waterford. Died of wounds.

Supplementary information: Son of John and Catherine Walsh, of 13 Bakehouse Lane, Waterford. From the *Waterford News* May 1916:

WATERFORD SOLDIER'S DEATH.

The death took place on Monday last at the St John and St Elizabeth Hospital, London, as a result of wounds received in action, of Private John Walsh, 5054, 2nd Leinster Regiment. Deceased was brother of Mr James Walsh, clerk in the office of Mr George Nolan, solicitor, O'Connell Street. He joined the army on the 22nd October, 1915, and went to the front on the 21st February last. He was wounded in France on the 29th April, and passed away, as stated, on Monday last in London. He was buried yesterday with full military honours, his brother, Mr James Walsh, being chief mourner at the funeral.

Grave or Memorial Reference: 6. (Screen Wall). Cemetery: Kensal Green (St Mary's) Roman Catholic Cemetery, UK.

WALSH, John: Rank: Private. Regiment or Service: Royal Munster Fusiliers. Unit: 8th Battalion. Age at death: 18. Date of death: 11 May 1916. Service No: 4399. Born in Waterford. Enlisted in Waterford while living in Waterford. Died of wounds.

Supplementary information: Son of Thomas and Bridget Walsh, of 40 Gracedieu Road, Waterford. Grave or Memorial Reference: V.C. 37. Cemetery: Bethune Town Cemetery in France.

WALSH, Joseph: Rank: Private. Regiment or Service: US Army. Unit: 11th Engineer Regiment. Date of death: 28 July 1918.

Supplementary information: From the WWI Long Island (Brooklyn) War Dead:

Walsh, Joseph, 1877 Putnam Avenue. Horseshoer Joseph Walsh, whose name appears under the head of those who died from accident or other cause, is one of three brothers who were wounded in the present war and one of two brothers who, after receiving wounds on the field of battle, were later killed by accident. The address given: 1877, Putnam Avenue is that of his aunt, Mrs B. Hughes. Joseph was born in Waterford, Ireland, thirty five years ago and came to live in Brooklyn fifteen years ago. He enlisted in the army in 1916, saw service on the Mexican border and went to France with the Eleventh Engineers, about the first Regiment to go across.

Soon after arriving in France he was struck by shrapnel in the side and also received a bayonet thrust in the wrist. He met his death while driving a truck which ran into a pole behind the lines. His companion was also killed at the same time. Two brothers were in the British army and both were wounded. One brother, Thomas, after having been invalided to Canada, was riding in a train when it was wrecked and he was killed. A letter to his aunt says Joseph is buried in Grave 54, American Plot, Chateaureaux, France.

Wounded several times in action, Private Joseph Walsh a gallant young Irish-American soldier met death by accident in France. Walsh, who had lived fifteen years in Brooklyn, left two brothers in Ireland, both of whom enlisted in the British Army and mad the supreme sacrifice, one on the field in France and the other, wounded and sent to a hospital in Canada, killed in a train wreck. Walsh enlisted as a horse-shoer, but the Irish blood in him called for fighting and he went to the front, where enemy shrapnel "got him." Wounded several times, he recovered sufficiently to return to duty and drove a motor truck close behind the fighting lines. A collision of his truck with a telegraph pole resulted in his death as heroic as if he had fallen in battle.

Grave or Memorial Reference: Plot A, Row, 18, Grave, 32. Cemetery: St Mihiel American Cemetery, Thiaucourt in France.

WALSH, Joseph: Rank: Private. Regiment or Service: Royal Irish Regiment. Unit: 2nd Battalion. Date of death: 19 October 1914. Service No: 4693. Born in Carrick-on-Suir, Co. Waterford. Enlisted in Waterford. Died. He has no known grave but is listed on Panels 11 and 12 on the Le Touret Memorial in France.

WALSH, John: Rank: Private. Regiment or Service: Royal Irish Regiment. Unit: 2nd Battalion. Date of death: 11 June 1917. Age at death: 45. Service No: 5276. Born in Drumcannon, Co. Waterford. Enlisted in Waterford while living in Tramore, Co. Waterford. Died of wounds.

Supplementary information: Son of Patrick and Statia Walsh. From the the *Waterford News*, January 1917:

A PRISONER IN GERMANY.
Mr P. Walsh, Jail Street, Waterford, has received a postcard photograph of his son, Private John Walsh, R.I.R., who is a prisoner of war in Limburg (Lahn). Private Walsh is one of a group of five, all of whom seem in good form, in spite of their dreary imprisonment.

Grave or Memorial Reference: I.G.2. Cemetery: Hazebrouck Communal Cemetery, Nord, in France.

WALSH, John: Rank: Private. Regiment or Service: Royal Irish Regiment. Unit: 2nd Battalion. Date of death: 21 March 1918. Service No: 7645. Born in Waterford. Enlisted in Waterford. Killed in action. He has no known grave but is listed in Panels 30 to 31 on the Pozières Memorial in France.

WALSH, John: Rank: Private. Regiment or Service: East Lancashire Regiment. Unit: 1st Battalion. Date of death: 11 April 1918. Age at death: 42. Service No: 18724. He won the Military Medal and is listed in the *London Gazette*. Born in Aglish, Co. Waterford. Enlisted in Merthyr, Glam. Killed in action.

Supplementary information: Husband of Mary Walsh, of 7 New House, Garden City, Penydaren, Merthyr Tydfil, Glamorganshire. He has no known grave but is listed on Panel 5 and 6 on the Ploegsteert Memorial in Belgium.

WALSH, Martin: Rank: Private. Regiment or Service: Royal Irish Regiment. Unit: 2nd Battalion. Date of death: 22 February 1915. Service No: 5913. Born in Trinity Without, Waterford. Enlisted in Waterford. Died at Home. Grave or Memorial Reference: N. 172918. Cemetery: Brompton Cemetery, UK.

WALSH, Martin: Rank: Sailor. Regiment or Service: Mercantile Marine. Unit: SS *Penvearn* (Galmouth). Age at death: 21. Date of death: 1 March 1918.

Supplementary information: Son of Patrick and Honora Walsh, of Passage East, Waterford. He has no known grave but is listed on the Tower Hill Memorial in the UK.

WALSH, Michael: Rank: Lance Corporal. Regiment or Service: Royal Irish Fusiliers. Unit: 2nd Battalion. Date of death: 10 February 1915. Service No: 10625. Born in Cappoquin, Co. Waterford. Enlisted in Armagh. Killed in action. Grave or Memorial Reference: He has no known grave but is listed on Panel 42 on the Ypres (Menin Gate) Memorial in Belgium.

WALSH, Nicholas: Rank: Private. Regiment or Service: Irish Guards. Unit: No. 2 Coy. 1st Battalion. Age at death: 28. Date of death: 2 August 1917. Service No: 10775. Born in Duncannon, Co. Waterford. Enlisted in Whitehall in Middlesex. Killed in action.

Supplementary information: Son of Michael and Caroline Walsh of 13 Ponton Street, Nine Elms Lane, Battersea, London. Native of Duncannon, Co. Wexford. From an in a Wexford newspaper:

Duncannon Soldier Killed; Private Nicholas Walsh, of Duncannon, has been officially reported killed in action at the front, and the announcement has caused profound regret amongst a wide circle of friends. He joined the R. I. Regiment at the outbreak of the war and had since been on active service. In notifying his death to his relatives, his Captain paid a glowing tribute to the deceased's gallantry.

Grave or Memorial Reference: Panel 11. Memorial: Ypres (Menin Gate) Memorial in Belgium.

WALSH, P.: Rank: Private. Regiment or Service: Royal Irish Regiment. Unit: 'B' Coy. 5th Battalion. Age at death: 28. Date of death: 24 November 1918. Service No: 1288.

Supplementary information: Son of Ellen Dear (formerly Walsh), of 62 Sallypark, Waterford, and the late John Walsh. Grave or Memorial Reference: S.II.MM. 10. St Sever Cemetery Extension, Rouen in France.

WALSH, Patrick: Rank: Cattleman. Regiment or Service: Mercantile Marine. Unit: Steamship *Formby*. Date of death: 22 May 1915. The only information I have on this sailor is contained in the below. He is not in any of the War Dead databases. From the *Waterford News*, 1915:

WATERFORD CATTLEMAN DROWNED.

A Cattleman named Patrick Walsh employed by the Clyde Shipping Company, fell overboard from the SS. *Formby* on Saturday night and was drowned.

The *Formby* left Waterford at ten minutes to 8 o'clock on Saturday for Birkinhead and the unfortunate occurrence took place opposite Glass House. It is not yet known exactly how the man happened to fall into the river, but immediately after the incident a boat was lowered from the *Formby* and a fisherman named Haberlin, who was in the vicinity at the time, also made an attempt to rescue the deceased. It appears, however, that no trace of him could be found.

It was known in the city on Saturday that a Cattleman had been drowned from the *Formby*. But which of the Cattlemen it was only definitely ascertained this morning when the following telegram was

received by the Clyde Shipping Company agent here from the captain of the vessel; "Cattleman Patrick Walsh lost overboard on Saturday evening while passing Glass House Mill. Launched boat but failed to trace him. Fisherman Haberlain also attempted rescue."

The deceased resided at Ferrtbank and leaves a grown-up family. It appears that a son of his was recently wounded in the Dardanelles and that another was wounded in France. He has also a third son in the merchant service. His tragic death was learned with regret in the city. The body of the deceased had not yet been recovered.

WALSH, Patrick: Rank: Able Seaman. Regiment or Service: Mercantile Marine. Unit: SS *Coningbeg* (Glasgow). Torpedoed by German Submarine U-62. There were no survivors. U-62 surrendered in November 1918. Age at death: 48. Date of death: 18 December 1917.

Supplementary information: Son of the John and Annie Keating. Husband of Norah Walsh (*née* O'Neill), of No. 9 Cottage, Passage East, Co. Waterford. Born at Passage East, Co. Waterford. He has no known grave but is listed on the Tower Hill Memorial in the UK. He is also listed on the Formby-Coningbeg Memorial, Adelphi Quay in Waterford City.

WALSH, Patrick: Rank: Private. Regiment or Service: Irish Guards. Unit: 1st Battalion. Age at death: 25. Date of death: 24 September 1916. Service No: 10081 (Commonwealth War Graves Commission), 10061 (Soldiers died in the Great War). Born in Kilmacow, Co. Kilkenny. Enlisted in Waterford. Died of wounds.

Supplementary information: Son of Peter and Johanna Walsh, of Miltown, Kilmacow, Waterford. Grave or Memorial Reference: II.C.56. Cemetery: Dartmoor Cemetery, Becordel-Becourt in France.

WALSH, Patrick: Rank: Private. Regiment or Service: Leinster Regiment. Unit: 2nd Battalion. Age at death: 19. Date of death: 20

October 1914. Service No: 10001. Born in Lismore, Co. Waterford. Enlisted in Cork. Killed in action. Son of Mrs Margaret Walsh, of New Street, Lismore, Co. Waterford. From the *Waterford News*, 1915:

LISMORE MEN LOST.
Mrs Herlihy, New-Street, Lismore, has been notified that her son Patrick, a Sergeant in the 1st Battalion, Leinster Regiment, was killed in action on 14th February. Corporal Sweeney and Private James Doherty, both of the Royal Irish Regiment, and Patrick Walsh, of the Leinster's, all Lismore men, are reported missing.

Grave or Memorial Reference: 10 on the Ploegsteert Memorial in Belgium.

WALSH, Patrick: Rank: Private. Regiment or Service: Royal Irish Regiment. Unit: 1st Battalion. Date of death: 29 January 1915. Service No: 5134. Born in St Patrick's, Waterford. Enlisted in Tipperary while living in Waterford. Died of wounds. Grave or Memorial Reference: B.8. Cemetery: Dickiebusch New Military Cemetery in Belgium.

WALSH, Patrick: Rank: Private. Regiment or Service: Royal Irish Regiment. Unit: 1st Battalion. Date of death: 9 May 1915. Service No: 5665. Born in Trinity Without, Waterford. Enlisted in Waterford. Died of wounds. Grave or Memorial Reference: II.A.95, Cemetery: Bailleul Communal Cemetery Extension (Nord) in France.

WALSH, Patrick: Rank: Private. Regiment or Service: Royal Irish Regiment. Unit: 2nd Battalion. Date of death: 28 April 1915. Service No: 6769. Born in St Patrick's, Waterford. Enlisted in Waterford. Killed in action. He has no known grave but is listed on Panel 4 on the Ploegsteert Memorial in Belgium.

WALSH, Patrick: Rank: Private. Regiment or Service: Royal Irish Regiment. Unit: 'C' Company, 2nd Battalion. Age at death: 39. Date of death: 24 May 1915. Service No: 6906. Born in Carrigeen, Co. Kilkenny (Soldiers died in the Great War) Carrigeen, Co. Waterford (Irelands Memorial Records). Enlisted in Waterford while living in Mooncoin, County Kilkenny. Killed in action.
Supplementary information: Son of John and Mary Walsh, of Ballygorey Cottage, Mooncoin, Co. Kilkenny. Enlisted August 1914. He has no known grave but is listed on Pier and Face 3 A on the Thiepval Memorial in France.

WALSH, Patrick: Rank: Private. Regiment or Service: Royal Irish Regiment. Unit: 2nd Battalion. Date of death: 21 August 1918. Age at death: 25. Service No: 7367. Born in St John's, Waterford. Enlisted in Waterford. Killed in action.
Supplementary information: Son of Patrick and Mary Walsh, of 1 Shee's Terrace, Bath Street, Waterford. Husband of Ellen Walsh, of 2 Grady's Lane, Barrack Street, Waterford. From the *Waterford News*, August 1915:

THE "NEWS" IN FRANCE.
We have received the following dated "Somewhere in France"

Dear Sir,
We write you those few lines hoping to find you in good health as it leaves ourselves out here. We get you paper regularly every week, and we need not tell you that we do be delighted to get it because by reading it we all get the news of the old town. It is a book to the boys of the old Urbs —acta to read your most valuable paper in the lull of the fighting. Furthermore, we wish to appreciate the boys of the old dart for responding to the patriotic call. Waterford, as you know, is playing no small part in this great struggle to uphold gallant little Belgium and crush tyranny. –We remain, dear sir, yours truly.

Lance Corporal Walsh, P, 7367; Private Tobin, M, 7588; Private Flynn, P, 7663; Private Kennedy, T, 7596; Private Heaney, T, 7506; Drummer.

From the *Waterford News*, February 1917:

LETTERS FROM THE FRONT.

Private Patrick Walsh, R. I. R., who is in France, writes to ask us if "some friend would kindly send on a football or something I the way of sport to help us to pass the time out of the trenches. There are about a dozen of us here from Waterford. "The address of this soldier may be had at the "News" office.

Has no known grave but is commemorated on Panel 5. Vis-En-Artois Memorial in France.

WALSH, Patrick: Rank: Stoker 1st Class. Regiment or Service: Royal Navy. Unit: H. M. S/M. G7. Age at death: 26. Date of death: 1 November 1918. Service No: K/13723. 'G&' was a Royal Navy Submarine.

Supplementary information: Son of Patrick and Mary Walsh, of Waterford. Grave or Memorial Reference: 28 on the Plymouth Naval Memorial, UK.

WALSH, Stephen: Rank: Private. Regiment or Service: Royal Irish Regiment. Unit: 2nd Battalion. Age at death: 32. Date of death: 23 March 1918. Service No: 9524. Born in Cashel, County Tipperary. Enlisted in Cashel. Died of wounds.

Supplementary information: Nephew of Michael McDonnell, of 30 St Mary's Road, Hennessy's Road, Waterford. Grave or Memorial Reference: I.A.10. Cemetery: Honnechy British Cemetery in France.

WALSH, Thomas: Rank: Company Quartermaster Sergeant. Regiment or Service: Royal Munster Fusiliers. Unit: 1st Battalion. Age at death: 36. Date of death: 25

April 1915. Service No: 5530 Awards: D.C.M.

Supplementary information: Son of William and Margaret Walsh, of Lisnabrin, Curraglass, Tallow, Co. Waterford. Killed at Suvla. Served in the South African Campaign and on the North West Frontier of India. From the *Waterford News*, September 1915:

ANOTHER WATERFORDMAN'S DEATH AT THE DARDANELLES.

Official intimation was received yesterday of the death of Sergeant Thomas Walsh, Royal Irish Regiment, who was killed at the Dardanelles on the 16th of August. The fallen soldier previous to joining the army was a printer by trade and served his time on one of the local newspapers. He enlisted in the Royal Irish Regiment and served the full time with the colours. On leaving the Army he resided at Manchester, but occasionally visited his native city when he used to stay with Mr Thomas Cleary, caretaker of the Y. M. S., of whose wife he was a nephew. On the outbreak of the war he rejoined his old Regiment and was sent out to the Gallipoli Peninsula six weeks ago. A pathetic yet consoling incident in connection with his death is that a letter had been received from him under the date the 15th August–the day previous to his death–in which he stated that from the Colonel down to the Private every Catholic member of the Battalion had just received Holy Communion. Whilst Divine Service was taking place five or six bombs were dropped by a hostile aeroplane near by, but marvellous to relate not a person was touched by them.

He has no known grave but is listed on Panel 190 to 196 on the Helles Memorial in Turkey.

WALSH, Thomas: Rank: Sergeant. Regiment or Service: Royal Irish Regiment. Unit: 5th Battalion. Age at death: 44. Date of death: 16 August 1915. Service No: 189. Born in St Johns, Waterford. Enlisted in Manchester while living in Waterford. Killed in action in Gallipoli.

Supplementary information: Nephew of Thomas Cleary, of 5 College Green, Waterford. From the *Waterford News*, September 1915:

TRIBUTE TO FALLEN WATERFORD SOLDIER.

In connection with the death of Sergeant Walsh, 5th Battalion, R.I. Regiment, who was killed in action recently in the Dardanelles, the following letter has been received from the officer commanding the company to which the fallen soldier belonged; --

From the officer commanding the company to which the N.C.O. mentioned below belonged.
To Mrs Cleary, caretaker, Young Men's Society, Parnell Street, Waterford.
Dear Sir,
I very much regret to have to inform you that No 189 Sergeant Walsh, 5th Battalion, R. I. Regiment, was killed in action on August 16th. It will be a consolation to you to know that this man died fighting like a man as he always lived. He was wounded in the arm about 2 o'clock, but continued in action and was shot dead fifteen minutes later. His last words ro a comrade next to him, Private Whelan, were, "Have confidence, Mike, and take good aim. " Sergeant Walsh was a thorough man, an excellent N. C. O., and I feel in losing him that I have lost a loyal friend. You have my deepest sympathy. –
Yours faithfully.
V. M. Scully, Captain.

Sergeant Walsh was a nephew of Mrs Cleary and had seen many years service. Prior to enlisting he was a printer by trade and served his time on one of the local newspapers. After leaving the army he resided in Manchester, but occasionally paid visits to his native city. On the outbreak of the war he rejoined and was sent to the Dardanelles. A letter received from him on the day previous to his death stated that ll the Catholic members of the Battalion, from the colonel down to the privates, had received Holy Communion. During the ceremony a hostile aeroplane dropped bombs in the vicinity but, marvellous to relate not a person was struck.

From the *Waterford News*, November 1915:

WATERFORD MAN AT THE DARDANELLES.
Sergeant-Major J. Conway, of 2 Newgate Street, Waterford, writes to a member of the *Munster Express* staff, Mr Ryan, from the Dardanelles. He speaks in glowing terms of the conduct of the soldiers from Waterford, and says that so far they have been fairly lucky. He mentions Sergeant Po Sullivan and L. Murphy as being in his tent. Sergeant J Coady, Butchers Lane, is in hospital in Cairo.

Sergeant-Major Conway names the following casualties of Waterford soldiers in Suvla; --Killed; Sergeant Thomas Walsh, Water Street; Private J Fitzgerald, Newport Lane; Private Peter Sullivan, Knockboy; Private Pat Sullivan, Ballytruckle. Wounded Corporal Henneberry, Hennessy's Road; Lance Corporal W Brown, Jail Street; Private W Brown, Stephen Street (stretcher bearer); Private P Kennedy, Kneefe's Lane; Private Rossiter, Castle Street; Private P Wilson, Grady's Yard; Private D Connors, address not known.

He concludes his letter by asking for the prayers of his friends, saying "It is the only comfort we can get out here, and in return the boys will send a prayer up from the battlefield every night."

He has no known grave but is listed on Panel 55 on the Helles Memorial in Turkey.

WALSH, William: Rank: Private. Regiment or Service: Devonshire Regiment. Unit: B Company, 2nd Battalion. Date of death: 24 April 1918. Age at death: 30. Service No: 13007. Born in Waterford. Enlisted in Wattstown, Glamorganshire. Died of wounds. Killed in action.

Supplementary information: Husband of Jessie Walsh, of 48 Pleasant View, Wattstown, Ynishir (Rhondda), Glamorganshire. Grave or Memorial Reference: II.P.11. Cemetery: Adelaide Cemetery, Villers–Bretonneux in France.

WALSH, William: Rank: Private. Regiment or Service: Royal Irish Regiment. Unit: 2nd Battalion. Age at death: 24. Date of death: 24 May 1915. Service No: 6487. Born in St Patrick's, Waterford. Enlisted in Waterford. Killed in action.

Supplementary information: Son of William and Johanna Walsh, of Philip Street, Waterford. He has no known grave but is listed on Panel 33 on the Ypres (Menin Gate) Memorial in Belgium.

WALSHE, Mary A.: Rank: Staff Nurse. Regiment or Service: Queen Alexandra's Imperial Military Nursing Service. Date of death: 21 August 1915. From the *Munster Express*, August 1915:

DEATH OF WATERFORD NURSE IN MALTA.

We regret to record the death of Miss Mary Walshe, daughter of the late Dr Walshe, Kilmacthomas, and sister of Mrs W O'Donoghue, Kilmacthomas, which occurred at Malta. The deceased young lady was a nurse in the County and City Infirmary, and volunteered for Red Cross work. She went to Malta some weeks ago, and the sad news of her death was cabled to Waterford by Dr Morrissey, of this city, who is in Malta. Sister Walshe was a skilled nurse, highly esteemed by all who knew her, and her death has evoked feelings of regret amongst the staffs of the County and City Infirmary, with whom she was most popular. For her sorrowing mother and other relatives deep sympathy will be felt will be felt in their bereavement. The following resolution was passed by the Committee of the County and City Infirmary at meeting held on Tuesday last;

– "That the Committee desire to express the great regret with which they heard of the death of Sister Mary Walshe, who was connected with the infirmary for the past 15 years, and who discharged the duties of surgical staff nurse for the last seven years in such an eminently satisfactory manner."

Grave or Memorial Reference: E.EA.A.661. Cemetery: Addolorata Cemetery in Malta.

WALSHE, Patrick: Rank: Corporal. Regiment or Service: Royal Irish Regiment. Unit: 2nd Battalion. Date of death: 14 July 1916. Service No: 10758. He won the Military Medal and is listed in the *London Gazette*. Born in Newtown Co. Waterford. Enlisted in Waterford while living in Kilmacthomas, Co. Waterford. Killed in action. He is listed on the Graves and Co. Roll of Honour Memorial. Located are located in Christ Church Cathedral (Church of Ireland), Henrietta Street, Waterford. He has no known grave but is listed on Pier and Face 3 A on the Thiepval Memorial in France.

WALSHE, William: Rank: Lance Corporal. Regiment or Service: Machine Gun Corps. Unit: Infantry, 64th Brigade. Date of death: 26 September 1916. Service No: 11589. Formerly he was with the Royal Irish Regiment where his number was 9687. Born in Mooncoin, Kilkenny. Enlisted in New Cross while living in Carrickbeg. Killed in action. He has no known grave but is listed on Pier and Face 5C and 132C on the Thiepval Memorial in France

WATERS, George Alexander: Rank: Fleet Surgeon. Regiment or Service: Royal Navy. Unit: HMS *Goliath*. Age at death: 52. Date of death: 13 May 1915. HMS *Goliath* was sunk by three torpedoes from German destroyer *Muvanet-I-Milet*, she blew up and capsized immediately taking 570 of her 750 crew including the Captain to a watery grave. Ten Waterford men died on the *Goliath* that day.

Supplementary information: Son of Eaton William and Mary Waters, of Tranmore, Waterford. M.D. Was present at the operations against the German light cruiser in the Rufiji River, German East Africa and at the bombardment of Dar-es-Salaam in 1914. Grave or Memorial Reference: 9. Memorial: Chatham Naval Memorial In England.

WHELAN, James: Rank: Private. Regiment or Service: Royal Irish Regiment. Unit: 1st Battalion. Age at death: 33. Date of death: 15 March 1915. Service No: 4674. Born in Portlaw, Co. Waterford. Enlisted in Waterford while living in Portlaw. Died of wounds.

Supplementary information: Son of John and Kate Whelan, of 61 William Street, Portlaw, Co. Waterford. Grave or Memorial Reference: J.34. Cemetery: Bailleul Communal Cemetery (Nord) in France.

WHELAN, John: Rank: Gunner. Regiment or Service: Royal Field Artillery. Unit: 117th Battery. 26th Brigade. Age at death: 35. Date of death: 30 October 1917. Service No: 28816. Born in Aglish, Waterford, Ireland. Enlisted in Cork. Killed in action.

Supplementary information: Son of Thomas and Margaret Whelan, of Tinniscart, Villierstown, Co. Waterford. Grave or Memorial Reference: IX.E.10. Cemetery: Vlamertinghe New Military Cemetery in Belgium.

WHELAN, John: Rank: Sergeant. Regiment or Service: Royal Irish Regiment. Unit: 2nd Battalion. Date of death: 24 May 1915. Service No: 9571. Born in St Patrick's, Waterford. Enlisted in Waterford. Died of wounds. Grave or Memorial Reference: I.F. 54. Cemetery: Bailleul Communal Cemetery Extension (Nord) in France.

WHELAN, Maurice: Rank: Driver. Regiment or Service: Royal Horse Artillery and Royal Field Artillery. Unit: 'A' Battery, 63rd

Brigade. Date of death: 4 July 1918. Service No: 80425. Born in Waterford. Enlisted in Llanelly, Carmarthenshire. Died. Grave or Memorial Reference: IX.A.15. Cemetery: Contay British Cemetery, Contay in France.

WHELAN, Michael: Rank: Stoker 1st Class. Regiment or Service: Royal Navy. Unit: HMS *Vivid.* Date of death: 1 January 1915 Age at death: 19. Service No; K23606. Born in Dungarvan, Co. Waterford.

Supplementary information: Son of Daniel and Ellen Whelan, of Ballycoe, Dungarvan, Co. Waterford. Grave or Memorial Reference: General L. 13.0. Cemetery: General L. 13.0. Cemetery: Ford Park Cemetery (Formerly Old Cemetery)(Pennycomequick), Devon, U.K.

WHELAN/WHEALAN, Michael: Rank: Corporal. Regiment or Service: Northumberland Fusiliers. Unit: 26th Battalion (Tyneside Irish). Date of death: 2 September 1917. Age at death: 37. Service No: 26/1297. Born in Waterford. Enlisted in Newcastle-on-Tyne. Killed in action.

Supplementary information: Won the Distinguished Conduct Medal and the Military Medal. Son of Patrick and Anastasia Whelan. Native of Cleator Moor, Cumberland. Grave or Memorial Reference: I.D.20. Cemetery: Hargicourt British Cemetery, Aisne in France.

WHELAN/WHELAND, Peter: Rank: Private. Regiment or Service: Royal Irish Regiment. Unit: 2nd Battalion. Date of death: 39. Age at death: 9 May 1915. Service No: 7113. Born in St John's Waterford. Enlisted in Waterford. Died of wounds.

Supplementary information: Son of Peter and Mary Whelan, of Waterford. Husband of Sarah Whelan, of 8 Peter Street, Waterford. Served in the South African Campaign. Grave or Memorial Reference: Plot 1, Row E, Grave, 21. Cemetery: Hop Store Cemetery, Ypres in Belgium.

WHELAN, T.: (Commonwealth War Graves Commission), **WHELAN, John** (Soldiers died in the Great War). Rank: Private. Regiment or Service: Royal Irish Regiment. Unit: 1st Battalion. Age at death: 28. Date of death: 20 May 1915. Service No: 4224. Born in Trinity Without, Waterford. Enlisted in Waterford. Died of wounds.

Supplementary information: Son of Mrs Margaret Whelan, of 4 Buttermilk Lane, Mayor Walk, Waterford. Grave or Memorial Reference: Screen Wall. W.43. Cemetery: Leeds (Lawns Wood) Cemetery, UK.

WHELAN, William: Rank: Private. Regiment or Service: Australian Pioneers. Unit: 2nd. Date of death: 15 March 1918. Enlisted 4 July 1916 in Melbourne, Victoria. Killed in action. Service No: 2730.

Supplementary information: Son of James and Statia Whelan. Native of Waterford Ireland.

In or near what Parish or Town were you born? Waterford, Ireland.

Are you a natural born British subject or a Naturalised British subject? Natural Born British Subject.

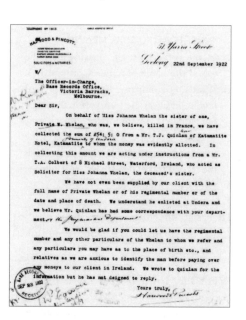

William Whelan

What is your age? 37 years 7 months.

What is your trade or calling? Labourer.

Are you, or have you been an Apprentice? No. If so where, to whom, and for what period?

Are you married? No.

Who is your next of kin? Parents deceased. (sister) Miss J Whelan, 78 Manor Road, Waterford.

Have you ever been convicted by the Civil Power? No.

Have you ever been discharged from any part of His Majesty's Forces, with Ignominy, or as Incorrigible and Worthless, or on account of conviction of felony, or of a Sentence of Penal Servitude, or have you been dismissed with Disgrace from the Navy? No.

Do you now belong to, or have you ever served in, His Majesty's Army, the Marines, the Militia, the Militia Reserve, the Territorial Reserve, Royal Navy or Colonial Forces?, No. If so, state which, and if not now serving, state cause of discharge

Have you stated the whole, if any, of your previous service? Yes.

Have you ever been rejected as unfit for his Majesty's Service? No. If so, on what grounds?

(For Married Men and Widowers with Children)---Do you understand that no Separation Allowance will be issued to you either before or after embarkation during your term of service? --

Age, 37 years, 7 months. Height 5 feet, 6 ¾ inches. Weight, 131 lbs. Chest measurement: 33-35 inches. Complexion, fresh. Eyes: grey. Hair: black. Religious denomination: R. C.

His will left his estate to Miss Minnie Quinlan, Undera Hotel, Undera, Victoria. This will was later revoked and all his estate was to be sent to his sister Johanna.

Grave or Memorial Reference: II.G.12. Cemetery, Pont-D'Achelles Military Cemetery, Nieppe in France.

WHITE, ?: Rank: Private. The only reference to this man is contained in the article below. He is not findable in any of the databases with this scant information.

Miss White, of Bracklin, Portarlington, who is at present engaged at the postal delivery instead of one of the postmen now on active service, was notified during the week that her brother, Private White, of the Canadian contingent, was killed in action in France recently. Private White was only 19 years of age and was home on leave about three months ago before he left for the firing line. Sincere sympathy is expressed with Miss White in her sad bereavement.

WHITE, Aloysius: Rank: Private. Regiment or Service: Middlesex Regiment. Unit: 11ᵗʰ Battalion. Date of death: 13 February 1917. Service No: G/716. Born in Dungarvon, Co. Waterford. Enlisted in Aldershot, Hants while living in Dublin. Died at Home. Grave or Memorial Reference: Gen 7346 (Screen Wall). Cemetery: Tottenham Cemetery, UK.

WHITE-MANNING, George Frederick: See **MANNING, George Frederick:**

WHITTY, Stephen: Rank: Able Seaman. Regiment or Service: Mercantile Marine. Unit: SS Coningbeg (Glasgow). Torpedoed by German Submarine U-62. There were no survivors. U-62 surrendered in November 1918. Age at death: 44. Date of death: 18 December 1917.
Supplementary information: Son of Thomas and Anastatia Whitty. Husband of Margaret Whitty (*née* Hayes), of 31 Roanmore Road, Ballybricke, Waterford. Born at Ballyhack, Co. Wexford. He has no known grave but is listed on the Tower Hill Memorial in the UK. He is also listed on the Formby-Coningbeg Memorial, Adelphi Quay in Waterford City.

WHITTLE, Edward: Rank: Private. Regiment or Service: Welsh Regiment. Unit: 9ᵗʰ Battalion. Date of death: 7 July 1916. Service No: 14604. Born in Waterford. Enlisted in Merthyr. Killed in action.
Supplementary information: Son of Richard and Mary Whittle, of 41 Bryn Street, Merthyr Tydvyl, Glamorganshire. He has no known grave but is listed on Pier and Face 7A and 10A on the Thiepval Memorial in France.

WHITEY/WHITTY, Thomas Anthony: Rank: Private. Regiment or Service: Royal Dublin Fusiliers. Unit: 'D' Coy. 7ᵗʰ Battalion. Age at death: 22. Date of death: 16 August 1915. Service No: 14202. Born in Waterford. Enlisted in Dublin. Killed in action in Gallipoli.
Supplementary information: Son of Mary E. Whitty, of 18, Harcourt Street, Dublin, and of the late Dr P.J. Whitty, of Waterford, and grandson of Thomas Hazleton, of Dublin. Born in Waterford. From the *Waterford News*, September 1915:

WATERFORD SOLDIER MISSING.
In the official list of "missing" will be found the name of Lance Corporal T. A. Whitty, D Company, 7ᵗʰ battalion, Royal Dublin Fusiliers. He took part in the fierce fight at Suvla Bay on August 16ᵗʰ.
Lance Corporal Whitty was one of the first who joined the D Company. He is the second son of the late Dr P. J. Whitty of Lady Lane, Waterford.

He has no known grave but is listed on Panel 190 to 196 on the Helles Memorial in Turkey.

WHYTE, John: Rank: Third Engineer. Regiment or Service: Mercantile Marine. Unit: SS *Gena*. Age at death: 24. Date of death: 24 May 1916.

Supplementary information: Son of James and Ellen Whyte, of Cutteen, Kilrossanty, Co. Waterford. Grave or Memorial Reference: III.C.22. Cemetery: Mazargues War Cemetery, in France.

WILLIAMS, Frederick Joseph: Rank: Sergeant. Regiment or Service: Welsh Regiment. Unit: 18th Battalion. Date of death: 9 April 1918. Service No: 57493. Born in Dungarvan, Co. Waterford. Enlisted in Newport, Monmouthshire. Killed in action. From the *Waterford News*, April 1915:

> Mr J. W. Williams, son of Mr J. F. Williams, solicitor, Dungarvan, and Mrs C. J. Biggs, son of Mr T. J. Biggs, B. S., Dungarvan, have successfully passed their examinations for entrance to the Royal Military College of Sandhurst.

Grave or Memorial Reference: He has no known grave but is listed on Panel 7 on the Ploegsteert Memorial in Belgium.

WILLS, William Henry: Rank: Sailmaker. Regiment or Service: Royal Navy. Unit: HMS *Rinaldo*. Age at death: 35. Date of death: 13 February 1918. Service No: 200149 (Dev). Son of Mrs Fanny Wills, of 9, Shanbally Terrace, Torpoint, Cornwall. Born at Ardmore, Waterford. Grave or Memorial Reference: Eur. Sec. 22B. Cemetery: Saldanha Public Cemetery, Western Cape, South Africa.

WIXTED, Thomas: Rank: Donkeyman. Regiment or Service: Mercantile Marine. Unit: SS *Coningbeg* (Glasgow). Torpedoed by German Submarine U-62. There were no survivors. U-62 surrendered in November 1918. Age at death: 50. Date of death: 18 December 1917.

Supplementary information: Son of the late Thomas and Mary Wixted. Husband of Mary Catherine Wixted (*née* Power), of 41 Francis Street, Waterford. Born in Waterford. He has no known grave but is listed on the Tower Hill Memorial in the UK. He is also listed on the Formby-Coningbeg Memorial, Adelphi Quay in Waterford City.